Mental Health Challenges and Work

There is a growing recognition that poorly designed work can degrade employees' mental health. Relatedly, there is also an acknowledgment that employees with existing mental health challenges—such as clinically significant depression and anxiety—may need particular support to thrive in the workplace. Yet, while research on this topic has blossomed, there are systematic challenges that must be addressed to promote continued advancement.

This book will go beyond the basics to investigate complex questions about the relationship between work and employees' mental health. For instance, how are employees' mental health challenges impacted by their gender or race? How can employees' mental health be protected in inherently stressful work? By juxtaposing curated research on mental health and work, this edited volume provides value by highlighting novel perspectives, as well as areas of opportunity to better understand how diverse employees manage mental health in the changing world of work.

Researchers and advanced students in management and psychology will find that this book provides a strong foundation for conducting future studies at the intersection of work and mental health.

Emily H. Rosado-Solomon is Assistant Professor of Management at Babson College, USA. She received her PhD from Rutgers University School of Management and Labor Relations.

Routledge Studies in Management, Organizations and Society

This series presents innovative work grounded in new realities, addressing issues crucial to an understanding of the contemporary world. This is the world of organized societies, where boundaries between formal and informal, public and private, local and global organizations have been displaced or have vanished, along with other nineteenth century dichotomies and oppositions. Management, apart from becoming a specialized profession for a growing number of people, is an everyday activity for most members of modern societies.

Similarly, at the level of enquiry, culture and technology, and literature and economics, can no longer be conceived as isolated intellectual fields; conventional canons and established mainstreams are contested. *Management, Organizations and Society* addresses these contemporary dynamics of transformation in a manner that transcends disciplinary boundaries, with books that will appeal to researchers, students and practitioners alike.

Recent titles in this series include:

Management, Organizations, and Paradoxes
Insights from the Central and Eastern European Region
Edited by Malgorzata Rozkwitalska-Welenc, Agnieszka Zakrzewska-Bielawska and Anna Maria Lis

Business Networks and Organizational Resilience
Relational Capital of Companies and Times of Crisis
Anna Aleksandra Walecka

Strategy and Leadership for Grand Societal Challenges
Bridging Theory and Practice
Edited by Alice Erthal and Douglas Wegner

Mental Health Challenges and Work
Advanced Topics and Future Research Directions
Edited by Emily H. Rosado-Solomon

For more information about this series, please visit: www.routledge.com

Mental Health Challenges and Work

Advanced Topics and Future Research Directions

Edited by Emily H. Rosado-Solomon

Routledge
Taylor & Francis Group
NEW YORK AND LONDON

First published 2026
by Routledge
605 Third Avenue, New York, NY 10158

and by Routledge
4 Park Square, Milton Park, Abingdon, Oxon, OX14 4RN

Routledge is an imprint of the Taylor & Francis Group, an informa business

ISBN: 978-1-032-78920-0 (hbk)
ISBN: 978-1-032-79248-4 (pbk)
ISBN: 978-1-003-49117-0 (ebk)

DOI: 10.4324/9781003491170

Typeset in Times New Roman
by Apex CoVantage, LLC

For Product Safety Concerns and Information please contact our EU representative:
GPSR@taylorandfrancis.com
Taylor & Francis
Verlag GmbH, Kaufingerstraße 24, 80331 München, Germany

Contents

Contributors

Neal M. Ashkanasy is Emeritus Professor of Management at the University of Queensland, Australia, former Editor-in-Chief of the *Journal of Organizational Behavior,* and former Associate Editor of *Academy of Management Learning and Education, Academy of Management Review, Emotion Review, Journal of Management Education.* He received his PhD in Social and Organizational Psychology from the University of Queensland.

Jordon Babcock is Vice President of Outpatient Operations for ALLY Psychiatry, USA. He received his MBA from Northern Illinois University.

Janine Bosak is Professor of Organizational Psychology/Behavior and Research Director of the Leadership and Talent Institute at Dublin City University, Ireland. She received her PhD in Psychology from the University of Bern in Switzerland.

Thomas W. Britt is Professor of Psychology at Clemson University, USA, Prisma Health Sciences Research Director for Clemson University, a faculty instructor at the US Army War College, and Editor-in-Chief for *Military Psychology*. He received his PhD in Social Psychology from the University of Florida.

Abigail Clemson is a student at Rutgers University School of Management and Labor Relations, USA.

Lauren Cox is a PhD student at the University of Queensland Business School, Australia.

Samantha G. Deane is a PhD student in the School of Management and Labor Relations at Rutgers University, USA.

Shoshana Dobrow is Associate Professor of Management at London School of Economics and Political Science, UK. She received her PhD in Organizational Behavior from Harvard University.

Marissa Edwards is Senior Lecturer at the University of Queensland Business School, Australia. She received her PhD in Management from the University of Queensland.

Renée D. Edwards is Assistant Director at the Heldrich Center for Workforce Development at Rutgers University, USA. She received her PhD in Public Policy and Comparative Politics from Washington State University.

Hadar Elraz is Senior Lecturer in Human Resource Management and Organisational Behaviour at Swansea University, UK. She received her PhD from Cardiff University.

Jiani Fan is a doctoral student at the University of Alabama, USA.

Tyler N.A. Fezzey is a doctoral candidate in Management at the University of Alabama, USA.

Patrick C. Flood is Full Professor of Organizational Behavior at Dublin City University, Ireland. He received his PhD from London School of Economics and Political Science.

Yseult Freeney is Professor of Organizational Psychology, Research Director of the Irish Institute for Digital Business, and Program Chair of the MSc Work and Organizational Psychology/Behavior program at Dublin City University, Ireland.

Allison S. Gabriel is Thomas J. Howatt Chair in Management and the Faculty Director of the Center for Working Well (CWW) at Purdue University, USA. She also serves as Associate Editor at the *Journal of Applied Psychology*. She received her PhD in Industrial/Organizational Psychology from the University of Akron.

Kelly P. Gabriel is a PhD candidate in Eller College of Management, University of Arizona, USA.

Neha Gopinath is Lecturer in the Department of Management at the University of St. Andrews, UK. She received her PhD in Business Administration from the University of Essex.

Danna Greenberg is Walter H. Carpenter Distinguished Professor of Organizational Behavior, Associate Dean of Faculty, and Chair of the Management Division at Babson College, USA. She is also former Associate Editor of *Academy of Management Learning and Education*. She received her PhD in Organizational Behavior from Boston College.

Patrick Groulx is Professor of Organizations and Human Resources at HEC Montréal, Canada. He received his PhD in Organizational Behavior from HEC Montréal.

Sheila K. Hanson is Associate Professor of Entrepreneurship and Management at the University of North Dakota and Resident Psychologist at the Northern Prairie Community Clinic, USA. She received her PhD in Clinical Psychology from the University of North Dakota.

Ravit Heskiau is Associate Teaching Professor at Northeastern University, USA. She received her PhD in Organizational Behavior and Human Resource Management from the University of Toronto.

Hooria Jazaieri is Assistant Professor of Management and the Director of the Leadership, Affective Science, Emotion, and Reputation (LASER) Laboratory at Santa Clara University, and a licensed psychotherapist in the State of California, USA. She received her PhD in Social Psychology from the University of California, Berkeley.

Niamh Kavanagh is a doctoral student at Dublin City University, Ireland.

Steven Kilroy is Associate Professor of Human Resource Management at Trinity College Dublin, Ireland. He received his PhD in Human Resource Management from Dublin City University.

Douglas L. Kruse is Distinguished Professor and Co-director of the Program for Disability Research at the School of Management and Labor Relations, Rutgers University, USA. He is also Associate Editor of the *Journal of Participation and Employee Ownership* and former Editor of the *British Journal of Industrial Relations*. He received his PhD in Economics from Harvard University.

Jamie J. Ladge is Professor at Boston College, USA, Distinguished Research Professor at the University of Exeter, and Associate Editor for the *Journal of Organizational Behavior.* She received her PhD in Management from Boston College.

Angela Martin is Professorial Research Fellow in Work and Mental Health Menzies Institute for Medical Research, University of Tasmania, New Zealand. She received her PhD in Organizational Psychology from Griffith University.

Sarah D. Meyer is a doctoral student in Industrial-Organizational Psychology at Clemson University, USA.

Maura J. Mills is Associate Professor of Management and Associate Director of the UA Masters in Management Program at the University of Alabama, USA. She also serves as Associate Editor for the journal *Industrial & Organizational Psychology: Perspectives on Science & Practice.* She received her PhD in Industrial and Organizational Psychology from Kansas State University.

Caleb Phillips is a doctoral candidate at the London School of Economics and Political Science, UK.

Tanesha L. Rorie is Associate Professor of Counseling at Malone University and Licensed Professional Counselor in the state of Ohio, USA. She received her PhD from Kent State University in Counselor Education and Supervision.

Katina B. Sawyer is Associate Professor of Management and Organizations at the University of Arizona, USA. She received her PhD in Industrial/Organizational Psychology and Women's Studies from the Pennsylvania State University.

Lisa Schur is Professor of Labor Studies and Employment Relations and Director of the Program for Disability Research at Rutgers University School of Management and Labor Relations, USA. She received her PhD in Political Science from University of California, Berkeley, and her JD from Northeastern University School of Law.

Ryan Travia is Associate Vice President for Student Success at Babson College, USA. He received his doctorate in Higher Education Management from the University of Pennsylvania.

Lucy Turner is Assistant Professor of Practice in Organizational Behavior and Former Associate Director of the Undergraduate Center for Career Development at Babson College, USA.

Lisa van der Werff is Associate Professor of Organizational Psychology, Director of Doctoral Studies, and Co-Director of Irish Institute of Digital Business at Dublin City University Business School, Ireland. She also serves as Deputy Editor in Chief for the *Journal of Trust Research.* She received her PhD in HRM and Organizational Behavior from Dublin City University.

Emma C. Vosika is a doctoral student in Industrial-Organizational Psychology with a concentration in Occupational Health Psychology at Clemson University, USA.

Acknowledgments

I wish to extend my gratitude to the numerous people who supported the development of this book. Most prominently, I am grateful to the chapter authors, who thoughtfully crafted their research to cohesively align with the other work encompassed in this volume. The importance and rigor of their work, along with their enthusiasm for this topic, made this process of editing this book truly joyful.

I am further grateful to Wendy Murphy and Danna Greenberg for encouraging me to undertake this project, and to my countless friends and colleagues for connecting me with chapter authors outside my immediate network. Additionally, I thank Martha Lanning for her copyediting of the chapters in Section I of the book.

Finally, I am grateful to my friends and family for their ongoing support of my research on mental health challenges and work. I am particularly indebted to my parents, Ruth and Rudy Rosado, my husband, David Solomon, and my son, Hudson. They have provided thousands of hours of generative discussion about my research and patiently supported me—and forgiven my occasional absence—while I continue to devote myself to this work.

1 Introduction to Mental Health Challenges and Work

Emily H. Rosado-Solomon

Introduction

Each chapter in this book starts with statistics about the importance of attending to mental health challenges and work, with myriad statistics about the prevalence of mental illness, as well as the increasing impact of societal stresses and work on employees' mental health. According to a new study of US workers, at least 50% of respondents report experiencing "moderate to severe" levels of burnout, depression, and anxiety symptoms with 90% experiencing at least one mild symptom of a mental health challenge (Mind Share Partners, 2025). This is congruent with messages in broader society; in 2024, the United States Surgeon General issued a formal advisory on the "Mental Health & Well-Being of Parents" (Murthy, 2024)—many of whom hold paid employment. Less formally, celebrities and non-celebrities alike are increasingly discussing their own mental health challenges (Calhoun & Gold, 2020; Mind Share Partners, 2025), further shaping the recognition of mental health challenges as a ubiquitous concern. While it is redundant to repeat all the statistics here, it is sobering to say the least and undeniable that mental health challenges have an exorbitant human and financial cost for organizations and those they employ (see Rosado-Solomon et al., 2023, for a review). The scale of this challenge is so vast that it cannot be ignored, and academics have the opportunity to play an important role in creating knowledge that can be leveraged to improve employees' mental health.

In comparison to the enormity of this challenge, a book may not seem like a worthy defense. The challenges can feel overwhelming, and admittedly any one research study or book is insufficient to "fix" anything. Yet I argue that this book can play an important part in moving the needle in academics' ability to gain useful insight about work and mental health challenges, defined as "an umbrella term for both diagnosed mental illness and undiagnosed/subclinical poor mental health, which may manifest as symptoms associated with conditions such as anxiety, depression, obsessive–compulsive disorder, and bipolar disorder" (Rosado-Solomon et al., 2023, p. 752). In this book, mental health challenges also manifest as burnout, which is a specific form of poor mental

DOI: 10.4324/9781003491170-1

health that comprises emotional exhaustion, depersonalization or cynicism, and reduced professional efficacy (Maslach & Jackson, 1981; Maslach et al., 1997) that shares several overlapping themes with other forms of poor mental health (Kelloway et al., 2023).

A quote that motivates my own research on mental health challenges is from an ancient Jewish text called the Pirket Avot, and it says, "Do not be daunted by the enormity of the world's grief . . . *You are not obligated to complete the work, but neither are you free to abandon it*" (emphasis added). To that end, in an effort to advance knowledge about mental health challenges and work in spite of the enormity of the problems, this book collects insights from a cross-disciplinary, international group of 39 authors with three primary goals for contributing to the literature on mental health challenges and work.

First, elements of this book aim to provide an overview of "advanced topics" in the field of mental health and work that go beyond the frequently repeated (and often impossible) instructive to avoid "too much" stress. This requires research that examines nuance: the unique mental health challenges of people with different attributes and in different contexts, the detailed methodological and conceptual considerations of related constructs, and the way that these dynamics manifest in actual organizations. For those who are new to this field and wish to quickly see where the cutting edge is, this volume aims to serve as a useful overview. This book creates value by strategically aggregating work from a variety of scholars with diverse disciplinary and topical perspectives on related issues. In this aggregation, the book aims to create a resource that is more than the sum of its parts: juxtaposing complementary work that might not otherwise be found by scholars who reside in a specific disciplinary niche. In doing this, the hope is that scholars—both those with deep expertise in this topic and those who are newer to studying mental health challenges—will not have to go searching for fragmented bits of knowledge, thereby expediting the research that is to build off this in the years to come.

A related aim of this book is to extend the current thinking on mental health challenges and work by aggregating a body of cutting-edge work, adding novel perspectives and insights beyond the well-known findings in this space. This is accomplished in two ways. First, the book includes chapters on topics that are understudied in management research, such as the unique mental health challenges of employees who are already marginalized or work with industry-specific challenges. The literature on many of these topics remains understudied even as the practical challenges of these topics affect millions of workers, making them particularly worthy of study.

Additionally, a section of this book is devoted to extending the literature by examining how mental health challenges are impacted by major trends in the changing nature of work. Indeed, much has been made of how work is becoming increasingly relational and collaborative (Thornhill-Miller et al., 2023) while simultaneously featuring increased feelings of isolation as virtual work becomes more normative (Van Zoonen, & Sivunen, 2022). The chapters in this section represent the tip of the iceberg for what scholars will need to investigate as work continues to evolve in the years to come.

The final goal of this book is to serve as a call to action, providing motivation and resources for scholars who wish to devote their time and expertise to investigating mental health challenges and work. Based on countless conversations with other academics, the motivation piece seems comparatively easy. Especially after the COVID-19 pandemic, which led to ubiquitous mental health challenges in the workplace (Giorgi et al., 2020), everyone knows someone whose work has been impacted by a mental health challenge, often including themselves. Indeed, as academics we face unique challenges that can cause or exacerbate mental health challenges (for a review, see Martin et al., this volume), making this research deeply personal to many scholars.

Yet some academics I have talked to expressed doubt that they could "get up to speed" on this emerging literature in management sufficiently well to enter the space. In fairness, there are indeed a number of challenges. Even the most experienced researchers recognize that there are outstanding questions about the most foundational elements of understanding mental health challenges and work. What are mental health challenges, anyway? How do different forms of mental health challenges—poor mental health, burnout, mental illness, and others—relate to one another, and what is the importance of clarifying and maintaining theoretical precision for promoting future research? What insights can be drawn from other disciplines, especially psychology, to enrich management research so that it is not "reinventing the wheel"? What does all this mean for what organizations can, or should, do to support employees' mental health? And how might existing organizational practices inform researchers about potentially needed research in this area?

This book addresses many of these questions and provides a foundation on which researchers might build their own inquiries. Moreover, through both juxtaposition of contrasting research and explicit articulation, the book also hopes to clarify elements of the research where there are divergent perspectives. This should not be misinterpreted as an attempt to "take a side" in any particular debate but rather to articulate various perspectives, highlight their commonalities and divergence, and help researchers make an informed choice about how and where to situate their research. These issues impact all elements of the research process, including theorizing, methodological choices, interpretation of findings, and implications for practice and future research. It is the intention of this book to enable a body of future research that is rigorous in aligning these elements while preserving a necessary diversity of thought and approach in this field.

To reach these goals, the volume is divided into five sections, each composed of chapters that relate to a central theme. While each of the chapters makes a valuable contribution in its own right, its order has been designed to lead readers—especially those with limited previous knowledge in this space—to form a cohesive, integrated body of knowledge. To promote this integration, I first set expectations by describing the format of the book briefly, and then providing foundational knowledge to assist readers with limited exposure to concepts surrounding mental health challenges and work.

Volume Structure

The progression of this book, in general, moves from most research-focused to most practice-focused, with the three sections in the middle having significant implications for both research and practice. The first section contains two chapters that bring insights from extant psychology research into the management domain. In different ways, this integration enriches knowledge by breaking down disciplinary siloes and leveraging established knowledge in novel ways. In the first chapter, Hanson and Rosado-Solomon provide an overview of how clinical psychology can help researchers make more informed methodological choices in designing their research. This chapter was inspired by Rosado-Solomon and colleagues' (2023) observation, based on their review of 556 studies in this space, that there was a lack of methodological clarity in some extant work on this subject. This chapter is an attempt to help future researchers avoid the same challenges by drawing on clinical psychology principles to help guide future research decisions in ways that are in keeping with established norms and best practices.

The second chapter of this section provides an exemplar of how a particular field of management research might be extended by drawing on knowledge from clinical psychology. Dobrow and colleagues provide this exemplar by focusing on the narcissism and work literature, which has a long and well-known history of research by organizational scholars. The authors first survey recent trends in narcissism research across premier management journals, finding that there are impactful norms that create pockets of knowledge that are fully saturated while other areas remain barely explored. They then integrate insights about pathological narcissism from clinical psychology to demonstrate how such knowledge could enrich the set of questions and empirical techniques that management researchers might use to generate novel insights.

The second section of this book contains four chapters that investigate the mental health challenges of employees with specific attributes, collectively highlighting the importance of taking an intersectional approach to examining mental health challenges. These chapters have been chosen explicitly as exemplars of how different mental health challenges can be associated with employees' diverse attributes. In the first chapter of this section, Heskiau and colleagues examine the unique challenges associated with maternal mental health and work. These challenges include, but go beyond, challenges associated with balancing work and nonwork, gender and work-related challenges, and pregnancy discrimination to form a complex constellation of themes that could inform future work on this subject. In the next chapter, Fezzey and colleagues explore the unique mental health challenges of star employees, or those that are uniquely exceptional performers in their work. In this chapter, they note that these challenges are pervasive because they are sometimes related to good objective work performance, yet can cause distress for employees even as organizations might benefit from the employees' performance. In the third chapter of this section, Rorie focuses on African American mental health and work. This is an important example of how historical and sociocultural factors combine to create unique mental health challenges for employees from a given racial background. Finally, Turner and colleagues examine mental health challenges of early-career employees. This topic is particularly complex because it reflects both challenges associated with the career stage, such as the inherent stress of role transition between school and work, while also being complicated by generational differences, reflecting the unique perspective of Generation Z on mental health challenges. Taken together, these four chapters showcase the range of issues—and need for nuance—that attend focusing on mental health challenges in specific populations of workers.

The third section of this book explicitly considers how mental health challenges operate given various elements of the changing nature of work. As the norms, conditions, and challenges of work continue to change at an exceptionally fast rate, it is incumbent upon management scholars to inquire about how these changes can impact employees' mental health, for better or worse. This section begins with Kavanagh and colleagues' examination of trust and vulnerability in mental health disclosure decisions, which is particularly relevant in the era of rising relational orientation of work and expectations of authenticity at work (Pillemer, 2024). In the following chapter, Elraz examines how employees manage their mental health through computer-mediated communication, which is increasingly ubiquitous in the workplace in a way that is not reflected in extant research on mental health challenges and work. In the final chapter of this section, Sawyer and Gabriel take a broad perspective and reflect on how cumulative trauma impacts employees over the career lifecycle. As scholars increasingly recognize that nonwork trauma, both within employees' immediate environment (e.g., abuse, poverty) and in society more broadly (natural disasters, war), influences employees' experiences (Maitlis, 2020), this chapter provides an important foundation for how the resultant mental health challenges might manifest throughout a career.

The fourth section of this book looks at the unique mental health challenges that arise in specific work contexts. As with the previous sections, chapters have been chosen to showcase the divergent experiences that employees might face, with the aim of broadening readers' conceptualization of how mental health challenges might be impacted by various elements of work. In the first chapter of this section, Britt and colleagues present an overview of mental health challenges associated with work in high-risk occupations, in which they synthesize a diverse body of research on this field. In the second chapter, Martin and colleagues examine the mental health challenges that are uniquely relevant to academia.

Although discourse is increasing surrounding the importance of college students' mental health, research has not kept pace in examining how faculty's mental health is also impacted by academic work. In the third chapter, Gopinath examines mental health challenges in an entrepreneurship context. While research has acknowledged that entrepreneurial business founders and solo-venture entrepreneurs face unique mental health challenges (Stephan, 2018), this chapter investigates the mental health of those in the entrepreneur's orbit, who are impacted by the focal entrepreneur as well as their own circumstances and reaction to the unique environment of a small business. Finally, Jazaieri discusses the mental health challenges of leaders in organizations. Blending her expertise in leadership research and experience as a clinical psychologist, she illuminates the factors that might uniquely exacerbate leaders' mental health challenges, and invites readers to consider a broader perspective to support leaders' mental health going forward.

The final section of this book contains three chapters. Two of these examine efforts to support employees' mental health in a specific organization, while a third looks more generally at the complex interplay between HR functions and burnout. In the first of these chapters, Deane and colleagues present a case study of the wellness program at EY. In doing this, they explicate an important but often overlooked truism, which is that mental health challenges—and consequently mental health support—are inextricably linked to a broader ecosystem of overall wellness concerns. Following that, Kilroy and colleagues explore the relationship between human resource management (HRM) functions and burnout, which represents a common and problematic mental health challenge in organizations. In this chapter, they articulate how HRM practices can both promote good mental health and unintentionally exacerbate mental health challenges. In the final chapter, Rosado-Solomon and Babcock present a case study of a behavioral health facility's efforts to support their employees' mental health, with a focus on the unique context of caregiving during the COVID-19 pandemic. They demonstrate how HR practices can be leveraged to promote respect, which has not been prominently featured in the management literature on mental health challenges and work but is nevertheless crucial to well-being in organizations (Rogers & Ashforth, 2017). These efforts impacted the mental health of the employees within the organization and had important downstream impacts on the mental health of the psychiatric patients they serve. The book concludes with an integrative chapter that solidifies the pieces of the research foundation presented in this book and looks forward toward the next decade of research in this field.

Defining and Disambiguating Mental Health Challenges: Notes on Terminology

There is a variation of terminology on mental health challenges, some of which are defined in meaningfully different ways by different scholars (Bianchi et al.,

2015; Kelloway et al., 2023). This can make it hard to aggregate and compare related research to form a cohesive body of knowledge upon which to build (Rosado-Solomon et al., 2023). While a full review of terminology is beyond the scope of this introduction, it is important to distinguish mental health from mental illness. Mental health is a "general state of psychological wellness" (Rosado-Solomon et al., p. 752), which is conceptually similar to terms such as well-being and "emotional well-being" that are used synonymously across chapters in this volume. In contrast, mental illness refers to specific conditions that impact the way people think, feel, or act, such as major depressive disorder or generalized anxiety disorder which meet certain diagnostic criteria as defined in established psychological reference texts, such as the DSM-5, which change periodically but nevertheless represent a general consensus in the psychiatric community (Regier et al., 2013). Confusion often comes when distinguishing between poor mental health and mental illness, which are overlapping but conceptually distinct constructs (Follmer & Jones, 2018). Disambiguating these terms is important because it highlights the fact that people with chronic mental illness may have varied mental health, such that employees can experience good mental health while still existing with conditions of a chronic mental illness (Davidson & Roe, 2007; Rosado-Solomon et al., 2023). Concepts such as burnout and strain represent specific forms of poor mental health that often occur as a result of workplace stressors, and are therefore particularly relevant to organizational scholars (for additional information, see Hanson & Rosado-Solomon, this volume). Notwithstanding ongoing debate about the contours of these terms and their relationships to one another, readers are encouraged to utilize these general distinctions as a basis for understanding the interrelated nature of research in this volume.

Conclusion

In outlining the motivation for this book and setting expectations about structure and terminology, I hope to prepare readers for finding points of integration and complementarity as they read the chapters contained in this volume. Despite the enormity of the challenge of supporting employees' mental health at work, my hope is that this book inspires researchers to continue investigating the nuances of this important topic.

References

Bianchi, R., Schonfeld, I. S., & Laurent, E. (2015). Burnout–depression overlap: A review. *Clinical Psychology Review*, *36*, 28–41.

Calhoun, A. J., & Gold, J. A. (2020). "I feel like I know them": The positive effect of celebrity self-disclosure of mental illness. *Academic Psychiatry*, *44*, 237–241.

Davidson, L., & Roe, D. (2007). Recovery from versus recovery in serious mental illness: One strategy for lessening confusion plaguing recovery. *Journal of Mental Health*, *16*(4), 459–470.

Follmer, K. B., & Jones, K. S. (2018). Mental illness in the workplace: An interdisciplinary review and organizational research agenda. *Journal of Management, 44*(1), 325–351.

Giorgi, G., Lecca, L. I., Alessio, F., Finstad, G. L., Bondanini, G., Lulli, L. G., Arcangeli, G., & Mucci, N. (2020). COVID-19-related mental health effects in the workplace: A narrative review. *International Journal of Environmental Research and Public Health, 17*, 7857–7879.

Kelloway, E. K., Dimoff, J. K., & Gilbert, S. (2023). Mental health in the workplace. *Annual Review of Organizational Psychology and Organizational Behavior, 10*(1), 363–387.

Maitlis, S. (2020). Posttraumatic growth at work. *Annual Review of Organizational Psychology and Organizational Behavior, 7*(1), 395–419.

Maslach, C., & Jackson, S. E. (1981). The measurement of experienced burnout. *Journal of Organizational Behavior, 2*, 99–113.

Maslach, C., Jackson, S. E., & Leiter, M. P. (1997). Maslach burnout inventory: Third edition. In C. P. Zalaquett & R. J. Wood (Eds.), *Evaluating stress: A book of resources* (pp. 191–218). Scarecrow Education.

Mind Share Partners. (2025). *2025 Mental health at work report (report)*. https://www.mindsharepartners.org/2025-mental-health-at-work-report.

Murthly, V. H. (2024). *Parents under pressure: The U.S. surgeon general's advisory on the mental health and well-being of parents* (report). https://www.hhs.gov/sites/default/files/parents-under-pressure.pdf.

Pillemer, J. (2024). Strategic authenticity: Signaling authenticity without undermining professional image in workplace interactions. *Organization Science, 35*(5), 1641–1659.

Regier, D. A., Kuhl, E. A., & Kupfer, D. J. (2013). The DSM-5: Classification and criteria changes. *World Psychiatry, 12*(2), 92–98.

Rogers, K. M., & Ashforth, B. E. (2017). Respect in organizations: Feeling valued as "we" and "me". *Journal of Management, 43,* 1578–1608.

Rosado-Solomon, E. H., Koopmann, J., Lee, W., & Cronin, M. A. (2023). Mental health and mental illness in organizations: A review, comparison, and extension. *Academy of Management Annals, 17*(2), 751–797.

Stephan, U. (2018). Entrepreneurs' mental health and well-being: A review and research agenda. *Academy of Management Perspectives, 32*(3), 290–322.

Thornhill-Miller, B., Camarda, A., Mercier, M., Burkhardt, J. M., Morisseau, T., Bourgeois-Bougrine, S., Vinchon, F., El Hayek, S., Augereau-Landais, M., Mourey, F., Feybesse, C., Sundquist, D., & Lubart, T. (2023). Creativity, critical thinking, communication, and collaboration: Assessment, certification, and promotion of 21st century skills for the future of work and education. *Journal of Intelligence, 11*(3), 54.

Van Zoonen, W., & Sivunen, A. E. (2022). The impact of remote work and mediated communication frequency on isolation and psychological distress. *European Journal of Work and Organizational Psychology, 31*(4), 610–621.

Section I

Issues of Measurement and Construct Clarity

2 Conceptualizing and Measuring Mental Health

A Clinical Psychology Perspective for Workplace Research

Sheila K. Hanson and Emily H. Rosado-Solomon

Introduction

Scholarship on work and mental illness has expanded, although challenges have stymied research integration across fields of study, especially heterogeneous construct definitions and measurements of mental health including mental illness, related symptoms, and nonclinical states of poor mental health (Rosado-Solomon et al., 2023). The heterogeneity obscures relationships between similar constructs and impedes any ability to uncover complementarity. Poor understanding of construct alignment and measurement may cause researchers to misinterpret their findings. Lack of precise measuring and conceptualizing mental health challenges can produce inefficient research, with resources spent on duplicate studies of extant knowledge instead of building on previous research.

These concerns predominate in management research, where increasing attention has gone to mental health challenges in a disjointed way. This construct heterogeneity is less prevalent in clinical psychology, which has a longer history of studying mental health challenges and more standardization of conceptual boundaries across studies. Diagnostic criteria for each identified mental illness are defined in the *Diagnostic and Statistical Manual of Mental Disorders, 5th edition* (*DSM-V-TR*). Periodic updates reflect changes in psychologists' understanding of various mental illnesses (Regier et al., 2013). The updating promotes alignment between construct and measurement, which enables diagnostic criteria to reflect current scientific understanding. This alignment is crucial to ensure that constructs defined in the manual represent accurately the disorders they are intended to diagnose, in turn fostering measurement precision. Clinical instruments have been developed to assess various mental illnesses using clinically derived approaches to diagnose and treat problems. Given the established body of research on mental health and mental illness in clinical psychology, we propose incorporating a clinical psychology perspective, which is essential to inform management scholars who conduct research on mental health and mental illness in the workplace.

DOI: 10.4324/9781003491170-3

This chapter has three goals. First, the chapter defines and differentiates mental illness and (poor) mental health, comparing mainstream definitions in clinical psychology to concepts published in management literature. Second, the chapter describes how and why measurement tools are used to study mental health and illness, noting challenges for adopting clinical instruments in nonclinical contexts and their use by persons who are not clinically trained. Third, the chapter highlights research implications for organizational scholars and management. In summary, this chapter provides a useful overview of measurement issues for organizational researchers.

Define and Differentiate Mental Illness and (Poor) Mental Health

Mental Health

Mental health is defined as "a state of mental well-being that enables people to cope with the stresses of life, to realize their abilities, to learn well and work well, and to contribute to their communities" (World Health Organization [WHO], 2022, p. 8). Other terms to describe positive states of mental health include mental well-being (Pollard, 2001) and thriving (Porath et al., 2012). A nuanced discussion of positive mental health constructs (e.g., thriving; Goh et al., 2022) is beyond the scope of this chapter, although such constructs are somewhat related to mental health challenges. Mental health is an integral component of health and well-being and "is more than the absence of mental disorder" (WHO, 2022, p. 8). Clinical psychologists provide mental health services somewhat analogous to physical health services that prevent or intervene with physical illness and promote health. Clinical psychologists focus on diagnosis and treatment of mental illness with a goal to enhance mental health in a holistic sense, as they work to improve coping skills, functioning, and quality of life to the degree possible (Cuijpers et al., 2014; Davidson & Roe, 2007). In research, clinical psychologists might refer to poor mental health as a relative term or use the phrase "negative mental health outcomes" (e.g., Emmer et al., 2024) to describe a range of issues.

Mental illness and poor mental health are related but distinct concepts often conflated in management literature (Follmer & Jones, 2018; Rosado-Solomon et al., 2023). Poor mental health is a broad concept that may not meet the threshold for a clinical diagnosis but still impacts well-being and functioning. It may include experiences of strain (Karasek, 1979), burnout (Maslach & Jackson, 1981), or general psychological distress (e.g., Hardy et al., 2003) without a diagnosed mental disorder. Unlike mental illness, poor mental health may or may not involve significant impairment. Some management studies use "mental health" as a catch-all term encompassing diagnosed mental illness and general psychological well-being (Rosado-Solomon et al., 2023). Others focus on mental well-being as distinct from poor mental health, recognizing that people can have generally good mental well-being while still experiencing symptoms of mental illness, just as people can be in generally good physical health (exercising, eating well, etc.) while simultaneously experiencing a physical health concern (e.g., a broken ankle; Rosado-Solomon et al., 2023).

Two work-specific constructs, job strain and burnout, often appear in management studies on poor mental health (Bliese et al., 2017) and in clinical psychology literature (Deling et al., 2024). Scholars debate the relationship between these constructs and mental health challenges that are clinically derived (Bianchi et al., 2015). Some scholars note that job strain may have a causal relationship with mental illness (or symptoms thereof) (e.g., Madsen et al., 2017), whereas others view burnout and job strain as states of poor mental health that are problematic in their own right and that may lead to outcomes related more to the organization, such as turnover and impaired job performance. (For reviews on the consequences of burnout and strain, see Edú-Valsania et al., 2022, and Bliese et al., 2017, respectively.)

Mental Illness

To distinguish between mental health and mental illness, it is useful to consider how mental illness is defined. In clinical psychology, mental illness refers to diagnosable mental disorders characterized by significant disturbances in cognition and emotion regulation, or behavior that reflects dysfunction in psychological, biological, or developmental processes causing distress and impairment (American Psychiatric Association [APA], 2013). Mental illnesses are specific, diagnosable conditions like major depressive disorder (MDD) or generalized anxiety disorder (GAD).

Some types of mental illness share symptoms with constructs reflecting poor mental health. Bianchi and colleagues (2015) have shown significant empirical overlap between burnout and depression, with commonalities across various measures. However, a key distinction is that mental illness impairs two or more life domains (APA, 2013), whereas burnout is domain-specific and need not produce substantive impairment (Koutsimani et al., 2019). In other cases, there is a distinction between mental illness and poor mental health. For example, there is not only a strong association between worry and poor mental health but also significant heterogeneity. The presence of worry and poor mental health does not translate to a diagnosed mental illness such as GAD or MDD (Vîslă et al., 2022).

Given these differences, we now turn to measurement approaches in clinical psychology to explain the distinction between, and consequently the research implications of, various mental health constructs.

Measurement Tools Used to Study Mental Health and Illness: How and Why

Clinical psychologists use various measurement tools to study mental health and illness. Three ways to track and assess mental health conditions include screening, diagnosis, and monitoring of symptom severity and treatment outcomes.

Some tools are used with only one type of assessment; other tools can be used in multiple ways depending on their intended purpose. All are crucial for both clinical practice and research, providing standardized procedures to assess and track mental health conditions. We first review, then clarify, the implications of this framework for management researchers who wish to investigate mental health challenges.

Screening Tools

Screening tools are designed to identify, often by short questionnaires, individuals who may have mental health conditions. Two common examples are the generalized anxiety disorder-7 (GAD-7) and the Patient Health Questionnaire-9 (PHQ-9) developed for use in primary care settings. The GAD-7 is used widely to screen for anxiety symptoms indicating possible anxiety disorders (Spitzer et al., 2006). The PHQ-9 (Kroenke et al., 2001) is a self-report measure that aligns closely with DSM-5 criteria for MDD. It is commonly used to screen for depression but does *not* provide sufficient evidence of a MDD, as its purpose is to screen for depressive disorders with high sensitivity (Pettersson et al., 2015). Screening tools should not be interpreted as signaling a certain mental illness because a different diagnosis (e.g., bipolar disorder) may better explain symptoms in a full diagnostic assessment. These two examples of screening tools are often used in primary care settings and mental health clinics. They can be administered quickly and can provide early indication of potential issues to follow with comprehensive assessment.

The self-report tools above, as well as others, capture an individual's perception and understanding of their mental health (Smith, 2019). Self-report assessments are advantageous in clinical settings for quick screening and for referral to healthcare providers (Kroenke et al., 2001). They are efficient for collecting data on large populations because they are easy to administer and scalable online (Kolc et al., 2023). They are also useful because they do not require a clinician to have specialized expertise in psychology to administer an assessment, making them ideal for a primary care physician to refer patients to a specialist if needed. However, these tools are susceptible to bias and inaccuracy. Self-report measures may reflect a respondent's current mood (even though instructions specify reflection over the past two weeks), social desirability bias, or lack of insight into their own symptoms and mental health (Atkinson et al., 1997). This can lead to underreporting or overreporting of symptoms. An individual may underreport symptoms that are stigmatized or socially undesirable, such as substance abuse or certain psychiatric symptoms, to present themselves in a more favorable light (Gnambs & Kaspar, 2015). Deliberately inaccurate reporting is often referenced as "faking good" or "faking bad" to influence outcomes such as psychological readiness for military service (e.g., Boss et al., 2015). Individuals may infer meaning from the research instrument itself (Schwarz, 1999). For these reasons, supplementing self-report measures with clinical interviews can enhance interpretation. Developing rapport and creating a supportive, non-judgmental environment in clinical interviews can encourage accurate reporting (Rogers, 1957), as individuals are more likely to disclose true experience when they feel valued (Miller & Rollnick, 2013).

Although not as frequently used in clinical psychology, measures of burnout and job strain may be described as analogous to screening tools. They assess the extent to which one displays symptoms, but they are not often used to determine whether a person experiences burnout or strain. (For benchmarks of relative levels, see Maslach et al., 1996.) For readers interested in measuring these constructs, Edú-Valsania et al. (2022) present a review of burnout measurement and Hurrell et al. (1998) a review of measuring job strain.

Diagnostic Approaches

A second approach to measurement is diagnosis, which helps clinicians determine whether a person meets the criteria for an established mental illness. Self-report measures are used as a component of diagnosis, but diagnoses are not based solely on self-report measures. Self-report tools, clinician-rated measures, and clinical judgment approaches in mental health assessment offer unique insights and viewpoints. Self-report measures ask individuals to provide subjective information about symptoms of their own mental health through structured questionnaires or surveys (Schwarz, 1999). In contrast, clinician-rated measures rely on trained professionals evaluating the presence and severity of symptoms based on clinical judgment and observations during interviews or standardized assessments (Groth-Marnat, 2009). Clinical psychologists evaluate symptoms and functioning while incorporating behavioral observations and considering diagnostic criteria using clinical judgment (Groth-Marnat, 2009). This procedure is usually not possible for management researchers to replicate without an interdisciplinary team. It requires trained clinical judgment and integration of multiple information sources such as self-report measures, behavioral observations, and clinical interviews.

Diagnostic tools support clinicians in making formal diagnoses of mental health conditions. Clinical psychologists use standardized assessment tools validated through extensive research and often normed with multiple samples. Assessment and diagnosis often involve structured or semi-structured interviews and validated questionnaires that correspond to diagnostic criteria. Clinical interviews using clinician-rated measures are generally considered the gold standard for diagnosing mental health conditions in both research and practice (e.g., Subica et al., 2014).

In addition to measuring symptom presence and severity, clinician evaluation of an individual's mental health history is key to diagnosing mental illness. Many types of mental illness have similar symptoms, and it is necessary to distinguish which symptoms are most associated with which conditions. A process called differential diagnosis can make this distinction. It is part of a larger diagnostic picture beyond individual assessment tools and measures. Sometimes, diagnostic tools used to measure symptoms (e.g., Barkley's Adult ADHD Rating Scale; Barkley, 2011) may mislead management researchers. Without supporting clinical data, a practitioner could misinterpret clinical levels of ADHD symptoms as ADHD, when these symptoms are explained by a different condition, such as generalized anxiety (Alarachi et al., 2024). Both self-report and clinician-rated measures play pivotal roles in mental health assessment and differential diagnosis. They offer complementary perspectives that contribute to understanding an individual's mental health status and treatment needs. Formal diagnosis is comprehensive. It includes quantitative data (self-reports, clinical assessment) and qualitative data (structured interviews, behavioral observation). Although management scholars do not conduct diagnostic assessment in their research, understanding the process serves as a useful way to highlight the divide between assessing symptoms and evaluating chronic mental illness.

Symptom and Outcome Monitoring Tools

In addition to screening and diagnostic tools, clinical psychologists use standardized assessment tools to measure changes in symptom severity over time and to monitor treatment effectiveness in reducing symptoms. Regular use of these measures can help guide therapeutic interventions and track progress. Assessment tools are essential in clinical practice to confirm diagnoses, plan treatment, and monitor progress. The same assessment tools may be used to screen symptoms, clarify diagnoses, and monitor symptoms in the same person over time to track individual changes. Thus, assessment tools may be used in similar but meaningfully nuanced ways, requiring care and consideration by trained mental health professionals.

An example of a symptom management tool is the Beck Depression Inventory (BDI-II; Beck et al., 1996a). It is a self-report to assess the intensity of depressive *symptoms*, and it is widely used in both clinical and research settings. As a screening tool, the BDI-II can assess the presence and severity of depressive symptoms in clinical settings. It consists of 21 items that measure various symptoms of depression, including mood, pessimism, sense of failure, and physical symptoms such as fatigue and loss of appetite (Beck et al., 1996a). As a symptom-tracking tool, BDI-II may be used to track symptoms, monitor symptom changes over time during treatment, and adjust interventions accordingly (Gorman, 2015). As a research tool, the BDI-II represents *symptoms* rather than clinically diagnosed depressive disorders verified by clinicians. Clinical psychologists develop an evidence base for their clinical interventions, so both the BDI and BDI-II have served in randomized clinical trials to evaluate intervention effectiveness for depression (see Cuijpers et al., 2014).

Challenges in Using Clinical Instruments

Although assessments developed in a clinical setting are attractive to management scholars because of their rigorous development and validation, management researchers should consider certain challenges before adopting a clinically derived instrument. We now review some of the most notable challenges.

Contextual Validity

Clinical instruments are designed and validated within clinical settings to assess specific mental health constructs and disorders. Clinicians ensure that instruments have appropriate psychometric properties and clinical utility for their intended purpose. Extensive psychometric testing in clinical samples establishes the reliability, validity, sensitivity, and specificity of clinical instruments. For example, the original BDI was developed in 1961 to detect, assess, and monitor changes in depressive symptoms among individuals in psychiatric inpatient and outpatient settings (Beck et al., 1961). A second version of the inventory (BDI-II) was developed using a psychiatric adult outpatient sample and a control group (Beck et al., 1996b). Although the BDI-II provides information about the presence and severity of depressive symptoms, a formal diagnosis should *not* be made without clinical assessment by a qualified mental health professional (Beck et al., 1996b). When using clinical assessment tools in nonclinical contexts like a workplace, the relevance and interpretation of clinical measures as with the BDI-II could differ significantly. The comorbidity of other conditions like Post-Traumatic Stress Disorder (PTSD) in service members and veteran populations may be important (Reis et al., 2020).

On the other hand, some measures were not intended for clinical use. For example, in personality research, many Big Five personality instruments (those that measure extraversion, neuroticism, conscientiousness, openness to experience, and agreeability; Walton et al., 2008) do not have the content or sensitivity to assess the entire range of each construct (Dilchert et al., 2014). Therefore, commonly used personality instruments are not appropriate from which to make clinical research inferences, even for those that demonstrate extreme levels of a given trait. Although clinical psychologists have moved toward dimensional personality assessment, this does not mean that high levels of a personality trait automatically translate to a diagnosed mental illness (e.g., Narcissistic Personality Disorder [NPD]; Day et al., 2024). Rather, clinical psychologists use other assessment tools, such as the MMPI-3, to assess personality pathology and other forms of psychopathology together with a clinical interview (Ben-Porath & Tellegen, 2020).

Clinical Expertise and Scope

Management researchers lack the clinical training necessary to determine appropriate assessment tools, and then administer them and interpret the results. For example, using clinical instruments such as the Structured Clinical Interview for

DSM Disorders (SCID) and the Minnesota Multiphasic Personality Inventory (MMPI) series requires extensive training or supervision. A research version of the SCID-5 is available (First et al., 2015). Administering and interpreting with the MMPI-3 require specialized education and training on its structure, scales, and interpretation guidelines (Ben-Porath & Tellegen, 2020). An error in understanding assessment results can lead to misdiagnosis or inappropriate treatment recommendations (Ben-Porath & Tellegen, 2020).

Inadequate training may cause failure to contextualize test administration, such as by missing cultural or situational factors, which can skew results. Overreliance on tests and measures can lead to overlooking important information from clinical interviews, history, or other assessments, resulting in biased or incomplete conclusions (Graham, 2021). Practitioners and researchers must understand the limitations of assessment tools. For instance, tools designed for screening and symptom monitoring have a short temporal referent; in other words, they are meant to address symptoms over a time period of about two weeks. Scores should not be interpreted to represent events outside the temporal referent, such as a work event that occurred in prior years (Rosado-Solomon et al., 2023). As another example, persons with clinically significant symptoms of anxiety or depression do not necessarily have a diagnosed mental illness (e.g., GAD or MDD), so it is not appropriate to make inferences about participants having mental illness based on symptom measures. Clinically significant symptoms according to the DSM-V/V-TR refer to symptoms that are severe and frequent enough to impact negatively an individual's ability to function in multiple life domains, such as work and social settings (APA, 2013, 2022). An example of misguided inference might be assuming a person with high levels of depressive symptoms has experiences similar to those of someone with clinical depression, such as when facing stigma or navigating identity-related issues. In their review of mental health and work, Rosado-Solomon and colleagues (2023) found several studies that made just such an inference, highlighting the need for more nuanced insight when interpreting results.

Cultural Sensitivity

Clinical instruments are often developed and validated within specific cultural and clinical populations, and their applicability and validity may vary across different cultural and organizational contexts (Van de Vijver & Tanzer, 2004). Differences in cultural norms, work environments, and organizational structures affect how individuals perceive and respond to items on these instruments. Clinical instruments may not be culturally sensitive or appropriate for diverse workplace populations, potentially leading to biased or inaccurate results (Follmer & Jones, 2018). For example, in populations with East Asian heritage, depression is more likely to manifest as somatic symptoms (headache, body aches) than in Western contexts, where affective symptoms (sadness, low mood) are more likely (Sue & Sue, 1987). In samples disproportionately affected by known systematic trends, researchers should consider whether a given assessment tool is likely to capture phenomena of interest. This example underscores the need to use assessment tools that are validated and normed for relevant populations, especially in cross-cultural or international research. Several common assessment tools have been validated in multiple languages and various cultural contexts, including the BDI-II (Wang & Gorenstein, 2013) and the PHQ-9 (Murray et al., 2022).

Ethical Considerations

Unique ethical considerations may dictate the selection of clinical instruments for a management setting, especially in studies lacking clinician involvement. Popular scales include items that may produce sensitive information, and management researchers must think about how to handle information if it indicates a risk of harm. The PHQ-9, commonly used to measure symptoms of depression, asks about an individual's thoughts of self-harm (Wu et al., 2020). Especially in cases where researchers might be able to trace the identity of a respondent, such as with a master coding sheet, researchers must consider what they will do if they learn of a participant's thoughts of self-harm (e.g., suicidal ideation), as there may be an ethical obligation to act on this information. Such planning is typically done in clinical psychology research, where a protocol is developed for potential scenarios before research begins (Goodsmith et al., 2021). Alternatively, researchers may consider using a measure that does not risk producing such information. Institutional Review Boards (IRBs) will sometimes weigh in on guidelines for research on sensitive topics. Continuing the previous example, the PHQ-8 is a well-validated version of the PHQ-9, identical to the original measure omitting the item on thoughts of self-harm (Wu et al., 2020).

Using clinical instruments in nonclinical settings may raise ethical concerns about the use of diagnostic tools outside clinical practice. It is essential to consider potential consequences, such as implying the relevance of a mental health challenge to participants who may not share the view that it aligns with their professional or personal identities (American Psychological Association, 2017), resulting in alarm, distress, or confusion. Using clinical instruments in a workplace may raise ethical issues of privacy, confidentiality, or discrimination. Employees may feel uncomfortable disclosing sensitive mental health information to employers (Dimoff & Kelloway, 2019) or may be tempted to "fake good" if they do not trust researchers to maintain confidentiality. These potential outcomes suggest the negative consequences of accidental confidentiality breach for data on mental health challenges. Such a scenario could open liability for researchers and employees if the material is identified by participants' employers, or if it influences workplace decisions or violates employment laws and regulations (Dimoff & Kelloway, 2019).

Research Implications

In this chapter, we focus on quantitative research strategies that involve clinical psychology and that use clinical measurement tools and approaches to assess mental health and mental illness in workplace research. This is an opportunity for management scholars to address the importance of mental health and mental illness at work, introducing another field of study, clinical psychology, into management research.

Misuse of tests and measurements, whether through inadequate training or misinterpretation, can lead to harmful consequences for those being assessed in workplace research studies with implications for workplace settings. Management scholars who wish to conduct workplace research can focus on improving conceptual precision with clinical measures and tools. Studies that use Experience Sampling Methodology (ESM; Gabriel et al., 2019) to gather repeated measures of symptoms should rely on assessment tools that have been validated for symptom monitoring. Likewise, studies that investigate more static relationships, such as the impact of a major work event on long-term mental health, might select a different tool that better captures enduring symptoms. Most importantly, it is critical to provide strong transparency about the research methods, measures used, and rationale for those choices in order to help readers interpret and utilize the evidence in the studies.

Extensive training is needed to navigate measurement considerations. Interdisciplinary research teams could integrate both the management and the clinical psychology perspectives. Including a "native speaker" in clinical psychology may be of benefit in conducting new research and reviewing existing research. There is evidence of this approach in multidisciplinary reviews (Howard et al., 2022), but fields often operate independently (Rosado-Solomon et al., 2023). Yet there is precedent for interdisciplinary practice, as clinical psychologists often work side by side with psychiatrists and other medical professionals to leverage the expertise of more than one field. Bringing together interdisciplinary research teams of management scholars and clinical psychologists is one way to leverage assessment tools aiming toward best practice and ethical use. We view it as aspirational and desirable for clinical psychologists to partner with management researchers for shared benefit. Joining forces captures the expertise in both fields, informing research design, execution, and results.

Conclusion

This chapter integrates clinical psychology and scholarly management perspectives, differentiating mental illness from poor mental health. In describing the assessment processes of screening, the diagnostic and symptom management tools used by clinical psychologists, and the challenges of using clinical instruments in management research, this chapter brings to light multiple implications for research and practice. The chapter shares a pragmatic overview of measurement considerations for organizational researchers through the lens of clinical psychology research and practice.

References

Alarachi, A., Merrifield, C., Rowa, K., & McCabe, R. E. (2024). Are we measuring ADHD or anxiety? Examining the factor structure and discriminant validity of the Adult ADHD Self-Report Scale in an adult anxiety disorder population. *Assessment, 31*(7), 1508–1524.

American Psychiatric Association (APA). (2013; 2022). *Diagnostic and statistical manual of mental disorders* (5th ed.; DSM-5) and DSM-5-Text Revision (DSM-5-TR).

American Psychological Association. (2017). *Ethical principles of psychologists and code of conduct*. https://www.apa.org/ethics/code/

Atkinson, M., Zibin, S., & Chuang, H. (1997). Characterizing quality of life among patients with chronic mental illness: A critical examination of the self-report methodology. *American Journal of Psychiatry, 154*(1), 99–105.

Barkley, R. A. (2011). *Barkley Adult ADHD Rating Scale-IV (BAARS-IV)*. Guilford Press.

Beck, A. T., Steer, R. A., Ball, R., & Ranieri, W. F. (1996b). Comparison of Beck Depression Inventories-IA and –II in psychiatric outpatients. *Journal of Personality Assessment, 67*, 588–597.

Beck, A. T., Steer, R. A., & Brown, G. K. (1996a). *Manual for the Beck Depression Inventory-II*. Psychological Corporation.

Beck, A. T., Ward, C. H., Mendelson, M., Mock, J., & Erbaugh, J. (1961). An inventory for measuring depression. *Archives of General Psychiatry, 4*(6), 561–571.

Ben-Porath, Y. S., & Tellegen, A. (2020). *MMPI-3 manual for administration, scoring, and interpretation*. University of Minnesota Press.

Bianchi, R., Schonfeld, I. S., & Laurent, E. (2015). Burnout–depression overlap: A review. *Clinical Psychology Review, 36*, 28–41.

Bliese, P. D., Edwards, J. R., & Sonnentag, S. (2017). Stress and well-being at work: A century of empirical trends reflecting theoretical and societal influences. *Journal of Applied Psychology, 10*, 389–402.

Boss, P., König, C. J., & Melchers, K. G. (2015). Faking good and faking bad among military conscripts. *Human Performance, 28*(1), 26–39.

Cuijpers, P., Karyotaki, E., Weitz, E., Andersson, G., Hollon, S. D., & van Straten, A. (2014). The effects of psychotherapies for major depression in adults on remission, recovery and improvement: A meta-analysis. *Journal of Affective Disorders, 159*, 118–126.

Davidson, L., & Roe, D. (2007). Recovery from versus recovery in serious mental illness: One strategy for lessening confusion plaguing recovery. *Journal of Mental Health, 16*(4), 459–470.

Day, N. J. S., Green, A., Denmeade, G., Bach, B., & Grenyer, B. F. S. (2024). Narcissistic personality disorder in the ICD-11: Severity and trait profiles of grandiosity and vulnerability. *Journal of Clinical Psychology, 80*(8), 1917–1936.

Deling, L., Legerski, J.-P., & Hanson, S. K. (2024). Burnout in applied behavior analyst technicians: The role of personality and stress. *Current Psychology (New Brunswick, N.J.), 43*(13), 11627–11641

Dilchert, S., Ones, D. S., & Krueger, R. F. (2014). Maladaptive personality constructs, measures, and work behaviors. *Industrial and Organizational Psychology, 7*(1), 98–110.

Dimoff, J. K., & Kelloway, E. K. (2019). With a little help from my boss: The impact of workplace mental health training on leader behaviors and employee resource utilization. *Journal of Occupational Health Psychology, 24*(1), 4–19.

Edú-Valsania, S., Laguía, A., & Moriano, J. A. (2022). Burnout: A review of theory and measurement. *International Journal of Environmental Research and Public Health, 19*(3), 1780.

Emmer, C., Dorn, J., & Mata, J. (2024). The immediate effect of discrimination on mental health: A meta-analytic review of the causal evidence. *Psychological Bulletin, 150*(3), 215–252.

First, M. B., Williams, J. B. W., Karg, R. S., & Spitzer, R. L. (2015). *Structured clinical interview for DSM-5—Research version* (SCID-5 for DSM-5, Research Version; SCID-5-RV). American Psychiatric Association.

Follmer, K. B., & Jones, K. S. (2018). Mental illness in the workplace: An interdisciplinary review and organizational research agenda. *Journal of Management, 44*(1), 325–351.

Gabriel, A. S., Podsakoff, N. P., Beal, D. J., Scott, B. A., Sonnentag, S., Trougakos, J. P., & Butts, M. M. (2019). Experience sampling methods: A discussion of critical trends and considerations for scholarly advancement. *Organizational Research Methods, 22*(4), 969–1006.

Gnambs, T., & Kaspar, K. (2015). Disclosure of sensitive behaviors across self-administered survey modes: A meta-analysis. *Behavior Research Methods, 47*(4), 1237–1259.

Goh, Z., Eva, N., Kiazad, K., Jack, G. A., De Cieri, H., & Spreitzer, G. M. (2022). An integrative multilevel review of thriving at work: Assessing progress and promise. *Journal of Organizational Behavior, 43*(2), 197–213.

Goodsmith, N., Zhang, L., Ong, M. K., Ngo, V. K., Miranda, J., Hirsch, S., Jones, F., Wells, K., & Chung, B. (2021). Implementation of a community-partnered research suicide-risk management protocol: Case study from community partners in care. *Psychiatric Services, 72*(3), 281–287.

Gorman, J. M. (2015). Comorbid depression and anxiety spectrum disorders. *Depression and Anxiety, 32*(9), 699–701.

Graham, J. R. (2021). *MMPI-3: Assessing personality and psychopathology*. Oxford University Press.

Groth-Marnat, G. (2009). *Handbook of psychological assessment*. John Wiley & Sons, Inc.

Hardy, G. E., Woods, D., & Wall, T. D. (2003). The impact of psychological distress on absence from work. *Journal of Applied Psychology, 88*(2), 306.

Howard, M. C., Follmer, K. B., Smith, M. B., Tucker, R. P., & Van Zandt, E. C. (2022). Work and suicide: An interdisciplinary systematic literature review. *Journal of Organizational Behavior, 43*(2), 260–285.

Hurrell, J. J., Nelson, D. L., & Simmons, B. L. (1998). Measuring job stressors and strains: Where we have been, where we are, and where we need to go. *Journal of Occupational Health Psychology, 3*(4), 368–389.

Karasek, R. A. (1979). Job demands, job decision latitude, and mental strain: Implications for job redesign. *Administrative Science Quarterly*, 285–308.

Kolc, K. L., Tan, Y. X. K., Lo, A. Z. Y., Shvetcov, A., Mitchell, P. B., & Perkes, I. E. (2023). Measuring psychiatric symptoms online: A systematic review of the use of inventories on Amazon Mechanical Turk (mTurk). *Journal of Psychiatric Research, 163*, 118–126.

Koutsimani, P., Montgomery, A., & Georganta, K. (2019). The relationship between burnout, depression, and anxiety: A systematic review and meta-analysis. *Frontiers in Psychology, 10*, 1–19.

Kroenke, K., Spitzer, R. L., & Williams, J. B. (2001). The PHQ-9: Validity of a brief depression severity measure. *Journal of General Internal Medicine*, *16*(9), 606–613.

Madsen, I. E., Nyberg, S. T., Hanson, L. M., Ferrie, J. E., Ahola, K., Alfredsson, L., Batty, G. D., Bjorner, J. B., Borritz, M., Burr, H., Chastang, J. F., de Graaf, R., Dragano, N., Hamer, M., Jokela, M., Knutsson, A., Koskenvuo, M., Koskinen, A., Leineweber, C., . . .& IPD-Work Consortium. (2017). Job strain as a risk factor for clinical depression: Systematic review and meta-analysis with additional individual participant data. *Psychological Medicine*, *47*(8), 1342–1356. https://pubmed.ncbi.nlm.nih.gov/28122650/

Maslach, C., & Jackson, S. E. (1981). The measurement of experienced burnout. *Journal of Organizational Behavior*, *2*(2), 99–113.

Maslach, C., Jackson, S. E., & Leiter, M. P. (1996). *Maslach Burnout Inventory manual* (3rd ed.). Mind Garden.

Miller, W. R., & Rollnick, S. (2013). *Motivational interviewing: Helping people change* (3rd ed.). Guilford Press.

Murray, A. L., Hemady, C. L., Do, H., Dunne, M., Foley, S., Osafo, J., Sikander, S., Madrid, B., Baban, A., Taut, D., Ward, C. L., Fernando, A., Thang, V. V., Eisner, M., Hughes, C., Fearon, P., Valdebenito, S., Tomlinson, M., Pathmeswaran, A., & Walker, S. (2022). Measuring antenatal depressive symptoms across the world: A validation and cross-country invariance analysis of the Patient Health Questionnaire-9 (PHQ-9) in eight diverse low-resource settings. *Psychological Assessment*, *34*(11), 993–1007. https://pubmed.ncbi.nlm.nih.gov/36227303/

Pettersson, A., Boström, K. B., Gustavsson, P., & Ekselius, L. (2015). Which instruments to support diagnosis of depression have sufficient accuracy? A systematic review. *Nordic Journal of Psychiatry*, *69*(7), 497–508.

Pollard, T. M. (2001). Changes in mental well-being, blood pressure and total cholesterol levels during workplace reorganization: The impact of uncertainty. *Work & Stress*, *15*(1), 14–28.

Porath, C., Spreitzer, G., Gibson, C., & Garnett, F. G. (2012). Thriving at work: Toward its measurement, construct validation, and theoretical refinement. *Journal of Organizational Behavior*, *33*(2), 250–275.

Regier, D. A., Kuhl, E. A., & Kupfer, D. J. (2013). The DSM-5: Classification and criteria changes. *World Psychiatry*, *12*(2), 92–98.

Reis, D. J., Namekata, M. S., Oehlert, M. E., & King, N. (2020). A preliminary review of the Beck Depression Inventory-II (BDI-II) in Veterans: Are new norms and cut scores needed? *Psychological Services*, *17*(3), 363–371.

Rogers, C. R. (1957). The necessary and sufficient conditions of therapeutic personality change. *Journal of Consulting Psychology*, *21*(2), 95–103.

Rosado-Solomon, E. H., Koopmann, J., Lee, W., & Cronin, M. A. (2023). Mental health and mental illness in organizations: A review, comparison, and extension. *Academy of Management Annals*, *17*(2), 751–797.

Schwarz, N. (1999). Self-reports: How the questions shape the answers. *American Psychologist*, *54*(2), 93–105.

Spitzer, R. L., Kroenke, K., Williams, J. B. W., & Löwe, B. (2006). A brief measure for assessing generalized anxiety disorder the GAD−7. *Archives of Internal Medicine*, *166*, 1092–1097.

Subica, A. M., Fowler, J. C., Elhai, J. D., Frueh, B. C., Sharp, C., Kelly, E. L., Allen, J. G., & Reynolds, C. R. (2014). Factor structure and diagnostic validity of the Beck Depression Inventory-II with adult clinical inpatients: Comparison to a gold-standard diagnostic interview. *Psychological Assessment*, *26*(4), 1106–1115.

Sue, D., & Sue, S. (1987). Cultural factors in the clinical assessment of Asian Americans. *Journal of Consulting and Clinical Psychology*, *55*(4), 479–487.

Van de Vijver, F. J. R., & Tanzer, N. K. (2004). Bias and equivalence in cross-cultural assessment: An overview. *European Review of Applied Psychology*, *54*(2), 119–135.
Vîslă, A., Stadelmann, C., Watkins, E., Zinbarg, R. E., & Flückiger, C. (2022). The relation between worry and mental health in nonclinical population and individuals with anxiety and depressive disorders: A meta-analysis. *Cognitive Therapy and Research*, *46*(3), 480–501.
Walton, K. E., Roberts, B. W., Krueger, R. F., Blonigen, D. M., & Hicks, B. M. (2008). Capturing abnormal personality with normal personality inventories: An item response theory approach. *Journal of Personality*, *76*, 1623–1647.44
Wang, Y. P., & Gorenstein, C. (2013). Psychometric properties of the Beck Depression Inventory-II: A comprehensive review. *Revista Brasileira de Psiquiatria*, *35*(4), 416–431.
World Health Organization. (2022). *World mental health report: Transforming mental health for all*. World Health Organization. https://www.who.int/publications/i/item/9789240049338
Wu, Y., Levis, B., Riehm, K. E., Saadat, N., Levis, A. W., Azar, M., Rice, D. B., Boruff, J., Cuijpers, P., Gilbody, S., Ioannidis, J. P. A., Kloda, L. A., McMillan, D., Patten, S. B., Shrier, I., Ziegelstein, R. C., Akena, D. H., Arroll, B., Ayalon, L.,. . . Thombs, B. D. (2020). Equivalency of the diagnostic accuracy of the PHQ-8 and PHQ-9: A systematic review and individual participant data meta-analysis. *Psychological Medicine*, *50*(8), 1368–1380. https://pubmed.ncbi.nlm.nih.gov/31298180/

3 The Nature of Narcissism

A Review and Expansion of Research on Narcissism in the Workplace

Shoshana Dobrow, Caleb Phillips, and Emily H. Rosado-Solomon

Introduction

> The world outwardly rewards narcissists . . . they're charming, manipulative, and goal-oriented, they go on more dates and become titans of industry. But while they may control everything around them, they are yet to accept themselves. "Underneath all the noise is insecurity."[1]

These lines underscore the significance of narcissism, which fundamentally affects human interactions (American Psychological Association [APA], 2022) and can have powerful, widespread impact. Moreover, the prevalence of narcissism has increased in recent decades, reflecting broad sociocultural trends (e.g., Twenge et al., 2008). As such, narcissism, a "relatively stable individual difference consisting of grandiosity, self-love, and inflated self-views" (Campbell et al., 2011, p. 269), has increasingly captivated the attention of scholars (e.g., Miller et al., 2017) and popular discourse (e.g., Caron, 2024) alike. Narcissism is highly salient in the workplace, where management scholars have found it exerts a "pervasive influence" on organizational life (Campbell et al., 2011, p. 281).

The extent to which this influence is positive or negative has been murky, according to the most recent review of narcissism in management research (Campbell et al., 2011). This review highlights several key ways narcissism exerts influence at the individual, interpersonal, and organizational levels. The authors argue that narcissism should be considered a trade-off, with effects varying by context (i.e., the extent to which the environment is novel or chaotic vs. stable or long term; Campbell et al., 2011). Across many outcomes, time horizon plays a critical role, with higher narcissism often positive in the short term but negative in the long term. For instance, higher narcissism is linked to leadership emergence in the short term but questionable leadership effectiveness in the long run (Grijalva et al., 2015). Organizational selection processes

DOI: 10.4324/9781003491170-4

that prioritize short-term performance, likability in an interview, and projections of self-confidence can favor people higher in narcissism. Yet over time, higher narcissism often harms interpersonal relationships (Campbell et al., 2011). For organizational outcomes, in the short term, leaders higher in narcissism can generate better firm performance but eventually "destroy systems that they and others depend on to survive and thrive" (Campbell et al., 2011, p. 280).

Campbell and colleagues' (2011) review provides a useful definition of narcissism (above). Yet it also highlights "confusion about the construct" (p. 269) as a core issue in management research on narcissism; hence, we view this as a working definition for purposes of the present chapter. The review concludes by emphasizing that "from our perspective, the single most important theme in research on narcissism in organizations is that there is more research needed" (p. 281). Management scholars have heeded this call, publishing over 900 articles about narcissism since 2011, with exponential growth since 2018.

This surge in research reflects narcissism's growing importance in academic and public discourse. Yet it has yielded a fragmented body of work with significant knowledge gaps alongside well-studied areas. This chapter addresses these gaps with a two-step approach. First, to assess recent findings about narcissism since the last major review (Campbell et al., 2011), we conducted a systematic review. We focused on publications in leading management journals to identify key patterns, including those related to construct definition, outcomes of interest, and research methods. Second, we integrated our findings with extant research from another discipline that has paid considerable attention to narcissism: clinical psychology. Despite sharing a strong interest in narcissism, the management and clinical psychology literatures have remained distinct (Campbell et al., 2011), as with other psychological constructs appearing in both (Rosado-Solomon et al., 2023). We hope this integration will enhance and shape future narcissism research, as well as exemplify the benefit to management research of incorporating insights from clinical psychology.

Methods

Literature Search, Inclusion Criteria, and Coding Procedure

We conducted a systematic review of management research on narcissism after the last major review of this topic (Campbell et al., 2011), resulting in a 13-year study timeframe (2011–2023, inclusive). The search terms, sources, and screening criteria we specified yielded a final sample of 73 papers (see Figure 3.1).[2] All coauthor team members participated in preliminary coding, refinement of the coding scheme, and systematic coding of variables of interest across studies, ensuring multiple viewpoints contributed to each coding stage.

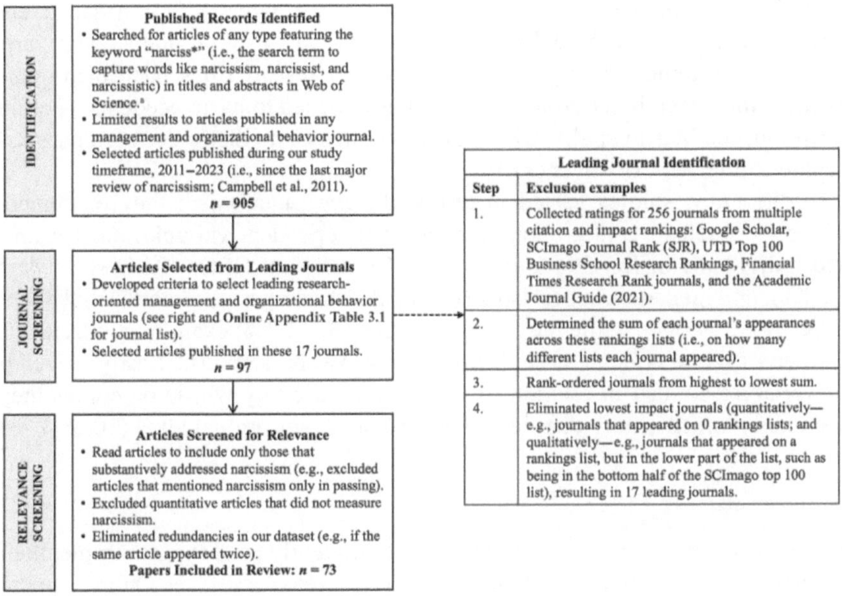

[a]This step, which searched for all article types in all disciplines between 2011 and 2023, yielded 7,044 articles.

Figure 3.1 Search Terms, Sources, and Screening Criteria for the Literature Search.

Narcissism in Management Literature: Overview of Findings

How Has Narcissism Been Studied?

We provide descriptive information about the papers reviewed and how narcissism has been studied in the Online Appendix, Table 3.1.[3]

About the Papers

The 73 papers appeared in 14 leading journals, with between 1 and 10 papers per journal (see Figure 3.1 for journal selection criteria). Studies were predominantly quantitative, using varied methodological approaches. Notably, our sample contained no qualitative studies. Roughly two-thirds of the studies used an organizational behavior/management lens, while one-third used a strategy lens.

About Narcissism

A majority of papers examined narcissism as the focal construct or independent variable (n = 51; 70%), with the next largest set (n = 17; 23%) studying narcissism as a moderator. Only one study viewed narcissism as a dependent variable, in a dynamic model where narcissism was also an independent variable. These findings highlight that management research has been disproportionately interested in narcissism's impact as opposed to its antecedents. (For an exception, see Martin et al., 2016, on narcissism as a mediator between parental income and leader effectiveness.)

Additionally, studies varied in terms of *whose* narcissism they examined. Of the 49 studies treating narcissism as an independent variable, most examined individuals in formal authority (n = 31; 63.3%): CEOs (32.7%), leaders (22.4%), and managers/supervisors (8.2%). A few studies were conducted about teams (n = 2; 4.1%), while the remainder (n = 16; 32.7%) examined individuals (e.g., employees, college alumni, students) in varied settings.[4] Lastly, dependent variables studied in relation to narcissism varied by whose outcomes they examined—mostly individual level (49.0%) or organizational level (30.6%).

Measures Used

We identified the narcissism measures most frequently used in our sample, their characteristics, and evaluated their strengths and weaknesses (see Online Appendix, Table 3.2). These measures (e.g., Narcissistic Personality Inventory (NPI); Raskin & Hall, 1979; Raskin & Terry, 1988) were developed to focus on and assess aspects of grandiose narcissism. Measures of vulnerable and other subtypes of narcissism, though routinely used in clinical psychology research, have not yet been deployed in management research (e.g., Hypersensitive Narcissism Scale, Wink & Gough, 1990; Pathological Narcissism Inventory, Pincus et al., 2009).

Pattern of Findings

About Narcissism's Impact

Our review of narcissism's relationships to outcomes revealed key patterns between two core facets of each study: *whose narcissism* (leaders, non-leader individuals, and teams) and *whose outcome* (impact on leader, non-leader individuals, team, and organization). First, research has disproportionately examined leader narcissism (n = 31) compared to non-leader narcissism (e.g., employees, college alumni, students; n = 16). Within the studies of leader narcissism, most have focused on leader narcissism's impact on *others* (n = 25), including on the firm (n = 15). Even when outcomes involve non-leader individuals like followers (n = 10), they typically concern organizations (e.g., prosocial and voice behaviors; Liu et al., 2017), rather than outcomes directly relevant to leaders or followers themselves (e.g., well-being). Much of this research has focused on reconciling complexities and nuances in relationships between leader narcissism and outcomes—the "bright" and "dark" side of leader narcissism (e.g., Reina et al., 2014), or how it leads to both positive and negative outcomes (Liu et al., 2022), reflecting the maturity of this line of work. Another nuanced aspect of leader narcissism explored in these studies is its interaction with other leader characteristics, such as the finding that leaders can have positive effects on followers when their narcissism is tempered by humility (Owens et al., 2015).

The limited research examining leader narcissism's impact on *leader outcomes* ($n = 7$) has focused on outcomes such as leader development, emergence, and effectiveness (see Grijalva et al., 2015, for a review). For instance, higher leader narcissism has been shown to predict leader emergence regardless of context, whereas its impact on leader performance depends on context (Nevicka et al., 2011). Grjalva and colleagues (2015) demonstrated that the relationship between leader narcissism and effectiveness depends on whether the effectiveness rating is observer- or self-reported. This set of outcomes has also included those that, while assessed about a leader (e.g., abusive supervision in Waldman et al., 2018), affect followers rather than leaders themselves. Though these studies examined both independent and dependent variables, all focused on leaders' roles—rather than their well-being, mental health, or career outcomes as individuals. As above, many of these studies examined complexities and nuances in the relationships between leader narcissism and outcomes, reflecting the advanced stage of research on these topics.

By contrast, the outcomes studied in relation to non-leader narcissism ($n = 15$) follow a different pattern. Although still generally relevant to organizations, these outcomes center on the non-leaders themselves rather than on other individuals or on the firm. They include greater variety, such as career outcomes (Wille et al., 2019), job performance (O'Boyle et al., 2012), and organizationally relevant attitudes and behaviors (e.g., citizenship behaviors in LeBreton et al., 2018 and workplace deviance in Ellen et al., 2021). This set of studies is robust in many ways, yet we note a few striking absences: research has paid less attention to individually relevant psychological or attitudinal variables such as job satisfaction and well-being, and to non-leader narcissism's impact on others.

Furthermore, the limited number of studies on narcissism in teams ($n = 2$) has investigated only team-level outcomes (e.g., cooperation and performance in Dierdorff & Fisher, 2022). This approach follows a pattern similar to that observed for leaders and non-leaders, where alignment exists between whose narcissism and whose outcomes are studied. As with research on leader narcissism, which has focused on outcomes not directly relevant to leaders themselves, research on team narcissism has focused on outcomes relevant only to the team or organization but not to individuals on the team.

Narcissism's Impact as a Moderator

When research examined narcissism as a moderator ($n = 17$), we identified a pattern similar to the main effect findings: leader narcissism ($n = 12$) remained the primary focus. Leader narcissism typically moderated relationships relevant to firms, whether regarding firm outcomes ($n = 8$; e.g., CEO narcissism as a moderator of the relationship between CEO political orientation and firm corporate social responsibility activities in Gupta et al., 2019) or leader outcomes ($n = 4$; e.g., leader narcissism as a moderator of the relationship between follower citizenship behavior and leader unethical behavior in Ahmad et al., 2021) but rarely outcomes directly about the leaders themselves or employees (e.g., well-being). A handful of studies examined non-leader narcissism ($n = 4$) as a moderator of relationships between individual independent and dependent variables (e.g., employee narcissism moderating the relationship between employees receiving help and their interpersonal deviance in Zhong et al., 2022) or team narcissism ($n = 1$) as a moderator of relationships between team independent and dependent variables (e.g., team member narcissism moderating the relationship between team leader narcissism and team member task performance in Han et al., 2020), again focusing on outcomes relevant to the organization but not to individuals themselves.

The Clinical Psychology Perspective on Narcissism

As in management research, narcissism has also captured the attention of scholars in clinical psychology. Indeed, in our review timeframe (2011–2023), while the management literature published more than 900 studies on narcissism, clinical psychology published close to 700 articles on narcissism.[5] We approached the clinical psychology literature at a high level, focusing on its relevance to and alignment with management research, rather than conducting a second systematic review. Core perspectives of each discipline have shaped their research on narcissism, with the management literature focusing on narcissism's impact in the workplace and clinical psychology focused differently. Specifically, clinical psychology is the branch of psychology that provides comprehensive mental and behavioral healthcare, research-based assessment, and intervention to prevent and treat emotional and behavioral disorders, primarily at the individual, couple, and family levels, as well as consultation on prevention and intervention at organizational levels (APA, 2022). With respect to narcissism, clinical psychology focuses more directly on narcissism itself, including its definition, assessment, etiology, and treatment to improve functioning in multiple life domains.

Both management and clinical psychology research view narcissism as a personality trait existing as a spectrum, with people showing varied levels of narcissistic characteristics. Low or moderate levels are below the threshold for clinical significance (hereafter referred to as "subclinical") and are considered generally unproblematic or even adaptive (Campbell et al., 2011). High levels can be maladaptive (hereafter referred to as "pathological")[6] and in some cases are classified as narcissistic personality disorder or NPD (Ellison et al., 2013; Levy, 2012). NPD is a severe, pathological form of high narcissism characterized by meeting at least five of nine diagnostic criteria outlined in the DSM-5, including arrogant, haughty behaviors and attitudes; lack of empathy; and excessive demand for admiration (APA, 2013). People with NPD exhibit widely varying levels of functioning, from "captains of industry [to those] unable to maintain steady employment," with a wider range of severity than any other personality disorder (Caligor et al., 2015, p. 416).

Clinical psychology researchers generally agree that two subtypes exist: grandiose, which presents as a "pervasive pattern of grandiosity" (Weinberg & Ronningstam, 2022, p. 368), and vulnerable, which presents as excessive fragility and intense need for acceptance from others (Pincus et al., 2014).[7] Both subtypes involve strong feelings of entitlement (Weinberg & Ronningstam, 2022). While the DSM-5 diagnostic criteria have been criticized for overemphasizing grandiose characteristics and underemphasizing vulnerable characteristics (Miller et al., 2013), these criteria nevertheless remain the primary method for clinically assessing NPD.

Key distinctions between the perspectives on narcissism in the management versus clinical psychology literatures have had significant implications for the nature of research undertaken in these fields. Clinical psychology research has focused on pathological narcissism as a stable condition that is perhaps malleable in the long term, whereas management research generally has not distinguished between subclinical and pathological narcissism, instead viewing it on a spectrum as a monolithic trait that does not change (e.g., Campbell et al., 2011). Correspondingly, the clinical psychology literature has acknowledged the genetic and contextual origins of narcissism, as well as interventions and treatments that might reshape or change it (Weinberg & Ronningstam, 2020, 2022). Recent meta-analytic evidence shows that narcissism decreases slightly as people age (Orth et al., 2024), supporting the argument that narcissism should be viewed as changeable.

Despite sustained attention to narcissism for over a hundred years (Freud, 1914/1957) and the acknowledgment that pathological narcissism may be treated, clinical psychology research on its antecedents and potential treatments has been limited (e.g., Miller et al., 2017). One reason for this lack of understanding is that core features of high narcissism, including a lack of authentic self-awareness, challenge the therapeutic process (Weinberg & Ronningstam, 2020). As such, pathological narcissism is often underdiagnosed (Ronningstam, 2011). The limited research on antecedents has identified a significant genetic component, with personality traits linked to adolescent narcissism observable in children as young as 3 (Carlson & Gjerde, 2009). Yet pathological narcissism can also emerge in reaction to certain early childhood experiences. In particular, childhood adversity, including various forms of abuse and trauma, is associated with higher rates of NPD later in life, as are certain parenting styles, including lenient discipline and invalidation (see Weinberg & Ronningstam, 2022).

In terms of interventions and treatments, most extant research utilizes individual case studies (e.g., Dimaggio & Weinberg, 2024), which limits a broad understanding of interventions due to lack of generalizability. The many distinctive challenges NPD creates in therapy settings have resulted in a situation where, for the limited subset of NPD patients who receive treatment, "existing treatments are only marginally helpful" (Weinberg & Ronningstam, 2020, p. 123). For example, when confronted with anything or anyone that does not foster their positive sense of self, people with NPD can react in a strongly negative manner (Di Pierro et al., 2019). Moreover, the interpersonal displays typical of people with NPD, such as detachment or paranoid reactions, can significantly impede the development of a therapeutic relationship with clinicians (Weinberg & Ronningstam, 2020).

Emerging research suggests techniques that may improve treatment of pathological narcissism. Certain psychotherapies show promise in reducing maladaptive symptoms, such as transference-focused psychotherapy [TFP-N] (Diamond et al., 2021), and goal-setting, due to its alignment with narcissists' strengths (Dimaggio & Weinberg, 2024). Moreover, flexibility in treating narcissism, including altering meeting frequency or temporarily decreasing required commitments from patients to build trust with the clinician (e.g., DiMaggio & Weinberg, 2024), can also be beneficial.

Enriching Narcissism Research

To enrich future research on narcissism in both management and clinical psychology, we propose incorporating insights into each from the other discipline. We first discuss four key themes identified by our review as needing greater attention: understanding of the construct, outcomes, methodological approaches, and interventions and treatments. We suggest ways management researchers might conduct novel future research based on insights from clinical psychology. Then, we propose that a reciprocal relationship exists between the management and clinical psychology literatures, and we recommend how strengths and insights from management research can enrich clinical psychology research.

Enriching Understanding of the Construct

Our review found that management research rarely distinguished among narcissism subtypes, instead implicitly treating grandiose narcissism as the sole form (see Online Appendix, Table 3.2). The singular exception in our sample is a study that conceptually differentiated grandiose and vulnerable narcissism but nonetheless focused only on grandiose narcissism in its focal data collection (Reina et al., 2014). Most studies in our review focused on individuals in positions of formal authority—CEOs, leaders, and managers—likely contributing to this emphasis. We suggest that the prominence of grandiose narcissism in these individuals, whose grandiosity, extraversion, assertiveness, and power-seeking tendencies may have helped them attain leadership roles (Brunell et al., 2008), has reinforced this bias. Clinical psychology, by contrast, emphasizes narcissism's dimensionality (Miller et al., 2021).[8] We propose that integrating insights from clinical psychology, particularly on the vulnerable subtype (e.g., Pincus et al., 2014), would benefit management research by broadening its theoretical mechanisms and range of variables.

Grandiose and vulnerable narcissism share characteristics of self-importance and entitlement. People with narcissism can oscillate between episodes of grandiosity and vulnerability, and high levels of the two may co-exist (e.g., Jauk et al., 2017). Yet the vulnerable form is marked by fragile self-esteem and hypersensitivity to rejection (Cain et al., 2008), with individuals often experiencing attachment anxiety, insecurity, and enmity (Besser & Priel, 2010; Rogoza et al., 2022) resulting in social withdrawal, decreased life satisfaction, and increased levels of anger and hostility (e.g., Zajenkowski et al., 2021). Vulnerable narcissism relates to hypercompetitiveness, neuroticism, disagreeableness, and antagonism (Luchner et al., 2011; Miller et al., 2017), potentially driving social comparison and a relentless pursuit of advancement in the workplace.

As narcissism is not homogeneous, we contend acknowledging and incorporating the existence of its subtypes would enrich management research conceptually and empirically. A more holistic view of narcissism including both vulnerable and grandiose could extend our understanding of narcissism's impact on those experiencing it and how to prevent negative impact on others in the workplace. For instance, in a study of managers, while grandiose narcissism did not predict work performance, vulnerable narcissism was linked to more counterproductive work behaviors and lower task performance (Dåderman & Kajonius, 2024). Future management research could further explore how narcissism subtypes differently impact key outcomes, which would also require broader measurement approaches (see following sections). Novel theorizing about narcissism subtypes is also possible; for example, as vulnerable narcissism is characterized by insecurity, detrimental effects could be driven more strongly by insufficient self-efficacy than with grandiose narcissism. We suggest future research questions for this and the themes that follow, with possible methodologies to extend those used in extant narcissism research, in the Online Appendix, Table 3.3.

Enriching Understanding of Outcomes

Our review highlights how research to date has offered a sophisticated, nuanced view of the impact of leader narcissism on specific outcomes relevant to organizations or leaders' roles. Yet research has rarely examined narcissism's relational impact—how it affects others—or its influence on broader, significant outcomes, including "traditional" organizational behavior constructs like job satisfaction, engagement, turnover, and well-being, for both leaders and those around them. Non-leader narcissism research has likewise centered on organizational outcomes while overlooking traditional organizational behavior variables despite earlier calls to address them (Mathieu, 2013). These patterns—of what narcissism research has and has not examined—align with findings from studies predating our review timeframe (e.g., for reviews, see Resick et al., 2009; Rosenthal & Pittinsky, 2006), indicating that psychological and attitudinal outcomes remain largely absent from the narcissism literature.

In contrast, clinical psychology views narcissism's impact as inherently relational. The DSM-5 definition of NPD classifies possible symptoms into two dimensions, self and interpersonal relations, each consisting of two areas of functioning—identity and self-direction for the self, and empathy and intimacy for the interpersonal—along with two personality traits: grandiosity and attention seeking (APA, 2013). Of note, beyond the clear relational nature of the interpersonal dimension, the self-dimension's criteria are also strongly relational: the identity area of functioning centers on individual appraisal of the self in relation to others. The self-direction area of functioning also involves goal-setting based on approval from others and viewing oneself as exceptional in relation to others. Even the two personality traits involve relations to others: a view that one is better than others for grandiosity, and extreme pursuit of admiration in attention seeking (Weinberg & Ronningstam, 2022).

We believe that integrating clinical psychology's relational view of narcissism and its impact could significantly enrich management research by, for instance, examining narcissism's impact on relations with other people, including but not limited to coworkers across hierarchical levels, teammates, clients, supervisors, protégés, or even boundary spanning to encompass others in work and nonwork domains. This is particularly salient for research on non-leader narcissism, where a relational focus is especially lacking. Also consistent with the clinical psychology literature, we encourage future management research to examine a broader range of outcomes in relation to the self, including the aforementioned traditional organizational behavior outcomes (e.g., job satisfaction, well-being).

Enriching Methodological Approaches

Our review recognized that studies have employed varied quantitative methodologies to examine narcissism, with none using qualitative methods. Furthermore, although the literature benefits from numerous studies employing more than one wave of data collection, these studies have typically examined narcissism's effect on an outcome at a later time point rather than examining narcissism longitudinally—collecting three or more measures of narcissism to understand its change over time, along with possible antecedents or consequences of change (Singer & Willet, 2003). Our review found that narcissism research has relied on a small number of measures. The Narcissistic Personality Inventory (Raskin & Hall, 1979; Raskin & Terry, 1988) was the most frequent self-report measure (37% of our sample), and the CEO Narcissism Index (Chatterjee & Hambrick, 2007) was the most frequent archival, unobtrusive measure (12% of our sample).

Other measures were used in a handful of studies apiece, and all assessed only grandiose narcissism.

Clinical psychology has excelled at developing clinical assessments of narcissism, beneficial for purposes including differentiating subclinical from pathological narcissism. Clinical psychology also acknowledges the existence and importance of narcissism's antecedents and potential for change—critical to diagnosing and treating pathological narcissism. Although systematic clinical psychology research on the antecedents—and especially the treatment—of NPD remains limited (Weinberg & Ronningstam, 2022), the available work has employed a broader range of methodological approaches than is typical in management studies on narcissism.

Integrating clinical psychology's methodologies for studying narcissism could enrich the taken-for-granted approaches in management research. First, we encourage management research to broaden its methodologies by incorporating those used or advocated in clinical psychology. The field would benefit from longitudinal studies examining the antecedents and change in narcissism over time, as well as from qualitative research, which—drawing on case study research widely used in the clinical tradition—could offer much-needed richness and depth to our understanding of how narcissism functions in the workplace. Repeated collection of existing measures, even with known limitations (see Online Appendix, Table 3.2), can still enrich our understanding of narcissism over time.

Second, we encourage expanding the range of narcissism assessments used in management research. This includes adapting established clinical measures and validating them for organizational settings. Clinical measures for other mental health conditions like those for depression have already been adapted for management research (e.g., Beck Depression Inventory-II, Beck et al., 1996). Similar adaptation of narcissism assessments could introduce useful methodological variety to a field long dominated by a narrow set of measures. Moreover, narcissism is inherently difficult to assess, and the typical subjects in management research—CEOs and leaders—are particularly hard to access for self-report (Cycyota & Harrison, 2006). Novel methods are emerging, such as an unobtrusive index measure calculated from five LinkedIn profile indicators (Junge et al., 2024), and other promising approaches, including natural language processing, have been proposed to capture CEO narcissism without direct input (Cragun et al., 2020). We echo calls for continued innovation in this area.

Lastly, we believe management research would benefit from incorporating clinical insights about narcissism subtypes into its measurement approaches. To move beyond a sole focus on grandiose narcissism, we encourage using clinical measures to assess vulnerable and other subtypes. Research on non-grandiose narcissism could be advanced through the methodological approaches noted earlier, such as using natural language processing to identify subtypes among leaders.

Enriching Understanding of Interventions

Despite the problems caused in organizations by people with untreated high narcissism (e.g., NPD)—such as abusive supervision (Waldman et al., 2018)—our review found no management studies investigating interventions directly targeting this problematic impact. As such, current management research offers little guidance for actionable interventions.

Clinical psychology's exploration of narcissism's developmental trajectory has yielded a key insight: early trauma may contribute to the emergence of clinically significant narcissism later in life (Weinberg & Ronningstam, 2022), but trauma-informed approaches have not been substantially connected to interventions for pathological narcissism. Broadly, a trauma-informed approach requires four competencies across all levels of an organization: (1) *realizing* trauma's existence and impact; (2) *recognizing* signs of trauma in context; (3) *responding* with trauma-informed care; and (4) *resisting re-traumatization* of stakeholders (Huang et al., 2014, pp. 9–10). Combining this approach with clinical insights about treating people with pathological narcissism—and those who interact with them—could inform novel intervention strategies, such as the use of goal-setting (e.g., Weinberg & Ronningstam, 2020).

We propose that management research on narcissism would be enriched by incorporating clinical insights into both uncovering and treating trauma. Applying a trauma-informed lens could deepen understanding of both people with high narcissism and those impacted by them. Organizations might leverage this approach by ensuring employee access to mental health resources, including adequate benefits and the time and flexibility to utilize them. When employees experience trauma due to interactions with colleagues with high narcissism in the organization, senior management might consider relocating or removing the latter to prevent further harm. Research shows that distancing from abusive supervision supports trauma processing (Masood et al., 2024), and trauma-informed responses that prioritize preventing re-traumatization can facilitate healing. To explore these possibilities, researchers could conduct natural field experiments to assess whether organizational provision of trauma-informed support for people harmed by narcissistic colleagues yields benefits both at the individual (e.g., well-being) and organizational (e.g., reduced turnover) levels.

Enriching Clinical Psychology Research

As noted earlier, we view management research as a potential source of enrichment for clinical psychology, as well as a beneficiary of it. About one-third of the studies we reviewed investigated the impact of those in formal authority on organizations (n = 15) or individuals with whom they interact (n = 10). This multilevel perspective (Klein & Kozlowski, 2000)—examining how people high in narcissism affect others and broader social systems—contrasts with clinical psychology's typical focus on the well-being or impairment of people with narcissism and their immediate relationships. We encourage clinical psychology to draw on management research's insights into the relational implications of pathological narcissism and to more explicitly consider its broader social implications. This perspective may be particularly generative in domains where interpersonal dynamics are central, such as couples and family counseling.

Another strength of management research is its emphasis on quantifying narcissism's effects—such as on creativity (Mao et al., 2021), advice taking (Kausel et al., 2015), and firm legal vulnerability (O'Reilly et al., 2018). We suggest that clinical psychology could be enriched by incorporating similarly outcome-focused approaches, for both people with narcissism and those affected by it. By better understanding the magnitude of narcissism's impact, clinical psychologists may be better positioned to evaluate the risks and benefits of different therapeutic strategies, including whether non-treatment may sometimes be appropriate.

Conclusion

Narcissism can pose serious challenges in organizations—not only for those who experience it directly but also for those around them: "Narcissism can be like a fire . . . the longer it burns, the more it destroys. If you want to avoid damage, there has to be some intervention" (Caron, 2024). With the significant rise in management research on narcissism since the last major review (Campbell et al., 2011), this chapter arrives at a critical moment to reassess what is—and is not yet—understood about this complex trait.

Our systematic review of 73 articles in leading management journals revealed key patterns and gaps in knowledge. By incorporating insights from clinical psychology, we sought to illuminate these gaps and encourage future research that expands our understanding of narcissism in organizational contexts. This interdisciplinary approach enriches theoretical and practical insights into narcissism and highlights the broader value of cross-field integration for addressing other complex constructs.

Looking ahead, we hope this chapter contributes to shaping future discourse on narcissism in management and beyond. By encouraging nuanced questions and innovative methods, it may guide efforts to manage narcissism's challenges and leverage its potential benefits. In so doing, we aim to offer a pathway toward healthier, more productive organizational environments.

Notes

1 Baer (2016) quoting the work of Wendy Behary.
2 A full list of studies is available from the first author upon request.
3 Online appendices can be viewed at http://bit.ly/4iMIhYe, or the information can be requested from the first author.

4 We categorized studies based on the terminology used by their authors to preserve the studies' intent, even though these categories may overlap conceptually (e.g., CEOs are also leaders).
5 Other related disciplines, such as social and industrial/organizational psychology, psychoanalysis, and psychiatry, have also addressed narcissism but are beyond the scope of this review.
6 We use this term to refer to people who display clinically significant levels of narcissism and some degree of impairment but may or may not have a clinical diagnosis.
7 These represent the two most popular conceptualizations of narcissism but not the only distinctions. For a broader discussion of other ways to differentiate narcissism, see Miller et al. (2021).
8 This review summarizes that narcissism should be conceptualized as hierarchical and comprising two distinguishable subtypes or dimensions, grandiose and vulnerable, which in turn comprise three dimensions: antagonism, part of both grandiose and vulnerable narcissism; agentic extraversion, characterizing grandiose narcissism only; and narcissistic neuroticism, characterizing vulnerable narcissism only (Miller et al., 2021). Scholars have proposed additional dimensions of narcissism, such as communal (Gebauer et al., 2012), a subtype of grandiose narcissism whereby individuals possess the same self-focused style as other people with grandiose narcissism, but overclaim how other-focused they are (e.g., viewing themselves as saintly figures in Yang et al., 2018, or boasting about their prosociality in Fatfouta & Schröder-Abé, 2018).

References

*References with an * are included in our review*

*Ahmad, M. G., Klotz, A. C., & Bolino, M. C. (2021). Can good followers create unethical leaders? How follower citizenship leads to leader moral licensing and unethical behavior. *Journal of Applied Psychology, 106*(9), 1374–1390.

American Psychiatric Association. (2013). *Diagnostic and statistical manual of mental disorders* (5th ed.). https://doi.org/10.1176/appi.books.9780890425596

American Psychological Association. (2022). *Clinical psychology. In APA directory of specialties and subspecialties*. https://www.apa.org/ed/graduate/specialize/clinical

Baer, D. (2016). Narcissists are lonely little creatures. *The Cut*. https://www.thecut.com/2016/09/why-do-people-become-narcissists.html

Beck, A. T., Steer, R. A., & Brown, G. (1996). Beck depression inventory–II [database record]. *APA PsycTests*. https://doi.org/10.1037/t00742-000

Besser, A., & Priel, B. (2010). Grandiose narcissism versus vulnerable narcissism in threatening situations: Emotional reactions to achievement failure and interpersonal rejection. *Journal of Social and Clinical Psychology, 29*(8), 874–902.

Brunell, A. B., Gentry, W. A., Campbell, W. K., Hoffman, B. J., Kuhnert, K. W., & Demarree, K. G. (2008). Leader emergence: The case of the narcissistic leader. *Personality & Social Psychology Bulletin, 34*(12), 1663–1676.

Cain, N. M., Pincus, A. L., & Ansell, E. B. (2008). Narcissism at the crossroads: Phenotypic description of pathological narcissism across clinical theory, social/personality psychology, and psychiatric diagnosis. *Clinical Psychology Review, 28*(4), 638–656.

Caligor, E., Levy, K. N., & Yeomans, F. E. (2015). Narcissistic personality disorder: Diagnostic and clinical challenges. *American Journal of Psychiatry, 172*(5), 415–422.

Campbell, W. K., Hoffman, B. J., Campbell, S. M., & Marchisio, G. (2011). Narcissism in organizational contexts. *Human Resource Management Review, 21*(4), 268–284.

Carlson, K. S., & Gjerde, P. F. (2009). Preschool personality antecedents of narcissism in adolescence and young adulthood: A 20-year longitudinal study. *Journal of Research in Personality, 43*(4), 570–578.

Caron, C. (2024). Narcissism is a trait that's hard to shake, study says. *New York Times*. https://www.nytimes.com/2024/07/11/well/mind/narcissism-age-empathy.html

Chatterjee, A., & Hambrick, D. C. (2007). It's all about me: Narcissistic chief executive officers and their effects on company strategy and performance. *Administrative Science Quarterly*, *52*(3), 351–386.

Cragun, O. R., Olsen, K. J., & Wright, P. M. (2020). Making CEO narcissism research great: A review and meta-analysis of CEO narcissism. *Journal of Management*, *46*(6), 908–936.

Cycyota, C. S., & Harrison, D. A. (2006). What (not) to expect when surveying executives: A meta-analysis of top manager response rates and techniques over time. *Organizational Research Methods*, *9*(2), 133–160.

Dåderman, A. M., & Kajonius, P. J. (2024). Linking grandiose and vulnerable narcissism to managerial work performance, through the lens of core personality traits and social desirability. *Scientific Reports*, *14*(1), Article 12213.

Diamond, D., Yeomans, F., & Keefe, J. R. (2021). Transference-focused psychotherapy for pathological narcissism and narcissistic personality disorder (TFP-N). *Psychodynamic Psychiatry*, *49*(2), 244–272.

*Dierdorff, E. C., & Fisher, D. M. (2022). Problematic personalities in teams: Implications for performance trajectories and resilience to unexpected change. *Personnel Psychology*, *75*(3), 589–617.

Dimaggio, G., & Weinberg, I. (2024). What do we need in order to successfully treat persons with pathological narcissism? How does change happen? Treatment principles and mechanisms of change emerging from single cases treated by experts: A commentary. *Journal of Clinical Psychology*, *80*(5). https://doi.org/10.1002/jclp.23652.

Di Pierro, R., Costantini, G., Benzi, I. M. A., Madeddu, F., & Preti, E. (2019). Grandiose and entitled, but still fragile: A network analysis of pathological narcissistic traits. *Personality and Individual Differences*, *140*, 15–20. https://doi.org/10.1016/j.paid.2018.04.003

*Ellen III, B. P., Alexander, K. C., Mackey, J. D., McAllister, C. P., & Carson, J. E. (2021). Portrait of a workplace deviant: A clearer picture of the Big Five and Dark Triad as predictors of workplace deviance. *Journal of Applied Psychology*, *106*(12), 1950–1961.

Ellison, W. D., Levy, K. N., Cain, N. M., Ansell, E. B., & Pincus, A. L. (2013). The impact of pathological narcissism on psychotherapy utilization, initial symptom severity, and early-treatment symptom change: A naturalistic investigation. *Journal of Personality Assessment*, *95*(3), 291–300.

Fatfouta, R., & Schröder-Abé, M. (2018). A wolf in sheep's clothing? Communal narcissism and positive implicit self-views in the communal domain. *Journal of Research in Personality, 76,* 17–21.

Freud, S. (1914/1957). On narcissism: An introduction. In J. Strachey, J. Freud, A. Strachey, & A. Tyson (Trans.), *The standard edition of the complete psychological works of Sigmund Freud* (Vol. 14). Hogarth Press.

Gebauer, J. E., Sedikides, C., Verplanken, B., & Maio, G. R. (2012). Communal narcissism. *Journal of Personality and Social Psychology*, *103*(5), 854–878.

*Grijalva, E., Harms, P. D., Newman, D. A., Gaddis, B. H., & Fraley, R. C. (2015). Narcissism and leadership: A meta-analytic review of linear and nonlinear relationships. *Personnel Psychology*, *68*(1), 1–47.

*Gupta, A., Nadkarni, S., & Mariam, M. (2019). Dispositional sources of managerial discretion: CEO ideology, CEO personality, and firm strategies. *Administrative Science Quarterly*, *64*(4), 855–893.

*Han, J. H., Liao, H., Kim, S., & Han, J. (2020). Narcissism and empowerment: How narcissism influences the trickle-down effects of organizational empowerment climate on performance. *Journal of Management Studies*, *57*(6), 1217–1245.

Huang, L. N., Flatow, R., Biggs, T., Afayee, S., Smith, K., Clark, T., & Blake, M. (2014). *SAMHSA's concept of trauma and guidance for a trauma-informed approach*. https://archive.hshsl.umaryland.edu/bitstream/handle/10713/18559/SAMHSA_Trauma.pdf?sequence=1

Jauk, E., Weigle, E., Lehmann, K., Benedek, M., & Neubauer, A. C. (2017). The relationship between grandiose and vulnerable (hypersensitive) narcissism. *Frontiers in Psychology, 8*, ID 1600. https://doi.org/10.3389/fpsyg.2017.01600

Junge, S., Graf-Vlachy, L., Hagen, M., & Schlichte, F. (2024). Narcissism at the CEO–TMT interface: Measuring executive narcissism and testing its effects on TMT composition. *Journal of Management, 51*(5), 1765–1802. https://doi.org/10.1177/01492063241226904

Kausel, E. E., Culbertson, S. S., Leiva, P. I., Slaughter, J. E., & Jackson, A. T. (2015). Too arrogant for their own good? Why and when narcissists dismiss advice. *Organizational Behavior and Human Decision Processes, 131*, 33–50.

Klein, K. J., & Kozlowski, S. W. J. (2000). *Multilevel theory, research, and methods in organizations: Foundations, extensions, and new directions*. Jossey-Bass.

*LeBreton, J. M., Shiverdecker, L. K., & Grimaldi, E. M. (2018). The dark triad and workplace behavior. *Annual Review of Organizational Psychology and Organizational Behavior, 5*(1), 387–414.

Levy, K. N. (2012). Subtypes, dimensions, levels, and mental states in narcissism and narcissistic personality disorder. *Journal of Clinical Psychology, 68*(8), 886–897.

*Liu, H., Chiang, J. T.-J., Fehr, R., Xu, M., & Wang, S. (2017). How do leaders react when treated unfairly? Leader narcissism and self-interested behavior in response to unfair treatment. *Journal of Applied Psychology, 102*(11), 1590–1599.

*Liu, X., Zheng, X., Li, N., Yu, Y., Harms, P. D., & Yang, J. (2022). Both a curse and a blessing? A social cognitive approach to the paradoxical effects of leader narcissism. *Human Relations, 75*(11), 2011–2038.

Luchner, A. F., Houston, J. M., Walker, C., & Houston, M. A. (2011). Exploring the relationship between two forms of narcissism and competitiveness. *Personality and Individual Differences, 51*(6), 779–782.

*Mao, J. Y., Quan, J., Li, Y., & Xiao, J. (2021). The differential implications of employee narcissism for radical versus incremental creativity: A self-affirmation perspective. *Journal of Organizational Behavior, 42*(7), 933–949.

*Martin, S. R., Côté, S., & Woodruff, T. (2016). Echoes of our upbringing: How growing up wealthy or poor relates to narcissism, leader behavior, and leader effectiveness. *Academy of Management Journal, 59*(6), 2157–2177.

Masood, H., Mercer, M., & Karakowsky, L. (2024). Future past tense of abusive supervision: A narrative inquiry. *Leadership & Organization Development Journal, 45*(5), 811–831.

Mathieu, C. (2013). Personality and job satisfaction: The role of narcissism. *Personality and Individual Differences, 55*(6), 650–654.

Miller, J. D., Back, M. D., Lynam, D. R., & Wright, A. G. C. (2021). Narcissism today: What we know and what we need to learn. *Current Directions in Psychological Science, 30*(6), 519–525.

Miller, J. D., Gentile, B., Wilson, L., & Campbell, W. K. (2013). Grandiose and vulnerable narcissism and the DSM–5 pathological personality trait model. *Journal of Personality Assessment, 95*(3), 284–290.

Miller, J. D., Lynam, D. R., Hyatt, C. S., & Campbell, W. K. (2017). Controversies in narcissism. *Annual Review of Clinical Psychology, 13*(1), 291–315.

*Nevicka, B., De Hoogh, A. H., Van Vianen, A. E., Beersma, B., & McIlwain, D. (2011). All I need is a stage to shine: Narcissists' leader emergence and performance. *Leadership Quarterly, 22*(5), 910–925.

*O'Boyle, E., Forsyth, D. R., Banks, G. C., & McDaniel, M. A. (2012). A meta-analysis of the Dark Triad and work behavior: A social exchange perspective. *Journal of Applied Psychology*, *97*(3), 557–579.

*O'Reilly, C. A. III, Doerr, B., & Chatman, J. A. (2018). "See you in court": How CEO narcissism increases firms' vulnerability to lawsuits. *Leadership Quarterly*, *29*(3), 365–378.

Orth, U., Krauss, S., & Back, M. D. (2024). Development of narcissism across the life span: A meta-analytic review of longitudinal studies. *Psychological Bulletin*, *150*(6), 643–665.

*Owens, B. P., Wallace, A. S., & Waldman, D. A. (2015). Leader narcissism and follower outcomes: The counterbalancing effect of leader humility. *Journal of Applied Psychology*, *100*(4), 1203–1213.

Pincus, A. L., Ansell, E. B., Pimentel, C. A., Cain, N. M., Wright, A. G., & Levy, K. N. (2009). Initial construction and validation of the Pathological Narcissism Inventory. *Psychological Assessment*, *21*(3), 365–379.

Pincus, A. L., Cain, N. M., & Wright, A. G. (2014). Narcissistic grandiosity and narcissistic vulnerability in psychotherapy. *Personality Disorders: Theory, Research, and Treatment*, *5*(4), 439–443.

Raskin, R. N., & Hall, C. S. (1979). A narcissistic personality inventory. *Psychological Reports*, *45*(2), 590–590.

Raskin, R. N., & Terry, H. (1988). A principal-components analysis of the Narcissistic Personality Inventory and further evidence of its construct validity. *Journal of Personality and Social Psychology*, *54*(5), 890–902.

*Reina, C. S., Zhang, Z., & Peterson, S. J. (2014). CEO grandiose narcissism and firm performance: The role of organizational identification. *Leadership Quarterly*, *25*(5), 958–971.

Resick, C. J., Whitman, D. S., Weingarden, S. M., & Hiller, N. J. (2009). The bright-side and the dark-side of CEO personality: Examining core self-evaluations, narcissism, transformational leadership, and strategic influence. *Journal of Applied Psychology*, *94*(6), 1365–1381.

Rogoza, R., Crowe, M. L., Jamison, L., Cieciuch, J., & Strus, W. (2022). Support for the three-factor model of narcissism and its personality underpinnings through the lens of the network psychometrics. *Psychological Assessment*, *34*(9), 880–890.

Ronningstam, E. (2011). Narcissistic personality disorder: A clinical perspective. *Journal of Psychiatric Practice*, *17*(2), 89–99.

Rosado-Solomon, E. H., Koopmann, J., Lee, W., & Cronin, M. A. (2023). Mental health and mental illness in organizations: A review, comparison, and extension. *Academy of Management Annals*, *17*(2), 751–797.

Rosenthal, S. A., & Pittinsky, T. L. (2006). Narcissistic leadership. *Leadership Quarterly*, *17*(6), 617–633.

Singer, J. D., & Willett, J. B. (2003). *Applied longitudinal data analysis: Modeling change and event occurrence*. Oxford University Press.

Twenge, J. M., Konrath, S., Foster, J. D., Campbell, W. K., & Bushman, B. J. (2008). Egos inflating over time: A cross-temporal meta-analysis of the Narcissistic Personality Inventory. *Journal of Personality*, *76*, 875–901.

*Waldman, D. A., Wang, D., Hannah, S. T., Owens, B. P., & Balthazard, P. A. (2018). Psychological and neurological predictors of abusive supervision. *Personnel Psychology*, *71*(3), 399–421.

Weinberg, I., & Ronningstam, E. (2020). Dos and don'ts in treatments of patients with narcissistic personality disorder. *Journal of Personality Disorders*, *34*(Supplement), 122–142.

Weinberg, I., & Ronningstam, E. (2022). Narcissistic personality disorder: Progress in understanding and treatment. *Focus*, *20*(4), 368–377.

*Wille, B., Hofmans, J., Lievens, F., Back, M. D., & De Fruyt, F. (2019). Climbing the corporate ladder and within-person changes in narcissism: Reciprocal relationships over two decades. *Journal of Vocational Behavior*, *115*, Article 103341.

Wink, P., & Gough, H. G. (1990). New narcissism scales for the California Psychological Inventory and MMPI. *Journal of Personality Assessment*, *54*(3–4), 446–462.

Yang, Z., Sedikides, C., Gu, R., Luo, Y. L., Wang, Y., Yang, Y., Wu, M., & Cai, H. (2018). Communal narcissism: Social decisions and neurophysiological reactions. *Journal of Research in Personality*, *76*, 64–73.

Zajenkowski, M., Rogoza, R., Maciantowicz, O., Witowska, J., & Jonason, P. K. (2021). Narcissus locked in the past: Vulnerable narcissism and the negative views of the past. *Journal of Research in Personality*, *93*, Article 104123.

*Zhong, M., Gao, Z., & Song, L. J. (2022). Pay it forward or keep it for myself? How narcissism shapes daily prosocial motivation and behavior after receiving help. *Journal of Vocational Behavior*, *135*, Article 103721.

Section II

Intersectionality

4 Managing Maternal Mental Health and Illness in the Workplace

From Vulnerability to Opportunity

Ravit Heskiau, Allison S. Gabriel, and Jamie J. Ladge

The interface between work and family life is the foundation of one of the largest areas of study in the organizational sciences (e.g., Allen & Martin, 2017), and spillover effects are considered at the core of work and family stress (Grzywacz et al., 2002). Yet little attention has been drawn to how mental health and mental illness[1] impact the intersection of work and parenting, especially for working mothers who often bear the bulk of childcare (Bianchi et al., 2012). Understanding how the integration of these two central life domains can affect and be affected by mental health is relevant and timely for two important reasons. One is the enhanced awareness, prevalence, and de-stigmatization of mental health and mental illness in the workplace (Okoli, 2023; Rosado-Solomon et al., 2023). The other is the stronger acknowledgment of the challenges stemming from integrating work and parenting, such as the stress associated with finding affordable and reliable childcare (Modestino et al., 2021) and balancing infant needs such as breastfeeding with work (Chawla et al., 2024; Gabriel et al., 2020).

Accordingly, we review the management literature pertaining to the intersection of motherhood, work, and mental health/illness, which led us to several important observations. First, we find that surprisingly little research examines mental health/illness as it relates to working mothers. Second, despite the complex and reciprocal relations between mental health and work–family, mental health is mostly examined as a distant outcome versus a potential antecedent or mechanism. Third, this literature focuses mostly on early-stage motherhood including pregnancy (e.g., Hackney et al., 2021; Hennekam, 2016; Ladge et al., 2012; Little et al., 2015) and the return to work (e.g., Chawla et al., 2024; Gabriel et al., 2023; Ladge & Greenberg, 2015; Ladge et al., 2018; Little & Masterson, 2023), rarely covering other stages or transitions associated with motherhood where mental health issues may be prevalent such as infertility, parenting teenagers, and becoming empty-nesters (Ladge & Greenberg, 2019). Based on these themes, we devise recommendations for future research and critical practical implications.

DOI: 10.4324/9781003491170-6

Management Scholarship on Maternal Mental Health and Work

The vast majority of literature at the intersection of motherhood, work, and mental health is in the medical, social work, women and family studies, psychology, and education literatures. However, there has been an emerging body of literature in the management and organizational sciences. Table 4.1 outlines the key sources of the research we reviewed. Later, we summarize key findings separated by pregnancy (the antepartum stage) and postpartum (post-childbirth) periods. We recognize that other mental health challenges can happen outside of pregnancy and childbirth for women but exclusively focus on these stages of motherhood in this review since these reflect the majority of the literature to date.

Pregnancy Work Environment and Prenatal/Postpartum Mental Health

There is a range of experiences that pregnant professionals face that can impact their mental health. Such experiences are often derived from perceived discrimination and biases, disclosure decisions, and stigma. For example, Jones (2013) utilized stigma theory to analyze the experiences of expectant mothers as they navigated the stigma associated with pregnancy in the workplace. This study focused on decisions related to revealing (i.e., actively and purposefully disclosing), concealing (i.e., avoiding the topic through self-editing and half-truths), and signaling (i.e., indirect and implicit communication) of pregnancy with others in the workplace. The relationship to psychological distress of the pregnant women was assessed over three weeks, and the findings suggested that concealing was associated with greater depression and anxiety, highlighting the importance of authenticity for new mothers' mental health.

Additionally, scholars have considered forms of mistreatment that pregnant women may experience at work. Hackney and colleagues (2021) studied the effects of pregnancy discrimination at work—the unfair treatment of mothers due to pregnancy, childbirth, or related medical conditions. The authors found that mothers' perception of pregnancy discrimination in the workplace was related to postpartum depression symptoms, as mediated by mothers' stress. Maternity harassment as workplace discrimination was also studied during COVID-19 in Japan (Kachi et al., 2021). In this study, nearly one-fourth of pregnant participants had experienced maternity harassment by supervisors and colleagues, defined as one of 16 adverse treatments (e.g., dismissal, forced resignation, demotion, unfavorable performance evaluations, mental and physical harassment). These experiences were significantly related to antepartum and postpartum depression, regardless of remote or in-person work. While these findings may be surprising given that most countries have laws to prevent discrimination, bias and unfair treatment persist, which can create mental and physical health challenges for pregnant workers (Gatrell et al., 2024).

Table 4.1 Sources Covering Motherhood, Work, and Mental Health/Illness in Management/Applied Psychology Scholarship

Citation	*Motherhood Stage*	*Theoretical Framework*	*Methodology*	*Mental Health/Illness Studied*
Chawla et al. (2024)	• Reentry	• Social cognitive model of career self-management	Time-lagged surveys	• Postpartum depressive symptoms
Falletta et al. (2020)	• Pregnancy • Postpartum • Reentry	None	Cross-sectional	• Anxiety • Depression
Gabriel et al. (2023)	• Postpartum	• Work–life shocks • Identity and sensemaking • Stigma management	Qualitative interviews, grounded theory	• Postpartum depression
Grandey et al. (2020)	• Menstruation • Maternity • Menopause	• Boundary theory • Stigma disclosure • Allostatic load model • Resource theories	Literature review	• Menstrual mood fluctuations • Menopausal major depression
Hackney et al. (2021)	• Postpartum	• Workplace stress • Job demands–resources model	Two longitudinal studies	• Prenatal stress • Postpartum depression
Jones (2013)	• Pregnancy	• Identity management • Stigma theory • Transactional theory of stress and coping	Three-week experience sampling	• Anxiety • Depression
Jones et al. (2022)	• Pregnancy • Postpartum	• Conservation of resources • Social support	Time-lagged surveys	• Prenatal stress • Postpartum depression
Kachi et al. (2021)	• Pregnancy • Postpartum	None	Cross-sectional	• Antepartum depression • Postpartum depression
Ortega and Reio (2016)	• Postpartum • Maternity leave	• Stress-buffering hypothesis	Interdisciplinary literature review	• Postpartum depression
Wilkinson (2022)	• Perinatal	• Bio-ecological systems • Rhythmanalysis	Literature review	• Perinatal mental health

(*Continued*)

Table 4.1 (Continued)

Citation	*Motherhood Stage*	*Theoretical Framework*	*Methodology*	*Mental Health/Illness Studied*
Wilkinson et al. (2024)	• Perinatal	• Work–life interface • Social identity (identity threat)	Biographical narrative interviews	• Prenatal depression • Postpartum depression • Postpartum psychosis • Perinatal obsessive–compulsive disorder • Perinatal eating disorders • Tokophobia (fear of childbirth) • Post-traumatic stress disorder
Zhang et al. (2016)	• Postpartum • Maternity leave • Reentry	None	Literature review	• General maternal mental health • Depressive symptoms

Considering this, research is beginning to unpack what can be done to help support pregnant women who may face such challenges. Jones et al. (2022) examined how the workplace social environment affects postpartum mental health via stress. Their findings suggest that coworker support was negatively related to next-day stress during pregnancy; however, no such relation was observed with supervisor support. Yet coworker support interacted with supervisor support to predict prenatal stress and depression upon return to work—higher levels of combined support yielded the best mental health outcomes. As such, future research will be needed to continue unpacking the adaptive forms—or combinations—of support for working mothers.

Postpartum Experiences Tied to Maternity Leave, Work Reentry, and Mental Health

Women can also struggle with mental health/illness challenges following childbirth that unfold during maternity leave and reentry to work (Chawla et al., 2024; Gabriel et al., 2023; Wilkinson, 2022). Around 40–80% of women experience baby blues, or mild and transient mood disturbances that occur in the immediate days after childbirth (O'Hara & McCabe, 2013). While common, these fluctuations can still prove challenging for women's overall mental health during this tumultuous postpartum period. More extreme mental illness can also occur, captured by postpartum depression (PPD) in about 15% of women (making it the most common postpartum complication; Post & Leuner, 2019) and postpartum psychosis, which only occurs in about 0.1–0.5% of women (Sit et al., 2006). Of these, organizational research has begun to pay attention to postpartum depressive experiences, as well as the effects of a postpartum depression diagnosis.

Gabriel et al. (2023) focused on the influence of being diagnosed with postpartum depression in a sample of 41 working women. Their qualitative research found that those diagnosed went through an extensive sensemaking process around this newfound identity—what the authors termed an imposing identity. This imposing identity was unwanted and given to women with the formal diagnosis of having this mental illness, influencing both pre-existing identities (e.g., being an employee) and provisional identities (e.g., being a working mother). Gabriel et al. (2023) also found that once women were diagnosed and treated, they were able to make sense of their imposing identity and learn to cope in ways that shaped their personal work–family narratives, shifting priorities to realign their work and family goals and demands, as well as engaging in acts of self-compassion toward themselves/others. Critically, antisupports that dismissed women's mental health at work and home made this coping challenging, showing that women are attuned to cues from others about how valid their mental health challenges are.

More research has focused on how cues from organizations shape women's mental health during reentry after maternity leave. For example, Zhang et al.

(2016) reviewed the effects of maternity benefits on mental health. They concluded that beneficial effects depend on mothers' preferences, needs, and the quality of the benefits. They found that while a short maternity leave can negatively affect maternal mental health, optimal duration depends on financial and health factors. Similarly, while workplace flexibility is negatively associated with maternal depression, it also depends on the policies and whether they result in additional family responsibilities. Furthermore, the beneficial effects of child-care benefits depend on the quality of care.

Turning to experiences during reentry, Falletta et al. (2020) examined mental health during the transition back to work. Over half of their participants reported feeling depressed for several days or more during the first month, and over two-thirds reported feeling anxious several days or more. Furthermore, depressive and anxious symptoms at work reentry were associated with reduced health. The authors emphasized the importance of maternity leave duration in light of new mothers' challenges such as marital strain, increased expenses, and sleep deprivation. Presenting similar experiences, Wilkinson et al. (2024) focused on maternal mental illness in the context of the UK police. They found that even after previous experience with mental illness, individuals were shocked to experience postpartum mental illness. Once acknowledged, mental illness constituted a threat to their employment-related identity, especially due to undermined sense of control. Participants were reluctant to use mental health services and concerned about the adverse effects of medication on their work. Organizational and professional cultures were key in terms of stigmatization of mental health, discouragement of disclosure, and how requests for flexibility were considered. Work–life conflicts exacerbated mental illness, which resulted in reduced confidence, concentration, and decision making, as well as increased risk aversion and presenteeism.

In light of the limited amount of mandated leave in countries such as the United States, researchers have tried to identify ways for organizations to support mothers' mental health. Wilkinson (2022) discussed the interaction of four elements: the body, the sociocultural context, individual agency, and time. The author emphasized the support of organizations during the bumpy process of medication adjustment as well as empowering managers with resources and accountability for mental health. As another example, Chawla et al. (2024) explored postpartum allyship, or acts that coworkers and managers can enact to both support and advocate for mothers as they reenter work. Their research found four types of allyship: (1) co-navigating the HR infrastructure; (2) creating physical and temporal spaces for motherhood; (3) validating the mother's identity; and (4) validating the worker's identity. In a study of 155 working mothers who recently returned to work, they found that higher postpartum allyship experiences were positively related to work-motherhood self-efficacy and lower feelings of guilt, which in turn reduced postpartum depressive symptoms.

Integrative Themes

While this area of research is still nascent, we note four important themes warranting further attention. First, there are seemingly *bidirectional relationships between maternal mental health and work.* As reviewed by Gabriel et al. (2023), mental health symptoms can affect productivity, concentration, and social relations at work. At the same time, work conditions, stress, discrimination, and stigma during pregnancy (Hackney et al., 2021; Jones, 2013) and reentry (Chawla et al., 2024) can all affect mental health. Thus, while it is crucial for researchers to consider maternal mental health/illness as an outcome, understanding how mental health challenges affect work/career choices is paramount (e.g., women deciding to leave certain occupations and/or organizations in order to restore their health; Gabriel et al., 2023).

Second, there are *multilevel effects of how work and maternal mental health intersect.* For example, there can be both daily stressors associated with work and motherhood that affect mental health (Gabriel et al., 2020; Jones, 2017), and stable aspects of the work environment that attenuate how these daily experiences relate to core mental health outcomes. As is the case in the organizational sciences, research in maternal mental health benefits should acknowledge the role of meso- and macro-systems, in addition to analyzing individuals' symptoms and perceptions.

Third, the literature highlights *the half glass full*—the silver lining of working mothers' mental illness. Gabriel et al. (2023) found that women experiencing PPD prioritized their needs and their relationships without guilt, took better care of themselves, and showed increased compassion toward themselves and others. Similarly, Wilkinson et al. (2024) referred to the role of work in recovery from maternal mental illness: being helpful, doing important work, helping others, and advocating for better new parents' support. Still, more research is needed to continue to balance out these perspectives given the challenges associated with maternal mental health.

Finally, *every working mother is different*, experiencing a unique set of symptoms, requiring a different range of supports (Gabriel et al., 2023; Ladge & Greenberg, 2019). The literature outside of management also demonstrates that factors such as family, characteristics of children, parenting styles, and socioeconomic variables need to be taken into consideration. Moreover, the optimal duration of maternity leave depends on its quality and other needs of the mother and family. Congruity between work roles and mothers' needs and preferences also affects the transition back to work (Ortega & Reio, 2016). Finally, mothers work in different modalities, and in-person as well as remote work have their risks and opportunities (Ladge & Greenberg, 2019).

Future Directions and Considerations

Our review supports the value of an interdisciplinary perspective, and we see several opportunities for critical advancement. For example, when it comes to mental illness, a broader view beyond anxiety and depression is crucial. Neuroscience is an area of connection to advance our understanding of causes and factors affecting mental illness, as well as parts of the brain and neurotransmitters involved in organizational phenomena (e.g., Ghosh, 2018). Additionally, when examining the mechanisms through which life events affect mental health, the role of self-conscious emotions is especially relevant. Shame is a negative self-evaluation related to one's moral character (Greenbaum et al., 2020) and has been studied as a harmful experience of working parents (Greenbaum et al., 2022). Future research could draw from the connections shown between shame and mental illness, such as depressive symptoms (Coelho et al., 2021; Kim et al., 2011), anxiety (Cândea & Szentagotai-Tătar, 2018), social anxiety (Carpenter et al., 2022), and obsessive–compulsive behavioral tendencies (Doron et al., 2012).

Emphasis is also needed on the positive interface between work and motherhood. Pride is felt when people appraise that they have lived up to actual or ideal self-representations and expectations (Tracy & Robins, 2004). Hence, experiences of maternal confidence (Ladge et al., 2018), as well as pride in managing the interface of motherhood and work, can enhance the mental health of working mothers. Moreover, provided that self-forgiveness is positively related to mental health (Davis et al., 2015) and negatively related to depression and anxiety (Kim et al., 2023), future research could study ways for organizations to promote self-forgiveness and self-compassion among working mothers (Ladge & Greenberg, 2019).

Furthermore, most of the existing literature includes mental health and illness as an outcome (e.g., Chawla et al., 2024; Jones et al., 2022). However, in many cases, predispositions can affect the interplay between work and motherhood. For example, mental illness can be related to a variety of adverse or abusive childhood experiences (McKay et al., 2021), which can shape the interface between work and motherhood. This relates more generally to the potential of mothers to enrich workplace diversity due to implementing different decision-making tools, as well as cognitive, coping, and leadership styles.

There is a clear need for research on motherhood across career stages. Very little research attention has been dedicated to mothering older adolescents. Older ages are associated with different demands that increase the risk of maternal mental conditions, for example, the increased mental health crisis among teens (Weigle & Shafi, 2024). Moreover, mental health of close family members, or even other mothers in the workplace, can affect working mothers through mental health or psychiatric social contagion (Horesh et al., 2022). Such contagion depends on the regulation of relationships and communication, which organizations can help individuals manage. Another understudied stage of career for mothers is retirement. Research highlights the importance of managing this transition considering other social and demographic factors; for example, forced versus voluntary retirement was found to relate to women's mental health after retirement, especially among minorities (Sheppard & Wallace, 2018).

Other understudied topics include individuals' experiences related to their maternal potential. Recent work has touched upon the mental hardship of the interface between work and fertility treatment (Mumford et al., 2023), as well as coping with miscarriage and related trauma (Schnitzler, 2024). Furthermore, awareness of mental health challenges during perimenopause and menopause—consisting of anxiety, depression, and negative impact on emotions and self-worth—has been increasing (O'Reilly et al., 2023). Despite the significant impact on women's work life, research on work implications is scarce. More research is needed on interventions and potential positive implications for women and workplaces (Verdonk et al., 2022), especially considering findings that employment predicts lower anxiety-related menopausal symptoms (Hunter et al., 1986). Indeed, employees' interest in menopause leave increased by 336% globally in 2023, the highest increase among desired benefits (Goodwin, 2023). While organizations offer support related to the challenges of menopause, these are far from being consistent or global.

Finally, it is important to evaluate mental health challenges of working mothers in light of changes in work modalities and technologies. More research is needed on how post-pandemic flexibility in the workplace, especially remote work, plays a role in maternal mental health. The outcomes of remote work for mothers can be mixed provided social isolation and blurred boundaries between life domains (Lyzwinski, 2024; Sarangi et al., 2022). Furthermore, the integration of artificial intelligence could play a role in the mental health of mothers through affecting job security and professional identity. On the positive side, more research is needed on using technology to effectively augment (e.g., Wilson & Daugherty, 2018) the work experience of working mothers toward greater self-efficacy and effectiveness. To support this, as well as the other ideas highlighted here, experimental research is needed to assess the effectiveness of initiatives aimed at supporting mothers. While support broadly is perceived to be helpful, explicit interventions tested within experimental paradigms will likely be fruitful.

Practical Implications

Organizations invest in interpersonal diversity to enhance organizational health; clearly, organizations also need to invest in managing intrapersonal diversity of their employees to support mental health and the mental health of working mothers. The first front of support is policy, both the legal landscape and organizational policies. Based on our review, organizations should augment the law through policies that support the healthy recovery of mothers, whether through paid or unpaid time off and other forms of flexibility (e.g., return to part-time work prior to full-time work). Other benefits can include access to quality medical care, mental health resources, hormonal therapy, and employee assistance plans. Despite increased organizational investment in mental health initiatives, in a recent American Psychological Association poll, the 2023 Work in America

Survey, only 43% of respondents reported that their employer offers health insurance with coverage for mental health and substance use disorders, and 15% reported that their employer offers company-wide mental health days. Specific benefits supporting the mental health of mothers are likely lower. Through surveying hundreds of companies and analyzing workforce composition data from the Equal Employment Opportunity Commission, Kalev and Dobbin (2022) showed how corporate programs, specifically flexible schedules, family leave, and childcare support increase productivity, reduce turnover, and improve employees' mental health. In addition to these, they promote diversity, especially at management levels, more than diversity-targeting programs. Since new mothers' mental health is also affected by physical comfort, designing jobs to align with the needs of mothers supports both physical and mental health, increasing a sense of control.

Additionally, to adequately support the evolving nature of motherhood, social–emotional resources may prove effective. These can include affinity groups for mothers at different stages to enhance self-perceptions and benefit from social learning. Helping mothers build professional and personal networks within and outside of the organization, as well as offering mentorship programs could be another fruitful avenue, whether formal or informal. Prenatal peer support (Jones et al., 2014) and mentorship (Law et al., 2022) have been shown effective in the case of prenatal mental health and illness; however, these studies were conducted in nonprofessional settings and require investigation in the context of the workplace, where mentorship can be better targeted and result in stronger mutual benefits.

As our review critically demonstrated, all of these could create backlash in the absence of a supportive and open organizational culture. While both motherhood and mental health have been associated with reduced stigma in the workplace in recent years, de-stigmatization is the first step in enhancing the usage of initiatives and benefits. The second step is ensuring working mothers are aware of the available supports and career paths (e.g., Chawla et al., 2024). The next step is perceived relevance; self-stigma can be a major obstacle, and organizational initiatives need to be tailored and communicated so mothers see the relevance to their journey and have a voice in helping craft the policies and initiatives that exist within organizations. Therefore, useful initiatives will result from participation of mothers in the process of design and implementation.

Finally, leadership plays an important role in legitimizing and prioritizing the mental health of mothers. This can be done through leaders who regularly utilize benefits, discuss mental health, and exhibit family-supportive behaviors (Crain & Stevens, 2018). However, organizations and leaders should go beyond this and promote the transfer and expansion of resources mothers possess. Specifically, they should strive to capitalize on strengths of working mothers, such as coping skills, time and relationship management, and unique social networks.

Conclusion

In this chapter, we focused on management literature at the intersection of motherhood, work, and mental health/illness. Our review highlights the complexity of the relations between maternal mental health and the workplace, thus emphasizing the roles of coworkers, leaders, organizational cultures, families, and communities in proactively supporting the mental health of mothers and leveraging the strengths they bring to the workplace. Along with discussing important themes in the existing literature, we identify notable gaps and research opportunities across different motherhood and career stages.

Note

1 We follow Follmer and Jones (2018) and view mental health as transient fluctuations in psychological health/well-being, and mental illness as a disorder that is formally diagnosed by a medical provider.

References

Allen, T. D., & Martin, A. (2017). The work-family interface: A retrospective look at 20 years of research in JOHP. *Journal of Occupational Health Psychology*, *22*(3), 259–272. https://doi.org/10.1037/ocp0000065

American Psychological Association. *2023 work in America survey*. https://www.apa.org/pubs/reports/work-in-america/2023-workplace-health-well-being

Bianchi, S. M., Sayer, L. C., Milkie, M. A., & Robinson, J. P. (2012). Housework: Who did, does or will do it, and how much does it matter? *Social Forces*, *91*(1), 55–63. https://doi.org/10.1093/sf/sos120

Cândea, D. M., & Szentagotai-Tătar, A. (2018). Shame-proneness, guilt-proneness and anxiety symptoms: A meta-analysis. *Journal of Anxiety Disorders, 58,* 78–106. https://doi.org/10.1016/j.janxdis.2018.07.005

Carpenter, T., Stebbins, O., Fraga, K., & Erickson, T. M. (2022). Shame-proneness uniquely predicts social evaluative symptoms: Considering the sociometer theory of shame. *Journal of Social and Clinical Psychology, 41*(3), 238–263. https://doi.org/10.1521/jscp.2022.41.3.238

Chawla, N., Gabriel, A. S., Prengler, M., Rogers, K., Rogers, B., Tedder-King, A., & Rosen, C. C. (2024). Allyship in the fifth trimester: A multi-method investigation of women's postpartum return to work. *Organizational Behavior and Human Decision Processes, 182*, 104330. https://doi.org/10.1016/j.obhdp.2024.104330

Coelho, H. L., Trindade, I. A., Mendes, A. L., & Ferreira, C. (2021). The mediating role of shame and fear of compassion on the relationship between major life events and depressive symptoms. *Current Psychology, 40*(9), 4553–4562. https://doi.org/10.1007/s12144-019-00396-6

Crain, T. L., & Stevens, S. C. (2018). Family-supportive supervisor behaviors: A review and recommendations for research and practice. *Journal of Organizational Behavior, 39*(7), 869–888. https://doi.org/10.1002/job.2320

Davis, D. E., Ho, M. Y., Griffin, B. J., Bell, C., Hook, J. N., Van Tongeren, D. R., DeBlaere, C., Worthington, E. L., Jr., & Westbrook, C. J. (2015). Forgiving the self and physical and mental health correlates: A meta-analytic review. *Journal of Counseling Psychology*, *62*(2), 329–335. https://doi.org/10.1037/cou0000063

Doron, G., Sar-El, D., & Mikulincer, M. (2012). Threats to moral self-perceptions trigger obsessive compulsive contamination-related behavioral tendencies. *Journal of Behavior Therapy and Experimental Psychiatry*, *43*(3), 884–890. https://doi.org/10.1016/j.jbtep.2012.01.002

Falletta, L., Abbruzzese, S., Fischbein, R., Shura, R., Eng, A., & Alemagno, S. (2020). Work reentry after childbirth: Predictors of self-rated health in month one among a sample of university faculty and staff. *Safety and Health at Work*, *11*(1), 19–25. https://doi.org/10.1016/j.shaw.2019.12.006

Follmer, K. B., & Jones, K. S. (2018). Mental illness in the workplace: An interdisciplinary review and organizational research agenda. *Journal of Management*, *44*(1), 325–351. https://doi.org/10.1177/0149206317741194

Gabriel, A. S., Ladge, J. J., Little, L. M., MacGowan, R. L., & Stillwell, E. E. (2023). Sensemaking through the storm: How postpartum depression shapes personal work–family narratives. *Journal of Applied Psychology*, *108*(12), 1903–1923. https://doi.org/10.1037/apl0001125

Gabriel, A. S., Volpone, S. D., MacGowan, R. L., Butts, M. M., & Moran, C. M. (2020). When work and family blend together: Examining the daily experiences of breastfeeding mothers at work. *Academy of Management Journal*, *63*(5), 1337–1369. https://doi.org/10.5465/amj.2017.1241

Gatrell, C., Ladge, J. J., & Powell, G. N. (2024). Profane pregnant bodies versus sacred organizational systems: Exploring pregnancy discrimination at work (R2). *Journal of Business Ethics*, *192*(3), 527–542. https://doi.org/10.1007/s10551-023-05518-6

Ghosh, S. K. (2018). Happy hormones at work: Applying the learnings from neuroscience to improve and sustain workplace happiness. *NHRD Network Journal*, *11*(4), 83–92. https://doi.org/10.1177/2631454118806139

Goodwin, B. (2023, July). Popular workplace demands in 2023: Menopause leave tops the list. *Employee Benefits and Wellness Excellence Essentials*, *10*(7), 21–22.

Grandey, A. A., Gabriel, A. S., & King, E. B. (2020). Tackling taboo topics: A review of the three Ms in working women's lives. *Journal of Management*, *46*(1), 7–35. https://doi.org/10.1177/0149206319857144

Greenbaum, R., Bonner, J., Gray, T., & Mawritz, M. (2020). Moral emotions: A review and research agenda for management scholarship. *Journal of Organizational Behavior*, *41*(2), 95–114. https://doi.org/10.1002/job.2367

Greenbaum, R. L., Deng, Y., Butts, M. M., Wang, C. S., & Smith, A. N. (2022). Managing my shame: Examining the effects of parental identity threat and emotional stability on work productivity and investment in parenting. *Journal of Applied Psychology*, *107*(9), 1479–1497. https://doi.org/10.1037/apl0000597

Grzywacz, J. G., Almeida, D. M., & McDonald, D. A. (2002). Work–family spillover and daily reports of work and family stress in the adult labor force. *Family Relations*, *51*(1), 28–36. https://doi.org/10.1111/j.1741-3729.2002.00028.x

Hackney, K. J., Daniels, S. R., Paustian-Underdahl, S. C., Perrewé, P. L., Mandeville, A., & Eaton, A. A. (2021). Examining the effects of perceived pregnancy discrimination on mother and baby health. *Journal of Applied Psychology*, *106*(5), 774–783. https://doi.org/10.1037/apl0000788

Hennekam, S. (2016). Identity transition during pregnancy: The importance of role models. *Human Relations*, *69*(9), 1765–1790. https://doi.org/10.1177/0018726716631402

Horesh, D., Hasson-Ohayon, I., & Harwood-Gross, A. (2022). The contagion of psychopathology across different psychiatric disorders: A comparative theoretical analysis. *Brain Sciences*, *12*(1), 67. https://doi.org/10.3390/brainsci12010067

Hunter, M., Battersby, R., & Whitehead, M. (1986). Relationships between psychological symptoms, somatic complaints and menopausal status. *Maturitas*, *8*(3), 217–228. https://doi.org/10.1016/0378-5122(86)90029-0

Jones, C. C. G., Jomeen, J., & Hayter, M. (2014). The impact of peer support in the context of perinatal mental illness: A meta-ethnography. *Midwifery*, *30*(5), 491–498. https://doi.org/10.1016/j.midw.2013.08.003

Jones, K. P. (2013). *From baby bump to stressful slump: An episodic model of identity management behaviors in pregnant employees* [Dissertation, George Mason University].

Jones, K. P. (2017). To tell or not to tell? Examining the role of discrimination in the pregnancy disclosure process at work. *Journal of Occupational Health Psychology*, *22*(2), 239–250. https://doi.org/10.1037/ocp0000030

Jones, K. P., Brady, J. M., Lindsey, A. P., Cortina, L. M., & Major, C. K. (2022). The interactive effects of coworker and supervisor support on prenatal stress and postpartum health: A time-lagged investigation. *Journal of Business and Psychology*, *37*(3), 469–490. https://doi.org/10.1007/s10869-021-09756-1

Kachi, Y., Fujiwara, T., Eguchi, H., Inoue, A., Baba, S., Ohta, H., & Tsutsumi, A. (2021). Association between maternity harassment and depression during pregnancy amid the COVID-19 state of emergency. *Journal of Occupational Health*, *63*(1), e12196. https://doi.org/10.1002/1348-9585.12196

Kalev, A., & Dobbin, F. (2022). The surprising benefits of work/life support. *Harvard Business Review, 100*(5), 98–107.

Kim, H. J., Seo, J., Bang, M., & Lee, S. H. (2023). Self-forgiveness is associated with increased volumes of fusiform gyrus in healthy individuals. *Scientific Reports*, *13*(1), 5505. https://doi.org/10.1038/s41598-023-32731-0

Kim, S., Thibodeau, R., & Jorgensen, R. S. (2011). Shame, guilt, and depressive symptoms: A meta-analytic review. *Psychological Bulletin*, *137*(1), 68–96. https://doi.org/10.1037/a0021466

Ladge, J. J., Clair, J. A., & Greenberg, D. (2012). Cross-domain identity transition during liminal periods: Constructing multiple selves as professional and mother during pregnancy. *Academy of Management Journal*, *55*(6), 1449–1471. https://doi.org/10.5465/amj.2010.0538

Ladge, J. J., & Greenberg, D. N. (2015). Becoming a working mother: Managing identity and efficacy uncertainties during resocialization. *Human Resource Management*, *54*(6), 977–998. https://doi.org/10.1002/hrm.21651

Ladge, J., & Greenberg, D. N. (2019). *Maternal optimism: Forging positive paths through work and motherhood.* Oxford University Press. https://doi.org/10.1093/oso/9780190944094.001.0001

Ladge, J. J., Humberd, B. K., & Eddleston, K. A. (2018). Retaining professionally employed new mothers: The importance of maternal confidence and workplace support to their intent to stay. *Human Resource Management*, *57*(4), 883–900. https://doi.org/10.1002/hrm.21889

Law, K. H., Jackson, B., Tan, X. H., Teague, S., Krause, A., Putter, K., Du'cane, M., Gibson, L., Bulles, K. F., Barkin, J., & Dimmock, J. A. (2022). Strengthening peer mentoring relationships for new mothers: A qualitative analysis. *Journal of Clinical Medicine*, *11*(20), 6009. http://doi.org/10.3390/jcm11206009

Little, L. M., Major, V. S., Hinojosa, A. S., & Nelson, D. L. (2015). Professional image maintenance: How women navigate pregnancy in the workplace. *Academy of Management Journal*, *58*(1), 8–37. https://doi.org/10.5465/amj.2013.0599

Little, L. M., & Masterson, C. R. (2023). Mother's reentry: A relative contribution perspective of dual-earner parents' roles, resources, and outcomes. *Academy of Management Journal*, *66*(6), 1741–1767. https://doi.org/10.5465/amj.2019.1344

Lyzwinski, L. N. (2024). Organizational and occupational health issues with working remotely during the pandemic: A scoping review of remote work and health. *Journal of Occupational Health*, *66*(1), uiae005. http://doi.org/10.1093/joccuh/uiae005

McKay, M. T., Cannon, M., Chambers, D., Conroy, R. M., Coughlan, H., Dodd, P., Healy, C., O'Donnell, L., & Clarke, M. C. (2021). Childhood trauma and adult mental disorder: A systematic review and meta-analysis of longitudinal cohort studies. *Acta Psychiatrica Scandinavica, 143*(3), 189–205. https://doi.org/10.1111/acps.13268

Modestino, A., Ladge, J. J., Swartz, A., & Lincoln, A. (2021, April 29). Childcare is a business issue. *Harvard Business Review*. https://hbr.org/2021/04/childcare-is-a-business-issue

Mumford, C., Wilkinson, K., & Carroll, M. (2023). "Potential parenthood" and identity threats: Navigating complex fertility journeys alongside work and employment. *Gender, Work and Organization, 30*(3), 982–998. https://doi.org/10.1111/gwao.12953

O'Hara, M. W., & McCabe, J. E. (2013). Postpartum depression: Current status and future directions. *Annual Review of Clinical Psychology, 9*, 379–407. https://doi.org/10.1146/annurev-clinpsy-050212-185612

Okoli, C. (2023). Board of directors' column: (de) Stigmatization of mental illness and mental health care. *Journal of the American Psychiatric Nurses Association, 29*(5), 432–435. https://doi.org/10.1177/10783903231191105

O'Reilly, K., McDermid, F., McInnes, S., & Peters, K. (2023). "I was just a shell": Mental health concerns for women in perimenopause and menopause. *International Journal of Mental Health Nursing*, published online. https://doi.org/10.1111/inm.13271

Ortega, C. C. L., & Reio, T. G. Jr. (2016). Interventions for women with postpartum depression symptoms: An integrative literature review for human resource development. *Human Resource Development Review, 15*(2), 131–150. https://doi.org/10.1177/1534484316641523

Post, C., & Leuner, B. (2019). The maternal reward system in postpartum depression. *Archives of Women's Mental Health, 22*(3), 417–429. https://doi.org/10.1007/s00737-018-0926-y

Rosado-Solomon, E. H., Koopmann, J., Lee, W., & Cronin, M. A. (2023). Mental health and mental illness in organizations: A review, comparison, and extension. *The Academy of Management Annals, 17*(2), 751–797. https://doi.org/10.5465/annals.2021.0211

Sarangi, A., Kim, D., & Rafael, J. (2022). The mental health impact of work from home: A literature review. *The Southwest Respiratory and Critical Care Chronicles, 10*(45), 10–18. https://doi.org/10.12746/swrccc.v10i45.1085

Schnitzler, K. (2024). The intersect of miscarriage and work: Concealment, minimization and discriminatory practice. In K. Wilkinson & H. Woolnough (Eds.), *Work-life inclusion: Broadening perspectives across the life-course* (pp. 81–94). Emerald Publishing Limited. https://doi.org/10.1108/978-1-80382-219-820241007

Sheppard, F. H., & Wallace, D. C. (2018). Women's mental health after retirement. *Journal of Psychosocial Nursing and Mental Health Services, 56*(7), 37–45. https://doi.org/10.3928/02793695-20180619-07

Sit, D., Rothschild, A. J., & Wisner, K. L. (2006). A review of postpartum psychosis. *Journal of Women's Health, 15*(4), 352–368. https://doi.org/10.1089/jwh.2006.15.352

Tracy, J. L., & Robins, R. W. (2004). Putting the self into self-conscious emotions: A theoretical model. *Psychological Inquiry, 15*(2), 103–125. https://doi.org/10.1207/s15327965pli1502_01

Verdonk, P., Bendien, E., & Appelman, Y. (2022). Menopause and work: A narrative literature review about menopause, work and health. *Work, 72*(2), 483–496. https://doi.org/10.3233/WOR-205214

Weigle, P. E., & Shafi, R. M. (2024). Social media and youth mental health. *Current Psychiatry Reports, 26*(1), 1–8. https://doi.org/10.1007/s11920-023-01478-w

Wilkinson, K. (2022). Maternal (perinatal) mental health and employment: An agenda for research and practice. *Human Resource Management Journal, 33*(2), 346–361. https://doi.org/10.1111/1748-8583.12434

Wilkinson, K., Lennie, S. J., & Duddin, K. (2024). Perinatal mental health and employment: Exploring the work-illness intersection in the context of UK policing. In K. Wilkinson & H. Woolnough (Eds.), *Work-life inclusion: Broadening perspectives across the life-course* (pp. 95–108). Emerald Publishing Limited. https://doi.org/10.1108/978-1-80382-219-820241008

Wilson, H. J., & Daugherty, P. R. (2018). Collaborative intelligence: Humans and AI are joining forces. *Harvard Business Review*, *96*(4), 114–123.

Zhang, J., Thomas, C., Dirr, B., Cone, R., & Spitzmueller, C. (2016). Global maternity benefits and their impact on maternal and child well-being. In C. Spitzmueller & R. A. Matthews (Eds.), *Research perspectives on work and the transition to motherhood* (pp. 149–169). Springer International Publishing. https://doi.org/10.1007/978-3-319-41121-7_8

5 High-Flyers Under High Pressure

A Critical Review of Mental Health Concerns among High Achievers at Work

Tyler N.A. Fezzey, Jiani Fan, and Maura J. Mills

Recent scholarship underscores the significant impact of modern work demands on employee mental health, with ample evidence pointing to the negative consequences of several contemporary work practices (Greenwood & Anas, 2021; Kim et al., 2022). As organizations grapple with the challenges of a constantly connected digital workforce and an "always-on" culture, there is an increasing need to develop strategies to address these issues effectively (Fezzey et al., 2025). This urgency is further magnified by the rise in work-related stressors—such as the expectation to be responsive to work communications outside of traditional working hours and increasing interruptions permeating nonwork time (e.g., Grotto & Mills, 2023; Grotto et al., 2022, 2024)—leading to an uptick in both mental and physical health concerns among employees (Rosado-Solomon et al., 2023). With mental illnesses affecting approximately 17–20% of the workforce and contributing to an estimated $16 trillion in economic losses between 2010 and 2030 through absenteeism and diminished productivity (see Patel et al., 2018), the implications for both individuals and organizations are profound.

In this chapter, we examine mental health challenges faced by high-achieving employees, who are often presumed to be unlikely candidates for work-related mental health issues (Moneta, 2011). Notably, these individuals' high performance keeps them off the radar of organizational concern, often precluding others from recognizing that they might be struggling. Despite the common assumptions that traits such as competitiveness, need for achievement, and Type A personality protect against mental health problems like depression and burnout, emerging evidence suggests that these high-achieving employees may actually be at unique risk (e.g., Fezzey & Swab, 2024a, 2024b).

We pay particular attention to mental health in this segment of employees, examining the interplay between individual characteristics and organizational environments. We consider how organizational policies and practices, ostensibly designed to boost performance, can adversely affect employees' mental well-being. By focusing on both the individual dispositions that contribute to high achievement and the institutional practices that may inadvertently harm

DOI: 10.4324/9781003491170-7

mental health, this chapter aims to shed light on the complex dynamics that can create stress in high performers while simultaneously masking the negative impact from their peers and supervisors. In doing so, we contribute to the burgeoning body of literature on mental health challenges in the workplace, emphasizing the need for a multifaceted approach that recognizes the nuanced ways work-related stressors impact distinct employee groups, including those traditionally viewed as more resilient to occupational stress.

High-Performers and Mental Health

"High-achieving," "high-performing," and "star" are terms commonly used to describe individuals who possess a combination of traits and behaviors that predispose them toward workplace success. Many traits and individual differences contribute to workplace success; however, research has identified a core set that is particularly predictive. This chapter centers on this core set, including Type A personality (Rosenman et al., 1988), need for achievement (Conroy et al., 2009), trait competitiveness (Spence & Helmreich, 1983), perfectionism (Harari et al., 2018), and overachievement (Eldad, 2019) as key constructs. While a few studies have found that these personalities may be particularly resilient to stress (e.g., Hsu et al., 2010), we argue that this resilience against negative mental health symptomology is not infallible.

Mental health is conceptualized as a spectrum ranging from a state of flourishing, described as being "filled with positive emotion and to be functioning well psychologically and socially" (Keyes, 2002, p. 210), to a state of languishing, characterized by "emptiness and stagnation, constituting a life of quiet despair" (p. 210). Notably, flourishing is often associated with *good performance* (Montano et al., 2017), suggesting a direct link between positive mental health and high functioning. This, however, implies that high performance is largely incompatible with mental health challenges. Furthermore, decrements in performance have also been commonly cited as a "sign of struggle," a signal that managers should recognize as a signal of deteriorating employee well-being (e.g., Dimoff & Kelloway, 2016). We seek to challenge the idea that high performance and negative mental health cannot (or are unlikely to) coincide. That is, excellence in performance does not preclude the experience of mental health difficulties, and it may actually contribute to them.

Occupational stressors play a pivotal role in shaping employee well-being and performance. The resulting occupational strain can manifest in various forms, including burnout and depression (e.g., Dimoff & Kelloway, 2016). While the range of potential outcomes is vast, occupational stressors impact employees idiosyncratically. Certain groups, such as those with pre-existing mental health conditions, are more visibly affected by these stressors. However, this focus can inadvertently obscure the unique challenges high-flying employees face. Known for their apparent ability to thrive under pressure, tolerate longer working hours, and manage higher job demands, the mental health of these high performers can be easily overlooked and masked by their outward success (Eldad, 2019).

The differential impacts of occupational stressors on employees often give rise to what is known as the *stress paradox* (Crum et al., 2013), whereby stress can have negative impacts, such as compromising health and work outcomes (e.g., distress), or can facilitate positive growth, such as contributing to improvements in eudaimonic well-being and performance (e.g., eustress). In line with this paradox, theoretical frameworks have proposed categorizing stressors into hindrance demands and challenge demands (Podsakoff et al., 2007), with each type eliciting distinct responses and outcomes. Hindrance demands are typically linked to lower satisfaction, commitment, and performance, as well as increased turnover and withdrawal behaviors. In contrast, challenge demands are associated with more positive job attitudes, motivation, and enhanced performance. Integrating ideas from existing research on the challenge and threat framework (e.g., Blascovich, 2013; To et al., 2020), high-flyers may be predisposed to interpret stressors as challenges rather than threats or hindrances, enabling them to maintain or even improve their performance in the face of strain. This can explain how high-flyers still perform well despite exposure to and experience with occupational stressors, often making their suffering challenging to identify. However, organizations must understand that high performance does not mitigate strain responses or subsequent adverse outcomes. As such, it is essential to explore the distinctive ways in which stress adversely affects high-flyers and highlight how these differ from other employee groups.

As aforementioned, high-performing employees are crucial to the operational success of organizations. However, the mental health concerns associated with these individuals often remain under-recognized, a phenomenon usually attributed to their apparent success and resilience (Kelloway et al., 2023). These individuals are frequently faced with undertaking the most challenging projects, compensating for less capable or less motivated peers, and taking on a range of supplementary job tasks, all of which can contribute to elevated workload and stress levels. Indeed, it is often the very attributes that facilitate high performers' success in their professional roles that simultaneously predispose them to unique mental health challenges. We present our full conceptual model (Figure 5.1) to further unpack such experiences at work.

Individual Characteristics of High-Flyers

Type A Personality

Despite some evidence of their resilience to work-related stress, Type A individuals are susceptible to adverse mental health outcomes resulting from such stress (e.g., Conrad et al., 2014).[1] The Type A pattern includes behavioral dispositions such as excessive competitiveness, overt behaviors such as impatience,

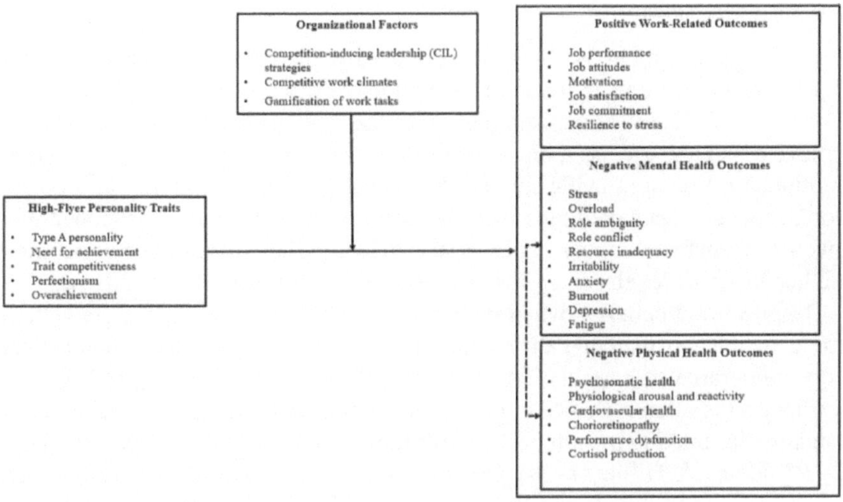

Figure 5.1 Conceptual Model of High-Flyer Personality Traits and Related Outcomes.

Note: Although this chapter primarily focuses on the mental health challenges faced by high-flyers, we acknowledge the reciprocal relationship between negative mental health outcomes and negative physical health outcomes, as indicated by the dashed lines. This interconnectedness is well-documented, with mental health issues often exacerbating physical health problems and vice versa. For further discussion on this bidirectional relationship, see Kelloway and Day (2005) and Kelloway et al. (2023)

and negative emotional responses such as hostility and anger (Wilmot et al., 2019). Research shows that these individuals tend to perform well (Watson et al., 2006) and experience high job satisfaction (Bruk-Lee et al., 2009). However, findings also argue that Type A behavior is closely associated with adverse work outcomes such as increased role ambiguity, conflict, and resource inadequacy (Shaheen, 2012). Moreover, Type A behavior is a significant negative moderator in the dynamics between job stressors and workplace outcomes such as satisfaction, commitment, psychosomatic health problems, and motivation to turnover (Billing & Steverson, 2013). Type A employees (nurses, in particular) also report significantly greater experiences of job stress, ambiguity, conflict, overload, and considerations of turnover than those with Type B personalities. Furthermore, Type A individuals display more stress symptoms such as irritability, somatic complaints, and anxiety (Nakao, 2017).

In addition to the psychological implications, Type A behaviors are associated with significant physical health concerns, such as elevated cholesterol levels and potential cardiovascular health issues (Lee & Watanuki, 2007). Type A behaviors have also been connected to central serous chorioretinopathy, a condition characterized by the abnormal accumulation of fluid under the retina, potentially leading to permanent vision impairment (Conrad et al., 2014; Varghese et al., 2022).

Need for Achievement

Need for achievement is often described as a positive trait associated with high performance and motivation as well as positive mental health outcomes (Conroy et al., 2009). For example, evidence has suggested that the need for achievement can serve as a buffer against all three components of burnout (i.e., emotional exhaustion, cynicism, and reduced efficacy; Moneta, 2011). Furthermore, some studies have found that high achievement striving is associated with lower-performance anxiety (Chen et al., 2018), higher work–home enrichment and health status levels, and a lower vulnerability to stress (Russo, 2015).

Despite these benefits, when people strive for achievement, they develop a strong belief and fear that they must prove themselves worthy, making them more vulnerable to further performance dysfunction (Lee et al., 1996). Such dysfunction is often reflected in high achievement-striving individuals' elevated standards for making meaningful contributions and carrying out tasks satisfactorily (Goldberg & Hillier, 1979). Contrary to the findings of Moneta (2011), Lee and colleagues (1996) found that individuals high in achievement striving are especially prone to burnout due to their tendency to be substantially overworked.

Competitiveness

Although competitiveness is often recognized as a catalyst for enhancing individual performance (Tauer & Harackiewicz, 2004), it is essential to consider its potential downsides (Fezzey & Swab, 2024a, 2024b). Meta-analysis has demonstrated that there are direct positive relationships between trait competitiveness and elevated levels of stress and anxiety, as well as a higher likelihood of turning over (Fezzey et al., 2023; Yearick, 2018). Further research highlights the link between hypercompetitive attitudes (i.e., being indiscriminately competitive, even in non-competitive situations) and increased prevalence of depression, anxiety, and stress symptoms (Chan & Cheung, 2022), with this effect being notably significant among women. Moreover, comparative analyses of competitiveness and cooperativeness reveal that competitiveness is inversely related to psychological well-being, unlike cooperativeness, which tends to foster a healthier state of mind (Kirkcaldy et al., 1998; Peng et al., 2021). Hypercompetitiveness is also characterized by significant disagreeableness and hostility (Ryckman et al., 1994), which negatively influences not only the individual's health but also the well-being of their team members (Chan & Cheung, 2022). Furthermore, studies focusing on adolescents demonstrate that a discrepancy between competitiveness and competitive climate contributes to heightened levels of depression and anxiety (Liu et al., 2024).

The impact of competitiveness on stress is further magnified by an increased willingness to work extended hours, driven by a desire to outdo others. This compulsion to outperform peers often results in feelings of being overburdened and stressed (Sato et al., 2009). Supporting this position, Iwata and colleagues (1992) found evidence among banking professionals in managerial positions that managers with higher competitiveness tend to work longer hours than their less competitive colleagues, reinforcing the link between competitiveness, work engagement, and stress. Further evidence of the relationship between competitiveness and stress has been found using both psychometric measures (e.g., Rhodewalt et al., 1991) and lab experiments (Buckert et al., 2017). Experimental results have triangulated this relationship across three stress indicators: cortisol production, heart rate variability, and blood pressure (Buckert et al., 2017).

Competitive individuals are also likely to adopt a differentiation mindset, which places them in opposition to others, leading to interpersonal problems that prompt further stress and related adverse outcomes (Stapel & Koomen, 2005). In line with this, research shows that competitive individuals encounter increased difficulties forming close interpersonal connections with others (e.g., Luchner et al., 2011; Thornton et al., 2011) due to their tendency to manage interpersonal relationships poorly (e.g., Swab & Johnson, 2023). Given that interpersonal relationships are critical for job satisfaction (Santana & Loureiro, 2019), this inability to form close ties amplifies mental health concerns for these high-striving individuals. Finally, while some competitiveness is likely necessary to be a high performer (e.g., Fezzey & Swab, 2024a, 2024b; Locander et al., 2020), excessive levels can be highly maladaptive. Hypercompetitive individuals are described as highly neurotic and disagreeable (Mudrack et al., 2012) and are marked by low self-esteem, insecure attachments, neuroticism, and low psychological health (e.g., Ryckman et al., 2009).

Perfectionism

Striving for perfection and subsequently engaging in performativity to do so generates anxiety (Knights & Clarke, 2018). This anxiety becomes further amplified because perfectionists cannot separate themselves from work (e.g., Flaxman et al., 2012). Perfectionism has also been found to have substantive, generalizable correlations with stress, anxiety, and depression (Harari et al., 2018). These stress responses have been validated in experimental conditions as well. While mentally and physically detaching from work is necessary for employee health recovery, well-being, and work performance (Agolli & Holtz, 2023), evidence has shown that perfectionists often think about work during their leisure time (e.g., Flaxman et al., 2018), making it difficult for them to detach and recover from work-related stressors. Furthermore, a study conducted on academics found that more perfectionist academics report significantly higher fatigue, emotional exhaustion, and anxiety in post-respite weeks due to their tendency for perseverative cognition (i.e., work-related worry and rumination; Flaxman et al., 2012).

Importantly, these negative consequences pour over into employees' personal lives. More specifically, perfectionism predicts work–family conflict over and above the Big Five, trait affectivity, and achievement motivation, especially among maladaptive perfectionists (i.e., individuals having especially diminishing feelings of accomplishment due to unrealistic performance standards; Conrad et al., 2014). This work–life conflict subsequently leads to lower job engagement and higher turnover intention (Jaharuddin & Zainol, 2019). Finally, perfectionism has also been indirectly associated with poor sleep quality and poor workday functioning via the excessive tendency to worry and ruminate about work (Flaxman et al., 2018).

Overachievement

Conceptually similar to perfectionism, complexities associated with overachievement further illustrate the challenges individuals face at the apex of the achievement spectrum. Overachievers, though lacking a universally accepted definition, are often characterized by their relentless pursuit of success coupled with perpetual dissatisfaction with their accomplishments (see Guidry et al., 2022). While striving for success is inherently positive, pursuing overachievement may lead to a focus on striving for professional accomplishments at the expense of personal well-being. The propensity of overachievers to take on excessive workloads is a direct pathway to burnout. Research has elucidated a correlation between overachievement and elevated incidences of self-doubt and anxiety (Zhao & Wichman, 2015). The relentless pursuit of lofty, often unattainable goals, compounded by a pervasive fear of failure, constitutes a significant occupational stressor for these employees (Eldad, 2019). Such individuals are prone to extending their work hours, prioritizing professional commitments over their personal relationships, and neglecting self-care practices and leisure activities in pursuit of task completion. This imbalance significantly undermines work–life harmony, correlating with diminished satisfaction in both life and job domains and engendering higher levels of anxiety and depression (Haar et al., 2014).

Risk of Stigma

A tantamount issue impacting the mental health of all high-flying employees is the stigma they might feel around seeking support, coupled with an internalized and occasionally externally induced pressure to maintain their status as high performers. Such individuals may hesitate to solicit assistance, perceiving it as a threat to their reputation as competent and reliable employees. This reluctance is particularly pronounced among those in leadership positions or those exhibiting hypercompetitiveness, perfectionism, and overachievement, as they may equate seeking help with a demonstration of weakness, incompetence, or failure. This leads to a continued effort to excel in their roles (e.g., working extended, unrewarded hours) without seeking necessary support. Furthermore, the high-performance level of these employees comes from their tendency to prioritize their work-related tasks over other tasks. This may cause them to overlook their mental well-being in favor of addressing tasks deemed more critical. While this approach may yield short-term benefits, neglecting early signs of the need for mental health interventions can precipitate long-term adverse outcomes.

The Role of Context

As important as individual difference variables are in influencing mental health, they provide an incomplete picture without simultaneous consideration of the occupational environments in which these individuals operate. The adage that "hard workers get rewarded with more hard work" rings particularly true for high-flying employees, who often find themselves navigating increasingly demanding work conditions as a testament to their success. Such conditions create a landscape ripe with professional hurdles, where the pressure to adopt new roles or responsibilities while maintaining high performance becomes a significant source of stress. It is also essential to recognize that several organizational practices aimed at boosting performance may inadvertently exacerbate mental health challenges among high performers. These include competition-inducing leadership (CIL) strategies (Friess et al., 2023), the cultivation of competitive work climates (Fletcher et al., 2008), and the gamification of work tasks (Hammedi et al., 2021). Each of these elements, though designed to enhance performance, can contribute to an environment that paradoxically undermines the mental well-being of its most capable employees.

Competition-Inducing Leadership

Recent research elucidates the complex dynamics of competition-inducing leadership (CIL), a set of leader behaviors designed to foster interpersonal competition among employees, and its nuanced impact on employee motivation and well-being (Friess et al., 2023; Heidemeier & Bittner, 2012). While CIL can inspire employees by setting higher goals and delineating pathways to achievement (Atefi et al., 2018), it may simultaneously exert undue performance pressure, eliciting negative emotions (Habel et al., 2021) and diminishing job satisfaction (Reina et al., 2018), which influence health as well as performance. Furthermore, despite positively affecting team performance, stimulated intra-team competition is negatively related to psychological safety and positively related to team conflict (Brouwer, 2016). This two-sided nature becomes particularly problematic in environments where employee recognition is contingent upon outperforming peers, leading to inter-employee rivalries, increased mental stress, and physiological arousal (To et al., 2018). Moreover, leaders who engage in CIL often implement stress-inducing strategies, such as pay-for-performance schemes or zero-sum reward systems, which may further exacerbate stress levels among high-achieving employees (Fezzey & Swab, 2024a).

Organizational Culture and Climate

The impact of organizational culture and climate on employee stress and well-being is well documented. An illustration of this can be found in the intentional establishment of competitive climates within organizations to enhance performance. While the results of competitive climates on employee performance are mixed (e.g., Wolf et al., 2021), studies have consistently shown that competitive environments foster stress among employees regardless of their innate trait of competitiveness (Fletcher et al., 2008). Interestingly, while employees with a high level of trait competitiveness may naturally gravitate toward and thrive in competitive settings (e.g., in sales roles), they are not immune to the adverse effects of increased stress levels that these environments promote (Fletcher et al., 2008).

Gamification

Competitive, high-stress work environments like those described earlier are becoming increasingly common due to *gamification*, which applies the principles of a game to a work context to increase an individual worker's motivation, effectiveness, and performance (Cardador et al., 2017). Gamification is perceived to have long-term benefits through increased engagement and intrinsic motivation (Harris et al., 2023; Kolb & Kolb, 2010), but more recent articles have explored the downside of gamification. For example, Hammedi and colleagues (2021) found that gamified processes decrease front-line employees' job satisfaction and well-being. While high-achieving employees might be the ones who respond most positively to gamification in the short term, the potential long-term detriment might significantly outweigh the benefits.

Practical Implications

The evidence highlighted in this chapter clarifies that the unique mental health challenges faced by high achievers in the workplace cannot go unaddressed, and organizations must help their high-performing employees navigate these issues (Leka et al., 2011). There is a compelling incentive for managers to support high-performing employees in managing stress, as this can help sustain the high-performance levels of their top employees. Given that developing individual capabilities to cope with work-related stress has been linked to enhanced performance and well-being (Zhong et al., 2018), managers must provide this support. Accordingly, we propose several targeted interventions later that are aimed at safeguarding the mental health of not only those whose performance is adversely affected by stressors but also the high achievers who may be particularly inclined (and able) to conceal their struggles.

Positive emotions play a crucial role in moderating stress and facilitating stress recovery (for a review of positive psychology at work, see Mills et al., 2013). Research indicates that optimism can interact with the achievement-striving dimension of Type A to counteract anxiety (Lee et al., 1993), suggesting that employers can focus on creating work environments where employees feel optimistic, which in turn can help buffer against anxiety. That said, organizations should steer clear of toxic positivity (i.e., portraying a positive attitude in a way that appears platitudinous; Goodman, 2022), which may be particularly frustrating for high achievers, as they often work hard to remain intently aware of the nuances of their workplace and are thus more likely to pick up on inconsistencies, compromising their trust in the organization. However, organizations can nonetheless facilitate environments that are more likely to foster positive employee emotions for high achievers by ensuring safe spaces for failure and prioritizing an environment where striving for excellence is valued over avoiding failure.

More broadly, evidence suggests that high-flyers often compromise their relationships in their quest for achievement (e.g., Luchner et al., 2011; Thornton et al., 2011), significantly contributing to their stress levels. The relentless pursuit of professional goals frequently necessitates the forfeiture of quality time with friends and family, leading to heightened feelings of isolation. Contrary to the sacrificial nature of such pursuits, research indicates that nurturing robust social networks is conducive to sustained success (Wang & Uzzi, 2022). Consequently, introducing organizational initiatives to facilitate interpersonal interactions among employees can serve as a pivotal mechanism for cultivating social support systems. Moreover, organizations should enforce policies that encourage employees, especially those in high-demand roles, to take adequate time off from work and maintain a clear demarcation between work and personal life.

The responsibility for mental health maintenance is shifting from solely an employee's burden to a critical organizational concern (see Thomas et al., 2024). We agree that this represents a proper shift in the responsibility for promoting positive mental health. We recommend that organizations adopt options such as workplace wellness programs to foster a health-conscious organizational culture (Fezzey et al., 2025; Tetrick & Winslow, 2015). With this in mind, we recognize that budget constraints and logistical issues often hinder the implementation of some interventions outlined earlier. Nonetheless, innovations in employee health coverage have made prevention, intervention, and accommodation of mental health in organizations far more feasible than previously possible.[2]

Conclusion

The evolving modern workscape (Mills et al., 2018) is increasingly characterized by an array of work-related stressors, contributing to widespread mental health outcomes. While much of the focus in organizational research and practice has traditionally centered on employees who show signs of struggle through missed performance benchmarks, our review highlights mental health considerations for those at the opposite end of the spectrum: the consistently high-performing individuals. As we have unpacked herein, these individuals are all too often overlooked in discussions of workplace mental health, where they fall victim to implicit assumptions that they are inherently well-equipped to handle pressures due to their apparent success and thus largely immune to mental health concerns. Not only is this inaccurate, but it can also be highly detrimental. In this chapter, we have sought to unravel the complex reality these high-flyers face. We have also critically analyzed how certain organizational policies and practices, though ostensibly crafted to foster high performance, may inadvertently exacerbate mental health challenges. By bringing these issues to the foreground, we aspire not only to broaden the understanding of mental health in the workplace but also to catalyze a shift in how organizations approach the well-being of their top performers. We hope that this chapter illuminates the often-hidden mental health struggles of high-performing employees, urging a reevaluation of current practices. In doing so, we advocate for a more inclusive research agenda that recognizes the unique mental health needs of this critical workforce segment.

Notes

1 While this section discusses individual characteristics commonly found among high-flyers, it is important to note that these traits are presented to illustrate general trends only and should not be interpreted as implying personal responsibility for any associated mental health challenges.

2 Although beyond the primary scope of this chapter, readers are encouraged to see Stratton et al. (2022), Thomas et al. (2024), and elsewhere in this volume for further discussion of organizational-level approaches.

References

Agolli, A., & Holtz, B. C. (2023). Facilitating detachment from work: A systematic review, evidence-based recommendations, and guide for future research. *Journal of Occupational Health Psychology*, *28*, 129–159.

Atefi, Y., Ahearne, M., Maxham III, J. G., Donavan, D. T., & Carlson, B. D. (2018). Does selective sales force training work? *Journal of Marketing Research*, *55*, 722–737.

Billing, T. K., & Steverson, P. (2013). Moderating role of Type-A personality on stress-outcome relationships. *Management Decision*, *51*, 1893–1904.

Blascovich, J. (2013). Challenge and threat appraisal. In *Handbook of approach and avoidance motivation* (pp. 431–445). Psychology Press.

Brouwer, R. (2016). When competition is the loser: The indirect effect of intra-team competition on team performance through task complexity, team conflict and psychological safety. *2016 49th Hawaii International Conference on System Sciences (HICSS)*, 1348–1357.

Bruk-Lee, V., Khoury, H. A., Nixon, A. E., Goh, A., & Spector, P. E. (2009). Replicating and extending past personality/job satisfaction meta-analyses. *Human Performance*, *22*, 156–189.

Buckert, M., Schwieren, C., Kudielka, B. M., & Fiebach, C. J. (2017). How stressful are economic competitions in the lab? An investigation with physiological measures. *Journal of Economic Psychology*, *62*, 231–245.

Cardador, M. T., Northcraft, G. B., & Whicker, J. (2017). A theory of work gamification: Something old, something new, something borrowed, something cool? *Human Resource Management Review*, *27*, 353–365.

Chan, C. Y., & Cheung, K. L. (2022). Exploring the gender difference in relationships between narcissism, competitiveness, and mental health problems among college students. *Journal of American College Health*, *70*, 1169–1178.

Chen, C.-C., Hung, C.-H., Chen, P.-L., & Hsueh, J.-H. (2018). Double-edged sword: Different learning behavior patterns for junior high school mathematics. *Journal of Research in Education Sciences*, *63*, 105–130.

Conrad, R., Geiser, F., Kleiman, A., Zur, B., & Karpawitz-Godt, A. (2014). Temperament and character personality profile and illness-related stress in central serous chorioretinopathy. *The Scientific World Journal, 2014*, 1–7.

Conroy, D. E., Elliot, A. J., & Pincus, A. L. (2009). The expression of achievement motives in interpersonal problems. *Journal of Personality*, *77*, 495–526.

Crum, A. J., Salovey, P., & Achor, S. (2013). Rethinking stress: The role of mindsets in determining the stress response. *Journal of Personality and Social Psychology*, *104*, 716–733.

Dimoff, J. K., & Kelloway, E. K. (2016). Resource utilization model: Organizational leaders as resource facilitators. In W. A. Gentry & C. Clerkin (Eds.), *The role of leadership in occupational stress* (pp. 141–160). Emerald Group Publishing.

Eldad, K. (2019). The superstar paradox—How overachievers miss the mark in life and at work. *Psychology Research*, *9*, 339–343.

Fezzey, T. N. A., Fan, J., Mills, M. J., & Howes, S. S. (2025). A commentary on Thomas et al. (2024). How high achievers and hypercompetitive cultures may be inadvertently dissuading mental health offering usage. *Group & Organization Management*. https://doi.org/10.1177/10596011251314212

Fezzey, T. N. A., Harms, P., & DeSimone, J. A. (2023). Development and validation of the brief competitiveness inventory. In *Academy of management proceedings* (Vol. 2023, No. 1, p. 16354). Academy of Management.

Fezzey, T. N. A., & Swab, R. G. (2024a). How bad do you want it? A bibliometric review of individual competitiveness. *Journal of Management History*, *30*, 60–86.

Fezzey, T. N. A., & Swab, R. G. (2024b). The competitive conundrum: Exploring multilevel competitive influences on stress and well-being. *Research on Occupational Stress and Well Being*, *22*, 17–52.

Flaxman, P. E., Ménard, J., Bond, F. W., & Kinman, G. (2012). Academics' experiences of a respite from work: Effects of self-critical perfectionism and perseverative cognition on post respite well-being. *Journal of Applied Psychology*, *97*, 854–865.

Flaxman, P. E., Stride, C. B., Söderberg, M., Lloyd, J., Guenole, N., & Bond, F. W. (2018). Relationships between two dimensions of employee perfectionism, postwork cognitive processing, and work day functioning. *European Journal of Work and Organizational Psychology*, *27*, 56–69.

Fletcher, T. D., Major, D. A., & Davis, D. D. (2008). The interactive relationship of competitive climate and trait competitiveness with workplace attitudes, stress, and performance. *Journal of Organizational Behavior*, *29*, 899–922.

Friess, M., Alavi, S., Habel, J., & Richter, B. (2023). When sales leaders induce competition among sales employees: A source of motivation or exhaustion? *Journal of Personal Selling & Sales Management*, 1–19.

Goldberg, D. P., & Hillier, V. F. (1979). A seated version of the General Health Questionnaire. *Psychological Medicine, 9,* 139–145.

Goodman, W. (2022). *Toxic positivity: Keeping it real in a world obsessed with being happy*. TarcherPerigee.

Greenwood, K., & Anas, J. (2021). It's a new era for mental health at work. *Harvard Business Review*, 4–13.

Grotto, A. R., & Mills, M. J. (2023). Crossing the line: The violating effects of illegitimate interruptions from work and the differential impact on work-to-family conflict by gender. *Journal of Organizational Behavior*, *44*, 700–716.

Grotto, A. R., Mills, M. J., & Eatough, E. M. (2022). Switching gears: A self-regulatory approach and measure of nonwork role re-engagement following after-hours work intrusions. *Journal of Business and Psychology*, *37*, 491–507.

Grotto, A. R., Mills, M. J., & Eatough, E. M. (2024). Manage boundaries better with your team. *MIT Sloan Management Review*. https://sloanreview.mit.edu/article/manage-boundaries-better-with-your-team/

Guidry, C. M., Medina, M. S., Bennett, K. K., & Schwier, N. C. (2022). The other side of "challenging learners": Strategies for teaching and precepting the overachiever and high performer. *American Journal of Health-System Pharmacy*, *79*, 17–22.

Haar, J. M., Russo, M., Suñe, A., & Ollier-Malaterre, A. (2014). Outcomes of work–life balance on job satisfaction, life satisfaction and mental health: A study across seven cultures. *Journal of Vocational Behavior*, *85*, 361–373.

Habel, J., Alavi, S., & Linsenmayer, K. (2021). Variable compensation and salesperson health. *Journal of Marketing*, *85*, 130–149.

Hammedi, W., Leclercq, T., Poncin, I., & Alkire, L. (2021). Uncovering the dark side of gamification at work: Impacts on engagement and well-being. *Journal of Business Research*, *122*, 256–269.

Harari, D., Swider, B. W., Steed, L. B., & Breidenthal, A. P. (2018). Is perfect good? A meta-analysis of perfectionism in the workplace. J*ournal of Applied Psychology*, *103*, 1121–1144.

Harris, J. N., Swab, R. G., Mercer, I. S., & Tomczyk, D. A. (2023, March). Role-playing as experiential learning: Using dungeons and dragons to teach management concepts. In *Developments in business simulation and experiential learning: Proceedings of the Annual ABSEL conference* (Vol. 50).

Heidemeier, H., & Bittner, J. (2012). Competition and achievement goals in work teams. *Human Performance*, *25*, 138–158.

Hsu, H. Y., Chen, S. H., Yu, H. Y., & Lou, J. H. (2010). Job stress, achievement motivation and occupational burnout among male nurses. *Journal of Advanced Nursing*, *66*, 1592–1601.

Iwata, N., Suzuki, K., Saito, K., & Abe, K. (1992). Type A personality, work stress and psychological distress in Japanese adult employees. *Stress and Health, 8,* 11–21.

Jaharuddin, N. S., & Zainol, L. N. (2019). The impact of work-life balance on job engagement and turnover intention. *South East Asian Journal of Management*, *13*, 106–117.

Kelloway, E. K., & Day, A. L. (2005). Building healthy workplaces: What we know so far. *Canadian Journal of Behavioural Science/Revue canadienne des sciences du comportement*, *37*, 223–235.

Kelloway, E. K., Dimoff, J. K., & Gilbert, S. (2023). Mental health in the workplace. *Annual Review of Organizational Psychology and Organizational Behavior*, *10*, 363–387.

Keyes, C. L. (2002). The mental health continuum: From languishing to flourishing in life. *Journal of Health and Social Behavior*, *43*, 207–222.

Kim, K. Y., Messersmith, J. G., Pieper, J. R., Baik, K., & Fu, S. (2022). High performance work systems and employee mental health: The roles of psychological empowerment, work role overload, and organizational identification. *Human Resource Management*, *62*, 791–810.

Kirkcaldy, B. D., Furnham, A., & Martin, T. (1998). National differences in personality, socio-economic, and work-related attitudinal variables. *European Psychologist*, *3*, 255–262.
Knights, D., & Clarke, C. (2018). Living on the edge? Professional anxieties at work in academia and veterinary practice. *Culture and Organization*, *24*, 134–153.
Kolb, A. Y., & Kolb, D. A. (2010). Learning to play, playing to learn: A case study of a ludic learning space. *Journal of Organizational Change Management*, *23*, 26–50.
Lee, C., Ashford, S. J., & Jamieson, L. F. (1993). The effects of Type A behavior dimensions and optimism on coping strategy, health, and performance. *Journal of Organizational Behavior*, *14*, 143–157.
Lee, C., Jamieson, L. F., & Earley, P. C. (1996). Beliefs and fears and Type A behavior: Implications for academic performance and psychiatric health disorder symptoms. *Journal of Organizational Behavior*, *17*, 151–177.
Lee, J.-M., & Watanuki, S. (2007). Cardiovascular responses of Type A and Type B behavior patterns to visual stimulation during rest, stress and recovery. *Journal of Physiological Anthropology*, *26*, 1–8.
Leka, S., Jain, A., Iavicoli, S., Vartia, M., & Ertel, M. (2011). The role of policy for the management of psychosocial risks at the workplace in the European Union. *Safety Science*, *49*, 558–564.
Liu, W., Wen, H., Zhu, C., Quan, X., Wang, X., & Zhang, C. (2024). The joint impact of trait competitiveness and competitive climate on depressive symptoms and anxiety among adolescents. *Journal of Youth and Adolescence, 53,* 79–88.
Locander, D. A., Locander, J. A., & Weinberg, F. J. (2020). How salesperson traits and intuitive judgments influence adaptive selling: A sensemaking perspective. *Journal of Business Research, 118,* 452–462.
Luchner, A. F., Houston, J., Walker, C., & Houston, M. (2011). Exploring the relationship between two forms of narcissism and competitiveness. *Personality and Individual Differences*, *51*, 779–782.
Mills, M. J., Fleck, C. R., & Kozikowski, A. (2013). Positive psychology at work: A conceptual review, state-of-practice assessment, and a look ahead. *The Journal of Positive Psychology*, *8*, 153–164.
Mills, M. J., Pervez, A., & Mandeville, A. M. (2018). We're not there yet: Gender and the work-family interface in the modern workscape. In J. Nicklin (Ed.), *Work-life balance in the 21st century: Perspectives, practices, and challenges* (pp. 17–54). Nova Science Publishers.
Moneta, G. B. (2011). Need for achievement, burnout, and intention to leave: Testing an occupational model in educational settings. *Personality and Individual Differences*, *50*, 274–278.
Montano, D., Reeske, A., Franke, F., & Hüfmeier, J. (2017). Leadership, followers' mental health and job performance in organizations: A comprehensive meta-analysis from an occupational health perspective. *Journal of Organizational Behavior*, *38*, 327–350.
Mudrack, P. E., Bloodgood, J. M., & Turnley, W. H. (2012). Some ethical implications of individual competitiveness. *Journal of Business Ethics*, *108*, 347–359.
Nakao, M. (2017). Somatic manifestation of distress: Clinical medicine, psychological, and public health perspectives. *BioPsychoSocial Medicine*, *11*, 33–34.
Patel, V., Saxena, S., Lund, C., Thornicroft, G., Baingana, F., Bolton, P., Chisholm, D., Collins, P. Y., Cooper, J. L., Eaton, J., Herrman, H., Herzallah, M. M., Huang, Y., Jordans, M. J. D., Kleinman, A., Medina-Mora, M. E., Morgan, E., Niaz, U., Omigbodun, O., Prince, M., . . . UnÜtzer, J. (2018). The Lancet Commission on global mental health and sustainable development. *Lancet (London, England)*, *392*, 1553–1598.
Peng, H., Bell, C., & Li, Y. (2021). How and when intragroup relationship conflict leads to knowledge hiding: The roles of envy and trait competitiveness. *International Journal of Conflict Management*, *32*, 383–406.

Podsakoff, N. P., LePine, J. A., & LePine, M. A. (2007). Differential challenge stressor-hindrance stressor relationships with job attitudes, turnover intentions, turnover, and withdrawal behavior: A meta-analysis. *Journal of Applied Psychology*, *92*, 438–454.

Reina, C. S., Rogers, K. M., Peterson, S. J., Byron, K., & Hom, P. W. (2018). Quitting the boss? The role of manager influence tactics and employee emotional engagement in voluntary turnover. *Journal of Leadership & Organizational Studies*, *25*, 5–18.

Rhodewalt, F., Sansone, C., Hill, C. A., Chemers, M. M., & Wysocki, J. (1991). Stress and distress as a function of Jenkins activity survey-defined Type A behavior and control over the work environment. *Basic and Applied Social Psychology*, *12*, 211–226.

Rosado-Solomon, E. H., Koopmann, J., Lee, W., & Cronin, M. A. (2023). Mental health and mental illness in organizations: A review, comparison, and extension. *Academy of Management Annals*, *17*, 751–797.

Rosenman, R. H., Swan, G. E., & Carmelli, D. (1988). Definition, assessment, and evolution of the Type A behavior pattern. In B. K. Houston & C. R. Snyder (Eds.), *Type A behavior pattern: Research, theory, and intervention* (pp. 8–31). John Wiley & Sons.

Russo, M. (2015). Work–home enrichment and health: An analysis of the mediating role of persistence in goal striving and vulnerability to stress. *International Journal of Human Resource Management, 26,* 2486–2502.

Ryckman, R. M., Thornton, B., & Butler, C. J. (1994). Personality correlates of the Hypercompetitive Attitude Scale: Validity tests of Horney's theory of neurosis. *Journal of Personality Assessment*, *62*, 84–94.

Ryckman, R. M., Thornton, B., & Gold, J. A. (2009). Assessing competition avoidance as a basic personality dimension. *The Journal of Psychology: Interdisciplinary and Applied*, *143*, 175–192.

Santana, S., & Loureiro, S. M. C. (2019). Analysing drivers and outcomes of job and professional satisfaction at health centres in Portugal. *Benchmarking: An International Journal*, *26*, 1357–1375.

Sato, Y., Miyake, H., & Thériault, G. (2009). Overtime work and stress response in a group of Japanese workers. *Occupational Medicine*, *59*, 14–19.

Shaheen, N. (2012). Type A behaviour and work-family conflict in professional women. *Pakistan Journal of Social and Clinical Psychology*, *9*, 70–74.

Spence, J. T., & Helmreich, R. L. (1983). Achievement-related motives and behavior. In J. T. Spence (Ed.), *Achievement and achievement motives: Psychological and sociological approaches* (pp. 10–74). Freeman.

Stapel, D. A., & Koomen, W. (2005). Competition, cooperation, and the effects of others on me. *Journal of Personality and Social Psychology*, *88*, 1029–1038.

Stratton, E., Lampit, A., Choi, I., Malmberg Gavelin, H., Aji, M., Taylor, J., Calvo, R. A., Harvey, S. B., & Glozier, N. (2022). Trends in effectiveness of organizational eHealth interventions in addressing employee mental health: Systematic review and meta-analysis. *Journal of Medical Internet Research, 24*, 1–26.

Swab, R. G., & Johnson, P. D. (2023). Attachment, competitiveness, and workplace aggression: A model of aggressive intent and examination of the competitive orientation scale. *Psychological Reports*. https://doi.org/10.1177/00332941231203568

Tauer, J. M., & Harackiewicz, J. M. (2004). The effects of cooperation and competition on intrinsic motivation and performance. *Journal of Personality and Social Psychology*, *86*, 849–861.

Tetrick, L. E., & Winslow, C. (2015). Workplace stress management interventions and health promotion. *Annual Review of Organizational Psychology and Organizational Behavior*, *2*, 583–603.

Thomas, B. J., Follmer, K. B., & Meglich, P. (2024). Giving Organization stakeholders better help: A taxonomy for making sense of workplace mental health offerings. *Group & Organization Management*, 1–44.

Thornton, B., Ryckman, R. M., & Gold, J. A. (2011). Hypercompetitiveness and relationships: Further implications for romantic, family, and peer relationships. *Psychology*, *2*, 269–274.

To, C., Kilduff, G. J., Ordoñez, L., & Schweitzer, M. E. (2018). Going for it on fourth down: Rivalry increases risk taking, physiological arousal, and promotion focus. *Academy of Management Journal*, *61*, 1281–1306.

To, C., Kilduff, G. J., & Rosikiewicz, B. L. (2020). When interpersonal competition helps and when it harms: An integration via challenge and threat. *Academy of Management Annals*, *14*, 908–934.

Varghese, J., Kesharwani, D., Parashar, S., & Agrawal, P. (2022). A review of central serous chorioretinopathy: Clinical presentation and management. *Cureus*, *14*, e27965.

Wang, D., & Uzzi, B. (2022). Weak ties, failed tries, and success. *Science*, *377*, 1256–1258.

Watson, W. E., Minzenmayer, T., & Bowler, M. (2006). Type A personality characteristics and the effect on individual and team academic performance. *Journal of Applied Social Psychology*, *36*, 1110–1128.

Wilmot, M. P., Haslam, N., Tian, J., & Ones, D. S. (2019). Direct and conceptual replications of the taxometric analysis of Type A behavior. *Journal of Personality and Social Psychology*, *116*, e12–e26.

Wolf, T., Jahn, S., Hammerschmidt, M., & Weiger, W. H. (2021). Competition versus cooperation: How technology-facilitated social interdependence initiates the self-improvement chain. *International Journal of Research in Marketing*, *38*, 472–491.

Yearick, K. A. (2018). *Competitive personality and work outcomes: A meta-analysis and scale development* (Doctoral dissertation, University of Illinois at Urbana-Champaign).

Zhao, Q., & Wichman, A. (2015). Incremental beliefs about ability ameliorate self-doubt effects. *SAGE Open*, *5*, 1–10.

Zhong, S., Shalev, I., Koh, D., Ebstein, R. P., & Chew, S. H. (2018). Competitiveness and stress. *International Economic Review*, *59*, 1263–1281.

6 Mental Health of African Americans and Implications for Organizations

Tanesha L. Rorie

Mental health challenges affect African Americans at similar rates compared to the non-Hispanic White individuals (CDC, 2021). While the rates of utilization of mental health services for Black people who have a mental illness have increased up to 16% over the past four years (Panchal & Lo, 2024), it is still lower than non-Hispanic White people at 28%. People of color face unique experiences in the United States that impact their overall mental health experience. Specifically, Black/African American people have a long-standing history of oppression that has produced trauma for many people in this community. This chapter will outline the mental health experiences of Black people as well as sociocultural backgrounds and impacts to the mental health state of this group. Finally, implications for organizations and their employee assistance programs (EAPs) will be discussed.

Factors Impacting Mental Health Experience in the African American Community

The overall mental health state of Black people has shifted throughout the years in how African Americans experience mental health, how they consume mental health services, and how their experience is reflected in research. Over six million African Americans experience mental illness (SAMHSA, 2023). Substance use disorders exist in the Black community with alcohol being the top substance used at over 40% usage (SAMHSA, 2012). About 96% of Black people with a substance use order do not seek out treatment (SAMHSA, 2012) which is incredibly high in the number of untreated substance use disorders experienced by Black people. There are a number of factors that contribute to the pernicious nature of substance use in the Black community. Oftentimes, substance use disorders include co-occurring disorders alongside mood and trauma-related disorders. Treating the underlying issues in conjunction with the substance use disorder can often help in the area of reduction of use and recovery.

Around 5–10% of Black men experience major depressive disorder (Ward & Mengesha, 2013) with Black women experiencing depression at varying reported

DOI: 10.4324/9781003491170-8

rates due to the lack of research in this area for Black women (Hunn & Craig, 2009). Studies vary in a range of percentage rates from about 25% to 50% of Black women experiencing depressive symptoms to some degree (Holden et al., 2013; Quist et al., 2022). Depression in the Black community can be difficult to truly assess, as it is often underdiagnosed and typically diagnosed in primary care settings, where psychotropic medications are often pushed with little to no recommendation for counseling (Bailey et al., 2011; Robinson et al., 2005). Anxiety is also prevalent in the Black population, with many factors that have been researched in its contribution including racism (Davis et al., 2018; Graham et al., 2016) and academic experiences (Turner & Jimenez, 2022; Young & Young, 2016).

In addition to mood and substance use disorders, trauma-related disorders are also prevalent in the Black community. Trauma in the Black community dates back centuries ago starting with the effects of enslavement of African people which serves as the foundation of African American people in the United States. Post-traumatic slave disorder is a concept developed by Joy DeGruy (2005) that explores the ways in which generational traumas have been experienced since the period of enslavement as a result of enslavement, and the ways in which Black people have survived since that time as well. Epigenetics explains how the traumas and resources can be passed down across generations since the period of enslavement. Furthermore, post-traumatic slave disorder looks at how the oppressions that have been experienced by Black people have contributed to systemic issues like institutionalized racism.

In addition to the historical experiences of trauma, trauma has been examined in how Black people are exposed to it currently. Trauma exposure has been found to be more prevalent for Black people which can lead to diagnoses like post-traumatic stress disorder (Alim et al., 2006; Breslau et al., 1998; Richie, 2012; Roberts et al., 2011). Trauma in the Black community has been experienced in various forms including violence (e.g., physical and sexual; Richie, 2012), vicarious trauma (Pryce et al., 2021), and racism on various levels (Heard-Garris et al., 2018; Williams et al., 2021). Trauma can catapult a number of issues for Black people and if left untreated can lead to personality disorders (Macintosh et al., 2015; Pérez Benítez et al., 2010; Van der Kolk et al., 1994).

Utilization of Mental Health Services and Stigma

There has been an increase in the utilization of mental health services over the years (Panchal & Lo, 2024; Terlizzi & Schiller, 2022; Wilson, 2001). While this increase in utilization is apparent, there is still stigma around seeking out professional help for psychological distress (Alvidrez et al., 2008; Conner et al., 2010; Pederson et al., 2022). Stigma among the African American community has been rooted in a number of issues including cultural mistrust of healthcare professionals and the religious/spiritual connection that the community has to healing. Cultural mistrust has a long-standing history with communities of color, including African Americans. Projects such as the Tuskegee Syphilis study were based on deceitful practices and caused harm to many African Americans who trusted the facilitators and healthcare providers associated with this study (Thomas & Quinn, 1991). While this is just one example, there are many experiences where African Americans are put in harmful, compromising positions by healthcare professionals that continue to add to the level of mistrust within the community when it comes to healthcare, which includes mental health services.

Sociocultural Impacts

Because of its relevancy, it is crucial that we know and understand the impacts of mental health distress and illness so we can add to the comprehension of mental health disorders. While the experience of mental health is universal, how it is experienced across cultures varies due to the unique nature in which cultures are constructed and how society views individual cultures. For African Americans, mental health must be viewed based on this as it extends beyond just the experience of generalized stressors and adds complex layers to the experience of mental health. Additionally, there are specific intricacies in how Black people experience their identities as it relates to their race. When we are considering how one may identify, it is not enough to think about these identities separately as they do not exist on singular planes. There is much complexity to who we are as human beings and being Black adds not only another layer of uniqueness and beauty but also oppression as it relates to identities and how they intersect.

Dating back to the 1600s and the period of African enslavement in the United States, the treatment of Black people has been one of oppression, discrimination, and marginalization. The effect of enslavement is still being experienced today as racism still persists. We see racism in the form of white supremacy in the way our major systems are created and maintained (e.g., healthcare systems, educational settings, and working spaces) (Ampudia, 2024; Allcorn, 2007; Brady, 2017; Corneau & Stergiopoulos, 2012; Fullilove et al., 2024; Ieva et al., 2021; Lincoln & Stanley, 2021; Robert, 2003). Systems rooted in white supremacy inherently do harm in the ways in which Black people navigate through these systems. Consequently, there are continual efforts to educate, dismantle, and rebuild these systems to be more diverse, equitable, and inclusive.

Oppression has huge impacts on mental health as it is a form of trauma that can lead to severe and persistent mental illness, anxiety disorders, and depression (Wilcox, 2023). It is important to examine systems and identities as they may have an impact on Black mental health. Now, common identities and experiences will be explored to gain understanding of how they can be impactful to a person's mental health experience.

Family and Interpersonal Relationships

Black families are so important to the progression of Black people as they enhance optimal wellness and actively fight against many of the oppressions integral to systemic racism. Mental health experience has components rooted in familial culture and background. There is such diversity in Black families, reflecting blended, nuclear, and single-parent households. There has been much research looking at the structure of Black families and the linked implications for overall Black success. Currently, about 40% of Black families consist of married couples, 30% headed by a female, and 16% of households led by a non-family member (U.S. Census Bureau, 2023). Mental health symptoms and identity are just a few areas that are impacted by familial structures (Barrett & Turner, 2005; Jones et al., 2021). Family structure can also influence the exposure children may have to trauma (Behere et al., 2017) which can be an underlying issue for several mental health disorders. Additionally, familial dynamics within families can influence mental health symptoms. For example, support from mothers and mentorship has been shown to be a predictor of depressive symptoms in Black youth (Jones et al., 2021). Family can also serve as a resource in therapy and reduce risk when it comes to severe and persistent mental health disorders.

Interpersonal relationships have huge implications for the mental health of Black people. With a lot of collectivistic cultures, the influence on relationships is important for the overall advancement of the community. Each relationship serves a unique purpose and can be a resource in mental health treatment of Black people. Familial relationships can impact how people experience connection, attachment, and love (Bowlby, 1979). It also can serve as a source of trauma for many individuals as there can be traumatic experiences like abuse and unhealthy relationship dynamics that can make navigating familial relationships challenging for many. There is diversity in Black romantic relationships with about 32% national average for Black married adults (Washington & Walker, 2022), about 40% of Black adults who are either married or cohabiting, with another 38% having neither a romantic relationship nor a desire to have one (Mouzon et al., 2020), and about 4–5% of Black people exploring dynamics such as polyamory (Clardy, 2024; Smith, 2016).

Friendships can also come in various forms as there are many ways that individuals can grow to become friends. Whether that is through childhood sports or a Divine 9 fraternity/sorority (i.e., Black Greek letter organizations that make up the National Pan-Hellenic Council; National Museum of African American History and Culture, 2025), those connections can grow. Friendships can also be influential in how one goes about taking care of their own mental health. They can serve as significant sources of emotional support (Samter et al., 1997). Black female friendships, or "sisterhoods," often serve as spaces where Black women can come together and share their intersectional experiences of both being Black and female in safe environments with no gaslighting or relegation (Goins, 2011;

Leath et al., 2022). Black male friendships are also crucial in the realms of support for Black men as these are often vehicles for discussing aspects of identity and connecting in their roles as Black men (McClure, 2006).

Spiritual Connections

Spirituality is especially important in the Black community as it often serves as the foundation for many of the ways in which Black people engage in community and regard their own mental health/wellness. Much like every other aspect of Black culture, spirituality does not look the same for everyone. Religion is often considered a public expression of a traditional set of rules while spirituality is considered more of a private, personal experience for many people. Additionally, some people might consider religion a public expression of spirituality.

When it comes to the structure of religion, there are several religions that are practiced within the Black community. In fact, Black adults were found to be the most religious in the United States with higher percentages that believe in God and state that religion is important to them (Pew Research Center, 2021). Over two-thirds of Black Americans identify as Protestants with 6% identifying as Catholic and 3% associated with other Christian identities including non-denominational Christianity (Pew Research Center, 2021). There is another 3% of Black Americans that identify as Islam (Pew Research Center, 2021), with the Nation of Islam making up a small percentage of that make-up. Additionally, there is about one in five Black Americans who do not identify with a religion.

The "Black" Christian church has been researched in its connection to mental health and the treatment of mental illness (Blank et al., 2002; Campbell & Winchester, 2020; Robinson et al., 2018). Traditionally, many Black Americans have relied on their spirituality and religious ties to help them through difficult times (Black, 1999; Hunn & Craig, 2009) which has been a positive coping mechanism for many people. Now, there has been a shift in incorporating the art and science of mental health treatment with spiritual and religious practices.

Gender Roles and Intersectionality

Within the Black community, there are expectations regarding gender roles and the ways in which they are represented in the community. Furthermore, the many subcultures of the Black diaspora have different expectations regarding gender roles. Black women have been given the title of "strong Black women" which comes with many connotations for what it means to navigate through life's tasks. It is often seen as a banner of pride. However, there are a number of issues in what this represents from a mental health standpoint as it can lead to Black women being the go-to when support or resolution is needed. It also leads to Black women experiencing increased pressure which can lead to psychological distress, depression, and anxiety (Castelin & White, 2022; Donovan & West, 2015; Liao et al., 2020). One of the impacting factors is the way in which race and gender intersect. Black women are in an interesting position of experiencing oppression from the standpoint of being Black and also the standpoint of being a woman. Kimberle Crenshaw (2013) coined the phrase intersectionality to explain this intersection and its relevance in identity politics. However, intersectionality can be extended to all aspects of identity including sexual/affectional orientation, social class, and ability status.

For Black men, there are many aspects of masculinity that are portrayed across cultures. For example, the experience around emotions and the expectations for emotions including this thought that "men don't cry" or there is limited expression around any other emotion other than anger (Jackson & Harvey Wingfield, 2013; Lindsey et al., 2017; Wilkins, 2012). This concept of "machismo" is applicable across cultures including Hispanic/Latiné cultures which reflects the components of what makes a man masculine and challenging the myths associated with it (Torres et al., 2002). These expectations themselves can serve as barriers in help-seeking behaviors for Black men (Mahalik, 2003).

Finally, the uniqueness of the experience of being trans* in the Black community is worth discussing. Trans* folx of color have the experience of identifying in the minority for multiple identities (e.g., gender identity and racial/ethnic identity) and experience the nuances of the subcultures within the LGBTQ+ community. Less than 2% of Black adults identify as Trans (Cox, 2023). However, about one in three Black adults state they know of Black trans person in their lives to some capacity (Cox, 2023). When examining these numbers, it is important to note that these numbers may be underreported as there may be individuals who are not willing to disclose these identities for safety purposes. Being a trans* person of color has numerous concerns as this group is often targeted for hate crimes. The experience of transmisia in addition to racism can lead to severe depression, anxiety, and increased rates of suicide attempts. These forms of oppression can occur at all levels including micro-levels and macro-levels. Organizations such as Trans People of Color Coalition are focused on these unique experiences and the unique injustices they face in the intersections of race and gender.

In addition to trans* experience, there is also the experience of sexual/affectional orientation within the Black community. The minority experience of sexual/affectional experience (i.e., Lesbian, Gay, Bisexual, Queer) is unique because of the homomisia and homophobia that have traditionally existed within the community. With about 12% of the LGBTQ+ community identifying as Black, there are implications here for physical and mental health experience. There is about a 10% increase in the experience of depression for Black LGBTQ+ (Choi et al., 2021) and overall greater odds of being diagnosed with chronic health issues (Choi et al., 2021).

Implications for Organizations and Administrators

The overall wellness of Black people is inclusive of mental and emotional health. However, it extends into many areas of life including physical, spiritual, financial, etc. Wellness is an individualized experience and looks unique to each person's stage of development and season of life. Organizations and EAP administrators need to know what mental health and wellness of Black people look like as they can be important sources of support for Black people in workspaces.

Self-care practices have been seen as "radical acts" for Black people as often quoted by the great Audre Lorde. Recently, there has been a shift in how we are considering self-care. It is not always the Westernized ways we see self-care (e.g., yoga and spa days). It could be those activities or it could be establishing personal boundaries and practicing grounding techniques to make it through the day. Tricia Hersey (2022) has been instrumental in the encouragement and advocacy of rest for Black people. She challenges the idea of rest being a privilege and highlights the right we have to unapologetically embrace rest as a form of self-care. Furthermore, Wyatt and Ampadu (2022) explore an intentional model around self-care that challenges these beliefs that self-care translates to solely actions. Rather, they use Miller and colleagues' (2019) self-care model to explain self-care for Black people going beyond actions and exploring it in five layers: self-care support, self-care orientation, self-care motivation, self-care behaviors, and self-care skills. Self-care and wellness are open opportunities for everyone to explore the ways in which they restore and love on themselves. Self-care for Black people is crucial to the dismantling of White supremacist ideologies and systemic racism. Administrators of organizations and EAPs should integrate wellness practices into their organizations to increase the likelihood of using self-care strategies. For example, providing wellness initiatives as incentives to premium reductions for benefits can be helpful. Also, supporting mental health days as paid time off can add to the rest of Black people.

Now, more than ever, there are efforts across mainstream platforms that call for mental health education and advocacy in the utilization of services for Black people. Social media has produced waves of mental health advocacy that highlight the importance of mental healthcare and help reduce the stigma. Organizations such as Therapy for Black Girls, Therapy for Black Men, and Clinicians of Color are platforms where Black therapists are listed which can help streamline the process of finding a therapist of similar background. Nonprofit organizations such as the Loveland Foundation are targeted toward providing free therapy sessions for Black womxn and girls. Increasing ease in the process of finding a therapist can help in the reduction of stigma and increase of utilization. Knowing these resources can help in the connection of mental health therapists for Black employees and colleagues.

It is important to note that it could be a combination of treatment approaches that work well for Black people as each person is unique in their experience of mental health issues. There has also been the topic of match between race of the therapist and the client. While the research supports the fact that cultural competency and humility are most important in a therapist, there is a level of comfort that is experienced when a Black client is matched with a Black therapist.

Resources listed earlier have allotted the opportunity for there to be a place where Black people can find Black therapists or even therapists of color. However, with the numbers skewed toward White therapists, the likelihood of experiencing cross-racial interactions within therapeutic settings is high. With that said, it is important to find a therapist who has done their own self-reflection to examine and work through their own prejudices and biases as racial perception has impact when it comes to cross-racial interactions (Walker & Bruns, 2022). Furthermore, it is important that therapists acknowledge the -isms and social injustices that exist within our society as they do contribute to the mental health of Black people. This same reflective work applies to managers and EAP administrators as they must be considerate of how their identity may impact cross-racial professional relationships.

Conclusion

Black mental health is complex in that it is an experience for every Black person with many levels of consideration in how their mental health is experienced. Layers of systemic issues impact mental health experience which makes it important to examine how systems are affecting Black people. This chapter explored many dynamics of Black culture to highlight the ways in which they may have an effect on mental health in the form of not only illness but also wellness. Black wellness is a strengths-based mindset and approach to the upliftment of Black people by taking a preventative approach to mental illness, thereby accenting the positive ways Black people can pour into themselves. The challenge is considering how our systems are intentionally dismantling these oppressive practices in addition to how they are uplifting Black wellness.

References

Alim, T. N., Graves, E., Mellman, T. A., Aigbogun, N., Gray, E., Lawson, W., & Charney, D. S. (2006). Trauma exposure, posttraumatic stress disorder and depression in an African-American primary care population. *Journal of the National Medical Association, 98*(10), 1630.

Allcorn, S. (2007). The psychological nature of oppression in an American workplace. *Organisational and Social Dynamics, 7*(1), 39–60.

Alvidrez, J., Snowden, L. R., & Kaiser, D. M. (2008). The experience of stigma among Black mental health consumers. *Journal of Health Care for the Poor and Underserved, 19*(3), 874–893.

Ampudia, C. (2024). Unfair labor practices targeting minorities in the working class: A critical examination of systemic oppression across sectors. *Available at SSRN 4815662.*

Bailey, R. K., Patel, M., Barker, N. C., Ali, S., & Jabeen, S. (2011). Major depressive disorder in the African American population. *Journal of the National Medical Association, 103*(7), 548–559.

Barrett, A. E., & Turner, R. J. (2005). Family structure and mental health: The mediating effects of socioeconomic status, family process, and social stress. *Journal of Health and Social Behavior, 46*(2), 156–169.

Behere, A. P., Basnet, P., & Campbell, P. (2017). Effects of family structure on mental health of children: A preliminary study. *Indian Journal of Psychological Medicine, 39*(4), 457–463.

Black, H. K. (1999). Poverty and prayer: Spiritual narratives of elderly African-American women. *Review of Religious Research*, 359–374.

Blank, M. B., Mahmood, M., Fox, J. C., & Guterbock, T. (2002). Alternative mental health services: The role of the Black church in the South. *American Journal of Public Health, 92*(10), 1668–1672.

Bowlby, J. (1979). The Bowlby-Ainsworth attachment theory. *Behavioral and Brain Sciences, 2*(4), 637–638.

Brady, J. (2017). Education for whom?: Exploring systems of oppression and domination. *Canadian Journal for New Scholars in Education/Revue canadienne des jeunes chercheures et chercheurs en éducation, 8*, 116–126.

Breslau, N., Kessler, R. C., Chilcoat, H. D., Schultz, L. R., Davis, G. C., & Andreski, P. (1998). Trauma and posttraumatic stress disorder in the community: The 1996 Detroit Area Survey of Trauma. *Archives of General Psychiatry, 55*(7), 626–632.

Campbell, R. D., & Winchester, M. R. (2020). Let the church say . . .: One congregation's views on how the Black church can address mental health with Black Americans. *Social Work & Christianity, 47*(2).

Castelin, S., & White, G. (2022). "I'm a strong independent Black woman": The strong Black woman schema and mental health in college-aged Black women. *Psychology of Women Quarterly, 46*(2), 196–208.

Centers for Disease Control (CDC). (2021). *Summary health statistics: National health interview survey: 2018*. https://ftp.cdc.gov/pub/Health_Statistics/NCHS/NHIS/SHS/2018_SHS_Table_A-8.pdf.

Choi, S.K., Wilson, B., & Mallory, C. (2021). Black LGBT adults in the us: LGBT well-being at the intersection of race. *UCLA School of Law: Williams Institute*. Retrieved April 16, 2025, from https://williamsinstitute.law.ucla.edu/wp-content/uploads/LGBT-Black-SES-Jan-2021.pdf.

Clardy, J. L. (2024). Polyamory in Black: A companion justification for minimal marriage. *Journal of Applied Philosophy*. https://doi.org/10.1111/japp.12749

Conner, K. O., Copeland, V. C., Grote, N. K., Koeske, G., Rosen, D., Reynolds III, C. F., & Brown, C. (2010). Mental health treatment seeking among older adults with depression: The impact of stigma and race. *American Journal of Geriatric Psychiatry, 18*(6), 531–543.

Corneau, S., & Stergiopoulos, V. (2012). More than being against it: Anti-racism and anti-oppression in mental health services. *Transcultural Psychiatry, 49*(2), 261–282.

Cox, K. (2023). Black Americans' views on transgender and nonbinary issues. *Pew Research Center.* https://www.pewresearch.org/2023/02/16/black-americans-views-on-transgender-and-nonbinary-issues/.

Crenshaw, K. W. (2013). Mapping the margins: Intersectionality, identity politics, and violence against women of color. In *The public nature of private violence* (pp. 93–118). Routledge.

Davis, M., Stadulis, R., & Neal-Barnett, A. (2018). Assessing the effects of the acting White accusation among Black girls: Social anxiety and bullying victimization. *Journal of the National Medical Association, 110*(1), 23–28.

DeGruy, J. (2005). *Post traumatic slave syndrome: America's legacy of enduring injury and healing*. Joy DeGruy Publications.

Donovan, R. A., & West, L. M. (2015). Stress and mental health: Moderating role of the strong Black woman stereotype. *Journal of Black Psychology, 41*(4), 384–396.

Fullilove, M. T., Dix, E., Hankerson, S. H., Lassiter, J., & Jordan, A. (2024). Systems that promote mental health in the teeth of oppression. *The Lancet Psychiatry, 11*(1), 65–74.

Goins, M. N. (2011). Playing with dialectics: Black female friendship groups as a homeplace. *Communication Studies, 62*(5), 531–546.
Graham, J. R., West, L. M., Martinez, J., & Roemer, L. (2016). The mediating role of internalized racism in the relationship between racist experiences and anxiety symptoms in a Black American sample. *Cultural Diversity and Ethnic Minority Psychology, 22*(3), 369.
Heard-Garris, N. J., Cale, M., Camaj, L., Hamati, M. C., & Dominguez, T. P. (2018). Transmitting trauma: A systematic review of vicarious racism and child health. *Social Science & Medicine, 199*, 230–240.
Hersey, T. (2022). *Rest is resistance: A manifesto.* Little Brown Spark.
Holden, K. B., Bradford, L. D., Hall, S. P., & Belton, A. S. (2013). Prevalence and correlates of depressive symptoms and resiliency among African American women in a community-based primary health care center. *Journal of Health Care for the Poor and Underserved, 24*(4), 79–93.
Hunn, V. L., & Craig, C. D. (2009). Depression, sociocultural factors, and African American women. *Journal of Multicultural Counseling and Development, 37*(2), 83–93.
Ieva, K., Hannon, M. D., & Vereen, L. G. (2021). The intentionality of confronting racism, systemic oppression, and cyclical trauma in counselor education: A self study. *Teaching and Supervision in Counseling, 3*(2), 11.
Jackson, B. A., & Harvey Wingfield, A. (2013). Getting angry to get ahead: Black college men, emotional performance, and encouraging respectable masculinity. *Symbolic Interaction, 36*(3), 275–292.
Jones, K. V., Boyd, D. T., & Quinn, C. R. (2021). The impact of mother support and natural mentoring on the depressive symptoms of black youth. *Journal of Child and Family Studies, 30*, 2589–2600.
Leath, S., Mims, L., Evans, K. A., Parker, T. A., & Billingsley, J. T. (2022). "I can be unapologetically who I am": A study of friendship among Black undergraduate women at PWIs. *Emerging Adulthood, 10*(4), 837–851.
Liao, K. Y. H., Wei, M., & Yin, M. (2020). The misunderstood schema of the strong Black woman: Exploring its mental health consequences and coping responses among African American women. *Psychology of Women Quarterly, 44*(1), 84–104.
Lincoln, Y. S., & Stanley, C. A. (2021). The faces of institutionalized discrimination and systemic oppression in higher education: Uncovering the lived experience of bias and procedural inequity. *Qualitative Inquiry, 27*(10), 1233–1245.
Lindsey, M. A., Brown, D. R., & Cunningham, M. (2017). Boys do (n't) cry: Addressing the unmet mental health needs of African American boys. *American Journal of Orthopsychiatry, 87*(4), 377.
MacIntosh, H. B., Godbout, N., & Dubash, N. (2015). Borderline personality disorder: Disorder of trauma or personality, a review of the empirical literature. *Canadian Psychology/Psychologie Canadienne, 56*(2), 227.
Mahalik, J. R. (2003). Why won't he go to the doctor?: The psychology of men's help seeking. *International Journal of Men's Health, 2*(2), 93–109.
McClure, S. M. (2006). Improvising masculinity: African American fraternity membership in the construction of a Black masculinity. *Journal of African American Studies, 10*, 57–73.
Miller, A. E., Green, T. D., & Lambros, K. M. (2019). Foster parent self-care: A conceptual model. *Children and Youth Services Review, 99*, 107–114.
Mouzon, D. M., Taylor, R. J., & Chatters, L. M. (2020). Gender differences in marriage, romantic involvement, and desire for romantic involvement among older African Americans. *PLoS One, 15*(5), e0233836.
National Museum of African American History and Culture. (2025). *The historical legacy of the divine nine.* Retrieved July 5, 2025, from https://nmaahc.si.edu/explore/stories/divine-nine-black-fraternities-sororities

Panchal, N., & Lo, J. (2024, August 1). *Exploring the rise in mental health care use by demographics and insurance status*. https://www.kff.org/mental-health/issue-brief/exploring-the-rise-in-mental-health-care-use-by-demographics-and-insurance-status/
Pederson, A. B., Hawkins, D., & Conteh, N. (2022). Ethnic identity and mental health stigma among Black adults in the United States. *Ethics, Medicine and Public Health, 25*, 100774.
Pérez Benítez, C. I., Yen, S., Shea, M. T., Edelen, M. O., Markowitz, J. C., McGlashan, T. H., Ansell, E. B., Grilo, C. M., Skodol, A. E., Gunderson, J. G., & Morey, L. C. (2010). Ethnicity in trauma and psychiatric disorders: Findings from the collaborative longitudinal study of personality disorders. *Journal of Clinical Psychology, 66*(6), 583–598.
Pew Research Center. (2021, February 16). *Faith among Black Americans*. Retrieved July 6, 2025, from https://www.pewresearch.org/religion/2021/02/16/faith-among-black-americans/#black-americans-more-religious-than-the-u-s-public-overall
Pryce, D. K., Olaghere, A., Brown, R. A., & Davis, V. M. (2021). A neglected problem: Understanding the effects of personal and vicarious trauma on African Americans' attitudes toward the police. *Criminal Justice and Behavior, 48*(10), 1366–1389.
Quist, A. J., Han, X., Baird, D. D., Wise, L. A., Wegienka, G., Woods-Giscombe, C. L., & Vines, A. I. (2022). Life course racism and depressive symptoms among young black women. *Journal of Urban Health*, 1–12.
Richie, B. E. (2012). Arrested justice: Black women, violence, and America's prison nation. In *Arrested Justice*. New York University Press.
Robert, P. (2003). Disability oppression in the contemporary US capitalist workplace. *Science & Society, 67*(2), 136–159.
Roberts, A. L., Gilman, S. E., Breslau, J., Breslau, N., & Koenen, K. C. (2011). Race/ethnic differences in exposure to traumatic events, development of post-traumatic stress disorder, and treatment-seeking for post-traumatic stress disorder in the United States. *Psychological Medicine, 41*(1), 71–83.
Robinson, M. A., Jones-Eversley, S., Moore, S. E., Ravenell, J., & Adedoyin, A. C. (2018). Black male mental health and the Black church: Advancing a collaborative partnership and research agenda. *Journal of Religion and Health, 57*, 1095–1107.
Robinson, W. D., Geske, J. A., Prest, L. A., & Barnacle, R. (2005). Depression treatment in primary care. *Journal of the American Board of Family Practice, 18*(2), 79–86.
Samter, W., Whaley, B. B., Mortenson, S. T., & Burleson, B. R. (1997). Ethnicity and emotional support in same-sex friendship: A comparison of Asian-Americans, African-Americans, and Euro-Americans. *Personal Relationships, 4*(4), 413–430.
Smith, C. N. (2016). Open to love: Polyamory and the Black American. *Journal of Black Sexuality and Relationships, 3*(2), 99–129.
Substance Abuse and Mental Health Services Administration (SAMHSA). (2012). *Center for behavioral health statistics and quality, national survey on drug use and health, 2008–2012* (2008–2010 Data—Revised March 2012).
Substance Abuse and Mental Health Services Administration (SAMHSA). (2023). *Key substance use and mental health indicators in the United States: Results from the 2022 National Survey on Drug Use and Health (HHS Publication No. PEP23-07-01-006, NSDUH Series H-58)*. Center for Behavioral Health Statistics and Quality, Substance Abuse and Mental Health Services Administration. https://www.samhsa.gov/data/report/2022-nsduh-annual-national-report
Terlizzi, E. P., & Schiller, J. S. (2022). Mental health treatment among adults aged 18–44: United States, 2019–2021. *NCHS Data Brief*, No. 444. National Center for Health Statistics. https://dx.doi.org/10.15620/cdc:120293.
Thomas, S. B., & Quinn, S. C. (1991). The Tuskegee Syphilis Study, 1932 to 1972: Implications for HIV education and AIDS risk education programs in the black community. *American Journal of Public Health, 81*(11), 1498–1505.

Torres, J. B., Solberg, V. S. H., & Carlstrom, A. H. (2002). The myth of sameness among Latino men and their machismo. *American Journal of Orthopsychiatry*, *72*(2), 163–181.

Turner, F. D., & Jimenez, S. (2022). The levels of multicultural distress, academic stress, depression, anxiety, and stress of Black undergraduate students compared with Asian, Latinx, and White undergraduate students. *Journal of Negro Education*, *91*(4), 476–487.

U.S. Census Bureau. (2023). *American community survey 5-year estimates: Comparison profiles 5-year [household type (including living alone) (Black or African American alone]*. U.S. Department of Commerce. Retrieved July 5, 2025, from https://data.census.gov/table/ACSDT5Y2023.B11001B?q=Owner/Renter+(Householder)+Characteristics&g=010XX43US_010XX01US_010XX00US

Van der Kolk, B. A., Hostetler, A., Herron, N., & Fisler, R. E. (1994). Trauma and the development of borderline personality disorder. *Psychiatric Clinics of North America*, *17*(4), 715–730.

Walker, T. L., & Bruns, K. L. (2022). Cross-racial interactions in the counselor education classroom: The impact of racial perception. *Journal of Multicultural Counseling and Development*, *50*(2), 94–105.

Ward, E., & Mengesha, M. (2013). Depression in African American men: A review of what we know and where we need to go from here. *American Journal of Orthopsychiatry*, *83*(2pt3), 386–397.

Washington, C., & Walker, L. (2022, July 19). *District of Columbia had lowest percentage of married black adults in 2015–2019*. US Census Bureau. Retrieved July 5, 2025, from https://www.census.gov/library/stories/2022/07/marriage-prevalence-for-black-adults-varies-by-state.html

Wilkins, A. (2012). "Not out to start a revolution" race, gender, and emotional restraint among black university men. *Journal of Contemporary Ethnography*, *41*(1), 34–65.

Williams, T. R., Walker, T. L., & Wyatt, W. N. (2021). Conceptualizing racism through a systemic trauma lens: Impacts on Black college students. *Journal of Psychotherapy Integration*. Advance online publication. https://doi.org/10.1037/int0000206

Wilson, M. (2001). Black women and mental health: Working towards inclusive mental health services. *Feminist Review*, *68*(1), 34–51.

Wyatt, J. P., & Ampadu, G. G. (2022). Reclaiming self-care: Self-care as a social justice tool for Black wellness. *Community Mental Health Journal*, *58*(2), 213–221.

Young, J. R., & Young, J. L. (2016). Young, Black, and anxious: Describing the Black student mathematics anxiety research using confidence intervals. *Journal of Urban Mathematics Education*, *9*(1), 79–93.

7 From School to Work

Emotional Well-being and Emerging Adults

Lucy Turner, Ryan Travia, and Danna Greenberg

The school-to-work transition is often the first major transition that individuals experience in their careers. This transition is defined as the shift from formal education to formal employment (Ng & Feldman, 2007). For emerging adults, that is individuals who are between adolescents and the beginning of adulthood (18–29) (Arnett, 2014), this can be a highly turbulent transition as they face a less structured future in which they will need to establish new routines and a new professional identity (Arnett, 2014; Takeuchi et al., 2021). How emerging adults move through this transition has profound implications for their personal and professional lives.

Hence, one of the implicit, and often explicit, goals of higher education, particularly business education, is to help emerging adults develop the mindset and competencies that will support their transition to work. Students pursue a program of study, engage in co-curricular activities, and work with career centers to identify and prepare for the workforce. Career centers assist students to identify, prepare for, and apply to positions that meet their qualifications, course of study, and professional goals. Yet this approach assumes that students will have the mental capacity, initiative, and resilience to translate their experiences into the work opportunities they desire.

For a student who struggles with emotional well-being the process of moving from school to work may not be so straightforward. Recent findings from the National Healthy Minds Study found that in 2021 more than 60% of students met the criteria for one or more mental health problems, a nearly 50% increase from 2013 (Lipson et al., 2022). Emotional insecurity can introduce unique challenges to the school-to-work transition—a transition that is foundational to becoming a mature, thriving adult (Grosemans et al., 2020).

In this chapter, we focus on emerging adults and the unique well-being needs of these individuals as they transition from school to work. Drawing on qualitative interviews with career advisors and talent management professionals, who work closely with emerging adults during these transitions, we sought to identify the trends these industry experts are witnessing. In so doing, we provide insights for organizations and managers on how to better support the specific emotional well-being needs of emerging adults as they launch their professional lives.

DOI: 10.4324/9781003491170-9

Emotional Well-Being, Emerging Adults, and School-to-Work Transitions

Similar to other scholars, we use the broader construct of emotional well-being as we focus on the school-to-work transition. "Well-being is a construct understood as a multidimensional and holistic quality" (Travia et al., 2020). This includes, but is not limited to, physical, emotional, spiritual, intellectual, social, occupational, financial, and environmental components. While there is no universally accepted definition of well-being, "there is a general agreement that well-being includes having positive emotions (e.g., contentment, happiness), not having negative emotions (e.g., depression, anxiety), satisfaction with life, fulfillment, and positive functioning" (U.S. Centers for Disease Control and Prevention, n.d., first para).

Pertinent to this chapter, emerging adulthood corresponds with the life stage when individuals often experience heightened emotional well-being challenges (Arnett et al., 2014; Magier et al., 2025). Generation Z, which encompasses today's emerging adults, reports higher rates of anxiety, depression, and distress than any other age group (Chrikov et al., 2020; Coe et al., 2022). The isolationism and lack of connectedness that was heightened by the pandemic has further intensified the mental health challenges emerging adults face (Travia, 2022), as has the increased political uncertainty, the high cost of living, and the heightened sense of existential dread (Chrikov et al., 2020). Indeed, this generation reports feeling double and triple the level of emotional distress in comparison to Millennials, Gen Xers, and Baby Boomers (Coe et al., 2022).

Despite the rise in emotional well-being concerns among the emerging adult population, there remains a paucity of research that explores emotional well-being and school-to-work transitions (Jensen & Hermansen, 2023). Extant research has not examined emotional well-being during these transitions and how and why today's work context may be contributing to the rise in emotional well-being issues among emerging adults.

School-to-Work Transition

Scholars and practitioners define the school-to-work transition as the phase during which an individual exits formal learning and commences employment (Ng & Feldman, 2007). This transition is critical to career development as it sets the foundation for a positive work identity and a sustainable career (Blokker et al., 2023). Furthermore, how early-career professionals navigate the school-to-work transition establishes patterns that influence future career transitions (Akkermans et al., 2021). A negative school-to-work transition can have lasting consequences on an individual's future career development, later life outcomes, and financial and career achievement (Blokker et al., 2023).

While the school-to-work transition is shaped by both individual and contextual factors, relevant to this chapter we highlight the relationship between mental health and these transitions. Extant research shows that emerging adults who struggle with mental health often experience more challenges during the school-to-work transition. These individuals may experience delays in employment and may struggle to stay employed (Huegaerts et al., 2020). Individuals with mental health challenges may struggle with other issues at school and work that can affect how they approach the school-to-work transition. For instance, individuals who are struggling with mental health may be less optimistic, have lower self-esteem, or feel less self-control over their future, all of which has been found to negatively affect school-to-work transitions (e.g., Baay et al., 2014; Huegaerts et al., 2020). Emerging adults who are experiencing mental health challenges may also struggle with career decision making and engaging in proactive career behaviors—all of which can further exacerbate difficulty in school-to-work transitions (Blokker et al., 2019).

Building upon this emergent research, in this chapter we draw on the perspective of career advisors and talent managers to explore emotional well-being of emerging adults during the school-to-work transition.

Methodology

For this exploratory study, we engaged an inductive, qualitative approach drawing on Corbin and Strauss (2014). We wanted to learn from career advisors and talent management professionals' lived experiences working with and supporting emerging adults in their school-to-work transitions (Charmaz, 2006).

Upon receiving IRB approval, we interviewed career advisors and talent management professionals who were engaged with emerging adults as they were transitioning from school to work. These individuals worked with emerging adults in securing co-ops and internships, in overseeing corporate internship programs, and in hiring and onboarding large cohorts of recent graduates into management training programs. Through a combination of purposive and snowball sampling (Corbin & Strauss, 2014; Zickar & Keith, 2023), we conducted interviews with ten participants. Most participants were talent management professionals who held roles ranging from recruitment coordinator to early-career talent managers to vice president of talent acquisition. The career advisors worked with undergraduate and graduate students to secure internships and post-graduate employment.

The interviews were 45–60 minutes in length. We engaged a semi-structured interview protocol in which we asked participants about their work with emerging adults and the school-to-work transition, their perspectives regarding emotional well-being during this transition, and how managers, employers, and universities were responding to the unique needs of emerging adults. Drawing upon our detailed interview notes and interview recordings, we identified patterns across participant interviews. As this is exploratory research, we present these data as key themes rather than as a robust conceptual model.

Insights on Well-Being and School-to-Work Transitions

Our interviews with talent managers and career advisors reinforced the perspective that there are unique well-being issues today's emerging adults experience during the school-to-work transition. Furthermore, these informants highlighted distinct generational differences in how emerging adults approach emotional well-being that increases the prevalence and complexity of these issues in comparison with previous generations.

In introducing the focal topic of well-being, the researchers began by asking participants to define emotional well-being. Across participants, there was convergence that well-being referenced an emotional state and authenticity at work. One respondent stated that emotional well-being is "showing up as your best self professionally and personally" and when your "identity matches your environment." Another participant equated emotional well-being to both "mental health" and "emotional intelligence," also noting that it is "how you show up in your day-to-day." Respondents used terms such as "balance" and "thriving" to describe well-being. Across nearly all interviews, emotional well-being included "coming to work as your full self."

Participants also converged on two major themes regarding the emotional well-being of emerging adults during the school-to-work transition: *an increased prevalence and severity of emotional well-being challenges* and *shifting generational norms around self-disclosure that appear to be contributing to this increased prevalence.* Our participants also focused on two organizational factors that they believed were important to emotional well-being during this transition: *the rise of remote work* and *shifting needs from managers regarding emotional well-being.* Later, we discuss each of these insights in more detail.

Emotional Well-Being and Emerging Adults in School-to-Work Transitions

Increased Prevalence of Emotional Well-Being Challenges

All of our participants mentioned that emotional well-being issues in the school-to-work transition have increased following the COVID-19 pandemic. As one career advisor shared these were "pivotal years for these students to find themselves and that was taken from them" resulting in more emotional instability. As another respondent explained, "the sense of being overwhelmed is very common (in this generation)." Respondents described general emotional well-being issues as well as diagnosed mental health conditions, including depression, anxiety, and eating disorders.

Perhaps because of this increase in frequency of emotional well-being needs, participants described an increase in their need to intervene to support an emerging adult's emotional well-being during this transition. Career advisors reported that emerging adults in internships or co-op placements would discuss their emotional well-being with their advisors. One career advisor shared two stories of serving as a mediator by having conversation with students' employers on how the employers might modify the students' responsibilities so that the students could be successful at work and be emotionally healthier. Another career advisor shared, "I had a student who called me and was depressed because he just didn't feel like he was getting (understanding his role in) the job." The advisor reached out to the company to share the students' concerns, and the advisor was impressed that "the company triaged immediately to say, 'what can we do to make life easier for you to make it better'"—reflecting the manager's understanding of the importance of emotional well-being. A talent management professional responsible for their company's college internship program also found themselves intervening to support students' emotional well-being. This talent manager described how a highly successful intern had found they had "bit off more than they could chew and it was taking a hit on their emotional well-being." In coaching the intern on company supports, it became clear the intern needed more substantive support than was available through the company. The talent manager explained that the student "didn't even know that leaving the internship was an option and that it would be OK." The student ultimately finished the internship earlier and returned home to receive the support they needed.

This increase in emotional well-being needs among emerging adults is consistent with broader research. A recent study of more than 1,000 adults between the ages of 22 and 28 with at least a bachelor's degree shows there is a rise in incidents of emotional well-being challenges for young professionals. This study found more than half (51%) of young professionals reported needing help for emotional or mental health problems in the past year with women reporting worse mental health than men (Mary Christie Institute, 2023). This study also found that nearly half of young professionals said mental health is a priority at their workplace but less than half of their organizations had adequate resources to support employees (Mary Christie Institute, 2023).

Shifting Generational Norms Around Self-Disclosure and Well-Being

Beyond a general rise in emotional well-being needs among emerging adults, our participants also focused on shifting generational norms around self-disclosure that brought these issues to the forefront. Our participants described a cultural shift in that the current generation of emerging adults seems more interested in bringing their whole selves to work and not masking or suppressing their emotional well-being needs. As one talent management professional explained, "This generation is very open about how they feel and are fine appearing to not be feeling well. There is much less masking compared to other generations." Another career advisor noted, "This generation is seeking employment where they can be their authentic selves." This participant went on to explain that authenticity included being open about emotional instability, support from mental health professionals, and medication for ADHD, anxiety, and depression.

Participants also observed a generational difference in how emerging adults managed their work responsibilities vis-à-vis their well-being. One talent management professional commented, "I think that this generation is just very open about feeling mid (just OK)- like appearing to not be feeling well, whereas I feel like the way I was raised and the way I grew up I felt like it didn't matter if you didn't feel well, you get dressed, you show up, you, you know, just push on." Respondents also perceived that emerging adults put greater emphasis on work/life integration and having a meaningful life—not just meaningful work. As one talent manager shared, "The early career professionals have much stronger boundaries around, 'I am done at 6:00pm and if there is an experiment that needs to go longer, I will absolutely do it. But then I need comp time on another day.' Where like, I think our generation and older, like we didn't, we didn't necessarily set those boundaries."

Participants also observed that emerging adults were seeking out jobs and internships with companies that would support their emotional well-being. They looked for companies that had employee resource groups, diversity and inclusion initiatives, and mental health support. Participants described how even during the early stages of the interview process, emerging adults would ask about company culture and benefits and would discuss work/life boundaries they desired. Unlike previous generations, who might have prescribed a philosophy of paying your dues, emerging adults were authentic and open about their immediate desires for work/life boundaries and a work environment that would support their well-being.

Organizational Factors Affecting Emerging Adult's School-to-Work Transitions

When discussing the emotional well-being of emerging adults, participants emphasized two organizational factors that were pertinent to the school-to-work transition. The increase in *remote work* was one change that was negatively affecting emerging adults' emotional well-being. Remote work seemed to lead to increased loneliness and anxiety thereby hindering a successful school-to-work transition. *Managerial support* was also an important factor that could ease the anxiety emerging adults experienced during this transition. We discuss each of these factors in detail.

The Impact of Remote Work

The negative effects of remote work, a work characteristic that has risen since the COVID-19 pandemic, have been discussed by both academics and practitioners (Mortensen, 2023; Van Zoonen & Sivunen, 2022). The decrease in social interaction and increase in isolation from work colleagues that accompanies remote work can negatively affect all employees' well-being. This effect may be heightened for emerging adults who are leaving the safety of their academic and friend community and need to make new connections in the professional world. Remote work also lacks the physical characteristics that signal a professional environment which further hampers the transition to professional work (Rodoplu Şahin et al., 2022).

The talent managers and career advisors we interviewed were adamant in their concerns about remote work and its negative impact on emerging adults' school-to-work transitions. Every respondent used the word "isolation" to describe the effects of remote work on emerging adults. One talent manager explained, "What I worry about from a well-being perspective is if someone started their career as a remote employee, it could be really isolating." Career advisors were particularly attentive to the career losses of remote work and how this would impact emerging adult's professional confidence and development. They noted that remote work reduced opportunities for essential early-career developmental tasks such as networking, learning professionalism, and developing a more holistic understanding of an organization and different career opportunities. As one talent manager explained, "Early career employees don't have a resource pool yet. They don't have the relationships they can bounce ideas off-of, vent to, etc. Their peer group is just as clueless as them and they don't have people they can pull from." Lacking this career learning, emerging adults may become stalled and unable to develop a career direction, which in turn can negatively affect well-being. One career advisor speculated, "I suspect there's a higher prevalence of mental health issues if you are working fully remote . . . there's a greater chance of feeling isolated or less connected."

Participants also described how the lack of access to in-person team building and social activities could further impede the school-to-work transition. They observed that companies would "sell" their culture to students but failed to consider how to integrate remote new employees into the company culture and in-person office experiences. One respondent shared, "If you are remote . . . those benefits are actually not as cool, right? Like it's like, oh, well, that's great. . . . But I don't have as much access to it, so [I] certainly feel less connected." Lack of access to these activities also means a reduced opportunity for emerging adults to build informal mentoring relationships and expand their professional network—both of which are critical to successfully transitioning to work. As one talent manager explained, "Remote work can be isolating for early-career employees, making it harder to build connections. In-person roles offer perks and bonding experiences." Despite these drawbacks, participants also highlighted a tension in that they found many emerging adults were seeking remote work opportunities and it was hard to help them recognize the negative effect remote work could have on their transitions.

Absence of Managerial Support

Managerial support is critical to the well-being of all employees but even more so for emerging adults. When managers are supportive of emerging adults and the unique dynamics surrounding school-to-work transitions, it may ease the stressors of this transition and enhance emotional well-being.

Unfortunately, our findings raise concerns about managers' competency in supporting emerging adults' emotional well-being. In explaining the problem, one talent manager shared,

> What is expected of managers needs to be modeled from the very top. So, if you have a situation where you're saying you expect your managers to really support their employees with their emotional well-being, then the CEO, the C suite, everyone under them also needs to be modeling that behavior.

Some participants advocated for more comprehensive management training so that managers could be better prepared to provide support, onboarding, and mentoring to emerging adults. In the absence of managerial support, career advisors found they were forced to play this surrogate role during students' internships and first jobs.

An additional complexity to providing effective managerial support to emerging adults arises from the individualized attention that so many emerging adults desire. One talent manager who worked with emerging adults in their first jobs and in their internships shared that she felt she needed to provide "white glove service" as she focused on forming strong personal relationships and tailoring support to emerging adults' well-being needs. Participants emphasized the importance of emotional intelligence for managing the complex issues emerging adults brought to the workplace. One talent manager shared, "What I observed is those managers that were able to demonstrate empathy, were far more successful in building that initial trust." Emotional intelligence was also a focus of career advisors who emphasized active listening, empathy, and building trust when working with this population. One career advisor explained,

> I think students want to be accepted and they want to be valued, and they want to be heard. I think that's the one thing that I really stress, and I try to create is a safe environment where students can really express their opinions without being judged and to be seen and to be heard.

Participants noted that managers rarely had the time or skills to provide this level of individualized support to the emerging adults who worked for them.

Recommendations for Enhancing Emotional Well-Being During the School-to-Work Transition

Attending to employees' emotional well-being has become integral to an organization's wellness approach and talent management strategy as it enables individuals to thrive at work, strengthens work relationships, and enhances organizational productivity. For emerging adults who are transitioning from school to work, attending to emotional well-being is paramount. Beyond being the start of one's career, the school-to-work transition is a "major development task" separating youth from adulthood (Marshall & Symonds, 2021) and one in which today's emerging adults may face a prolonged period of uncertainty given the instabilities of the work world (Ling & O'Brien, 2013). Effectively managing these issues is essential for emerging adults if they are to successfully navigate this transition and begin building a strong foundation for their professional lives. On the basis of our findings and extant scholarship, we have identified strategies organizations, managers, and emerging adults might pursue to assist in the school-to-work transition.

Organizational Supports for Emerging Adults' Emotional Well-Being

Our findings suggest that organizations can better support emerging adults' emotional well-being by developing comprehensive, holistic benefits that go beyond healthcare and PTO. For instance, organizations can provide mental health resources along with benefits that help emerging adults cope with early life stressors such as financial management or finding affordable housing or elder care. Employee resource groups, shared interest meet-up events, and company-wide volunteer activities also can help emerging adults build personal and professional connections, which can buffer the stress of the school-to-work transition. Finally, emphasis on inclusion and sustainability initiatives can enhance meaning and purpose in the workplace and thereby support emerging adults' sense of belonging and desire to build meaningful careers.

Organizations also need to consider the impact on emotional well-being, particularly for emerging adults, as they design their flexible work policies. Many participants noted that workplaces were trending toward hybrid work models, which balance the individual benefits of remote work with the organizational need for in-person connection. However, there are many complexities to implementing a hybrid work model, including different employees coming in on different days or new employees being in-person and more senior employees being remote (Rockmann & Pratt, 2015). In creating hybrid work norms, managers might consider how to implement a hybrid work structure that supports workplace productivity and employees' well-being. Questions managers might consider include: how do we ensure that early-career individuals are in-person with more-experienced employees so informal mentoring and professional development is happening? How many days of in-person work are needed to form social connections and a supportive community for employees? Beyond in-person work, what else might we introduce to help emerging adults forge new personal and professional relationships? These activities can go beyond typical team building to include professional development or career mentoring. Managing hybrid work in a creative, thoughtful, proactive manner can enhance employees' productivity, social connections, and overall well-being.

Managerial Support for Emerging Adults' Emotional Well-Being

With today's emerging adults, managers need to be adept at supporting the emotional needs of their early-career employees. Almost half (43%) of young professionals say they would reach out to their supervisor if they had a mental health problem—particularly if it was affecting their job performance/productivity (Mental Health & Wellbeing of Young Professionals Study, 2023). Furthermore, individuals who had supervisors who proactively reached out to them about their mental health were more likely to report good or excellent mental health (Mary Christie Institute, 2023).

Managers are not and should not become mental health professionals. However, they can become more adept at managing early-career individuals in a way that supports their emotional well-being. Our respondents noted the difficulty in developing this managerial competency. As they shared, "(There is) so much work to be done here. It's hard to find the time to be a strong, supportive people manager with today's workload levels." Managers need more training and coaching on how to support the emotional well-being of emerging adults and when to suggest the need for more professional support. This includes being prepared for and appropriately responsive to broader and more frequent self-disclosure and conversations around well-being as this generation seeks to bring their whole selves to work instead of masking their needs. "More than one in four young employees said they have reached out to someone at work about a mental health problem, and of those, the vast majority (91%) felt they received a supportive response" (Mary Christie Institute, 2023). When managers are skilled at facilitating these conversations, it benefits individual employees' well-being, their connection with the organization, and their transition to work.

Managers might also consider how they can broaden the network of developmental support they provide for early-career individuals. Beyond the traditional one-on-one mentoring, managers might form mentoring circles in which emerging adults are grouped with mid-career professionals and more senior executives for career and professional guidance (Murphy & Kram, 2014). Mentoring circles enable emerging adults to build a breadth of supportive work relationships that can enhance their emotional well-being and professional development (Darwin & Palmer, 2009). In this way, emerging adults are not simply turning to their peers for support—a concern that was raised by our participants.

Emerging Adults Managing Their Own Well-Being

Beyond what organizations and managers can do, emerging adults also need to take responsibility for becoming more aware of the stressors of the school-to-work transition to better manage their own emotional well-being. Emerging adults can be more proactive in learning about and preparing for the school-to-work transition. Internships and formal work experiences not only are important for learning about career interests but also can provide an early test of how one might transition from school to work. This early information can help an emerging adult better prepare for a more permanent transition.

Emerging adults can also take time to become more self-aware regarding their individual concerns and needs during this transition. Questions they might consider include the following: What are some of my personal concerns and anxieties about leaving school and how will I manage those? If I am moving to a new place how will I build new routines and social connections? In what ways might remote work or hybrid work enhance or detract from my emotional well-being and what can I do to mitigate the detractors? and How will I form new professional and personal connections with different generations to support my school-to-work transition? We also encourage emerging adults to proactively identify self-care strategies and potential resources they can access to manage their well-being in advance of any challenges they may face.

Conclusion

Our findings reflect and extend our current understanding of the emotional well-being needs of emerging adults and how to support these individuals in the school-to-work transition. This has always been a difficult, and important, life transition, but it is one that has been further complicated by the COVID-19 pandemic. Organizations, managers, and early-career professionals will need to work together to ensure that emerging adults manage their well-being during this transition in such a way that they are able to build productive, meaningful careers.

References

Akkermans, J., Blokker, R., Buers, C., Van der Heijden, B. I. J. M., & De Vos, A. (2021). Ready, set, go! In A. Marshall & J. Symonds (Eds.), *Adult development at the school-to-work transition: International pathways and processes* (pp. 77–103). Oxford University Press, Oxford, UK.

Arnett, J. J. (2014). *Emerging adulthood: The winding road from the late teens through the twenties*. Oxford University Press.

Arnett, J. J., Žukauskienė, R., & Sugimura, K. (2014). The new life stage of emerging adulthood at ages 18–29 years: Implications for mental health. *The Lancet Psychiatry*, *1*(7), 569–576.

Baay, P. E., Van Aken, M. A., Van der Lippe, T., & De Ridder, D. T. (2014). Personality moderates the links of social identity with work motivation and job searching. *Frontiers in Psychology*, *5*, 1044.

Blokker, R., Akkermans, J., Marciniak, J., Jansen, P. G., & Khapova, S. N. (2023). Organizing school-to-work transition research from a sustainable career perspective: A review and research agenda. *Work, Aging and Retirement*, *9*(3), 239–261.

Blokker, R., Akkermans, J., Tims, M., Jansen, P. G. W., & Khapova, S. N. (2019). Building a sustainable start: The role of career competencies, career success, and career shocks in young professionals' employability. *Journal of Vocational Behavior, 112*, 172–184.

Centers for Disease Control and Prevention. (n.d). *Well-being concepts*. https://archive.cdc.gov/#/details?url=https://www.cdc.gov/hrqol/wellbeing.htm

Charmaz, K. (2006). *Constructing grounded theory: A practical guide through qualitative analysis*. Sage Publications.

Chrikov, I., Soria, K. M., Horgos, B., & Jones-White, D. (2020). Undergraduate and graduate students' mental health during the COVID-19 pandemic [Internet]. *SERU Consortium Reports, University of California - Berkeley and University of Minnesota, 1*, 1–10. http://conservancy.umn.edu/handle/11299/215271.

Coe, E., Cordina, J., Enomoto, K., Jacobson, R., Mei, S., & Seshan, N. (2022, January 14). Addressing the unprecedented behavioral-health challenges facing Generation Z. *McKinsey & Company*. https://www.mckinsey.com/industries/healthcare/our-insights/addressing-the-unprecedented-behavioral-health-challenges-facing-generation-z

Corbin, J., & Strauss, A. (2014). *Basics of qualitative research: Techniques and procedures for developing grounded theory*. Sage Publications.

Darwin, A., & Palmer, E. (2009). Mentoring circles in higher education. *Higher education Research & Development, 28*(2), 125–136.

Grosemans, I., Hannes, K., Neyens, J., & Kyndt, E. (2020). Emerging adults embarking on their careers: Job and identity explorations in the transition to work. *Youth & Society, 52*(5), 795–819.

Huegaerts, K., Wagener, M., & Vanroelen, C. (2020). Is mental health a predictor for a smooth school-to-work-transition? A 20-month follow-up study of Brussels youth. *Applied Research in Quality of Life, 15*, 1549–1567.

Jensen, M. R., & Hermansen, Å. (2023). Adolescence mental Health disorders and precarious school-to-work trajectories: The role of family background and gender. *YOUNG, 31*(4), 315–338.

Ling, T. J., & O'Brien, K. M. (2013). Connecting the forgotten half: The school-to-work transition of noncollege-bound youth. *Journal of Career Development, 40*(4), 347–367.

Lipson, S. K., Zhou, S., Abelson, S., Heinze, J., Jirsa, M., Morigney, J., Patterson, A., Singh, M., & Eisenberg, D. (2022). Trends in college student mental health and help-seeking by race ethnicity: Findings from the national healthy minds study, 2013–2021. *Journal of Affective Disorders, 30*(6), 138–147.

Magier, M. J., Law, M., Martini, T., Pennisi, S., Lucibello, K. M., & Patte, K. A. (2025). "I don't feel fully prepared": A qualitative study of recently graduated students' mental health experiences of the transition out of university. *Journal of Adolescence, 97*(2), 451–466.

Mary Christie Institute. (2023). *The mental health and wellbeing of young professionals survey*. https://marychristieinstitute.org/wp-content/uploads/2023/01/The-Mental Health-and-Wellbeing-of-Young-Professionals-Survey.pdf

Marshall, E. A., & Symonds, J. E. (Eds.). (2021). *Young adult development at the school-to-work transition: International pathways and processes*. Oxford University Press.

Mortensen, M. (2023, July 18). Tension is rising around remote work. *Harvard Business Review Digital*.

Murphy, W., & Kram, K. (2014). *Strategic relationships at work: Creating your circle of mentors, sponsors, and peers for success in business and life*. McGraw-Hill.

Ng, T. W., & Feldman, D. C (2007). The school-to-work transition: A role identity perspective. *Journal of Vocational Behavior, 71*(1), 114–134.

Rockmann, K. W., & Pratt, M. G. (2015). Contagious offsite work and the lonely office: The unintended consequences of distributed work. *Academy of Management Discoveries, 1*(2), 150–164.

Rodoplu Şahin, D., Aslan, M., Demirkaya, H., & Ateşoğlu, H. (2022). The effect of COVID-19 on employees' mental health. *Scientific Reports*, *12*(1), 15067.

Takeuchi, T., Takeuchi, N., & Jung, Y. (2021). Toward a process model of newcomer socialization: Integrating pre-and post-entry factors for newcomer adjustment. *Human Resource Development Quarterly*, *32*(3), 391–418.

Travia, R. M. (2022, July). Executive perspective: From alcohol czar to COVID czar: Managing through the COVID-19 pandemic. *College Health and Wellness in Action*. https://acha.readz.com/from-alcohol-czar-to-covid-czar-managing-through-the-covid-19-pandemic

Travia, R. M., Larcus, J. G., Andes, S., & Gomes, P. G. (2020). Framing well-being in a college campus setting. *Journal of American College Health*, *70*(3), 758–772.

Van Zoonen, W., & Sivunen, A. E. (2022). The impact of remote work and mediated communication frequency on isolation and psychological distress. *European Journal of Work and Organizational Psychology*, *31*(4), 610–621.

Zickar, M. J., & Keith, M. G. (2023). Innovations in sampling: Improving the appropriateness and quality of samples in organizational research. *Annual Review of Organizational Psychology and Organizational Behavior*, *10*(1), 315–337.

Section III

Navigating Mental Health Challenges in the New World of Work

8 Exploring the Role of Trust and Vulnerability in Mental Health Disclosure

Niamh Kavanagh, Lisa van der Werff, and Yseult Freeney

Introduction

Mental health challenges are highly stigmatized, and research shows that those experiencing poor mental health are regularly discriminated against or mistreated in the workplace (Hershcovis et al., 2020), often due to power or dependency imbalances inherent in particular relational contexts and competitive environments (McChesney & Foster, 2024). Against this backdrop, disclosing mental health challenges at work is a prominent concern for employees, and a myriad of factors influence their decision to disclose (Hennekam et al., 2021). A decision not to disclose mental health challenges does not necessarily protect employees from this discrimination, as their behavior is often misattributed by others and self-stigmatized (Colella & Santuzzi, 2024). Choosing to conceal an "invisible" disability (Bapuji et al., 2024) can prevent employees from accessing appropriate accommodations and support and create a fear of being "found out," consuming significant mental energy (Toth & Dewa, 2014). Competitive environments can complicate the decision to disclose, where those with mental health challenges may fear curtailed career opportunities, micro-management, and exclusion (Wheat et al., 2010). As a social identity, disclosing a mental health issue can result in a form of categorization by colleagues, with an "us" versus "them" attitude developing in the workplace (Turner & Oakes, 1986) and stigmatization compounded by gossip and social exclusion (Brohan et al., 2012).

Despite disclosure being an inherently relational phenomenon (Gibson, 2018), where an employee decides to share a personal mental health challenge with others at work, there is virtually no research on mental health disclosure that adopts a relational lens. Given the potential vulnerability involved, exploring the role of trust in mental health disclosures provides us with more insight into these decision-making processes. Trust represents a willingness to be vulnerable and is a choice based on positive expectations of the other party (Rousseau et al., 1998). In mental health disclosures, employees decide to accept the vulnerability that others' knowledge of their illness may create, particularly concerning interactions with them following disclosure. Exploring how organizations,

DOI: 10.4324/9781003491170-11

leaders, and team members create a trusting work environment, where employees feel comfortable and safe sharing mental-health-related information, is vital for employees and management, given the current climate and prevalence of mental health issues globally. This chapter zooms in on the relational factors at play in deciding to disclose a mental health challenge at work (Follmer & Jones, 2022), with a particular focus on the role of trust in peers, managers, and the employing organization in enabling disclosure (Gillespie et al., 2023). Our chapter starts with a review of the extant literature on mental health disclosure and then draws on the trust, distrust, and vulnerability literatures (e.g., Weibel et al., 2023) to develop a theoretical framework of mental health disclosure decisions that is anchored in the relational architecture of organizations. Our framework is illustrated by quotes from the lived experience of mental health disclosure decisions across multiple workplace contexts—private sector, public sector, and not-for-profit.[1] Our chapter sets out a vision for future research to advance scholarship and inform practical guidance on how organizations can proactively manage vulnerability to create a trusting work environment where employees feel more supported in sharing personal mental-health-related information with relevant others in the workplace.

Disclosure

The disclosure dilemma represents a significant challenge for employees with mental health challenges (MHCs). Traditional views of disclosure as a binary choice (conceal or reveal; Goffman, 1963) have been criticized as reductive and overly simplistic (Chaudoir & Fisher, 2010). As a result, process-based theories emerged to capture the nuances of disclosure as an intricate and dynamic process (Hastuti & Timming, 2021). These models encompass the entire disclosure process, from factors that influence the decision to disclose or not, the dimensions involved in the disclosure event, to consequences post-disclosure. While disclosure can be involuntary, where an employee is forced to disclose due to treatment requirements, or inadvertent, resulting from observable symptoms or behaviors (Toth & Dewa, 2014), this chapter focuses on voluntary disclosure, the primary focus of process-based models of disclosure.

Several factors are considered before disclosure, with internal motivators and external environmental and relational factors acting as precipitators of disclosure, and moderators of its outcomes (Hastuti & Timming, 2021). Individual factors include identity factors (Follmer & Jones, 2022), perception of self or self-stigma (Ragins, 2008), and symptomatology—where those with more severe or visible symptoms have an increased likelihood of disclosure (Follmer et al., 2020). Relational factors include perceived stigma or support (Brohan et al., 2012), the relationship between the discloser and the intended recipient, and the recipient's attitude and personality (Toth et al., 2022). Organizational factors include broader organizational support, established policies and practices, and organizational diversity climate (Toth et al., 2022). Researchers have further differentiated antecedents into motivationally focused goal types, including approach-focused goals—pursuing positive outcomes such as pragmatic accommodation seeking, a desire for authenticity or activism motivations, or avoidance-focused goals—avoiding adverse outcomes such as stigma or discrimination (Toth et al., 2022). Research suggests that approach-focused goals lead to more positive outcomes for disclosure (McGrath et al., 2023).

Disclosure is a continuum in which individuals must decide which aspects of their MHC to disclose, whom to share with (widely or with select individuals), and when to share (e.g., at the hiring stage or during employment; McGrath et al., 2023). Outcomes range from the positive, that is, an increase in accommodations (Hastuti & Timming, 2021) or improved workplace culture (Elraz, 2018), to the negative, including experiences of stigma and discrimination (McGrath et al., 2023). Individual- and organization-focused outcomes have received most attention in the literature, with limited focus placed on dyadic outcomes. Of the literature on dyadic outcomes, interpersonal relationships can be impacted (Barth & Wessel, 2022), with some research suggesting trust-related impacts (Toth et al., 2022). Process-based disclosure models can also incorporate a feedback loop in which the outcomes of one disclosure event feed into the pre-disclosure factors of the next (Toth et al., 2022). This feedback loop is valuable as disclosure events are rarely experienced only once for those with MHCs, and the process is repeated with different social actors and with alternative motivations. Ultimately, the disclosure process is interpersonal and hinges on the relationship and interaction between a discloser and their confidante(s). As such, a more relational perspective can be useful in expanding our understanding of this phenomenon.

Trust, Distrust, and Vulnerability

Trust is commonly defined as "a psychological state comprising the intention to accept vulnerability based upon positive expectations of the intentions or behavior of another" (Rousseau et al., 1998, p. 395). The positive expectations aspect has traditionally been considered as driven by our trust propensity—a dispositional willingness to trust other people in general—and perceptions of trustworthiness (Mayer et al., 1995). Drawing on the work of Mayer et al. (1995), trustworthiness is a perception of the characteristics of the other party, composed of three evaluations. Does the other person have the ability to meet our expectations? Do they have our best interests at heart, and are they benevolent? Do they have integrity and do their actions align with their words? Although trustworthiness and trust propensity have been the primary focus of empirical attention (Baer & Colquitt, 2018), the literature also recognizes the role of motivation and emotion in driving the positive expectations on which trust decisions are based (van der Werff et al., 2019).

The second part of the trust definition, a willingness to be vulnerable, is less explored and the focus of much current debate and attention (e.g., Schafheitle et al., 2023) as scholars strive to understand what vulnerability is and how it impacts trusting. Recent theoretical explorations of vulnerability define it as perceiving and feeling exposed and susceptible to harm or loss (Fulmer et al., 2025). Misztal (2011) delineates two forms of vulnerability: discontinuity vulnerability, which relates to uncertainty in knowing what will happen next, and socio-emotional vulnerability, which relates to our dependence on others for fulfillment and self-worth. Recent trust theory argues that in situations where vulnerability is highly salient, trust decisions will be made very carefully, with trustors searching for cues to help them decide whether or not they are willing to accept that vulnerability (Weibel et al., 2023).

Theories of trust portray proximal outcomes of trust as a psychological state as risk-taking within a relationship (Mayer et al., 1995) or trust-informed, voluntary actions, and intentions to act (Dietz & Den Hartog, 2006). This trust-informed intention to act is often operationalized as reliance or disclosure behaviors (Gillespie, 2003). Indeed, one of the items in a popular scale of trust disclosure asks participants to consider the extent to which they are willing to "Confide in this person about personal issues that are affecting your work." As such, we propose that mental health disclosure in the workplace represents a particular form of trusting decision, and in the next section, integrating literature on process-based disclosure theories (e.g., Chaudoir & Fisher, 2010) with that of trust and vulnerability, we develop a framework for considering the process of mental health disclosure through the trust lens. We support this with some empirical data gathered from individuals with experiences of MHCs while working (see Table 8.1).

Theoretical Framework

Antecedents and Trust: Individual and Interpersonal Factors

Voluntarily disclosing an MHC is a relational act of trust involving vulnerability and risk. Several relational antecedents factor into the decision to disclose, and parallels can be drawn between trust and disclosure literatures.

Vulnerability

Vulnerability represents a complex, yet integral, part of disclosure. Misztal (2011) highlights the interplay between trust and vulnerability, where vulnerability not only demands trust but also increases susceptibility to risk. This conceptualization is equally relevant to the disclosure dilemma. Feeling vulnerable is a common feeling both when individuals live with MHCs and when they disclose sensitive information (Numans et al., 2021). Living with a concealed

Table 8.1 Role of Trust in Anticipating Disclosure Outcomes

Felt Trust			
Supporting Quotes	*Trust Codes*	*Anticipated Outcome*	*Decision*
people looking at you completely differently, that I can't do the job, that would have been the biggest fear	Low ability	Felt (un) trustworthiness	Conceal MHC
You don't want people minding you, for me that would be worse, they see a weaker version because that's the way I saw myself	Benevolent ableism		
this sense of macho-ness. The biggest thing for mental health is that it exposes that you're not confident, you're not the macho person, you're not a superhero, you're vulnerable like anybody else	Perceived weakness		
I have seen that, yeah, in my place where it's that kind of reaction to talk about mental health and illnesses, that they are just taking the mickey^ and it's something to talk about or laugh about.	De-legitimizing MHC (witness)	Lack of (Felt) Trust in MHC	
And then I got a letter from HR . . . they thought I was taking the mickey, they said that stress wasn't a thing and it was like the new version of back-ache which was also a taking-the-mickey^ thing to write on your sick notes	De-legitimizing MHC (experience)		
I want to be an honest person and be upfront about it, and I feel like I should talk about this at work. . . . I wanted to be honest and be heard and be accepted	Being honest and authentic		Disclose MHC
Interpersonal Trust			
We are not a happy family. We do not support each other. We are not helpful to each other and don't trust each other	Lack of support	Perceived low benevolence	Conceal MHC
-the environment can be difficult and isolating and people are not very kind to each other.	Lack of kindness		
I'm thinking if he knows that, he'll say it to her, she may say it to somebody else, all of a sudden it's known, it's everywhere, and all of a sudden "he's mad"	Gossip	Perceived low integrity	

(*Continued*)

Table 8.1 (Continued)

Felt Trust			
Supporting Quotes	*Trust Codes*	*Anticipated Outcome*	*Decision*
I expected that the aims and objectives would permeate the organization completely and that everybody would have a very strong and obvious empathy and commitment to the goals of the [organization]. I don't find that at all', [P.14].	Espoused values not lived out		
But I know the people I work with very well and knew that they were all kind and caring and understanding. So that helped me and made me more confident in telling them.	Kindness	Expected benevolence	Disclose MHC
I think my manager did realise I was struggling because my husband rang through to her. . . . She had confided in me that she had had problems before as well and that she had gone for help	Shared experience		
. . . my manager had been supportive in the past to others' [P.2], 'A work colleague has previously disclosed and her experience was positive' [P.5]	Vicarious experience		

^ *taking the mickey: make fun of someone (quote 1) or having someone on, making them think something untrue is true (quote 2).*

identity, such as an undisclosed MHC, renders individuals more vulnerable to negative psychological stressors (Hastuti & Timming, 2021); however, there is also a relational vulnerability associated with voluntarily making these challenges visible to others (Rüsch et al., 2017). The inherent vulnerability associated with having MHCs acts as an antecedent to disclosure, particularly for those with more severe symptoms. Disclosing also creates a vulnerability to the social evaluations of others, where different facets of their trustworthiness might be questioned. In situations where vulnerability is particularly salient, trust decisions are likely to be taken more carefully (Weibel et al., 2023). Individuals must weigh current versus future possible states of vulnerability as they debate disclosure. In our interviews with employees with MHCs, participants often shared this weighing process with a focus on how others might perceive them: "that kind of colored my idea of what people in authority would think of you, that you weren't able to achieve or you weren't to be relied upon or trusted to do certain roles." As illustrated in Table 8.1, anticipated vulnerability can inhibit disclosure, where individuals shared fears about not being trusted to do their jobs or to be relied upon, whether through being perceived as weak or being protected due to benevolent ableism.

Identity and Authenticity

A desire for authenticity is frequently referenced as an antecedent to and motivator for disclosure (Toth et al., 2022) and is a crucial aspect of perceptions of trustworthiness (Palanski & Yammarino, 2007). Individuals with MHCs often struggle to balance the desire to be authentic while simultaneously protecting themselves from discrimination (Berkley et al., 2019). Concealing a part of themselves that is central to their identity leads to feelings of inauthenticity for an individual (Crabtree & Pillow, 2020). Authentic individuals are seen by others as more trustworthy (Avolio & Gardner, 2005), and revealing a stigmatized identity is said to improve relationships through relational authenticity (Berkley et al., 2019). The extent to which individuals perceive their MHC as central to their identity plays an important role. Self-verification theory holds that people are driven to have others see them as they see themselves (Swann, 1987). Identity centrality greatly influences self-verification, and this drives a need for identity congruence across different areas of a person's life, predicting greater disclosure likelihood (Ragins, 2008). Therefore, authenticity acts as an antecedent both by a motivation for self-congruence and to improve others' perception of their integrity. Employees with MHCs must assess the degree to which their desire for authenticity outweighs any potential disadvantages of disclosing. As depicted in Table 8.1, individuals are motivated to be seen as acting with integrity in order to be trusted by others. They talk about the importance of honesty and authenticity as drivers of sharing their MHCs with others: "I want to be an honest person and be upfront about it, and I feel like I should talk about this at work. . . . I wanted to be honest and be heard and be accepted." However, even when individuals may be inclined to disclose to gain authenticity, they experience fears regarding how legitimately their illness will be viewed by others, increasing the likelihood of concealment. As one of our interviewees shared, "People looking at you differently, that I can't do the job, that would have been the biggest fear."

Assessing the Confidante

A commonly discussed antecedent to disclosure is the perceived response, support, and trust of a confidante (e.g., Hastuti & Timming, 2021). Anticipating a positive outcome—such as being shown kindness or seeing others treated with kindness (see Table 8.1)—contributes to greater disclosure likelihood (Ragins, 2008). From this perspective, the personal trust cues of others are a critical relational factor in the decision to disclose, and the discloser is assessing the ability, benevolence, and integrity of a confidante during this evaluation. A confidante's skills and competence to respond appropriately to disclosure might be used as a barometer for assessing their ability. For those with an MHC, this might include the disclosure to a superior for accommodation purposes and an assessment of the supervisor's ability to respond appropriately to them, provide suitable support, and proceed with managing them in a way that would not damage their career (Kirsh et al., 2018).

Benevolence is cited as a crucial trustworthiness factor in relation to disclosure-based trust (Tomlinson et al., 2020). The beliefs, attitudes, and behaviors of others toward those with MHCs are carefully assessed pre-disclosure, and stronger perceptions of emotional support and empathy are associated with a higher likelihood of disclosure (Ridge et al., 2019). In our interviews with employees with MHCs, they have shared how important expected benevolence is in influencing their disclosure decisions: "I know the people I work with very well and knew they were all kind and caring and understanding. So that helped me and made me more confident in telling them." Employees often reflected on how their vicarious experience of others disclosing was useful in informing those expectations.

The integrity of the confidante also plays an important role, as the discloser must assess the acceptability of the trustee's values and the extent to which their actions mirror them. Integrity has been shown to be a critical driver of trust behavior in higher-reliability contexts (Colquitt et al., 2011), and our interviewees agreed that expectations of low integrity in their confidante influenced their intentions to disclose: "I'm thinking if he knows that, he'll say it to her, she might say it to someone else, all of a sudden its known, it's everywhere, and all of a sudden [people think] 'he's mad.'" Research on the disclosure of concealable, stigmatized identities underscores the importance of integrity, with incongruence between organizational policies and supervisor behavior linked to a lower likelihood of disclosure (Capell et al., 2018). Participants in our research (see Table 8.1) spoke about incongruence between espoused organizational values and how these were experienced, while others spoke about the fear of being the focal point of gossip. Signaling strategies are often used to gather more information during the disclosure decision-making process and assess the trustworthiness cues of confidantes (Toth et al., 2022).

The Disclosure Event

The disclosure event is also complex in its relation to vulnerability and trust. The individual must make decisions about the target of the disclosure based on their interpretations of personal trust cues, decide what information is shared, how this is framed, and the timing of the act. The discloser is essentially signaling aspects of their own trustworthiness to others. The framing of the disclosure might be done from the perspective of identity management, with some "claiming" (emphasizing the positive factors of their hidden identity) and some "downplaying" (shifting attention from the identity; Lyons et al., 2018). Research on the disclosure of physical disabilities finds that claiming leads to higher evaluations of competence from others than downplaying or concealing (Lyons et al., 2018). However, stereotypes of those with MHCs often result in lower ratings of competence and warmth (Gärtner et al., 2022), so it is unclear whether this disrupts the positive impact of claiming. Others could perceive disclosure as signaling low competence for organizational requirements (Toth et al., 2022). Employees might attempt to frame their disclosure strategically to bypass this, downplaying symptoms so that competence will not be questioned (Follmer & Jones, 2022). Disclosure might also be framed in a way that attempts to signal benevolence to others, potentially by acting as a role model for others with MHCs (Ridge et al., 2019). The language and affect used in disclosure have a crucial relational impact, with more vulnerable and emotional self-disclosure leading to greater relationship intimacy and more positive disclosure outcomes (Chaudoir & Fisher, 2010). Signaling factors also play a role in the timing of disclosure. Research by Toth et al. (2022) demonstrated that concealment is often strategically used to convey competence to others, particularly during hiring and selection processes.

Response

Once a disclosure is made, the confidante has an opportunity to respond. The response they choose has implications for both parties at an individual level and for their relationship. Barth and Wessel (2022) use a critical incident technique to classify responses as supportive or unsupportive. The supportive responses they outline include ones that are likely to signal explicitly the confidante's benevolence toward the discloser, including emotional support and affirmation, but likely spill over to influence perceptions of ability and integrity too. For instance, a response that delegitimizes the MHC, where it is not taken seriously, leads to reduced felt trust on the part of the discloser. This has been a recurrent theme in our research with employees who share experiences of managers and HR representatives de-legitimizing their illness: "They didn't think I could have been stressed and that stress wasn't a real reason to be out of work."

Other types of supportive responses may tap into more social identity bases for trust (Kramer & Lewicki, 2010), where confidantes aim to signal that they, too, or someone close to them, has faced mental health issues. Some of our participants spoke about shared experiences, where the confidante had a history of an MHC, resulting in a greater sense of perceived benevolence on the part of the confidante (see Table 8.1). Although reciprocal sharing of information may support ongoing social exchange in the relationship, evidence regarding how appropriate it is in response to mental health disclosure is mixed (Chernichky-Karcher et al., 2022). Finally, the Barth and Wessel (2022) framework includes responses that focus on providing instrumental or informational support in ways that are likely to signal their ability to support the discloser and also have tangential effects for more character-based assessments of trustworthiness (i.e., that they want to support the discloser). This framework aligns well with evidence from the broader trust literature, which suggests that interpersonal emotion regulation strategies, like validation and engagement with the issue they have shared, are important determinants of trust in the confidante (Naughton et al., 2024). In contrast, unsupportive responses like downplaying symptoms, avoidance of the issue, or even withdrawal from the relationship and exclusion of the discloser have obvious negative consequences for trustworthiness assessments and may even cause a trust breach, requiring efforts to restore trust in order for the relationship to recover (Sharma et al., 2023). These disclosure responses will provide feedback to inform future disclosure decisions in this relationship and relationships with others in the organization.

While there might be considerable spillover in perceived trustworthiness in these disclosure response incidences, those perceptions may not perfectly reflect actual confidante trustworthiness. Even well-intentioned, benevolent confidante's responses can be constrained by the influence of stereotypes that influence fear or threat (Johnson et al., 2020) and the skill level in perspective-taking and emotion regulation. However, related literature suggests that individual disclosers may interpret the same response quite differently (Dakof & Taylor, 1990). It is clear that confidantes, particularly those in a position of relative power, have a delicate balance to strike between providing appropriate support and accommodations without further stigmatization (Szulc, 2024).

Conclusion and Avenues for Future Research

Our chapter aims to stimulate more research on the role of trust and vulnerability in supporting positive experiences of mental health disclosure in the workplace. As we reviewed the literature and developed our thoughts regarding this topic, we noted several important areas for further research that will help provide more actionable advice for people who wish to disclose mental health challenges at work, and for colleagues and managers who wish to respond to those disclosures in ways that support the individual and strengthen their relationships. In particular, research is needed on the experiences of vulnerability, which are central to understanding disclosure decisions and responses. This is a nascent area of research that is developing from the wider trust literature, and we look forward to seeing how upcoming contributions in this space (e.g., Fulmer et al., 2025; Schafheitle et al., 2023) can be helpful in the refinement of theory on mental health disclosure at work.

Furthermore, evidence from related fields of interpersonal processes suggests that it is unlikely the impact of this disclosure process ends within this dyad. Instead, we encourage future researchers to consider how confidante responses to vulnerable disclosures might impact wider trust within the organization. Evidence shows that employees perceive the treatment they receive from their colleagues and managers to be indicators of the prevailing level of trust in the workplace (Bendersky & Brockner, 2020). In addition, third parties who witness or learn of responses to disclosures of MHC are likely to be influenced in a similar way to those witnessing workplace mistreatment (Skarlicki & Rupp, 2010) and injustice (Kay et al., 2023).

Finally, given the scale of the issues related to MHC in the workplace, organizations, and their employees need more evidence-based guidance on supporting colleagues with MHC. While important challenges related to stigma and bias remain, one promising approach to this may be to invest in developing trust in our workplaces to encourage authentic disclosures and increase the chances that they will be met by an appropriate response that is interpreted as supportive.

Note

1 The illustrative data are drawn from a series of parallel qualitative research projects on the exploration of mental health disclosure and concealment in a range of organizational contexts. In total, the quotes represent 82 participants' interviews, all of whom had mental health issues and were in full-time employment. The participants were drawn from a range of corporate workplaces ($n = 28$), a non-for-profit organization ($n = 38$), and a national police force ($n = 16$). Further information is available from the third author.

References

Avolio, B. J., & Gardner, W. L. (2005). Authentic leadership development: Getting to the root of positive forms of leadership. *The Leadership Quarterly*, *16*(3), 315–338. https://doi.org/10.1016/j.leaqua.2005.03.001

Baer, M. D., & Colquitt, J. A. (2018). Why do People Trust?: Moving toward a more comprehensive consideration of the antecedents of trust. In *The Routledge companion to trust* (1st ed.). Routledge.

Bapuji, H., Ertug, G., Soundararajan, V., & Shaw, J. D. (2024). Invisible inequalities: Barriers, challenges, and opportunities. *Journal of Management*, *50*(3), 835–848. https://doi.org/10.1177/01492063231205294

Barth, S. E., & Wessel, J. L. (2022). Mental illness disclosure in organizations: Defining and predicting (un)supportive responses. *Journal of Business and Psychology*, *37*(2), 407–428. https://doi.org/10.1007/s10869-021-09753-4

Bendersky, C., & Brockner, J. (2020). Mistreatment from peers can reduce the effects of respectful treatment from bosses, and respectful peers can offset mistreatment from bosses. *Journal of Organizational Behavior*, *41*. https://doi.org/10/ggrtcg

Berkley, R. A., Beard, R., & Daus, C. S. (2019). The emotional context of disclosing a concealable stigmatized identity: A conceptual model. *Human Resource Management Review*, *29*(3), 428–445. https://doi.org/10.1016/j.hrmr.2018.09.001

Brohan, E., Henderson, C., Wheat, K., Malcolm, E., Clement, S., Barley, E. A., Slade, M., & Thornicroft, G. (2012). Systematic review of beliefs, behaviours and influencing factors associated with disclosure of a mental health problem in the workplace. *BMC Psychiatry*, *12*(1), Article 1. https://doi.org/10.1186/1471-244X-12-11

Capell, B., Tzafrir, S. S., Enosh, G., & Dolan, S. L. (2018). Explaining sexual minorities' disclosure: The role of trust embedded in organizational practices. *Organization Studies*, *39*(7), 947–973. https://doi.org/10.1177/0170840617708000

Chaudoir, S. R., & Fisher, J. D. (2010). The disclosure processes model: Understanding disclosure decision making and postdisclosure outcomes among people living with a concealable stigmatized identity. *Psychological Bulletin*, *136*(2), 236–256. https://doi.org/10.1037/a0018193

Chernichky-Karcher, S., Venetis, M. K., & Gettings, P. E. (2022). Revealing mental health information in friendships: The role of disclosure strategy and perceived recipient response on disclosure outcomes. *Health Communication*, *37*(7), 909–918. https://doi.org/10.1080/10410236.2021.1876325

Colella, A., & Santuzzi, A. (2024). Known and unknown mental illness: Uncovering the multiple routes to workplace inequities. *Journal of Management*, *50*(3), 898–927.

Colquitt, J. A., Lepine, J. A., Zapata, C. P., & Wild, R. E. (2011). Trust in typical and high-reliability contexts: Building and reacting to trust among firefighters. *Academy of Management Journal*, *54*(5), 999–1015. https://doi.org/10.5465/amj.2006.0241

Crabtree, M. A., & Pillow, D. R. (2020). Consequences of enactment and concealment for felt authenticity: Understanding the effects of stigma through self-distancing and motive fulfillment. *European Journal of Social Psychology*, *50*(6), 1227–1247. https://doi.org/10.1002/ejsp.2680

Dakof, G. A., & Taylor, S. E. (1990). Victims' perceptions of social support: What is helpful from whom? *Journal of Personality and Social Psychology*, *58*(1), 80–89. https://doi.org/10.1037/0022-3514.58.1.80

Dietz, G., & Den Hartog, D. N. (2006). Measuring trust inside organisations. *Personnel Review*, *35*(5), 557–588. https://doi.org/10/cnhtds

Elraz, H. (2018). Identity, mental health and work: How employees with mental health conditions recount stigma and the pejorative discourse of mental illness. *Human Relations*, *71*(5), 722–741. https://doi.org/10.1177/0018726717716752

Follmer, K. B., & Jones, K. S. (2022). Navigating depression at work: Identity management strategies along the disclosure continuum. *Group & Organization Management*, *47*(5), 963–1007. https://doi.org/10.1177/10596011211002010

Follmer, K. B., Sabat, I. E., & Siuta, R. L. (2020). Disclosure of stigmatized identities at work: An interdisciplinary review and agenda for future research. *Journal of Organizational Behavior*, *41*(2), 169–184. https://doi.org/10.1002/job.2402

Fulmer, C. A., Gillespie, N., Gwak, J., Liu, L. A., Schafheitle, S., & Hong, S. (2025, June 18–21). *Navigating vulnerability: A unified definition and roadmap forward* [Paper presentation]. First International Network on Trust Conference, Genoa, Italy.

Gärtner, L., Asbrock, F., Euteneuer, F., Rief, W., & Salzmann, S. (2022). Self-stigma among people with mental health problems in terms of warmth and competence. *Frontiers in Psychology*, *13*. https://doi.org/10.3389/fpsyg.2022.877491

Gibson, K. R. (2018). Can I tell you something? How disruptive self-disclosure changes who "we" are. *Academy of Management Review*, *43*(4), 570–589.

Gillespie, N. (2003). *Measuring trust in working relationships: The behavioral trust inventory*. [Paper presentation]. Academy of Management Conference, Seattle, WA, United States.

Gillespie, N., Guan, B., & Kay, A. (2023). *Measuring trust in work relationships: A validation of the Behavioural Trust Inventory across multiple studies*. First International Network of Trust Researchers 12th Conference, Helsinki, Finland.

Goffman, E. (1963). *Stigma: Notes on the management of spoiled identity*. Penguin Books.

Hastuti, R., & Timming, A. R. (2021). An inter-disciplinary review of the literature on mental illness disclosure in the workplace: Implications for human resource management. *The International Journal of Human Resource Management*, *0*(0), 1–37. https://doi.org/10.1080/09585192.2021.1875494

Hennekam, S., Follmer, K., & Beatty, J. (2021). Exploring mental illness in the workplace: The role of HR professionals and processes. *The International Journal of Human Resource Management*, *32*(15), 3135–3156. https://doi.org/10.1080/09585192.2021.1960751

Hershcovis, M. S., Cortina, L. M., & Robinson, S. L. (2020). Social and situational dynamics surrounding workplace mistreatment: Context matters. *Journal of Organizational Behavior*, *41*(8), 699–705. https://doi.org/10.1002/job.2479

Johnson, K. R., Ennis-Cole, D., & Bonhamgregory, M. (2020). Workplace success strategies for employees with autism spectrum disorder: A new frontier for human resource development. *Human Resource Development Review*, *19*(2), 122–151. https://doi.org/10.1177/1534484320905910

Kay, A. A., Masters-Waage, T. C., Reb, J., & Vlachos, P. A. (2023). Mindfully outraged: Mindfulness increases deontic retribution for third-party injustice. *Organizational Behavior and Human Decision Processes*, *176*. https://doi.org/10.1016/j.obhdp.2023.104249

Kirsh, B., Krupa, T., & Luong, D. (2018). How do supervisors perceive and manage employee mental health issues in their workplaces? *Work*, *59*(4), 547–555. https://doi.org/10.3233/WOR-182698

Kramer, R. M., & Lewicki, R. J. (2010). Repairing and enhancing trust: Approaches to reducing organizational trust deficits. *Academy of Management Annals*, *4*(1), 245–277. https://doi.org/10.5465/19416520.2010.487403

Lyons, B. J., Martinez, L. R., Ruggs, E. N., Hebl, M. R., Ryan, A. M., O'Brien, K. R., & Roebuck, A. (2018). To say or not to say: Different strategies of acknowledging a visible disability. *Journal of Management*, *44*(5), 1980–2007. https://doi.org/10.1177/0149206316638160

Mayer, R. C., Davis, J. H., & Schoorman, F. D. (1995). An integrative model of organizational trust. *Academy of Management Review*, *20*(3), 709–734. https://doi.org/10.5465/amr.1995.9508080335

McChesney, J., & Foster, L. (2024). Is it #okaytosay I have anxiety and depression? Evaluations of job applicants who disclose mental health problems on LinkedIn. *Journal of Business and Psychology*, *39*(3), 779–795. https://doi.org/10.1007/s10869-023-09907-6

McGrath, M., Krysinska, K., Reavley, N., Andriessen, K., & Pirkis, J. (2023). Disclosure of mental health problems or suicidality at work: A systematic review. *International Journal of Environmental Research and Public Health*, *20*. https://doi.org/10.3390/ijerph20085548

Misztal, B. (2011). Trust: Acceptance of, precaution against and cause of vulnerability. *Comparative Sociology*, *10*(3), 358–379. https://doi.org/10.1163/156913311x578190

Naughton, B., O'Shea, D., van der Werff, L., & Buckley, F. (2024). Influencing a nation: How a leader's interpersonal emotion regulation influences citizen compliance via trust and emotions during a global pandemic. *Emotion*, *24*(1), 196–212. https://doi.org/10.1037/emo0001262

Numans, W., Regenmortel, T. V., Schalk, R., & Boog, J. (2021). Vulnerable persons in society: An insider's perspective. *International Journal of Qualitative Studies on Health and Well-Being*, *16*(1). https://doi.org/10.1080/17482631.2020.1863598

Palanski, M. E., & Yammarino, F. J. (2007). Integrity and leadership: Clearing the conceptual confusion. *European Management Journal*, *25*(3), 171–184. https://doi.org/10.1016/j.emj.2007.04.006

Ragins, B. R. (2008). Disclosure disconnects: Antecedents and consequences of disclosing invisible stigmas across life domains. *The Academy of Management Review*, *33*(1), 194–215. https://doi.org/10.2307/20159383

Ridge, D., Broom, A., Kokanović, R., Ziebland, S., & Hill, N. (2019). Depression at work, authenticity in question: Experiencing, concealing and revealing. *Health*, *23*(3), 344–361. https://doi.org/10.1177/1363459317739437

Rousseau, D., Sitkin, S., Burt, R., & Camerer, C. (1998). Not so different after all: A cross-discipline view of trust. *Academy of Management Review*, *23*. https://doi.org/10.5465/amr.1998.926617

Rüsch, N., Rose, C., Holzhausen, F., Mulfinger, N., Krumm, S., Corrigan, P. W., Willmund, G.-D., & Zimmermann, P. (2017). Attitudes towards disclosing a mental illness among German soldiers and their comrades. *Psychiatry Research*, *258*, 200–206. https://doi.org/10.1016/j.psychres.2017.08.028

Schafheitle, S., Weibel, A., & Möllering, G. (2023). Inviting submissions to the Special Issue on trust and vulnerability (Deadline 31 August 2024). *Journal of Trust Research*, *13*(2), 252–254. https://doi.org/10.1080/21515581.2023.2246837

Sharma, K., Schoorman, F. D., & Ballinger, G. A. (2023). How can it be made right again? A review of trust repair research. *Journal of Management*, *49*(1), 363–399. https://doi.org/10.1177/01492063221089897

Skarlicki, D. P., & Rupp, D. E. (2010). Dual processing and organizational justice: The role of rational versus experiential processing in third-party reactions to workplace mistreatment. *Journal of Applied Psychology*, *95*(5), 944–952. https://doi.org/10.1037/a0020468

Swann, W. B. (1987). Identity negotiation: Where two roads meet. *Journal of Personality and Social Psychology*, *53*(6), 1038–1051. https://doi.org/10.1037/0022-3514.53.6.1038

Szulc, J. M. (2024). Leading with understanding: Cultivating positive relationships between neurotypical leaders and neurodivergent employees. *Employee Relations: The International Journal*, *ahead-of-print*(ahead-of-print). https://doi.org/10.1108/ER-12-2023-0621

Tomlinson, E. C., Schnackenberg, A. K., Dawley, D., & Ash, S. R. (2020). Revisiting the trustworthiness–trust relationship: Exploring the differential predictors of cognition- and affect-based trust. *Journal of Organizational Behavior*, *41*(6), 535–550. https://doi.org/10.1002/job.2448

Toth, K. E., & Dewa, C. S. (2014). Employee decision-making about disclosure of a mental disorder at work. *Journal of Occupational Rehabilitation*, *24*(4), 732–746. https://doi.org/10.1007/s10926-014-9504-y

Toth, K. E., Yvon, F., Villotti, P., Lecomte, T., Lachance, J. P., Kirsh, B., Stuart, H., Berbiche, D., & Corbière, M. (2022). Disclosure dilemmas: How people with a mental health condition perceive and manage disclosure at work. *Disability and Rehabilitation*. https://www.tandfonline.com/doi/full/10.1080/09638288.2021.1998667

Turner, J. C., & Oakes, P. J. (1986). The significance of the social identity concept for social psychology with reference to individualism, interactionism and social influence. *British Journal of Social Psychology*, *25*(3), 237–252. https://doi.org/10.1111/j.2044-8309.1986.tb00732.x

van der Werff, L., Legood, A., Buckley, F., Weibel, A., & de Cremer, D. (2019). Trust motivation: The self-regulatory processes underlying trust decisions. *Organizational Psychology Review*, *9*(2–3), 99–123. https://doi.org/10.1177/2041386619873616

Weibel, A., Schafheitle, S., & van der Werff, L. (2023). Smart tech is all around us—bridging employee vulnerability with organizational active trust-building. *Journal of Management Studies*, *n/a*(n/a). https://doi.org/10.1111/joms.12940

Wheat, K., Brohan, E., Henderson, C., & Thornicroft, G. (2010). Mental illness and the workplace: Conceal or reveal? *Journal of the Royal Society of Medicine*, *103*(3), 83–86. https://doi.org/10.1258/jrsm.2009.090317

9 Mental Health Management in Remote and Hybrid Working

Hadar Elraz

Introduction

The increased Remote and Hybrid working (RaHW) arrangements continue to reverberate and be the source of considerable discussion, especially when considering aspects of equality, diversity, and inclusion. Indeed, the latest figures indicate a rising number of mental health conditions (MHCs) globally since 1990 (Hammoudi et al., 2024). This increase might be related to downsizing, financial struggles, mortality, and ill-health. The current state of MHCs around the globe means that those experiencing MHCs face isolation, uncertainty, and profound insecurity. These factors have not only strained general health services but also specifically impacted mental health services due to the growing number of people seeking mental health support (Kelloway et al., 2023). Consequently, managing mental health in the workplace has become more challenging, particularly for individuals with pre-existing MHCs, who now face changes associated with the contemporary workplace, such as increased RaHW and work intensification (Kelloway, 2017).

While literature on how employees cope with RaHW is not new, what we know less about is how new forms of working impact the working experiences of people with MHCs. This chapter aims to address this gap by examining the way in which individuals with MHCs cope in the workplace and the mechanisms they use to sustain their employment.

The research is situated within the UK nonprofit sector. The UK nonprofit sector is a vital part of the country's social fabric. Unlike traditional businesses, a nonprofit organization's (NPO) primary goal is to address social issues and create positive change rather than generating profit for owners or shareholders. NPOs often facilitate the employment of marginalized populations with the aim to bring about greater sense of equality and social inclusion. NPOs offer a sustainable and impactful way to address some of the most pressing issues facing society today (Damm & Kane, 2024).

Data were qualitatively collected as a part of a collaboration with a large NPO aiming to gain an understanding of employees' experiences during and after

DOI: 10.4324/9781003491170-12

COVID-19, focusing on the shift to RaHW asking: how does RaHW impact the working experiences of employees with MHCs? What are their working experiences in relation to managing their MHCs and the disclosure of their MHCs?

Finding suggest that RaHW arrangements improved the management of MHCs but were equally a challenge in light of increasing workplace expectations over performance. Contributions to better understanding the complexities associated with invisible conditions in the workplace are offered alongside practical implications for managing MHCs at work.

Mental Health Conditions and Workplace Support When Remote and Hybrid Working

Several studies have addressed the specific impact that working from home during the pandemic has had on the mental health and well-being of employees. For example, Wilson et al. (2024) argue that imposed RaHW has led to an increase in common mental health issues, such as stress, depression, and anxiety among employees. They posit that the slowdown associated with the pandemic and the fear of redundancies have increased these MHCs (Wilson et al., 2024).

Although scholars have examined how RaHW has impacted employees' mental health and well-being, less attention has been paid to exploring the experiences of those with pre-existing MHCs. While individuals with MHCs can engage in sustained and successful work (Ellison et al., 2003; Granger, 2000; Goldberg et al., 2005), there is a relative dearth of knowledge exploring how these individuals cope with remote working.

MHCs, as well as other health conditions or disabilities that significantly impact individuals' ability to carry out day-to-day tasks, are protected in the U.K. under the Equality Act (2010). This legislation makes it unlawful to discriminate against these individuals and requires organizations to accommodate for these conditions by making reasonable adjustments in the workplace (Gardenswartz, 2024).

Research suggests that online platforms can generate greater equality for people with disabilities, as their disabilities may not be immediately visible, reducing the likelihood of stigma (Hyde & Todd, 1996; Paterson & Hughes, 1999). At the same time, however, studies on online disclosure have also suggest that having an ongoing "disabled" narrative online can be damaging for employees with disabilities (Annable et al., 2007), whereas others have explored whether discrimination varies across different platforms (Dai & Brady, 2019). Rohm et al. (2021) found that mothers' online disclosures of their disabilities reduced social distance compared to a control condition, illustrating the stigma-reducing potential of self-disclosure and blogging (Corrigan & Matthews, 2003; Rains, 2014).

Shpigelman and Gill (2014) propose that online disability disclosure is vastly understudied. Yet some studies have suggested that stigma from online disclosure may differ from in-person interactions (Furr et al., 2016). Medjesky (2008) found that individuals with disabilities struggle with online disclosure, while Furr et al. (2016) highlighted that the frequency and audience of disclosure are important factors in this context.

Despite these studies, there is still little known about how individuals with MHCs cope with RaHW. This chapter examines the impact of RaHW on employees with MHCs and the support mechanisms that can help them sustain their employment (Branning et al., 2021).

Methods

This research began as an attempt to understand employees' experiences after COVID-19, but the findings have implications beyond that unique period in understanding work. Data were collected to understand employees' experiences in the light of RaHW. All data were collected within one major NPO organization, employing a large number of staff with pre-existing MHCs. The research utilized workshops, interviews, and focus groups with a sample of 58 charity sector employees with MHCs, part of a UK ESRC-funded project. Participants were recruited from an NPO focused on health and well-being. All participants were recruited from the same organization. The analysis presented here forms part of a larger research project, which consisted of the following recorded and transcribed sessions: 8.5-hour-long workshops, 15 interviews lasting around 45 minutes each, and two one-hour-long focus groups. All data were collected online, with live sessions taking place over video conferencing.

Information about the project was disseminated to staff and externally to service users. Out of the 58 participants, 49 were employed by the organization, while 9 service users participated in the workshops and were employed in either other charity sector (4) or public sector (4) organizations. Twelve participants were male, two identified as trans, and the remaining 44 were female. There were no specific exclusion or inclusion criteria regarding the participants' MHCs, although most experienced common yet persistent conditions such as mood (22) and anxiety disorders (24), while others had OCD (4), borderline personality disorder (4), PTSD (3), and psychosis (1). The participants' occupations varied, ranging from working in mental health services (17), health and well-being (17), community care (14), and managerial and office work (11). Two participants did not state their occupation.

There was a strong degree of similarity in the questions asked in the workshops, interviews, and focus groups, which invited participants to share their experiences of mental health and work. Specifically, the questions aimed to gain insight into how participants managed their MHCs at work, what triggers they experienced while working, how they managed RaHW, the impact of COVID-19 on their working situation and MHCs, what they did to stay well, whether they disclosed their MHCs at work and if so then how and to whom, and how they managed relationships with colleagues and managers.

Data Analysis

An exploratory qualitative approach was utilized, with anonymized transcripts being thematically analyzed to identify commonalities and differences in the experiences drawn upon within the respondents' texts. To investigate the research question and explore the participants' subjective accounts of their day-to-day experiences in the workplace, an interpretivist inductive exploratory qualitative approach was utilized (Bluhm et al., 2011). The workshops, focus groups, and loosely semi-structured interviews provided an opportunity for participants to talk freely about the issues that mattered most to them (Denzin & Lincoln, 1994; Mertens, 1999). The iterative process of identifying themes and nuances in the analysis of the findings leads to the formation of thematically organized coded data (Atkinson et al., 2003). Participants' names were replaced by pseudonyms to preserve confidentiality and anonymity. After examining the findings from this initial stage, textual critical analysis techniques were employed to explore the key processes through which individuals understood MHCs and their management within the workplace while remote working during the COVID-19 pandemic and the shift to online and hybrid forms of working. Situating the analysis of the finding within broader debates on RaHW during and after COVID-19, attendant work intensification, downsizing and working with fewer people (Elshaer et al., 2024), increasing expectations over productivity, and pressure on employees to continuously function and behave in an idealized manner suggests that employees with MHCs are further disadvantaged from these workplace practices. The following key themes emerging from the findings are further discussed in the following sections: mental health management while working remotely (1.1. Agile and remote working, 1.2. Workplace support or lack thereof, 1.3. Accessing mental health support outside of work); changes in work demands (2.1 Increased workload, 2.2 performance expectations). Each of these analytical themes is discussed in further detail.

Findings

For people with MHCs, the impact of RaHW arrangements has produced somewhat contradictory results, which problematize the perceived benefits and challenges associated with RaHW. Key factors at the interface between MHCs and the shift toward RaHW include the following: (1) managing mental health and well-being while transitioning toward flexible working and (2) increased performance expectations.

Managing Mental Health and Well-being While Transitioning Toward Flexible Working

Overall, the participants have clearly made the point that the greater flexibility afforded by working from home has proven to be especially helpful and enhanced their health and well-being while working remotely. Statements such as the following were not uncommon: "being at home with the dog rather than being stuck in the office" (Interview participant); "the flexibility gives a sense of inner peace and calmness to the working schedule" [Focus group participants]; and "Talking to people is important as well as yoga and meditation" (Workshop participant).

Participants also stated that they employed a range of techniques, which at least for them proved to be useful for tackling the problems associated with both RaHW:

> I have the time and space to consider what do I need to do for myself, before I start the day. So, that's a big one for me really, [writing in my] journal and getting out regularly for breaks and walks. Even if it's a 10-minute walk it helps. Middle of the day, end of the day, just as long as I get out every day at least once or twice like that.
>
> (Interview participant)

However, while some enjoyed the time spent not commuting, insofar as it afforded them greater time and opportunity to focus on engaging in activities that help them manage their well-being, others reported increasing pressure from organizational norms around productivity. Previously, when the workday was over, employees could perhaps feel some sense of closure from work activities, but with RaHW the pressure felt more constant.

Increased Performance Expectations

While some enjoyed working from home and found it a relief not to engage in face-to-face contact with colleagues, other participants felt that RaHW robbed them of the instant face-to-face support that they had previously when working in the office. For some of these participants, this exacerbated their pre-existing MHCs and had a detrimental impact on their ability to manage their MHCs, especially insofar as they experienced challenges in gaining the right kinds of support when they needed it. Participants regularly stressed that they had experienced work overload, which is not surprising; redundancies and attendant work intensification are unfortunately not uncommon given global downsizing and working with fewer people (Elshaer et al., 2024). Indeed, the research participants have commented on the way in which this had impacted their MHCs.

Above all, the participants noted that the workplace has been stressful and that they suffered isolation as well as struggles to manage their stress and anxiety. However, what was even more constraining was that they felt even more tied to their work in various ways, including, among other things, always being online, constantly responding to emails and working harder with less social breaks, and sometimes working longer days than they did before the shift to RaHW. The participants felt a constant pressure to take on a greater workload and increasing performance expectations. This also drew attention to the difficulties they faced in trying to live up to other colleagues' expectations of them:

> When I came back to the role they thought that I was something that I am not and trying to live up to that, trying to meet these high expectations of people that are there now, and I'm thinking I am not . . . and then sometimes I think, "come on you've got to have the confidence," but it is managing other people's expectations of you that is a challenge.
>
> (Workshop participant)

Prevailing workplace expectations around productivity and pressure on employees create an expectation to continuously function and behave in an idealized manner:

> You know from our management we can't run on 9–10 out of 10 [effort level] on a permanent basis, just getting by on annual leave. If we tried to do that we would all be off for sick leave for 3 or 4 weeks at a time, and that's not institutionally sustainable. We have to allow ourselves to basically run on 7 or 8 out of 10.
>
> (Focus group participant)

In this respect, the participants raised concerns pertaining to them feeling they need to put on a front or how they struggle over the lack of empathy in target-centered organizational discourses and logics: "there is not really any room for empathy in targets" (Interview participant); and "I use body language to appear confident to cover up how I am really feeling" (Workshop participant).

With the prevailing working culture of doing more and additional pressure employees put on themselves to perform and appear resilient to work pressures, those with MHCs often feel exacerbated levels of pressure on themselves and against performance expectations, which consequently results in a struggle to perform or stay well. This was especially the case for those providing emotional support to others insofar as participants felt "the job requires strong mental well-being [thus] it's harder to discuss your own suffering" (Focus group participant). Indeed, those participants whose job involved caring for others also felt that their own mental health had been compromised as a result.

One senior member of staff said they felt they "couldn't be seen to be struggling" (Interview participant) with their own mental health.

It might be that people with MHCs are even more prone to such burnouts (Koutsimani et al., 2019; Escudero-Castillo et al., 2021), especially under extreme conditions such as in the instance of RaHW. This perspective can be discerned in the following account:

> I think taking that moment and speaking to yourself and saying, "what's going on underneath you know?" You need to take a moment here and enough is enough sometimes.
>
> (Interview participant)

Discussion

This chapter aimed to examine how employees with MHCs cope in the context of RaHW. While many employees with MHCs engage in sustained and successful work (Ellison et al., 2003; Granger, 2000; Goldberg et al., 2005), there is a relative dearth of knowledge about those with MHCs working remotely. By shedding light on their RaHW experiences, this chapter aimed to explore how employees with MHCs managed their work and MHCs and how this may differ from or be similar to working in person while caring for one's MHC.

The findings in this exploration demonstrated how RaHW impacted employees' management of their MHCs and workplace performance. While RaHW facilitates better management of their MHCs, participants equally highlighted the challenges associated with RaHW. Illuminating how participants coped with growing performance expectations and the impact this had on their work performance suggests how high-performance expectations endured regardless of their impact on the MHCs of these individuals. The insight generated here feeds into contemporary debates on contemporary RaHW culture, which embraces performance expectations unfettered by any nonwork issues (Costin et al., 2023). This demonstrates how workplace expectations are entangled within high performance and confident appearance and high-achieving expectations and how these serve to marginalize employees with MHCs or lead them to keep their experiences concealed to appear to meet high-performance demands.

While there is literature on the overall experiences of employees in the light of RaHW, there is less literature addressing how individuals with MHCs manage their health and work when RaHW. The insight provided here could facilitate a better understanding of their experiences and consequently, identify ways to better support these employees. Expanding this debate to include the experiences of employees with MHCs, the analysis here may also provide insight into the extent to which contemporary performance expectations exclude certain populations of workers, such as employees with MHCs.

Conclusion

The analysis presented in this chapter suggests that organizations as well as governments need to first be aware of the experiences of employees with MHCs as well as identify ways to encourage these employees to gain support in managing their condition, especially while RaHW. Future research should examine the working experiences of employees with MHCs across employment contexts to provide an even more comprehensive understanding of invisible conditions, as well as address the interface between marginalization and RaHW within the setting of MHCs. By examining how people with MHCs experience the workplace when RaHW, researchers and practitioners could gain a more comprehensive understanding of how contemporary workplace expectations are experienced by those managing MHCs and ways to bring about positive change and greater inclusion for all workers.

References

Annable, G., Goggin, G., & Stienstra, D. (2007). Accessibility, disability, and inclusion in information technologies: Introduction. *Information, Communication & Society*, *10*(1), 1–12.

Atkinson, P., Coffey, A., & Delamont, S. (2003). *Key themes in qualitative research: Continuities and changes*. Rowman Altamira.

Bluhm, D. J., Harman, W., Lee, T. W., & Mitchell, T. R. (2011). Qualitative research in management: A decade of progress. *Journal of Management Studies*, *48*(8), 1866–1891.

Branning, G., Waters, H. C., Houle, C. R., Worthy, S. L., Fink, B., & Hayes, K. (2021). Mental illness disclosure in the workplace: An opportunity for improvement. *American Health & Drug Benefits*, *14*(4).

Corrigan, P. W., & Matthews, A. K. (2003). Stigma and disclosure: Implications for coming out of the closet. *Journal of Mental Health*, *12*(3), 235–248.

Costin, A., Roman, A. F., & Balica, R. S. (2023). Remote work burnout, professional job stress, and employee emotional exhaustion during the COVID-19 pandemic. *Frontiers in Psychology*, *14*, 1193854.

Dai, M., & Brady, M. (2019). Disability disclosure in the workplace: A review and research agenda. *Journal of Vocational Rehabilitation*, *51*(3), 253–264.

Damm, C., & Kane, D. (2024). Classifying UK charities' activities by charitable cause: A new classification system. *Voluntary Sector Review*, *15*(2), 249–275.

Denzin, N. K., & Lincoln, Y. S. (Eds.). (1994). *Handbook of qualitative research*. Sage Publications, Inc.

Ellison, M. L., Russinova, Z., MacDonald-Wilson, K. L., & Lyass, A. (2003). Patterns and correlates of workplace disclosure among professionals and managers with psychiatric conditions. *Journal of Vocational Rehabilitation*, *18*(1), 3–13.

Elshaer, I. A., Azazz, A. M., Ghaleb, M. M., Abdulaziz, T. A., Mansour, M. A., & Fayyad, S. (2024). The impact of work-related ICT use on perceived injustice: Exploring the effects of work role overload and psychological detachment. *Journal of Open Innovation: Technology, Market, and Complexity*, *10*(1), 100208.

Escudero-Castillo, I., Mato-Díaz, F. J., & Rodriguez-Alvarez, A. (2021). Furloughs, teleworking and other work situations during the COVID-19 lockdown: Impact on mental well-being. *International Journal of Environmental Research and Public Health*, *18*(6), 2898.

Fialho, J. (2022). Benefits and challenges of remote work. In R. Pereira, I. Bianchi, & Á. Rocha (Eds.). *Digital technologies and transformation in business, industry and organizations* (pp. 1–15). Springer.

Furr, J. B., Carreiro, A., & McArthur, J. A. (2016). Strategic approaches to disability disclosure on social media. *Disability & Society, 31*(10), 1353–1368.

Gardenswartz, C. (2024). Mental health issues in the workplace. *Psychology Today*.

Goldberg, S. G., Killeen, M. B., & O'Day, B. (2005). The disclosure conundrum: How people with psychiatric disabilities navigate employment. *Psychiatric Rehabilitation Journal, 28*(3), 306–310.

Granger, B. (2000). The role of psychiatric rehabilitation practitioners in the treatment of people with psychiatric disabilities. *Psychiatric Rehabilitation Journal, 23*(3), 215–223.

Hammoudi Halat, D., Sami, W., Soltani, A., & Malki, A. (2024). Mental health interventions affecting university faculty: A systematic review and meta-analysis. *BMC Public Health, 24*(1), 3040.

Hyde, M., & Todd, R. (1996). The impact of disability on employment: A review of the evidence. *Journal of Vocational Rehabilitation, 6*(3), 189–201.

Kelloway, E. K. (2017). Mental health in the workplace: Towards evidence-based practice. *Canadian Psychology/Psychologie canadienne, 58*(1), 1–6.

Kelloway, E. K., Dimoff, J. K., & Gilbert, S. (2023). Mental health in the workplace. *Annual Review of Organizational Psychology and Organizational Behavior, 10*, 363–387.

Koutsimani, P., Montgomery, A., & Georganta, K. (2019). The relationship between burnout, depression, and anxiety: A systematic review and meta-analysis. *Frontiers in Psychology, 10*, 429219.

Medjesky, C. (2008). Online disclosure of disability: Implications for employment. *Journal of Vocational Rehabilitation, 29*(2), 123–134.

Mertens, D. M. (1999). Inclusive evaluation: Implications of transformative theory for evaluation. *The American Journal of Evaluation, 20*(1), 1–14.

Paterson, K., & Hughes, B. (1999). Disability studies and sociology: An introduction. *Disability & Society, 14*(5), 597–604.

Rohm, A., Möhring, M., Grengel, M., & Hastall, M. R. (2021). How self-disclosure in online postings affects female readers' stigmatisation towards mothers with a disability. *European Journal of Health Communication, 2*(2), 1–20.

Shpigelman, C. N., & Gill, C. J. (2014). The impact of disability disclosure on employment outcomes. *Journal of Vocational Rehabilitation, 41*(3), 123–134.

Wilson, H. K., Tucker, M., & Dale, G. (2024). Learning from the working from home experiment during COVID-19: employees motivation to continue working from home. *Journal of Organizational Effectiveness: People and Performance, 11*(4), 967–986.

10 The Impact of Cumulative Trauma Across the Employee Lifecycle

Katina B. Sawyer and Kelly P. Gabriel

This chapter explores the understudied population of individuals who have experienced ongoing, complex trauma and its impact on employment. We argue that scholars and practitioners should focus more on how accumulated traumatic experiences shape career life cycles in meaningful yet addressable ways. Centering research on these populations can help organizations create inclusive workplaces that support individuals who have faced significant hardships. In this chapter, we explore trauma and complex trauma, theorizing their cumulative impacts across key stages of the employee lifecycle—recruitment, selection, performance management, and training and development—summarized in Figure 10.1. We also consider potential positive outcomes for trauma survivors and offer guidance for scholars and practitioners to better support employees with complex trauma histories.

What Is Trauma?

To start, let us define what we mean by trauma. Trauma occurs when environmental demands exceed an individual's available resources to cope (Sar & Ozturk, 2005). Unlike normal stressors that one may encounter in their everyday lives, potentially traumatic elements of one's environment are uniquely distressing, capture attention, and require significant cognitive processing (Sar & Ozturk, 2005). Indeed, separating traumatic events from more normative stressors, the American Psychological Association (APA, 2018) defines traumatic events as those that are psychologically, emotionally, or physically threatening, leading to subsequent shock and overwhelm. Within organizational scholarship, trauma is primarily understood as resulting from "an extremely upsetting event" (Maitlis, 2009, p. 49), which impacts one's work life and which, "at least temporarily, overwhelms the individual's resources" (Briere & Scott, 2012, p. 3). These events may be interpersonal, such as abuse, or environmental, such as hunger or homelessness. Because traumatic events infuse individuals' lives with a sense of confusion and chaos about their understanding of the world and how it operates, it can disrupt individuals' baseline understanding of who they are (Tedeschi &

DOI: 10.4324/9781003491170-13

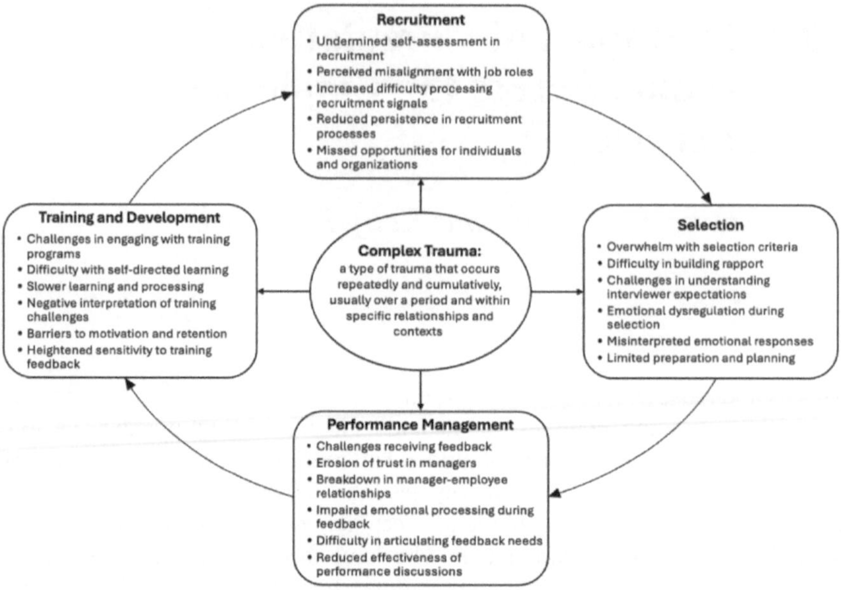

Figure 10.1 Summary of Potential Impact of Cumulative Trauma Across Employee Lifecycle.

Calhoun, 2004). As such, it is no surprise that trauma can have serious consequences for psychological and physical well-being. For example, some individuals may develop post-traumatic stress disorder (PTSD; Yehuda et al., 2015) after experiencing a traumatic event. PTSD symptoms can include intrusive memories, fear of the event recurring, and difficulty in connecting with others or oneself.

Importantly, trauma is subjective. There is no definitive list of events that will be experienced as traumatizing; rather, these outcomes hinge on individuals' access to available resources that may serve as a match to the potentially traumatizing events they encounter. Of course, certain events are so challenging to experience and process that they are likely to overwhelm even those who are rich in coping resources (e.g., witnessing or being victim to physical or sexual violence, experiencing an extreme natural disaster; APA, 2018). Ultimately, whether an event is experienced as traumatic depends on how it is perceived and processed by the individual.

What Is Complex Trauma?

To say that the literature in the organizational sciences has ignored the impacts of trauma on employees' working lives would be an understatement. Yet a focus on complex trauma, which may have unique effects on employees, has been particularly obscured from the literature. Research in management (unlike literature in other disciplines, like peace psychology and community studies; see Eagle & Kaminer, 2013, for a review) has primarily focused on acute trauma—singular events like shootings, natural disasters, job loss, or physical injury—which can lead to post-traumatic stress and, at times, post-traumatic growth (e.g., Conroy & O'Leary-Kelly, 2014; Haynie & Shepherd, 2011; Maitlis, 2020, 2022; Vough & Caza, 2017). Yet, in addition to acute trauma, individuals may experience recurring traumatic experiences over their lifetime (e.g., prolonged abuse, neglect, or living in a war zone), leading to complex trauma, "a type of trauma that occurs repeatedly and cumulatively, usually over a period of time and within specific relationships and contexts" (Courtois, 2008, p. 86). For example, employees may experience complex trauma from ongoing verbal or physical abuse by a supervisor, racist acts by coworkers, or distressing job-related conflicts, such as those in government or military roles.

Clinically, acute trauma is distinct from complex trauma (Herman, 1992) in that complex trauma creates ongoing disruptions to individuals' life trajectories, ultimately placing individuals into a state of continuous discontinuity. Complex trauma is experienced in systemic and multidimensional ways; indeed, experiences of trauma are pervasive and are often influenced by a multitude of social systems (Causadias & Umaña-Taylor, 2018). Over time, these experiences have compounded negative effects, including declines in physical and mental well-being (Pitman et al., 2012). Similar to the way acute trauma may lead to PTSD, complex trauma can provoke complex PTSD, which reflects the relational, affective, behavioral, and identity-related dysfunctions described in this chapter (Briere & Scott, 2015).

Complex trauma often arises from commonplace, but threatening, experiences (Van Nieuwenhove & Meganck, 2019), such as systemic "isms" (e.g., racism, sexism) that manifest in cumulative experiences of bias, discrimination, and mistreatment (e.g., Kira et al., 2008). Scholarship across disciplines has demonstrated that people of color often face recurring racial trauma (e.g., discrimination, microaggressions; Carter, 2007), impoverished individuals often face recurring socioeconomic trauma (e.g., hunger, homelessness; Seabrook & Avison, 2012), and women often face recurring gender-based trauma (e.g., sexual harassment, objectification; Deitz et al., 2015). Majority group members can also experience recurring trauma. Bullying and mobbing, which can target victims for reasons unrelated to identity, are also long-lasting, traumatic—yet commonplace—patterns of abuse that can significantly impact victims' careers (e.g., Leymann & Gustaffson, 1996; Matthiesen & Einarsen, 2004). Thus, recurring trauma impacts broad swaths of the working population.

Why Is It Important to Consider Cumulative Trauma Across the Employee Lifecycle?

Taking the above into account, individuals who have experienced complex trauma may face different challenges than their counterparts as they navigate their careers. We believe that a greater focus on complex trauma and its effects on employees is essential to develop more inclusive employee lifecycle theory and practice that accounts for the repeated, life-altering experiences many employees endure. Indeed, extant literature suggests that complex trauma may uniquely affect employees' careers in meaningful ways. Namely, complex trauma can uproot an employee's core sense of self when navigating their career; this departs from acute trauma, where individuals often retain the identities, assumptions, and goals they formed prior to the traumatic event and leverage them as they navigate the trials and tribulations of their working lives. Instead, continuous traumatic disruptions can impede the development of a coherent and stable "master status" (i.e., a set of core identities central to defining oneself; Maitlis, 2009, p. 68). As a result, those who experience complex trauma are more likely than those who experience acute trauma to suffer continued disturbances to their self-construal, creating difficulties in forming relationships, managing emotions, and maintaining a positive attitude about the self (Brewin et al., 2017).

Furthermore, career success often depends on social, economic, and psychological resources that help employees "get ahead" over time. Yet complex trauma can disrupt access to these key resources (Herman, 1992). For example, recurring trauma via ongoing discrimination can fracture social networks (Ibarra, 1995), limit economic opportunities (Lang & Spitzer, 2020), and damage an individual's sense of self (Neblett, 2019). Thus, complex trauma can create unavoidable, additional hurdles for employees navigating their careers.

While this may appear to be a lengthy list of struggles faced by individuals with complex trauma, in this chapter we highlight these issues not to point out potential flaws in those who have experienced trauma over time but rather to shed light on the hidden struggles that they are often forced to manage. While these issues may reflect differential challenges that these individuals may face across the career lifespan, we believe that employers must find ways to be more inclusive of such employees' struggles. Reimagining the career lifecycle from a trauma-informed lens is a key objective of this chapter, but doing so first requires acknowledging the limitations of current organizational systems. Indeed, researchers have suggested that addressing organizational inequities may involve balancing a recognition of challenges with a focus on strengths and solutions (e.g., Leslie et al., 2024). Thus, we now suggest limitations of commonplace employment practices for supporting those with complex trauma.

How Might Complex Trauma Impact Employees' Experiences in Recruitment?

Complex trauma can uniquely impact employees' experiences during recruitment. While navigating the job market is challenging for anyone, individuals with complex trauma may face heightened difficulties that exacerbate these challenges.

A key part of the recruitment process involves candidates forming opinions about potential jobs and organizations (Breaugh, 2013). As they learn about roles and organizational contexts, they process this information carefully, understanding that the decision to accept a job has significant work and life implications. As organizations send signals about job roles and work environments, job seekers use these cues to determine their job and organizational fit. While it is assumed that candidates can accurately assess their skills and suitability (Earnest et al., 2011), research shows that recruits often overestimate their abilities and believe they are qualified for roles they are not (e.g., Dunning, 2007). However, individuals with complex trauma often feel the opposite. Due to disruptions in their formation of a consistent self-concept from repeated traumatic events, they are more likely to doubt their job-related skills and abilities. Because repeated trauma causes individuals to question the world and their ability to control their circumstances (rightfully so, given much of what they experience may be beyond their control), they often see their capabilities as less than they truly are. Indeed, complex trauma is linked to lower self-esteem and a fragmented sense of self (Cook et al., 2005). Because individuals with complex trauma may struggle to see themselves as capable of performing a job, they may be less likely to apply for positions they are qualified for or may even withdraw during recruitment. As a result, qualified candidates with valuable skills may miss out on enriching opportunities, and organizations lose access to a richer, more diverse talent pool.

How Might Complex Trauma Impact Employees' Experiences With Selection?

The selection process may also prove particularly challenging for those who have experienced complex trauma. Similar to recruitment, employees gravitate toward roles that they feel match their abilities (Wilk & Sackett, 1996). As such, selection procedures (e.g., cognitive ability tests, personality assessments, interviews) can signal job requirements that may feel misaligned with their self-views, leading to feelings of overwhelm, reduced confidence, and disengagement during the process.

Those with complex trauma also face challenges during selection due to interpersonal attachment difficulties. A history of repeated unhealthy interactions with authority figures (e.g., caregivers, teachers; Cook et al., 2005) can hinder their ability to trust or form bonds with interviewers or potential supervisors. This may lead to perceptions that those leading the process are unsupportive of their candidacy or are working against them, adding to the stress of navigating employment hurdles. Additionally, instead of connecting and empathizing with authority figures, individuals with complex trauma may default to focusing inward or detaching, which can impede rapport-building, a key advantage in securing valued opportunities (Galinsky et al., 2008). In turn, it is possible that they may struggle to take an interviewer's perspective, as they often learned to mentally detach from authority figures as a survival strategy.

Emotion regulation challenges may also affect individuals with complex trauma during the selection process. The intense emotions triggered by repeated traumatic events can be difficult to process, leaving individuals grappling with unresolved feelings from past or ongoing experiences. This makes managing emotions during high-pressure situations, like interviews or assessments, even more difficult. Anxiety-inducing elements of selection, such as fear of failure or judgment (Proost et al., 2008), can exacerbate these difficulties. Already anxious about navigating job-related hurdles, individuals with complex trauma may find that their anxiety is amplified in demanding or self-doubt-inducing situations. Furthermore, individuals with complex trauma often struggle to accurately label their emotions (Cook et al., 2005), which can lead to misinterpretation. For instance, anxiety about pre-employment assessments might be misinterpreted as a fear of employment, dislike of the job, or frustration with the interviewer.

Finally, complex trauma, marked by life-altering events, often leads individuals to question the stability and predictability of the world around them (Pressley & Spinazzola, 2020). For those who have endured repeated trauma, the world can feel—and often is—deeply unpredictable. As a survival strategy, focusing solely on the present may be adaptive at times, but it can make planning for the future feel especially challenging, or even futile. This mindset can hinder applicants' ability to adequately prepare for organizational selection processes, even when these processes seem relatively straightforward.

How Might Complex Trauma Impact Employees' Experiences With Performance Management?

Performance management, which encompasses activities, policies, and feedback aimed at improving employee and organizational performance (DeNisi & Murphy, 2017), requires unique considerations for those who have experienced complex trauma. Performance management requires resilience, particularly when handling negative feedback—a challenging experience for any employee, even those without a history of trauma (Belschak & Den Hartog, 2009).

For individuals with complex trauma, challenges with attachment and emotion regulation can intensify the difficulty of processing and responding to negative feedback. As mentioned, those with complex trauma often have a history of unhealthy relationships, particularly with authority figures who are often responsible for inflicting or perpetuating trauma. This often leads to a functional level of suspicion or distrust of authority (Thoroughgood et al., 2020). In performance management, where supervisors hold power over feedback and employment decisions, such distrust can cause negative feedback to be processed both as distressing and suspicious. While managers may see candid feedback as an opportunity to build trust, without delivering such feedback with care, employees may perceive it as hostile or untrustworthy. Feeling defensive, these employees may resort to prior survival strategies, such as withdrawal or isolation, further distancing themselves from their managers and hindering productive communication.

With regard to emotional regulation, for those who have had to grapple with an onslaught of complex and upsetting emotions, it may be more difficult to process feedback as it is given, to communicate complicated feelings to managers, or to express how feedback processes might be improved moving forward. All of this stems from a persistent sense of emotional overwhelm caused by the repeated nature of complex trauma, where one traumatic experience often follows another, leaving little time for reflection, emotional processing, or the development of effective emotion management tools. Unlike those who experience acute trauma, individuals with complex trauma frequently carry unresolved emotions, which can make receiving feedback and building open and trusting relationships with managers more challenging.

Finally, while discussing both areas of improvement and encouragement is necessary for comprehensively addressing employees' strengths and weaknesses, receiving negative performance information may be particularly challenging for those with complex trauma. For example, a singular focus on problems or obstacles (e.g., management by objectives; Rodgers & Hunter, 1991) can seem overly bleak and have detrimental effects. Instead, a balance of positive and negative feedback may be needed in order to ensure such employees process areas of improvement more productively.

How Does Complex Trauma Impact Employees' Training and Development Experiences?

Training and development, which includes both formal and informal opportunities to learn and grow on the job (e.g., classroom training, job shadowing, online simulations; Sonnentag et al., 2004), can also pose challenges for those grappling with complex trauma. Similar to above, performance environments where skills are publicly displayed can heighten anxiety for all employees—but are especially daunting for those with a fragile self-concept. For example, research has shown that effective learning strategies are essential for retaining knowledge and skills, but that training anxiety can negate these benefits, with highly anxious individuals gaining less than their calmer counterparts (Warr & Downing, 2000). Thus, for those with complex trauma, low confidence in their abilities often heightens anxiety, making it difficult to fully benefit from these strategies despite their potential value.

Complex trauma can also hinder career planning, particularly as organizations are increasingly expecting employees to manage their own career development (despite the potential pitfalls of doing so; Westerman & Lundberg, 2023). Individuals who have experienced complex trauma may view the future as unpredictable and uncontrollable, making planning feel pointless. With limited experience in preparing for the future, they may face significant challenges in self-directed developmental contexts.

Additionally, because training and development require employees to process novel information and persist through learning challenges, those who have experienced complex trauma may struggle with maintaining motivation. Yet this is not for lack of ability or desire to be successful. First, these individuals may take longer to process information because they subconsciously assess new content for potential threats—a defense mechanism learned from past trauma (Crittenden & Heller, 2017). If a threat is perceived, the information may be discarded, dissociated from, or hyper-focused on. For example, trainees may respond to threatening content (e.g., overly challenging or taxing training content) with boredom or disconnection in the former cases, or stress and fixation in the latter. In either case, training content may trigger non-normative reactions uncommon in those without complex trauma. Second, individuals with complex trauma may interpret delays in progress as evidence of their lack of talent or skills. While others with stronger self-concepts see training struggles as temporary and specific (e.g., "I'm struggling now, but I'm still good at other things and I'll improve"), those with complex trauma, due to lower self-esteem and an unstable self-concept, are more likely to interpret setbacks as proof of their overall inadequacy and inability to improve.

Can Cumulative Trauma Experiences Have Positive Impacts on Employees?

We would be remiss if we neglected to mention that there are also positive potentialities for those who have experienced complex trauma. While people should not have to experience repeated traumatic events for the purpose of reaping these benefits, we do want to highlight these possibilities. For example, post-traumatic growth (Calhoun & Tedeschi, 2014) can develop after traumatic events. Post-traumatic growth entails growth in one's relationships, appreciation for oneself or one's life, spiritual growth and development, or a sense that one can overcome challenges (Henson et al., 2021). Thus, while trauma is challenging, there may be a "silver lining" in the longer term. Organizational researchers have highlighted the power of post-traumatic growth for promoting positive personal outcomes in an employment context as well (e.g., Maitlis, 2020).

Yet a search for complex post-traumatic growth does not return any search results. While we are not clinicians, we imagine individuals with complex trauma may have unique potential for growth. For instance, relationships sustained through repeated hardships may emerge especially strengthened, given that surviving repeated, uniquely difficult circumstances may send a strong signal to both relationship partners that their bond is resistant to being broken. Similarly, a strong sense of purpose and meaning in life may develop from overcoming significant repeated hardships; indeed the feeling of "being here for a reason" may gain credibility over time as seemingly insurmountable hurdles are overcome and individuals are still standing. Finally, embarking on a path to healing from complex trauma offers individuals the chance to redefine their self-concept, align with their values, and choose who they want to be, rather than being constrained by past trauma. It also offers the chance to break cycles of generational harm, intentionally cultivate healthier relationships, and inspire a ripple effect of positive change in families, communities, and organizations. While speculative, we see complex post-traumatic growth as a promising area for future scholarly inquiry.

How Can Scholars and Practitioners Better Support Those Who Have Experienced Complex Trauma?

While we have outlined the hidden challenges individuals with complex trauma may encounter throughout the career lifecycle, we want to conclude this chapter with recommendations for how scholars and practitioners can better support these employees.

First, we urge researchers to prioritize individuals with complex trauma in their scholarship. When existing theories do not adequately address understudied populations, building grounded theory is essential (Charmaz, 2013). Therefore, we encourage qualitative research to explore how those with complex trauma navigate recruitment, selection, performance management, training, and development processes, generating new theories that capture their unique experiences. Subsequent quantitative studies can then test the generalizability of these findings. We also emphasize the importance of the need for trauma-informed practices when engaging in research with this vulnerable population (Alessi & Kahn, 2023; Sawyer, 2021).

Second, we urge practitioners to better support employees with complex trauma by adopting trauma-informed practices throughout the career lifecycle. Talented individuals with complex trauma should receive the resources needed to reach their full potential at work. For this reason, we believe that training recruiters, managers, and other decision-makers in trauma-informed methods (i.e., a set of practices that supports the success of those who have experienced trauma)—already implemented in educational settings (Thomas et al., 2019)—can improve outcomes for this population.

While future research might be conducted to evaluate the merit of our recommendations, we do have several ideas. Regarding recruitment, organizations can train recruiters to recognize signs of self-doubt in candidates and provide encouragement to motivate them to apply, instead of viewing their doubts as a sign of incompetence. Furthermore, instead of leveraging intimidating or competitive tactics (i.e., those that emphasize how challenging it is to obtain a job in a particular organization, or how prestigious it is to work there), highlighting how some employees have gotten ahead in unconventional ways (e.g., with unrelated backgrounds or from less advantaged backgrounds) might give hope to those already immersed in self-doubt. In selection, providing clear explanations of the selection process and how candidates can best prepare may help those with complex trauma better anticipate and participate in the selection processes. Furthermore, removing unnecessarily stressful components from selection processes and offering stress reduction tips may help job candidates manage anxiety in the process. In performance management, when delivering negative feedback, ensuring that it is constructive, and balanced with more positive feedback, may garner more positive reactions. Having direct conversations about the intentionality behind negative feedback (i.e., to provide an opportunity to achieve one's full potential, as opposed to conveying that an employee does not have the talents or skills to be successful in the long term) may decrease suspicions and stave off diminishments in trust. Finally, in training and development, providing greater resources for co-crafted learning and development plans may be particularly valuable in this population.

Conclusion

Overall, we believe that scholars and practitioners alike could do more to explore and support the needs and desires of employees who have experienced complex trauma. We hope that this chapter serves as a starting point for a much-needed (in our view) dialogue about how to create more inclusive environments for those who have repeatedly faced some of life's toughest challenges.

References

Alessi, E. J., & Kahn, S. (2023). Toward a trauma-informed qualitative research approach: Guidelines for ensuring the safety and promoting the resilience of research participants. *Qualitative Research in Psychology*, *20*(1), 121–154. https://doi.org/10.1080/14780887.2022.2107967

American Psychological Association. (2018). Trauma. In *APA dictionary of psychology*. https://dictionary.apa.org/trauma

Belschak, F. D., & Den Hartog, D. N. (2009). Consequences of positive and negative feedback: The impact on emotions and extra-role behaviors. *Applied Psychology*, *58*(2), 274–303. https://doi.org/10.1111/j.1464-0597.2008.00336.x

Breaugh, J. A. (2013). Employee recruitment. *Annual Review of Psychology*, *64*(1), 389–416. https://doi.org/10.1146/annurev-psych-113011-143757

Brewin, C. R., Cloitre, M., Hyland, P., Shevlin, M., Maercker, A., Bryant, R. A.,. . .& Reed, G. M. (2017). A review of current evidence regarding the ICD-11 proposals for diagnosing PTSD and complex PTSD. *Clinical Psychology Review*, *58*, 1–15. https://doi.org/10.1016/j.cpr.2017.09.001

Briere, J., & Scott, C. (2012). *Principles of trauma therapy: A guide to symptoms, evaluation, and treatment*. Sage Publications.

Briere, J., & Scott, C. (2015). Complex trauma in adolescents and adults: Effects and treatment. *Psychiatric Clinics*, *38*(3), 515–527. https://doi.org/10.1016/j.psc.2015.05.004

Calhoun, L. G., & Tedeschi, R. G. (2014). The foundations of posttraumatic growth: An expanded framework. In L. G. Calhoun & R. G. Tedeschi (Eds.), *Handbook of posttraumatic growth* (pp. 3–23). Routledge.

Carter, R. T. (2007). Racism and psychological and emotional injury: Recognizing and assessing race-based traumatic stress. *The Counseling Psychologist, 35*(1), 13–105. https://doi.org/10.1177/0011000006292033

Causadias, J. M., & Umaña-Taylor, A. J. (2018). Reframing marginalization and youth development: Introduction to the special issue. *American Psychologist, 73*(6), 707–712. https://doi.org/10.1037/amp0000336

Charmaz, K. (2013). Grounded theory methods in social justice research. In N. K. Denzin & Y. S. Lincoln (Eds.), *Strategies of qualitative inquiry* (pp. 359–380). Sage Publications.

Conroy, S. A., & O'Leary-Kelly, A. M. (2014). Letting go and moving on: Work-related identity loss and recovery. *Academy of Management Review, 39*(1), 67–87. https://doi.org/10.5465/amr.2011.0396

Cook, A., Spinazzola, J., Ford, J., Lanktree, C., Blaustein, M., Cloitre, M., & Van der Kolk, B. (2005). Complex trauma. *Psychiatric Annals, 35*(5), 390–398. https://doi.org/10.3928/00485713-20050501-05

Courtois, C. A. (2008). Complex trauma, complex reactions: Assessment and treatment. *Psychological Trauma: Theory, Research, Practice, and Policy*, S(1), 86–100. https://doi.org/10.1037/1942-9681.S.1.86

Crittenden, P. M., & Heller, M. B. (2017). The roots of chronic posttraumatic stress disorder: Childhood trauma, information processing, and self-protective strategies. *Chronic Stress, 1*, 1–13. https://doi.org/10.1177/2470547016682965

Deitz, M. F., Williams, S. L., Rife, S. C., & Cantrell, P. (2015). Examining cultural, social, and self-related aspects of stigma in relation to sexual assault and trauma symptoms. *Violence against Women, 21*(5), 598–615. https://doi.org/10.1177/1077801215573330

DeNisi, A. S., & Murphy, K. R. (2017). Performance appraisal and performance management: 100 years of progress? *Journal of Applied Psychology, 102*(3), 421–433. https://doi.org/10.1037/apl0000085

Dunning, D. (2007). The inside view. In A. W. Kruglanski & E. T. Higgins (Eds.). *Social psychology, second edition: Handbook of basic principles* (pp. 69–90). New York: Guildford.

Eagle, G., & Kaminer, D. (2013). Continuous traumatic stress: Expanding the lexicon of traumatic stress. *Peace and Conflict: Journal of Peace Psychology, 19*(2), 85–99. https://doi.org/10.1037/a0032485

Earnest, D. R., Allen, D. G., & Landis, R. S. (2011). Mechanisms linking realistic job previews with turnover: A meta-analytic path analysis. *Personnel Psychology, 64*(4), 865–897. https://doi.org/10.1111/j.1744-6570.2011.01230.x

Galinsky, A. D., Maddux, W. W., Gilin, D., & White, J. B. (2008). Why it pays to get inside the head of your opponent: The differential effects of perspective taking and empathy in negotiations. *Psychological Science, 19*(4), 378–384. https://doi.org/10.1111/j.1467-9280.2008.02096.x

Haynie, J. M., & Shepherd, D. (2011). Toward a theory of discontinuous career transition: Investigating career transitions necessitated by traumatic life events. *Journal of Applied Psychology, 96*(3), 501–524. https://doi.org/10.1037/a0021450

Henson, C., Truchot, D., & Canevello, A. (2021). What promotes post traumatic growth? A systematic review. *European Journal of Trauma & Dissociation, 5*(4), 100195. https://doi.org/10.1016/j.ejtd.2020.100195

Herman, J. L. (1992). Complex PTSD: A syndrome in survivors of prolonged and repeated trauma. *Journal of Traumatic Stress, 5*(3), 377–391. https://doi.org/10.1002/jts.2490050305

Ibarra, H. (1995). Race, opportunity, and diversity of social circles in managerial networks. *Academy of Management Journal*, *38*(3), 673–703. https://doi.org/10.5465/256742
Kira, I. A., Lewandowski, L., Templin, T., Ramaswamy, V., Ozkan, B., & Mohanesh, J. (2008). Measuring cumulative trauma dose, types, and profiles using a development-based taxonomy of traumas. *Traumatology*, *14*(2), 62–87. https://doi.org/10.1177/1534765608319324
Lang, K., & Spitzer, A. K. L. (2020). Race discrimination: An economic perspective. *Journal of Economic Perspectives*, *34*(2), 68–89. https://doi.org/10.1257/jep.34.2.68
Leslie, L. M., Flynn, E., Foster-Gimbel, O. A., & Manchester, C. F. (2024). Happy talk: Is common diversity rhetoric effective diversity rhetoric? *Academy of Management Journal*, *67*(3), 595–624. https://doi.org/10.5465/amj.2021.1402
Leymann, H., & Gustafsson, A. (1996). Mobbing at work and the development of post-traumatic stress disorders. *European Journal of Work and Organizational Psychology*, *5*(2), 251–275. https://doi.org/10.1080/13594329608414858
Maitlis, S. (2009). Who am I now?: Sensemaking and identity in posttraumatic growth. In L. M. Roberts & J. Dutton (Eds.), *Exploring positive identities and organizations* (pp. 47–76). Psychology Press.
Maitlis, S. (2020). Posttraumatic growth at work. *Annual Review of Organizational Psychology and Organizational Behavior*, *7*(1), 395–419. https://doi.org/10.1146/annurev-orgpsych-012119-044932
Maitlis, S. (2022). Rupture and reclamation in the life story: The role of early relationships in self-narratives following a forced career transition. *Organizational Behavior and Human Decision Processes*, *169*, 104115. https://doi.org/10.1016/j.obhdp.2021.104115
Matthiesen, S. B., & Einarsen, S. (2004). Psychiatric distress and symptoms of PTSD among victims of bullying at work. *British Journal of Guidance & Counselling*, *32*(3), 335–356. https://doi.org/10.1080/03069880410001723558
Neblett, E. W., Jr. (2019). Racism and health: Challenges and future directions in behavioral and psychological research. *Cultural Diversity & Ethnic Minority Psychology*, *25*(1), 12–20. https://doi.org/10.1037/cdp0000253
Pitman, R. K., Rasmusson, A. M., Koenen, K. C., Shin, L. M., Orr, S. P., Gilbertson, M. W., Milad, M. R., & Liberzon, I. (2012). Biological studies of post-traumatic stress disorder. *Nature Reviews Neuroscience*, *13*(11), 769–787. https://doi.org/10.1038/nrn3339
Pressley, J., & Spinazzola, J. (2020). *Coping strategies for complex trauma survivors contending with the coronavirus (COVID-19) pandemic*. https://www.complextrauma.org/wp-content/uploads/2020/04/Complex-Trauma-Resource-9-Joseph-Spinazzola.pdf.
Proost, K., Derous, E., Schreurs, B., Hagtvet, K. A., & De Witte, K. (2008). Selection Test Anxiety: Investigating applicants' self-vs other-referenced anxiety in a real selection setting. *International Journal of Selection and Assessment*, *16*(1), 14–26. https://doi.org/10.1111/j.1468-2389.2008.00405.x
Rodgers, R., & Hunter, J. E. (1991). Impact of management by objectives on organizational productivity. *Journal of Applied Psychology*, *76*(2), 322–336. https://doi.org/10.1037/0021-9010.76.2.322
Sar, V., & Ozturk, E. (2005). What is trauma and dissociation? In G. F. Rhoades Jr. & V. Sar (Eds.), *Trauma and dissociation in a cross-cultural perspective* (pp. 7–20). Routledge.
Sawyer, K. (2021). When objectivity is out of reach: Learnings from conducting research with commercially sexually exploited women. *Academy of Management Perspectives*, *35*(3), 367–383. https://doi.org/10.5465/amp.2018.0088
Seabrook, J. A., & Avison, W. R. (2012). Socioeconomic status and cumulative disadvantage processes across the life course: Implications for health outcomes. *Canadian Review of Sociology*, *49*(1), 50–68. https://doi.org/10.1111/j.1755-618X.2011.01280.x

Sonnentag, S., Niessen, C., & Ohly, S. (2004). Learning at work: Training and development. In C. L. Cooper & I. T. Robertson (Eds.), *International review of industrial and organizational psychology volume 19* (pp. 249–290). John Wiley & Sons.

Tedeschi, R. G., & Calhoun, L. G. (2004). Posttraumatic growth: Conceptual foundations and empirical evidence. *Psychological Inquiry*, *15*(1), 1–18. https://doi.org/10.1207/s15327965pli1501_01

Thomas, M. S., Crosby, S., & Vanderhaar, J. (2019). Trauma-informed practices in schools across two decades: An interdisciplinary review of research. *Review of Research in Education*, *43*(1), 422–452. https://doi.org/10.3102/0091732X18821123

Thoroughgood, C. N., Sawyer, K. B., & Webster, J. R. (2020). Finding calm in the storm: A daily investigation of how trait mindfulness buffers against paranoid cognition and emotional exhaustion following perceived discrimination at work. *Organizational Behavior and Human Decision Processes*, *159*, 49–63. https://doi.org/10.1016/j.obhdp.2019.02.004

Van Nieuwenhove, K., & Meganck, R. (2019). Interpersonal features in complex trauma etiology, consequences, and treatment: A literature review. *Journal of Aggression, Maltreatment & Trauma*, *28*(8), 903–928. https://doi.org/10.1080/10926771.2017.1405316

Vough, H. C., & Caza, B. B. (2017). Where do I go from here? Sensemaking and the construction of growth-based stories in the wake of denied promotions. *Academy of Management Review*, *42*(1), 103–128. https://doi.org/10.5465/amr.2013.0177

Warr, P., & Downing, J. (2000). Learning strategies, learning anxiety and knowledge acquisition. *British journal of Psychology*, *91*(3), 311–333. https://doi.org/10.1348/000712600161853

Westerman, G., & Lundberg, A. (2023). Why Companies Should Help Every Employee Chart a Career Path. *MIT Sloan Management Review*, *64*(3), 79–84. https://doi.org/10.1348/000712600161853

Wilk, S. L., & Sackett, P. R. (1996). Longitudinal analysis of ability-job complexity fit and job change. *Personnel Psychology*, *49*(4), 937–967. https://doi.org/10.1111/j.1744-6570.1996.tb02455.x

Yehuda, R., Hoge, C. W., McFarlane, A. C., Vermetten, E., Lanius, R. A., Nievergelt, C. M., Hobfall, S. E., Koenen, K. C., Neylan, T. C., & Hyman, S. E. (2015). Posttraumatic stress disorder. *Nature Reviews Disease Primers*, *1*(15057), 1–22. https://doi.org/10.1038/nrdp.2015.57

Section IV

Psychological Hazards in Unique Contexts

11 Addressing Mental Health Challenges in High-Risk Occupations

An Organizational Imperative

Thomas W. Britt, Emma C. Vosika, and Sarah D. Meyer

The importance of employee mental health and well-being has been recognized at an unprecedented level in the past years in the popular press and in the disciplines of organizational psychology and organizational behavior. Organizational scientists, both researchers and practitioners, have emphasized the important role played by the organization and leaders of organizations in the mental health and well-being of employees, with some arguing that well-being or optimal functioning should be the "ultimate criterion" studied by organizational scientists (Tay et al., 2023). Although the mental health and well-being of employees are important to examine in all occupations (see Kelloway et al., 2023), employees who routinely work under high levels of exposure to different types of stressors are especially at risk for the development of mental health problems. Given that organizations know employees in high-risk occupations are going to encounter potentially traumatic events and high levels of operational stressors during their work, leaders of those organizations bear an increased responsibility for putting mechanisms in place that have been shown to blunt the negative impact of work demands and help employees who develop mental health concerns.

This chapter is devoted to better understanding the mental health challenges faced by employees in high-risk occupations and the role the organization plays in addressing these challenges. The chapter will first address the determination of which occupations are at higher risk for mental health problems and the evidence for the prevalence of mental health challenges in these occupations compared to other employee samples. Given the known mental health challenges in these occupations, the chapter then includes a discussion of the responsibility these organizations have for adopting a multi-pronged approach to address these concerns. Figure 11.1 highlights the strategies that will be discussed, including (1) reducing controllable demands and improving recovery; (2) equipping employees with the skills needed to address adversity through resilience training; (3) creating an organizational climate supportive of mental health and the treatment of mental health problems; (4) proactively treating early warning signs of poor mental health; and (5) allowing time away from work for mental health

DOI: 10.4324/9781003491170-15

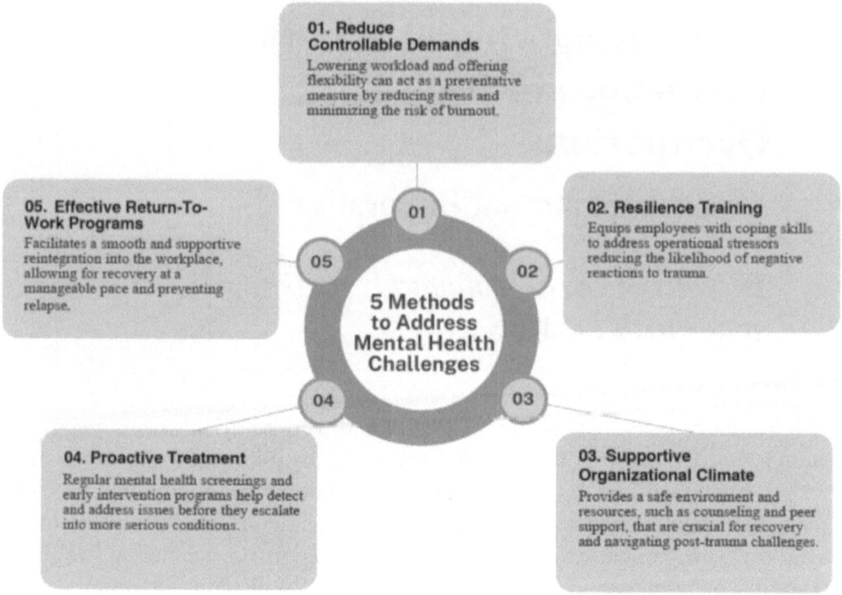

Figure 11.1 Five Strategies for Addressing Mental Health Challenges for Employees in High-Risk Occupations.

concerns and establishing effective return-to-work programs following mental health treatment.

High-Risk Occupations: Stressors and Mental Health Concerns

The term "high-risk occupation" is often utilized with the implicit understanding that these types of occupations are more likely to involve exposure to highly stressful and even traumatic events. Prototypical examples of high-risk occupations include military personnel, firefighters, police officers, emergency medical services employees, and healthcare professionals working in emergency settings. Employees working in these occupations are more likely to be exposed to traumatic events such as witnessing death and destruction, being in physical danger that could result in the employee's own death, and at times being helpless to intervene to prevent adverse outcomes (Britt & McFadden, 2012; Hoge et al., 2004; Sørensen et al., 2022). Consider emergency medicine professionals during the height of the COVID-19 pandemic who were required to decide which patients received ventilators versus those who did not and therefore died, or the firefighter who witnesses a child who died because of a house fire. Another recent example from 2024 involved first responders who were working at the Texas-Mexico border and witnessed parents drowning or being trapped and separated from their children (Chesky & Lozano, 2024).

Although traumatic events are clearly the most visible workplace experiences most associated with high-risk occupations, occupations can also be high risk if they are associated with pervasive exposure to less intense but nevertheless harmful stressors, including high workload and work hours, low control over demands and few resources, and financial concerns as a result of low pay, poor job security, or high debt associated with the profession (Parrish Meadows et al., 2011). For example, being an attorney would be considered a high-risk occupation given the intense and continuous workload required to be promoted and continually work for the firm (Eaton et al., 1990). Migrant workers also work long and unpredictable hours and must deal with the additional demands associated with their immigration status (Satyen & Becerra, 2022). Construction workers would be considered high risk given that in addition to the physical risks associated with the job, work is often uncertain, raising concerns about economic security (Liang et al., 2022). Jobs that pay poorly, such as childcare workers, fast food employees, and entry-level medical technicians, are also at heightened risk of mental health concerns as a function of poor financial security (Kiely et al., 2015).

Although organizational scholars have not settled on a definitive list of those occupations characterized by a greater risk for mental health problems, researchers have provided justification for why employees of a given occupation are at risk. These justifications specify the work demands employees in these occupations experience, with the demands varying in frequency, severity, and intensity. For example, Laditka et al. (2023) broke occupations into those that were characterized by low versus high risk for elevated risk based on the number of hours worked, the predictability of those hours, salary, and amount of control. As will be seen later in the chapter, understanding the nature of the adversity that employees face is important for reducing those demands that can be controlled and equipping employees to address those intractable demands that will be encountered during their work.

Given the various stressors present in high-risk occupations, it is not surprising that the prevalence of mental health problems in these occupations is greater than that of the general population. Studies examining mental health problems and concerns among employees in high-risk occupations typically examine whether employees exceed the threshold for a mental health problem according to diagnostic criteria, or report having symptoms of a mental health problem. Britt and McFadden (2012) reviewed evidence indicating that the prevalence of mental health problems was higher in military personnel, firefighters, police officers, and journalists covering combat operations. Laditka et al. (2023) found that employees in high-risk occupations were 20% more likely to develop significant distress as assessed by the Screening Scale for Psychological Distress (Kessler K6).

Prior research has identified numerous examples of specific occupations being at greater risk of mental health problems compared to other employees or the general population. Brandhorst and Compton (2022) noted that correctional officers, who experience chronic low-level stressors as well as traumatic stressors associated with witnessing violence, have a 39% greater suicide rate than employees from other occupations. A third or more of these officers also reported specific symptoms associated with PTSD and depression. Connolly et al. (2022) also reviewed evidence indicating that veterinary professionals in Austrasia have higher levels of depression, anxiety, stress, and burnout than the general population, presumably as a function of high workload and emotional labor, and low work–life balance. Schabram and Maitlis (2017) also pointed out that animal shelter workers experience increased demands, including high levels of euthanizing animals and exposure to animals who have been selected. Further back, Eaton et al. (1990) found support for attorneys having 3.6 greater odds of screening positive for major depression compared to other occupations. In addition to the primary effects of these mental health problems for the employee, secondary effects are often observed in terms of spousal abuse, divorce, and mental health problems for children (Britt & McFadden, 2012).

In summary, a large body of research suggests that employees in high-risk occupations, characterized by repeated exposure to stressors varying in severity, frequency, intensity, or duration, are at greater risk of developing mental health problems and concerns in comparison to employees in other occupations or the broader population. Furthermore, researchers have often characterized the demands in specific occupations that are hypothesized to be responsible for the higher rate of mental health problems or concerns. Given the extent of research supporting higher rates of mental health problems in high-risk occupations, as well as the secondary effects of mental health problems on such issues as domestic violence and divorce, organizational leaders bear responsibility for a multi-pronged approach to address mental health challenges in these occupations (see Figure 11.1). The linking of occupational demands to documented mental health problems among employees in high-risk occupations should reduce any temptation to hold the employees themselves as being responsible for the development of mental health problems in these high-stress occupational settings.

Reduce Controllable Demands and Improve Recovery

Given the likelihood of traumatic or frequent stressors for employees in high-risk occupations, it is critical for organizations to both reduce the controllable stressors facing employees and provide the necessary time for employees to recover from their work. Occupational health psychologists have emphasized the importance of primary prevention in organizational stress interventions, where the demands facing employees are reduced whenever possible (Kelloway et al., 2023). Unfortunately, organizational stress interventions rarely involve reducing the demands facing employees (Richardson & Rothstein, 2008). This is especially the case in high-risk occupations, where the nature of the work performed means employees being exposed to uncontrollable stressors. Consider healthcare professionals working within the context of a pandemic. Stressors such as an extremely high workload and potential exposure to the virus are inherent in the work performed (Britt et al., 2021). Given these inherent demands, organizations need to reduce those demands facing employees that can be addressed. For example, in the healthcare context, organizations can reduce demands such as lack of information and critical supplies by ensuring constant updates on the status of situation and ensuring that healthcare professionals have all the equipment and supplies needed to address different crises (National Academies of Sciences, 2019).

In addition to reducing controllable demands through primary prevention, organizational leaders also need to ensure that employees can recover from the uncontrollable demands they experience. Sonnentag et al. (2022) summarized extensive research showing the importance of both within-the-workday and between-workdays recovery for employees dealing with different types of organizational stressors. Recovery is especially important for employees in high-risk occupations exposed to traumatic or chronic stressors. Within military settings, removing service members from the battlefield for rest and restoration has long been recognized as an effective strategy for addressing mental health symptoms caused by exposure to traumatic stressors (Lamberg, 2004). Within the context of healthcare settings, emergency medicine professionals are often unable to take breaks during their shifts as a function of high levels of patient load (Klinefelter et al., 2023). Therefore, hospital administrators need to ensure sufficient time between shifts so that emergency medicine professionals can recover from the periods of high-intensity workload and therefore not experience a continuous loss of resources to deal with workplace demands, which will likely result in burnout and other mental health problems (Hobfoll et al., 2018).

Resilience Training to Maximize Adaptation Under Adversity

Given the degree of adversity facing employees in high-risk occupations, it is critical to train employees so they will be able to respond to the work-related stressors they will encounter in as adaptive a way as possible. Researchers generally use the term "resilience training" to refer to training that is designed to equip employees with the skills they will need to respond positively to adversity they are likely to encounter (Sarkar & Fletcher, 2017). Although meta-analyses have revealed that resilience training has beneficial effects on some indicators of functioning (e.g., Brassington & Lomas, 2021; Vanhove et al., 2016), most studies do not examine whether resilience training prior to significant adversity predicts a significant improvement in functioning following high levels of adversity. Studies also vary in the extent to which resilience training considers the unique adversity likely to be encountered in the high-risk occupation, as well as the specific resources and skills that need to be targeted for training.

Brassington and Lomas (2021) provided a systematic review of research on resilience training in high-risk occupations. They asserted that resilience training is generally beneficial for individuals in high-risk occupations. The closer resilience training is tailored to the specific needs of a given population and the timelier (i.e., closeness to a current or near-future event) its delivery, the greater its effectiveness in enhancing overall well-being. However, resilience training might be less effective for individuals who have already experienced the sequelae of trauma and may not be universally applicable to all employees in high-risk occupations (Crane et al., 2019; Hourani et al., 2016; Hoyt et al., 2018; Roy et al., 2017). Brassington and Lomas (2021) argued that some forms of resilience training may not benefit high-risk populations. For example, stress inoculation training (SIT), which involves exposing employees to less severe versions of workplace stressors so they may develop coping strategies, may be more beneficial and effective for workers *without* prior exposure to adverse events or PTSD (Hourani et al., 2016). Psychological skills training for coping with stressors may also not provide any benefit beyond PTSD-specific care (Hoyt et al., 2018) and may result in an initial worsening of PTSD symptoms before seeing any improvement (Roy et al., 2017). Finally, training designed to guide coping with work-related stressors may provide benefit to workers already experiencing the sequelae of trauma but requires a longer timeframe for results (Crane et al., 2019).

Ketelaars et al. (2024) conducted a systematic literature review on resilience training among employees involved in critical situation management (e.g., special forces soldiers, police investigators, and healthcare professionals) and concluded that the majority of resilience training research has focused on training people to deal with more long-term negative stress, as opposed to performing well in the particular critical situation. They suggested that this focus is unsatisfactory for managing critical situations such as those faced by high-risk occupations (e.g., triaging patients in an overwhelmed hospital during the COVID-19 pandemic). The authors argued that resilience should be regarded as a situated capability, influenced by the circumstances and environment of the work context, rather than a general capability. More specifically, they suggested a shift to focus on resilience in action, where resilience is both situated and situational (i.e., focusing on the contextual nature of resilience). Essentially, Ketelaars et al. (2024) suggest that future researchers and practitioners should focus on developing resilience training interventions that target real critical situations management. High-risk populations are unique, and so their resilience and other stress/health training should be tailored accordingly.

In summary, although resilience training has been shown to have some beneficial effects among employees in high-risk occupations, the extent to which such training protects employees from the level of adversity encountered is unclear. Furthermore, it is important to recognize the potential dark side of focusing on resilience and resilience training within high-risk occupations, as such an emphasis may communicate that employees are expected to demonstrate resilience no matter what level of adversity they encounter (Adler, 2013; Britt et al.,

2016b). Given the lack of longitudinal research demonstrating the effectiveness of resilience training for employees exposed to high levels of adversity, such training should be provided within the context of an overall organizational effort to improve the psychological health of employees and to ensure that employees who struggle receive help to address their mental health concerns.

Creating an Organizational Climate Supportive of Mental Health and Treatment Seeking

Given the exposure to traumatic and accumulated non-traumatic stressors found in high-risk occupations, an organizational culture supportive of mental health and seeking treatment for mental health concerns is critically important. At the broadest level, organizations should create a positive Psychosocial Safety Climate (PSC) surrounding the psychological health of employees. Dollard and Bakker (2010) referred to PSC as shared perception among employees of the "policies, procedures and practices for the protection of workers' psychological health and safety" (Dollard & Bakker, 2010, p. 580). A positive PSC communicates to employees that their psychological health matters and the organization will put policies in place to protect the mental health of employees. In addition to a broad focus on the importance of psychological health, Britt et al. (2020) argued that organizations should also develop a positive Climate of Support for Mental Health (CSMH), which refers to recognizing the development of mental health problems among fellow employees, supporting employees as they receive mental health treatment, and refraining from negative comments that stigmatize treatment seeking. Substantial research has shown that employees in organizations with greater support for psychological health report higher organizational commitment and well-being, as well as lower mental health symptoms (Lawrie et al., 2018). Please see Deane et al. (this volume) for an example of an organization developing a psychologically healthy climate.

In high-risk occupations, organizations can create a positive climate for psychological health and support for treatment seeking through recognizing the negative effects of exposure to stressors and normalizing the treatment of mental health problems before they become severe. Unfortunately, employees in many high-risk occupations are hesitant to even disclose mental health problems, let alone receive treatment for these difficulties. In a study of public service personnel including correctional workers, dispatchers, firefighters, paramedics, and police, Carleton et al. (2020) found employees would only access professional support or talk to a supervisor for mental health problems as a last resort. This finding seems consistent with other literature in reflecting a reluctance to disclose mental illness or utilize professional resources among public safety personnel (see also Newell et al., 2022). Reasons for not seeking help include the perceived stigma of mental health problems, negative attitudes toward mental health treatment, and practical barriers associated with navigating the process of receiving mental health treatment (Britt et al., 2016a; Carleton et al., 2020; Newell et al., 2022; Rutherford et al., 2023; Toth & Dewa, 2014). These concerns about treatment seeking are likely exacerbated among employees in high-risk occupations, given the expectations for resilience and employees not wanting to let their fellow team members down (Britt & McFadden, 2012).

Researchers have discussed a number of organizational interventions to improve the climate for mental health concerns and treatment seeking in high-risk occupations, including removing barriers to treatment, training supervisors to be more supportive of employees, and training employees to recognize mental health concerns in their peers. In their study of police officers, Newell et al. (2022) found that officers wanted greater confidentiality of treatment (e.g., separate entrances and exits), more convenient ways of accessing care (e.g., through phone apps), and easier ways to understand the resources available and processes for utilizing these resources. These include screening tools to help officers identify their mental health concerns, lists of resources covered by insurance, and simplified tools for booking appointments.

Related to these recommendations, Fragala and colleagues (2023) found success in the implementation of a "concierge service" to help connect employees with mental health services, used in combination with proactive mental health screening for employees. In comparison to a control condition, those employees who utilized the concierge service were more likely to obtain mental health services six months later. Proactively reaching out to employees in need through such a concierge service takes responsibility for finding help away from the employee, which should increase the likelihood that employees in high-risk occupations will receive the treatment they need. This type of service would be especially important for employees in high-risk occupations, as the demands experienced in the workplace likely provide employees with less time for negotiating the process of obtaining treatment for their mental health concerns.

In addition to removing barriers to treatment seeking, organizations should also train leaders and supervisors in how to better support employees who are struggling. Dimoff and Kelloway (2019a) developed supervisor training focused on recognizing mental health problems among employees, knowing how to respond to struggling employees, connecting employees with available resources, and helping employees navigate being away from work for mental health treatment and then returning to work once treatment was over. Although not involving supervisors and employees from high-risk occupations, the authors did find that compared to a randomly assigned control group, employees of leaders in the training condition reported that their leaders shared more information and resources related to mental health and encouraged them to utilize these resources. In addition, employees of leaders in the training condition indicated a greater willingness to actually examine and utilize these resources.

Examining the high-risk occupation of military personnel, Mohr, Hammer, and their colleagues trained unit leaders on how to better support their soldiers who were showing signs of mental health problems (Hammer et al., 2024; Mohr et al., 2024). Compared to a control group that did not receive the training, soldiers of leaders who received the training reported their leaders as performing more supportive behaviors related to mental health. Soldiers in the leader treatment condition also reported lower amounts of anger and loneliness in comparison to those in the control conditions. The results of these studies suggest that leaders can be trained to be more supportive of the mental health concerns shown by their employees.

In addition to training supervisors and leaders, organizational scientists have also developed mental health training programs, such as Mental Health First Aid, for all employees (see Kelloway et al., 2023). Although studies show that these programs are generally effective at improving mental health literacy and efficacy in helping others (Kitchener & Jorm, 2004; Wulf, 2022), the effects on the mental health of employees are lacking (Richardson et al., 2023). In terms of the effectiveness of these types of programs in high-risk occupations, Sayers et al. (2019) examined a peer support mental health intervention among coal miners and found that while help-seeking behavior increased following training, employees still felt that the disclosure of mental health problems to friends or colleagues would be met with stigma. Britt et al. (2018a) examined unit training to increase support for military personnel struggling with mental health problems. Compared to a no-training control group, three months following the training, those soldiers receiving the training reported more supportive behaviors toward fellow unit members struggling with mental health problems.

In summary, numerous studies have emphasized the importance of organizational climates that support mental health seeking treatment for mental health problems, as they impact the overall mental health of the organization and the likelihood that employees will seek necessary treatment. Interventions are available to improve the climate of support for psychological health, but more research is needed on changing the climate among employees who work in high-risk occupations.

Proactive Treatment Upon Early Warning Signs of Poor Mental Health

Given the known potential for the experience of mental health concerns among employees in high-risk occupations, organizational leaders need to be prepared for their employees to show signs they are struggling with the demands they are facing in the workplace. Dimoff and Kelloway (2019b) developed a structured measure to help managers and others identify when employees were struggling with mental health concerns. The Signs of Struggle questionnaire assesses employee distress, withdrawal behaviors, reduced attendance, decreases in job performance, and extreme behaviors such as suicidal ideation. The authors showed that peer ratings on these dimensions were highly correlated (r = .72) with employee self-ratings, indicating that peers are capable of picking up on when their fellow employees are struggling.

Getting employees help when their symptoms are relatively minor can help prevent symptoms from developing into more severe mental health problems (Bacharach & Bamberger, 2007; Bamberger, 2009). Britt et al. (2018b) examined military aviation personnel who experienced mental health problems, received treatment, and then applied for a waiver to return to flying status. The authors found that aviation personnel who sought treatment for an adjustment disorder (a less severe mental disorder) were more likely to be granted a waiver to return to duty in comparison to those who were diagnosed with more severe mental disorders, such as major depression or generalized anxiety disorder. Although organizations must still determine the most appropriate ways to monitor the mental health of their employees, encouraging employees to receive help for mental health concerns before they become severe ultimately benefits the employees themselves as well as the organization.

Time for Mental Health Treatment and Effective Return-to-Work Programs

Once employees have decided to get help for their mental health concerns, the organization needs to provide them with the necessary time to receive the treatment they need. Depending on the severity of the mental health concern, employees may be able to continue working while receiving mental health treatment, being provided time away from work as needed for therapy sessions. However, if the mental health problem is severe, employees may need to stop working altogether to have the problem addressed and then return to work ready to contribute to the mission of the organization (Blonk et al., 2006; Salomonsson et al., 2018). This may especially be the case if employees are being prescribed psychiatric medications, the side effects of which may interfere with work performance until the employee adjusts to the medication (Haslam et al., 2005; Knopf, 2014). Given the extent to which employees in high-risk occupations care about their work and team performance, it may be difficult for them to take time off work to get the help they need (Britt & McFadden, 2012). Organizational leaders need to emphasize the importance of making time for treatment for employees who are struggling and ensuring that the entire organization realizes that getting necessary help to address mental health difficulties ultimately increases the resilience of employees and the functioning of the team and organization (Britt & Jennings, 2017).

Although not necessarily involving employees in high-risk occupations, an emerging body of research has focused on interventions designed to improve the likelihood of returning to work among employees who are on sick leave for mental health problems. For example, Blonk et al. (2006) examined whether cognitive behavioral therapy with a focus on work-related issues was associated with a shorter time of returning to work among employees who were on leave from work for mental health problems. The authors found that compared to a control group, employees who had work-related issues integrated into therapy returned to work faster and had equivalent mental health symptoms. In a meta-analysis of 45 studies examining psychological interventions among employees who were on sick leave for mental health problems, Salomonsson et al. (2018) found that such interventions had a small but significant effect on the percentage of employees who were no longer on sick leave after the intervention. Interestingly, the type of psychological intervention (e.g., mental health therapy or work-related interventions) was not related to the outcome variables. Mental health treatment focused on a return to work is likely to be embraced by employees in high-risk occupations.

For those employees who take leave from work to receive mental health treatment, there is the important issue of those employees being supported when they return to work. Nielsen and Yarker (2023a, 2023b) have examined the experiences of employees who return to work following mental health treatment, including supervisor behaviors that make the transition back to work easier. Nielsen and Yarker (2023a) conducted interviews with employees in the months following their return from mental health treatment and found that employees made a more adaptive transition back to work when they had higher levels of social support from coworkers, more supportive supervisors, and a belief they were making a contribution to the organization. Nielsen and Yarker (2023b) conducted interviews with managers of employees returning to work from mental health treatment and found that managers felt their most beneficial behaviors involved effectively managing workload, being flexible regarding work arrangements, checking in regarding their employee's mental health status, and ensuring long-term social support for the employee.

Conclusion

Employees in high-risk occupations experience both high-intensity traumatic work events and chronic lower-intensity operational stressors. These workplace demands put these employees at greater risk of mental health problems. Organizational leaders bear responsibility for reducing controllable workplace demands, equipping employees to face adversity, creating a culture that supports psychological health, and encouraging the timely receipt of mental health treatment when problems are noticed. Leaders are also responsible for supporting employees during and following mental health treatment. Organizations and leaders taking a multi-pronged approach to addressing mental health concerns will ultimately reduce the mental health burden of employees in high-risk occupations, as well as improve the functioning of the overall organization.

References

Adler, A. B. (2013). Resilience in a military occupational health context: Directions for future research. In R. R. Sinclair & T. W. Britt (Eds.), *Building psychological resilience in military personnel: Theory and practice*. (pp. 223–235). American Psychological Association. https://doi.org.libproxy.clemson.edu/10.1037/14190-010.

Bacharach, S. B., & Bamberger, P. A. (2007). 9/11 and New York City firefighters' post hoc unit support and control climates: A context theory of the consequences of involvement in traumatic work-related events. *Academy of Management Journal*, *30*, 849–868. https://doi.org/10.5465/AMJ.2007.26279180

Bamberger, P. (2009). Employee help-seeking: Antecedents, consequences and new insights for future research. *Personnel and Human Resources Management*, *28*, 49–98. https://doi.org/10.1108/S0742-7301(2009)0000028005

Blonk, R. W. B., Brenninkmeijer, V., Lagerveld, S. E., & Houtman, I. L. D. (2006). Return to work: A comparison of two cognitive behavioural interventions in cases of work-related psychological complaints among the self-employed. *Work & Stress, 20,* 129–144. https://doi.org/10.1080/02678370600856615

Brandhorst, J. K., & Compton, C. A. (2022). Constructing barriers to Employee Assistance Program use by federal correctional officers. *Journal of Applied Communication Research*, *50*(5), 497–514.

Brassington, K., & Lomas, T. (2021). Can resilience training improve well-being for people in high-risk occupations? A systematic review through a multidimensional lens. *The Journal of Positive Psychology*, *16*(5), 573–592. https://doi.org.libproxy.clemson.edu/10.1080/17439760.2020.1752783

Britt, T. W., Adler, A. B., & Fynes, J. (2021). Perceived resilience and social connection as predictors of adjustment following occupational adversity. *Journal of Occupational Health Psychology*, *26*(4), 339–349. https://doi.org.libproxy.clemson.edu/10.1037/ocp0000286

Britt, T. W., & Jennings, K. S. (2017). Leadership and mental health treatment seeking in the workplace. In M. Crane (Ed.), *Workplaces that bounce back: A practical guide for managers seeking to build employee resilience* (pp. 71–85). Routledge. https://doi.org/10.4324/9781315648033–5

Britt, T. W., Jennings, K. S., Cheung, J. H., Pury, C. L. S., & Zinzow, H. M. (2018a). Unit training to increase support for military personnel with mental health problems. *Work & Stress*. https://doi.org/10.1080/02678373.2018.1445671

Britt, T. W., Jennings, K. S., Cheung, J. H., Pury, C. L. S., Zinzow, H. M., Raymond, M., & McFadden, A. C. (2016a). Determinants of mental health treatment seeking among soldiers who recognize their problem: Implications for high-risk occupations. *Work & Stress*, *40*, 318–336. https://doi.org/10.1080/02678373.2016.1246490

Britt, T. W., & McFadden, A. (2012). Understanding mental health treatment seeking in high stress occupations. In J. Houdmont, S. Leka, & R. Sinclair (Eds.), *Contemporary occupational health psychology: Global perspectives on research and practice* (pp. 57–73). Wiley-Blackwell Publishers. https://doi.org/10.1002/9781119942849.ch4

Britt, T. W., McGhee, J. S., & Quattlebaum, M. D. (2018b). Common mental disorders among U.S. Army aviation personnel: Prevalence and return to duty. *Journal of Clinical Psychology*, *74*, 2173–2186. https://doi.org/10.1002/jclp.22688

Britt, T. W., Shen, W., Sinclair, R. R., Grossman, M., & Klieger, D. (2016b). How much do we really know about employee resilience? *Industrial and Organizational Psychology: Perspectives on Science and Practice*, *9*, 378–404. https://doi.org/10.1017/iop.2015.107

Britt, T. W., Wilson, C. A., Sawhney, G., & Black, K. J. (2020). Perceived unit climate of support for mental health as a predictor of stigma, beliefs about treatment, and help-seeking behaviors. *Psychological Services*, *17*(2), 141–150. https://doi.org/10.1037/ser0000362.

Carleton, R. N., Afifi, T. O., Turner, S., Taillieu, T., Vaughan, A. D., Anderson, G. S., Ricciardelli, R., MacPhee, R. S., Cramm, H. A., Czarnuch, S., Hozempa, K., & Camp, R.

D. (2020). Mental health training, attitudes toward support, and screening positive for mental disorders. *Cognitive Behaviour Therapy*, *49*(1), 55–73. https://doi.org/10.1080/16506073.2019.1575900

Chesky, M., & Lozano, A. C. (2024, February 25). First responders in a Texas town are struggling to cope with the trauma of recovering bodies from the Rio Grande. *NBC News*. https://www.nbcnews.com/news/us-news/eagle-pass-texas-mexico-border-rio-grande-trauma-rcna138412

Connolly, C. E., Norris, K., Martin, A., Dawkins, S., & Meehan, C. (2022). A taxonomy of occupational and organisational stressors and protectors of mental health reported by veterinary professionals in Australasia. *Australian Veterinary Journal*, *100*(8), 367–376. https://doi.org/10.1111/avj.13167

Crane, M. F., Boga, D., Karin, E., Gucciardi, D. F., Rapport, F., Callen, J., & Sinclair, L. (2019). Strengthening resilience in military officer cadets: A group-randomized controlled trial of coping and emotion regulatory self-reflection training. *Journal of Consulting and Clinical Psychology*, *87*(2), 125–140. https://doi.org.libproxy.clemson.edu/10.1037/ccp0000356

Dimoff, J. K., & Kelloway, E. K. (2019a). With a little help from my boss: The impact of workplace mental health training on leader behaviors and employee resource utilization. *Journal of Occupational Health Psychology*, *24*(1), 4–19. https://doi.org/10.1037/ocp0000126

Dimoff, J. K., & Kelloway, E. K. (2019b). Signs of struggle (SOS): The development and validation of a behavioural mental health checklist for the workplace. *Work & Stress*, *33*(3), 295–313. https://doi.org/10.1080/02678373.2018.1503359

Dollard, M. F., & Bakker, A. B. (2010). Psychosocial safety climate as a precursor to conducive work environments, psychological health problems, and employee engagement. *Journal of Occupational and Organizational Psychology*, *83*, 579–599. https://doi.org/10.1348/096317909X470690

Eaton, W. W., Anthony, J. C., Mandel, W., & Garrison, R. (1990). Occupations and the prevalence of major depressive disorder. *Journal of Occupational and Environmental Medicine*, *32*(11), 1079–1087.

Fragala, M. S., Tong, C. H., Hunter, J. L., Jelovic, N. A., Hayward, J. I., Carr, S., Kim, P. M., Peters, M. E., & Birse, C. E. (2023). Facilitating mental health treatment through proactive screening and concierge services in the workplace. *Journal of Occupational and Environmental Medicine*, *65*(2), 160–166. https://doi.org/10.1097/JOM.0000000000002707

Hammer, L. B., Brockwood, K., Dimoff, J., Allen, S., Mohr, C., Dretsch, M., Lee, J., & Britt, T. W. (2024). Leadership training effects on service member problematic anger and well-being. *Military Medicine*, *189*(S3), 501–509. https://doi.org/10.1093/milmed/usae171

Haslam, C., Atkinson, S., Brown, S. S., & Haslam, R. A. (2005). Anxiety and depression in the workplace: Effects on the individual and organisation (a focus group investigation). *Journal of Affective Disorders*, *88*, 209–215. https://doi.org/10.1016/j.jad.2005.07.009

Hobfoll, S. E., Halbesleben, J., Neveu, J. P., & Westman, M. (2018). Conservation of resources in the organizational context: The reality of resources and their consequences. *Annual Review of Organizational Psychology and Organizational Behavior*, *5*, 103–128. https://doi.org/10.1146/annurev-orgpsych-032117-104640

Hoge, C. W., Castro, C. A., Messer, S. C., McGurk, D., Cotting, D. I., & Koffman, R. L. (2004). Combat duty in Iraq and Afghanistan, mental health problems, and barriers to care. *The New England Journal of Medicine*, *351*, 13–22. https://doi.org/10.1056/NEJMoa040603

Hourani, L., Tueller, S., Kizakevich, P., Lewis, G., Strange, L., Weimer, B., Bryant, S., Bishop, E., Hubal, R., & Spira, J. (2016). Toward preventing post-traumatic stress disorder: Development and testing of a pilot predeployment stress inoculation training program. *Military Medicine, 181*(9), 1151–1160. https://doi.org.libproxy.clemson.edu/10.7205/MILMED-D-15-00192

Hoyt, T., Barry, D., Kwon, S. H., Capron, C., De Guzman, N., Gilligan, J., & Edwards-Stewart, A. (2018). Preliminary evaluation of treatment outcomes at a military intensive outpatient program. *Psychological Services, 15*(4), 510.

Kelloway, E. K., Dimoff, J. K., & Gilbert, S. (2023). Mental health in the workplace. *Annual Review of Organizational Psychology and Organizational Behavior, 10*(1), 363–387. https://doi.org/10.1146/annurev-orgpsych-120920-050527

Ketelaars, E., Gaudin, C., Flandin, S., & Poizat, G. (2024). Resilience training for critical situation management. An umbrella and a systematic literature review. *Safety Science, 170*, 106311.

Kiely, K. M., Leach, L. S., Olesen, S. C., & Butterworth, P. (2015). How financial hardship is associated with the onset of mental health problems over time. *Social Psychiatry and Psychiatric Epidemiology, 50*, 909–918. https://doi.org/10.1007/s00127-015-1027-0

Kitchener, B. A., & Jorm, A. F. (2004). Mental health first aid training in a workplace setting: A randomized controlled trial [ISRCTN13249129]. *BMC Psychiatry, 4*. https://doi.org.libproxy.clemson.edu/10.1186/1471-244X-4-23

Klinefelter, Z., Hirsh, E., Britt, T. W., George, C. L., Sulzbach, M., & Fowler, L. A. (2023). Shift happens: Emergency physician perspectives on fatigue and shift work. *Clocks & Sleep, 5*, 234–248. https://doi.org/10.3390/clockssleep5020019

Knopf, A. (2014). Implement precision medicine right now: The trial-and-error method of selecting psychiatric medications is gradually being replaced by the precision of personalized medicine. *Behavioral Healthcare, 34*, 26–29.

Laditka, J. N., Laditka, S. B., Arif, A. A., & Adeyemi, O. J. (2023). Psychological distress is more common in some occupations and increases with job tenure: A thirty-seven year panel study in the United States. *BMC Psychology, 11*(1), 95. https://doi.org/10.1186/s40359-023-01119-0

Lamberg, L. (2004). Military psychiatrists strive to quell soldiers' nightmares of war. *JAMA: Journal of the American Medical Association, 292*(13), 1539–1540. https://doi.org/10.1001/jama.292.13.1539

Lawrie, E. J., Tuckey, M. R., & Dollard, M. F. (2018). Job design for mindful work: The boosting effect of psychosocial safety climate. *Journal of Occupational Health Psychology, 23*(4), 483–495. https://doi.org/10.1037/ocp0000102

Liang, Q., Zhou, Z., Ye, G., & Shen, L. (2022). Unveiling the mechanism of construction workers' unsafe behaviors from an occupational stress perspective: A qualitative and quantitative examination of a stress–cognition–safety model. *Safety Science, 145*. https://doi.org/10.1016/j.ssci.2021.105486

Mohr, C., Hammer, L., Dimoff, J., Allen, S., Lee, J., Arpin, S., McCabe, S., Brockwood, K., Bodner, T., Mahoney, L., Dretsch, M., & Britt, T. W. (2024). Supportive-leadership training to improve social connection: A cluster-randomized trial demonstrating efficacy in a high-risk occupational context. *Journal of Occupational Health Psychology*. Advance online publication. https://doi.org/10.1037/ocp0000384

National Academies of Sciences, National Academy of Medicine, & Committee on Systems Approaches to Improve Patient Care by Supporting Clinician Well-Being. (2019). *Taking action against clinician burnout: A systems approach to professional well-being*. https://doi.org/10.17226/25521

Newell, C. J., Ricciardelli, R., Czarnuch, S. M., & Martin, K. (2022). Police staff and mental health: Barriers and recommendations for improving help-seeking. *Police Practice and Research, 23*(1), 111–124. https://doi.org/10.1080/15614263.2021.1979398

Nielsen, K., & Yarker, J. (2023a). Thrivers, survivors or exiteers: A longitudinal, interpretative phenomenological analysis of the post-return-to-work journeys for workers with common mental disorders. *Applied Psychology: An International Review*. https://doi.org/10.1111/apps.12479

Nielsen, K., & Yarker, J. (2023b). What can I do for you? Line managers' behaviors to support return to work for workers with common mental disorders. *Journal of Managerial Psychology*, *38*(1), 34–46. https://doi.org/10.1108/JMP-09-2021-0500

Parrish Meadows, M., Shreffler, K. M., & Mullins-Sweatt, S. N. (2011). Occupational stressors and resilience in critical occupations: The role of personality. In *The role of individual differences in occupational stress and well being* (pp. 39–61). Emerald Group Publishing Limited.

Richardson, K. M., & Rothstein, H. R. (2008). Effects of occupational stress management intervention programs: A meta-analysis. *Journal of Occupational Health Psychology*, *13*, 69–93. https://doi.org/10.1037/1076-8998.13.1.69

Richardson, R., Dale, H. E., Robertson, L., Meader, N., Wellby, G., McMillan, D., & Churchill, R. (2023). Mental Health First Aid as a tool for improving mental health and well-being. *Cochrane Database of Systematic Reviews*, (8). https://doi.org/10.1002/14651858.CD013127.pub2

Roy, M. J., Costanzo, M. E., Highland, K. B., Olsen, C., Clayborne, D., & Law, W. (2017). An app a day keeps the doctor away: Guided education and training via smartphones in subthreshold post traumatic stress disorder. *Cyberpsychology, Behavior, and Social Networking*, *20*(8), cyber.2017.0221. https://doi.org/10.1089/cyber.2017.0221

Rutherford, K., Hiseler, L., & O'Hagan, F. (2023). Help! I need somebody: Help-seeking among workers with self-reported work-related mental disorders. *Journal of Occupational Rehabilitation*. https://doi.org/10.1007/s10926-023-10123-5

Salomonsson, S., Hedman-Lagerlöf, E., & Öst, L.-G. (2018). Sickness absence: A systematic review and meta-analysis of psychological treatments for individuals on sick leave due to common mental disorders. *Psychological Medicine*, *48*(12), 1954–1965. https://doi.org/10.1017/S0033291718000065

Sarkar, M., & Fletcher, D. (2017). How resilience training can enhance wellbeing and performance. In M. F. Crane (Ed.), *Managing for resilience: A practical guide for employee wellbeing and organizational performance* (pp. 227–237; 1–20 in PDF). Routledge/Taylor & Francis Group.

Satyen, L., & Becerra, A. F. (2022). Discrimination, stress, and well-being in the workplace: A comparison of Australian migrant and nonmigrant workers. *Journal of Employment Counseling*. https://doi.org/10.1002/joec.12184

Sayers, E. T., Rich, J., Rahman, M. M., Kelly, B., & James, C. (2019). Does help seeking behavior change over time following a workplace mental health intervention in the coal mining industry? *Journal of Occupational and Environmental Medicine*, *61*(6), e282–e290. https://doi.org/10.1097/JOM.0000000000001605

Schabram, K., & Maitlis, S. (2017). Negotiating the challenges of a calling: Emotion and enacted sensemaking in animal shelter work. *Academy of Management Journal*, *60*(2), 584–609. https://doi.org/10.5465/amj.2013.0665

Sonnentag, S., Cheng, B. H., & Parker, S. L. (2022). Recovery from work: Advancing the field toward the future. *Annual Review of Organizational Psychology and Organizational Behavior*, *9*, 33–60. https://doi.org/10.1146/annurev-orgpsych-012420-091355

Sørensen, L. N., Olesen, K. H., Midtgaard, C. D., & Willert, M. V. (2022). Risk of post-traumatic stress disorder following major disasters and critical incidents in police officers – a systematic review. *Journal of Police and Criminal Psychology*, *37*(4), 752–768. https://doi.org/10.1007/s11896-022-09547-1

Tay, L., Batz-Barbarich, C., Yang, L.-Q., & Wiese, C. W. (2023). Well-being: The ultimate criterion for organizational sciences. *Journal of Business and Psychology*, *38*, 1141–1157. https://doi.org.libproxy.clemson.edu/10.1007/s10869-023-09908-5

Toth, K. E., & Dewa, C. S. (2014). Employee decision-making about disclosure of a mental disorder at work. *Journal of Occupational Rehabilitation*, *24*(4), 732–746. https://doi.org/10.1007/s10926-014-9504-y

Vanhove, A. J., Herian, M. N., Perez, A. L., Harms, P. D., & Lester, P. B. (2016). Can resilience be developed at work? A meta-analytic review of resilience-building programme effectiveness. *Journal of Occupational and Organizational Psychology*, *89*(2), 278–307.

Wulf, I. C. (2022). Help-seeking and help-outreach intentions of healthcare workers—the role of mental health literacy and stigma in the workplace. *Frontiers in Education: Educational Psychology*, *7*. https://doi.org/10.3389/feduc.2022.856458

12 Academia

An Occupation With High Levels of Psychosocial Hazards That Can Increase the Risk of Mental Ill-Health

Angela Martin, Marissa Edwards, Lauren Cox, and Neal M. Ashkanasy

Introduction

Mental ill-health is prevalent in the contemporary university, with many students and faculty reporting high rates of stress, distress, and mental illness (for reviews, see Edwards et al., 2024; Lau & Pretorius, 2019; Nicholls et al., 2022). Evidence strongly suggests that academia is an unsafe occupation with high job-related stressors and limited resources to buffer stress (Wray & Kinman & 2020; see also Kinman & Court, 2010). Research also indicates that many individuals are struggling to cope with work demands, with one review finding university staff burnout levels "are comparable to 'high-risk' groups such as healthcare workers" (Guthrie et al., 2017 p. 2). While numerous academic institutions offer interventions such as counseling, health promotion, and well-being programs, most university leaders pay little attention to the role of occupation and work environment in preventing poor mental health (Cox et al., 2024).

In this chapter, we adopt an integrated approach to workplace mental health and well-being, focusing on (1) preventing harm to mental health that can occur from exposure to poor working conditions; (2) promoting mental health by enhancing positive features of work and organizations; and (3) responding to mental health problems in workers regardless of cause (LaMontagne et al., 2014). Universities have, however, been slow to apply this approach, particularly the "prevent harm" strategies. We argue in this chapter that academia is an important case that exemplifies the need for an integrated approach to workplace mental health with greater focus on preventing harm via psychosocial risk management.

Such an approach is not just critical to protecting academic staff, given the strong links between faculty and student well-being (Martin, 2008); it is also connected to the mission of universities. As Brewster et al. (2022) note, academics who are burnt out can have negative attitudes toward their students which in turn can impact the quality of education delivery and provision of student pastoral care.

DOI: 10.4324/9781003491170-16

Cox et al. (2024) comment further that, despite the large body of research indicating the extent of the problem, researchers have only explored preliminary solutions and possible interventions for supporting the mental health of academic staff. In this regard, mental health initiatives in universities appear usually to focus on students rather than staff and tend to be reactive in nature. This may be because of underlying attitudes that blame work stress on an individual's coping mechanisms and indicate that academic institutions are not yet sharing responsibility for the mental health of their people. This focus on individual strategies *in isolation* does not result in elimination of psychosocial risk (Way, 2020). Cox and her colleagues argue that what is required is a whole-of-university, multi-level, systematic approach that includes a strong focus on prevention.

In this chapter, we therefore seek to promote greater understanding of psychosocial hazards in academia and encourage increased deployment of psychosocial risk assessment within institutional approaches to support mental health and well-being. To accomplish this, we organize our chapter as follows. To begin, we discuss what psychosocial hazards are and why they are important in relation to mental (and physical) health. We then discuss what is known about a selection of prominent psychosocial hazards in universities and highlight those that remain under-explored. Finally, we offer some suggestions for future research and practice on psychosocial risk management in academia.

Psychosocial Hazards

Schulte and colleagues (2024) recently observed that there is an urgent and current need to prevent work-related psychosocial hazards for better population mental health. Work-related psychosocial hazards are associated with numerous adverse mental health outcomes such as anxiety and depression (Rugulies et al., 2023), and a range of adverse physical health outcomes including cardiovascular disease and musculoskeletal disorders (Niedhammer et al., 2021). Essentially, psychosocial hazards are factors in the work role or work environment that can cause stress, strain, or interpersonal problems for the worker.

There are a wide range of work-related psychosocial factors that pose a risk of harm (Cox & Griffiths, 2010). Depending on the jurisdictional context, voluntary guidelines or standards or regulatory expectations can assist or compel employers to manage these risks. For example, recent emergence of an international business standard "Psychological Health and Safety at Work" (ISO45003, 2021), an International Labor Organization/World Health Organization joint "Mental Health at Work Policy Brief" (ILO, 2022), and work, health and safety laws and regulations such as the "Code of Practice for Managing psychosocial hazards at work" (Safework Australia, 2022) all aim to guide employers toward best practice and legal compliance.

The number of psychosocial hazards considered in these guidance materials varies, with the ISO Global Standard being an example of a comprehensive

Table 12.1 Work-Related Psychosocial Hazards Recognized in the ISO Global Standard for Psychological Health and Safety

*Roles and Expectations**	*Job Security (Precarious Work)**	*Supervision***
Job control or autonomy*	Interpersonal relationships**	Civility and respect**
Job demands*	Leadership**	Work/life balance**
Organizational change management*	Organizational/workgroup culture**	Violence at work**
Remote and isolated work*	Recognition and reward**	Harassment**
Workload and work pace*	Career development**	Bullying and victimization**
Working hours and schedule*	Support**	Work environment, equipment, and hazardous tasks***

Note: These hazards can be grouped as aspects of work organization*; social factors at work**; and work environment, equipment, and hazardous tasks*** (ISO 45003 document).

guideline (21 hazards; see Table 12.1 for a summary). The ISO Global Standard separates hazards into three clusters: (1) aspects of how the work is organized; (2) social factors in the workplace; and (3) work environment, equipment, and hazardous tasks.

It is important to note that psychosocial hazards interact, and their effects can be multiplicative. For example, a worker with high job demands and low job control (a combination that is well known to produce "job strain") will experience greater psychological distress than a worker with high job control. It is estimated that approximately 17% of depression incidence in working women and 13% in working men could be prevented by eliminating job strain alone (LaMontagne et al., 2010). Psychosocial hazards can be acute (related to specific incidents and events) or chronic (long-term exposure). They are associated with both the development and exacerbation of mental health conditions (for a review, see Schulte et al., 2024).

In a recent systematic review, van der Molen et al. (2020) found that the psychosocial hazards of effort-reward imbalance, low organizational justice, and high job demands increase the risk of stress-related health problems by as much as 60–90%. In another recent study, Blomqvist et al. (2022) found that job insecurity (i.e., one example of a psychosocial hazard) is associated with an increased risk of suicide mortality even after controlling for other work factors and prevalent/previous mental health problems.

Robust theoretical and empirical work from the domains of organizational and occupational health psychology has explored the processes in which psychological harm can occur in relation to work characteristics that represent psychosocial hazards. This includes concepts such as burnout (Maslach & Leiter, 2023), the job demands and resources model (Bakker et al., 2023), and Psychosocial Safety Climate (PSC) theory (Law et al., 2011).

Psychosocial Hazards in Academia

While this is an emerging challenge for employers in all occupations and settings, we argue that academia is a profession with significant psychosocial hazards that increase the risk of mental illness. In one recent study, Wray and Kinman (2020) compared psychosocial hazards in the UK universities with general population benchmarks from the Health and Safety Executive (UK health and safety regulator). These authors found hazards for university employees were at higher levels than other industry benchmarks and were also increasing over time. The primary areas of concern they identified were job demands, control, role, and relationships.

In another study, researchers from the University of South Australia (2024) looked at data from an Australian longitudinal study of 6,291 faculty members from 38 universities over the past four years and found that "psychosocial safety climate" is poor and deteriorating in these institutions (Neser et al., 2023). The authors of this study reported rising emotional exhaustion and falling engagement over this time. They found that approximately 67% of those surveyed were deemed to be at high or very high risk of mental injury from working conditions. Benchmarking with other data sources, they also found that the university sector is performing far worse than other types of employers in these areas. Moreover, by comparing these results against a 2023 survey of 10,000 workers across multiple professions, the researchers also found that 54% of respondents were working in low-risk psychosocial environments. In universities, the figure was just 18%. The authors concluded that tertiary education ranked as the fifth worst of 53 occupational groupings for psychosocial safety.

In the next section of this chapter, we provide a brief review of selected research from the higher education context to exemplify the three major domains of work-related psychosocial hazards outlined earlier (ISO45003, 2021).

Aspects of Work Organization

According to ISO45003 (2021), work organization factors include roles and expectations, job control, job demands, organizational change, remote/isolated work, workload and work pace, working hours, and job security. According to Haddock-Fraser (2020), in line with the rise of new managerialism in Western universities in the last two decades, faculty today face significant demands at work, with increasing administrative burdens and less time available for teaching and research (see also Bowering & Reed, 2021). In another study, Coats et al. (2024) found that high job demand, low control, work/personal life imbalance, and pressure to publish are common psychosocial stressors in higher education.

Researchers (Kinman & Jones, 2003; Melin et al., 2014; Ross, 2022; Shaw, 2014) also found that academics are increasingly forced to manage high workloads and spend long hours at work (Corbyn, 2009; Flaherty, 2014; Sang et al., 2015), often completing "invisible" tasks not captured in workload models (see Kenny & Fluck, 2022; Ross, 2022). This can lead to high levels of role conflict, another important psychosocial risk. In another study, Jiang and her colleagues (2017) found that increasing student entitlement and related uncivil behaviors in the classroom links to educator strain and burnout.

Gender differences are important here; for example, Guarino and Borden (2017) found that female academics take on a greater share of service than men, and studies show that they are more likely to engage in pastoral care activities and "academic housework" (see also Järvinen & Mik-Meyer, 2024; Sümer & Eslen-Ziya, 2023). According to Heijstra et al. (2017), academic housework includes "tasks relating to giving back to the community, administrative and committee work, gender equality initiatives and various teaching and research-related activities such as student interactions and the organization of conferences" (p. 203). These "gendered" activities have potential to exacerbate role conflict because they take time from the primary responsibilities of research and teaching.

Karase (1979) noted long ago that job control was one of the most important psychosocial hazards. The need for some autonomy in how employees perform their jobs and to having input into decisions related to their job are fundamental to reducing some of the strain associated with high job demands. Academia has historically been high in job control, but recent research by Wray and Kinman (2020) showed that reduced autonomy and increased managerial control are major problems in contemporary academic life.

Researchers (see Organization for Economic Co-operation and Development, 2020) have also focused considerable attention on job insecurity and precarious work in academia. Universities today rely on large numbers of adjunct or casual staff, with an increasing number of employees experiencing irregular income patterns and periods of unemployment. With ongoing employment dependent on student numbers, government funding and grants, adjunct or "casual" staff are the first to lose their jobs when revenue declines (Baré & Bexley, 2017; Burch et al., 2023; Christian et al., 2021) and universities continue to favor a more agile (and expendable) academic workforce (see Australian Universities Accord Discussion Paper: February 2023, February 2023, p. 28).

Precarious work involves instability, lack of protection, insecurity, and social and economic vulnerability (Rodgers & Rodgers, 1989). As such, casual academic staff tend to source income across multiple institutions and juggle commitments across a combination of teaching, research, and project contracts (Smithers et al., 2023). This job insecurity impacts the mental health of academics in temporary roles (Castellacci & Viñas-Bardolet, 2021) and increases stress, maladaptive coping, and mental ill-health such as depression and anxiety (Reevy & Deason, 2014).

Ezzeddine and her co-authors (2023) noted that universities operate in a demanding, unpredictable, and volatile industry. Effective change management is therefore critical to reducing employee stress and promoting well-being in academia. The COVID-19 pandemic profoundly changed higher education and led to major shifts in learning environments, assessment approaches, and student, staff, and faculty experiences (see Tilak & Kumar, 2022). Even prior to the pandemic, academic work had been characterized as socially isolating and lonely (Belkhir et al., 2019). With increasing demand from employees to work remotely (McNaughton et al., 2022), we argue that universities should take steps to mitigate this risk in future.

Social Factors at Work

According to the World Health Organization (WHO, 2024), social aspects of work include interpersonal relationships, leadership, organizational/workgroup culture, recognition and reward, career development, support, supervision, civility and respect, work–life balance, violence at work, harassment, and bullying. The COVID-19 pandemic has highlighted further concerns regarding environmental stressors, particularly organizational stressors such as a lack of resources and low perceived organizational support. These hazards are now widespread and particularly concerning (Coats et al., 2024).

As Kinman and Jones (2003) observed in their review, changes in universities internationally mean that academics' perceptions of support and collegiality at work seem to have declined over time. The performance-driven culture means that academics are under considerable pressure to produce research outputs, and PhD students and early-career scholars who desire an academic career face a highly competitive job market. Perhaps unsurprisingly, research has revealed that many academics have poor work–life balance (e.g., Kinman & Jones, 2003; Drew & Marshall, 2020), and bullying (Tight, 2023) and sexual harassment (Bondestam & Lundqvist, 2020) are common. Aspects of violence on college campuses have also been discussed in the literature (e.g., gun violence in the United States, see Mournet et al., 2024; and technology-facilitated violence and attacks, see Gosse et al., 2024). However, direct and indirect exposure to potentially traumatic events associated with violence has received little attention from scholars to date and represents an important area for future research.

Given the numerous stressors that feature in the way work is organized, universities today must pay more attention to these social aspects of work, which can serve as protective factors rather than psychosocial hazards. Moreover, it should also be noted that work organization hazards can be antecedent factors in poor social behaviors. For example, bullying is more likely to occur in jobs with low control (Tuckey et al., 2009). Hence, a focus on social factors that do not come in combination with focus on work organization factors is unlikely to completely prevent these problems.

The Work Environment, Equipment, and Hazardous Tasks

WHO (2024) also defines psychosocial hazards in this domain in terms of inadequate equipment availability, suitability, reliability, maintenance, or repair; lack of space, poor lighting, and excessive noise; a lack of necessary tools, equipment, or resources to complete work tasks; and working in extreme conditions or situations.

The COVID-19 pandemic highlighted the need for research in this area in the context of academia. Specifically, many institutions had to rapidly convert their courses into remote teaching without the necessary training and infrastructure to do it optimally, creating challenges for educators and students (Turnbull et al., 2021). In one study, Mosleh et al. (2022) reported that around 60% of participants reported moderate stress during online teaching, and this was associated with significant personal and work-related burnout.

Unless the type of teaching or research involves "safety critical" elements (e.g., radiation exposures, see Asa et al., 2024) or is conducted in extreme conditions (e.g., field research in Antarctica, see Nicolas et al., 2022), research on these aspects is sparse. As relatively little is known about the effects of the physical work environment and physically hazardous tasks on academic mental health and well-being, we encourage researchers to consider the inter-relationships between the physical and psychosocial environment in future research.

Another factor has arisen in this domain in the role of office space and open plan offices (Ayoko et al., 2023; Sander et al., 2021). This has become an increasingly contested issue with studies (e.g., see Ayoko et al., 2023) demonstrating the stress experienced in open plan office environments. Further attention to these issues in the academic environment also seems warranted.

Directions for Future Research and Practice

The challenges experienced across all three major domains of work-related psychosocial hazards (aspects of work organization; social factors at work and the work environment, equipment, and hazardous tasks) clearly contribute to the considerable mental stress in contemporary academic working life. Our brief review in this chapter reveals that work in universities today is frequently characterized by high job demands, high role conflict, reduced autonomy, high workloads, and precarity. At the same time, many of the social factors that could protect mental health are limited with poor support, conflict, sexual harassment, and bullying consistently reported as highly problematic. We call for further research on the full range of psychosocial hazards included in ISO45003 within the academic setting, as well as the evaluation of strategies and interventions that attempt to eliminate hazards or mitigate harm.

However, the primary implication of this chapter is to encourage practical implementation of psychosocial hazard management systems such as ISO45003 in universities. This is so that any workplace mental health and well-being strategy and related interventions are comprehensive and integrated (i.e., cover prevention of harm as well as support for mental ill-health). Effective psychosocial risk management requires consistent implementation by line managers across an organization, strong leader commitment, and high level of worker participation. Clear roles, responsibilities, and authorities for managing psychosocial risk should be articulated at all levels of an institution.

The ISO45003 guidance suggests that organizations consider the following steps in conducting a psychosocial risk assessment:

a. provide information about potential hazards;
b. compare groups that differ in exposure to, or reporting of, psychosocial hazards;
c. consider the interaction of psychosocial risks with risks from other identified hazards;
d. prioritize hazards according to the level of risk;
e. consider the diversity of the workforce and the needs of particular groups, as well as the wider context of the organization; and
f. provide information on control measures and opportunities for improvement.

After identifying and assessing psychosocial risks, preventative or corrective measures should be put in place to eliminate or reduce the risk of harm. A monitoring and continuous improvement approach is then taken to assess the effectiveness of controls and to conduct regular cycles of risk assessment.

A recent review of interventions addressing psychosocial hazards that have been conducted in an academic setting showed limited focus on organizational factors (Cox et al., 2024). An exception was the "ARK Intervention Program" that was developed for the university sector and aims to improve the health and well-being of the employees of universities (Christensen et al., 2024). As Christensen and her co-authors describe it, the ARK Intervention Program focuses on both stresses and resources in the work environment and uses a participatory approach, whereby employees discuss the pros and cons of their work environment and develop actions for what they would keep and improve. This program is continuation of the work of Suárez-Reyes and Van den Broucke (2016), who found in a systematic review of health-promoting universities that actively involving university members in the planning, implementation, and evaluation of initiatives is key, allowing the interventions to be adapted to specific university contexts. The ARK intervention shows a lot of promise for the university sector; and we therefore encourage academic leaders to explore this approach in their own institutions.

Given we do not have much to guide us on psychosocial hazard-focused interventions in academic settings, however, we turn to the broader literature to suggest interventions that show good evidence in other occupational settings. In a recent systematic review of organizational-level interventions for improving the psychosocial work environment and workers' health and retention, Aust and colleagues (2023) reported strong evidence for interventions focusing on "changes in working time arrangements" and moderate evidence for "influence on work tasks or work organization," "healthcare approach changes," and "improvements of the psychosocial work environment."

We further argue that, in understanding the role of strong leader support for psychosocial risk assessment, the concept of psychosocial safety climate is critical. Law et al. (2011) define psychosocial safety climate in an organization as "shared perceptions of organizational policies, practices and procedures for the protection of worker psychological health and safety, that stem largely from management practices" (p. 1782). According to these authors, this climate is predictive of workplace bullying and harassment, job resources, psychological health, and employee engagement and can be improved through a focus on senior leaders' communication, consultation, prioritization of, and commitment to stress prevention. Ensuring this need is understood by university governance bodies, and getting psychosocial issues onto the risk registers/audit processes they manage is essential for a strong psychosocial safety climate.

Conclusion

Universities are not exempt from the various forms of occupational health and safety legislation that exist in many developed countries. Even in countries that do not have a strong legal imperative to take action on work-related psychosocial hazards, voluntary global business standards such as the ISO45003 can be implemented to ensure that mental safety is considered as important as physical safety. University leaders need to recognize that a climate of psychosocial safety is essential for the sustainability of academic institutions. This requires a systematic approach to psychosocial risk management that protects academics and their students from mental health harms they may experience in the pursuit of knowledge production and dissemination.

References

Asa, E., Eriksson, K., & Borell, J. (2024). Safety education at research facilities with radiation sources and short-term facility users: Current design and practice and possibilities for improvement, *Heliyon,* 10, e32675. https://doi.org/10.1016/j.heliyon.2024.e32675.

Aust, B., Møller, J. L., Nordentoft, M., Frydendall, K. B., Bengtsen, E., Jensen, A. B., Garde, A. H., Kompier, M., Semmer, N., Rugulies, R., & Jaspers, S. Ø. (2023). How effective are organizational-level interventions in improving the psychosocial work environment, health, and retention of workers? A systematic overview of systematic reviews. *Scandinavian Journal of Work, Environment & Health, 49*(5), 315–329. https://doi.org/10.5271/sjweh.4097.

Australian universities accord discussion paper: February 2023. (D23/344217). (2023, February). Department of Education. https://www.education.gov.au/australian-universities-accord/resources/australian-universities-accord-panel-discussion-paper

Ayoko, O. B., Ashkanasy, N. M., Li, Y., Dorris, A. D., & Jehn, K. A. (2023). An experience sampling study of employees' behaviors of withdrawal, conflict, and territoriality in an open-plan office. *Journal of Business Research, 155*, Part B, 113445. https://doi.org/10.1016/j.jbusres.2022.113445

Bakker, A. B., Demerouti, E., & Sanz-Vergel, A. (2023). Job demands–resources theory: Ten years later (January 2023). *Annual Review of Organizational Psychology & Organizational Behavior*, *10*(1), 25–53.

Baré, E., & Bexley, E. (2017). Redesigning the higher education workforce: A new architecture. In *Visions for Australian tertiary education*. Melbourne Centre for the Study of Higher Education. https://melbourne-cshe.unimelb.edu.au/__data/assets/pdf_file/0006/2263137/MCSHE-Visions-for-Aust-Ter-Ed-web2.pdf

Belkhir, M., Brouard, M., Brunk, K. H., Dalmoro, M., Ferreira, M. C., Figueiredo, B., Huff, A. D., Scaraboto, D., Sibai, O., & Smith, A. N. (2019). Isolation in globalizing academic fields: A collaborative autoethnography of early career researchers. *Academy of Management Learning & Education*, *18*(2), 261–285. https://doi.org/10.5465/amle.2017.0329

Blomqvist, S., Virtanen, M., LaMontagne, A., & Magnusson, H. (2022). Perceived job insecurity and risk of suicide and suicide attempts: A study of men and women in the Swedish working population. *Scandinavian Journal of Work Environ Health*, *48*(4), 293–301.

Bondestam, F., & Lundqvist, M. (2020). Sexual harassment in higher education—a systematic review. *European Journal of Higher Education*, *10*(4), 397–419. https://doi.org/10.1080/21568235.2020.1729833

Bowering, E., & Reed, M. (2021). Achieving academic promotion: The role of work environment, role conflict, and life balance. *Canadian Journal of Higher Education*, *51*(4), 1–25.

Brewster, L., Jones, E., Priestley, M., Wilbraham, S. J., Spanner, L., & Hughes, G. (2022). 'Look after the staff and they would look after the students' cultures of wellbeing and mental health in the university setting. *Journal of Further and Higher Education*, *46*(4), 548–560. https://doi.org/10.1080/0309877X.2021.1986473

Burch, S. Khosa, A., & Ozil, E. (2023). 'Some of them do treat you like an idiot': What it's like to be a casual academic. *The Conversation*. https://theconversation-com.cdn.ampproject.org/c/s/theconversation.com/amp/some-of-them-do-treat-you-like-an-idiot-what-its-like-to-be-a-casual-academic-201470

Castellacci, F., & Viñas-Bardolet, C. (2021). Permanent contracts and job satisfaction in academia: Evidence from European countries. *Studies in Higher Education*, *46*(9), 1866–1880. https://doi.org/10.1080/03075079.2019.1711041

Christensen, M., Fossum Fladmark, S., Zuberbühler, J. P., Innstrand, S. T., & Nielsen, K. (2024). The ARK program: A participatory organizational health intervention and development of meaning at work and work to home conflict over time for academics in Norway. In N. M. Ashkanasy, M. S. Edwards, A. J. Martin, & L. E. Cox (Eds.), *Research handbook of academic mental health* (pp. 475–492). Edward Elgar Publishing. https://doi.org/10.4337/9781803925080.00037

Christian, K., Johnstone, C., Larkins, J.-a., Wright, W., & Doran, M. R. (2021). A survey of early-career researchers in Australia. *eLife*, *10*, e60613. https://doi.org/10.7554/eLife.60613

Coats, S. F., Roemer, E. C., Kent, K. B., Zhang, Y., Davis, M. F., & Goetzel, R. Z. (2024). Scoping review of workplace mental health and well-being programs in higher education institutions. *Journal of Occupational and Environmental Medicine*, *66*(6), 461–466. https://doi.org/10.1097/JOM.0000000000003086

Corbyn, Z. (2009, September 24). Workload: It's not heavier, but it is more burdensome. *Times Higher Education*. https://www.timeshighereducation.com/news/workload-its-not-heavier-but-it-is-more-burdensome/408320.article

Cox, L. E., Martin, A. J., Bishop, J., Muurlink, O., & Mandrusiak, A. (2024). The landscape of mental health in higher education: The current state and where to next? In

N. M. Ashkanasy, M. S. Edwards, A. J. Martin, & L. E. Cox (Eds.), *Research handbook of academic mental health* (pp. 493–515). Edward Elgar Publishing. https://doi.org/10.4337/9781803925080.00038

Cox, T., & Griffiths, A. (2010). Work-related stress: A theoretical perspective. In S. Leka & J. Houdmont (Eds.), *Occupational health psychology* (pp. 31–56). Wiley-Blackwell.

Drew, E., & Marshall, C. (2020). Work-life balance in academia: Myth or reality? In *The gender-sensitive university* (pp. 52–66). Routledge.

Edwards, M. S., Cox, L. E., Martin, A. J., & Ashkanasy, N. M. (2024). Introduction and historical review. In M. S. Edwards, A. J. Martin, N. M. Ashkanasy, & L. E. Cox (Eds.), *Research handbook of academic mental health*. Edward Elgar Publishing.

Ezzeddine, R., Otaki, F., Darwish, S., & AlGurg, R. (2023). Change management in higher education: A sequential mixed methods study exploring employees' perception. *PLoS One*, *18*(7), e0289005.

Flaherty, C. (2014, April 8). So much to do, so little time. *Inside Higher Ed*. https://www.insidehighered.com/news/2014/04/09/research-shows-professors-work-long-hours-and-spend-much-day-meetings

Gosse, C., O'Meara, V., Hodson, J., & Veletsianos, G. (2024). Too rigid, too big, and too slow: Institutional readiness to protect and support faculty from technology facilitated violence and abuse. *Higher Education*, *87*(4), 923–941.

Guarino, C. M., & Borden, V. M. (2017). Faculty service loads and gender: Are women taking care of the academic family? *Research in Higher Education*, *58*, 672–694.

Guthrie, S., Lichten, C. A., van Belle, J. Ball, S. Knack, A., & Hofman, J. (2017). *Understanding mental health in the research environment: A rapid evidence assessment*. RAND Corporation, RR-2022-RS, 2017.

Haddock-Fraser, J. (2020). The unseen pressures of academia. In M. Antoniadou & M. Crowder (eds), *Modern day challenges in academia* (pp. 211–225). Edward Elgar.

Heijstra, T. M., Einarsdóttir, T. J., Pétursdóttir, G. M., & Steinþórsdóttir, F. S. (2017). Testing the concept of academic housework in a European setting: Part of academic career-making or gendered barrier to the top? *European Educational Research Journal*, *16*, 200–214. https://doi.org/10.1177/1474904116668884

International Labor Organization. (2022). *ILO/WHO Mental health at work policy brief*. Retrieved July 25, 2024, from https://www.who.int/publications/i/item/9789240057944

International Standards Organization. (2021). *ISO45003: Psychological health and safety at work—Guidelines for managing psychosocial risks*. https://www.iso.org/standard/64283.html

Järvinen, M., & Mik-Meyer, N. (2024). Giving and receiving: Gendered service work in academia. *Current Sociology*, 00113921231224754.

Jiang, L., Tripp, T. M., & Hong, P. Y. (2017). College instruction is not so stress free after all: A qualitative and quantitative study of academic entitlement, uncivil behaviors, and instructor strain and burnout. *Stress and Health*, *33*(5), 578–589.

Karasek, R. A. (1979). Job demands, job decision latitude and mental strain: Implications for job redesign. *Administrative Sciences Quarterly*, *24*, 285–308.

Kenny, J., & Fluck, A. E. (2022). Emerging principles for the allocation of academic work in universities. *Higher Education*, *83*, 1371–1388.

Kinman, G., & Court, S. (2010). Psychosocial hazards in UK universities: Adopting a risk assessment approach. *Higher Education Quarterly*, *64*(4), 413–428. https://doi.org/10.1111/j.1468-2273.2009.00447.x

Kinman, G., & Jones, F. (2003). Running up the down escalator: Stressors and strains in UK academics. *Quality in Higher Education*, *9*(1), 21–38.

LaMontagne, A. D., Martin, A., Page, K. M., Reavley, N. J., Noblet, A. J., Milner, A. J., Keegel, T., & Smith, P. M. (2014). Workplace mental health: developing an integrated intervention approach. *BMC Psychiatry*, *14*(1), 131. https://doi.org/10.1186/1471-244X-14–131

LaMontagne, A. D., Sanderson, K., & Cocker, F. (2010). *Estimating the economic benefits of eliminating job strain as a risk factor for depression*. Victorian Heath Promotion Foundation (VicHealth), Carlton, Australia. https://www.vichealth.vic.gov.au/media-and-resources/publications/economic-cost-of-job-strain

Lau, W., & Pretorius, L. (2019). Intrapersonal wellbeing and the academic mental health crisis. In L. Pretorius, L. Macaulay, & B. Cahusac de Caux (Eds.), *Wellbeing in doctoral education: Insights and guidance from the student experience* (1st ed., pp. 37–45). Springer. https://doi.org/10.1007/978-981-13-9302-0_5

Law, R., Dollard, M. F., Tuckey, M. R., & Dormann, C. (2011). Psychosocial safety climate as a lead indicator of workplace bullying and harassment, job resources, psychological health and employee engagement. *Accidental Analysis &Prevention*, *43*(5), 1782–1793. https://doi.org/10.1016/j.aap.2011.04.010.

Martin, A. (2008). Service climate and employee well-being in higher education. *Journal of Management & Organization*, *14*(2), 155–167. https://doi.org/10.5172/jmo.837.14.2.155

Maslach, C., & Leiter, M. (2023). *The burnout challenge: Managing people's relationships with their jobs*. Harvard University Press.

McNaughton, J., Whaley, C., & Wallace, C. (2022, October 12). What must leaders consider as they develop permanent remote work policies? *Times Higher Education*. https://www.timeshighereducation.com/campus/what-must-leaders-consider-they-develop-permanent-remote-work-policies

Melin, M., Astvik, W., & Bernhard-Oettel, C. (2014). New work demands in higher education. A study of the relationship between excessive workload, coping strategies and subsequent health among academic staff. *Quality in Higher Education*, *20*(3), 290–308.

Mosleh, S. M., Kasasbeha, M. A., & Aljawarneh, Y. M. (2022). The impact of online teaching on stress and burnout of academics during the transition to remote teaching from home. *BMC Medical Education*, *22*, 475. https://doi.org/10.1186/s12909-022-03496-3

Mournet, A. M., Kellerman, J. K., & Kleiman, E. M. (2024). Associations between feelings of safety, concerns about firearms on campus and suicidal thoughts and behaviours among college students. *Injury Prevention*, *30*, 171–175.

Neser, D., Lushington, K., Zadow, A., Potter, R., Parkin, A., Richter, S., Pignata, S., Afsharian, A., Bakker, A., & Dollard, M. F. (2023). Work, digital stress and well-being survey report. *The University of South Australia*. https://www.acgr.edu.au/wp-content/uploads/2024/04/Psychosocial-Saftey_AA_E-stress-2023-Dashboard-Report_12022024-1.pdf

Nicholls, H., Nicholls, M., Tekin, S., Lamb, D., & Billings, J. (2022). The impact of working in academia on researchers' mental health and well-being: A systematic review and qualitative meta-synthesis. *PLoS One*, *17*(5), e0268890. https://doi.org/10.1371/journal.pone.0268890

Nicolas, M., Martinent, G., Palinkas, L., & Suedfeld, P. (2022). Dynamics of stress and recovery and relationships with perceived environmental mastery in extreme environments, *Journal of Environmental Psychology*, *83*, 101853. https://doi.org/10.1016/j.jenvp.2022.101853.

Niedhammer, I., Bertrais, S., & Witt, K. (2021). Psychosocial work exposures and health outcomes: A meta-review of 72 literature reviews with meta- analysis. *Scandinavian Journal of Work, Environment & Health*, *47*(7), 489–508.

Organization for Economic Co-operation and Development. (2020). Executive summary. In *Resourcing higher education challenges, choices and consequences*. OECD Publishing.

Reevy, G. M., & Deason, G. (2014). Predictors of depression, stress, and anxiety among non-tenure track faculty [Original Research]. *Frontiers in Psychology*, *5*.

Rodgers, G., & Rodgers, J. (1989). *Precarious jobs in labour market regulation: The growth of atypical employment in Western Europe*. International Institute for Labour Studies.

Ross, J. (2022, August 18). Overworked academics give away one-third of their time. *Times Higher Education*. https://www.timeshighereducation.com/news/overworked-academics-give-away-one-third-their-tim

Rugulies, R., Aust, B., Greiner, B. A., Arensman, E., Kawakami, N., LaMontagne, A. D., & Madsen, I. E. H. (2023). Work-related causes of mental health conditions and interventions for their improvement in workplaces. *Lancet*, *403*, 1368–1381.

Safework Australia. (2022). *Model code of practice: Managing psychosocial hazards at work*. https://www.safeworkaustralia.gov.au/doc/model-code-practice-managing-psychosocial-hazards-work

Sander, E. J., Marques, C., Birt, J., Stead, M., & Baumann, O. (2021). Open-plan office noise is stressful: Multimodal stress detection in a simulated work environment. *Journal of Management & Organization*, *27*(6),1021–1037. https://doi.org/10.1017/jmo.2021.17

Sang, K., Powell, A., Finkel, R., & Richards, J. (2015). 'Being an academic is not a 9–5 job': Long working hours and the 'ideal worker' in UK academia. *Labour & Industry: A Journal of the Social and Economic Relations of Work*, *25*(3), 235–249.

Schulte, P. A., Sauter, S. L., Pandalai, S. P., Tiesman, H. M., Chosewood, L. C., Cunningham, T. R., Wurzelbacher, S. J., Pana-Cryan, R., Swanson, N. G., Chang, C-C., Nigam, J. A. S. Reissman, D. B., Ray, T. K., & Howard, J. (2024). An urgent call to address work-related psychosocial hazards and improve worker well-being. *American Journal of Industrial Medicine*, *67*(6), 499–514.

Shaw, C. (2014, May 8). Overworked and isolated—work pressure fuels mental illness in academia. *The Guardian*. https://www.theguardian.com/higher-education-network/blog/2014/may/08/work-pressure-fuels-academic-mental-illness-guardian-study-health

Smithers, K., Spina, N., Harris, J., & Gurr, S. (2023). Working every weekend: The paradox of time for insecurely employed academics. *Time & Society*, *32*(1), 101–122. https://doi.org/10.1177/0961463x221144136

Suárez-Reyes, M., & Van den Broucke, S. (2016). Implementing the Health Promoting University approach in culturally different contexts: A systematic review. *Global Health Promotion*, *23*(1_suppl), 46–56. https://doi.org/10.1177/1757975915623933

Sümer, S., & Eslen-Ziya, H. (2023). Academic women's voices on gendered divisions of work and care: 'Working till I drop . . . then dropping'. *European Journal of Women's Studies*, *30*(1), 49–65.

Tight, M. (2023). Bullying in higher education: An endemic problem? *Tertiary Education and Management*, *29*, 123–137. https://doi.org/10.1007/s11233-023-09124-z

Tilak, J. B. G., & Kumar, A. G. (2022). Policy changes in global higher education: What lessons do we learn from the COVID-19 pandemic? *Higher Education Policy*, *35*, 610–628. https://doi.org/10.1057/s41307-022-00266-0

Tuckey, M. R., Dollard, M. F., Hosking, P. J., & Winefield, A. H. (2009). Workplace bullying: The role of psychosocial work environment factors. *International Journal of Stress Management*, *16*(3), 215–232. https://doi.org/10.1037/a0016841

Turnbull, D., Chugh, R., & Luck, J. (2021). Transitioning to e-learning during the COVID-19 pandemic: How have higher education institutions responded to the challenge? *Education and Information Technologies*, *26*, 6401–6419. https://doi.org/10.1007/s10639-021-10633-w

van der Molen, H. F, Nieuwenhuijsen, K, Frings-Dresen, M. H. W., & de Groene, G. (2020). Work- related psychosocial risk factors for stress-related mental disorders: An updated systematic review and meta-analysis. *BMJ Open*, *10*(7), e034849.

Way, K. (2020). Psychosocial hazards. In *The core body of knowledge for generalist OHS professionals* (Vol. 2, pp. 1–50). Australian Institute of Health and Safety.
World Health Organization (WHO). (2024). *Achieving well-being: A global framework for integrating well-being into public health utilizing a health promotion approach.* WHO.
Wray, S., & Kinman, G. (2020). The psychosocial hazards of academic work: An analysis of trends. *Studies in Higher Education*, *47*(4), 771–782. https://doi.org/10.1080/03075079.2020.1793934

13 Well-Being in Small Entrepreneurial Firms

Balancing Relationships, Autonomy, and Leadership

Neha Gopinath

Introduction

The relationship between small entrepreneurial firms and well-being is complex and multidimensional. While prior studies have extensively examined the well-being of entrepreneurs themselves (Stephan et al., 2023; Wiklund et al., 2019), the experiences of those working for entrepreneurs have received significantly less attention. This chapter integrates both perspectives by examining how small entrepreneurial firms shape employee well-being while also considering how employee well-being, in turn, impacts business sustainability and innovation.

Employees in small firms operate in highly dynamic environments characterized by informality, resource constraints, and close relationships with both the entrepreneur and customers. These conditions create a work setting that can simultaneously enhance and diminish well-being. While employees often benefit from greater autonomy and direct involvement in decision-making (Schjoedt, 2009), they may also experience job insecurity, role ambiguity, and blurred work–life boundaries (Peterson & Wilson, 2002). Understanding how these factors influence well-being is crucial, as small firms play a vital role in economic growth and employment generation.

This chapter addresses the following research questions:

- How do employees experience and navigate well-being in small entrepreneurial firms?
- In what ways do autonomy, flexibility, and workplace structures contribute to both positive and negative well-being outcomes?
- How do employee well-being experiences influence the sustainability and operations of small entrepreneurial firms?

By presenting a case study of a small entrepreneurial firm in the United Kingdom, this chapter contributes to the growing discourse on workplace well-being. Findings highlight how working in such an environment fosters well-being

DOI: 10.4324/9781003491170-17

through creativity, autonomy, and close community ties, yet also presents risks such as stress, lack of formalized policies, and emotional burdens stemming from intense workplace relationships. These findings challenge the dominant view in entrepreneurship research that portrays small business environments primarily as positive spaces for mental health (Wiklund et al., 2019). Instead, they reveal a more complex and nuanced reality where entrepreneurial settings can be both enriching and precarious for employees.

By situating this study within broader debates on workplace well-being, this chapter not only advances theoretical understanding but also provides practical insights for entrepreneurs and policymakers aiming to create more sustainable and supportive work environments in small firms.

Literature Review—Small Entrepreneurial Firms and Well-being

Theoretical Foundations of Well-being

Well-being research encompasses both hedonic and eudaimonic perspectives. Hedonic well-being focuses on subjective happiness and life satisfaction (Diener, 1984), while eudaimonic well-being emphasizes personal growth and fulfillment (Ryan & Deci, 2001). These dimensions are particularly relevant in small firms, where employees experience both opportunities for autonomy and creativity, as well as stress from high job demands and informal structures. Self-determination theory (Ryan & Deci, 2001) further suggests that workplace well-being depends on fulfilling three intrinsic needs: autonomy, competence, and relatedness. While small firms may enhance autonomy, they may simultaneously challenge competence and relatedness due to unclear roles and informal managerial approaches.

Despite the emphasis on positive organizational behavior (POB) (Seligman & Csíkszentmihályi, 2000), research has increasingly recognized the importance of integrating stress and well-being research to fully understand work experiences (Cameron et al., 2003; Dewe et al., 2012). Workplace well-being is shaped not just by job satisfaction and engagement but also by factors such as work-related stress, job insecurity, and lack of organizational structure (Aspinwall & Staudinger, 2003; Lopez et al., 2018). This dual perspective—considering both positive and negative aspects—is crucial when studying employee experiences in small entrepreneurial firms. Before we explore employee experiences in small entrepreneurial firms, we need to look at the scholarly discourse that surrounds this topic in the entrepreneurship literature.

Well-being in Entrepreneurship

Recent scholarly discourse underscores the significance of entrepreneurs' well-being, recognizing it as a pressing contemporary issue (Stephan et al., 2023; Stephan, 2018; Wiklund et al., 2019). Stephan et al. (2023) have introduced a novel perspective on entrepreneurial well-being, applying Williamson's hierarchy of institutions theory (2000) to elucidate the role of contextual factors such as national settings and institutional frameworks. Moreover, researchers are increasingly investigating how well-being impacts entrepreneurial engagement (Foo et al., 2009; Foo, 2011; Hahn et al., 2012), focusing primarily on the entrepreneur's viewpoint. Studies highlight various facets of entrepreneurial well-being and positive affect (Baron, 2008; Uy et al., 2013), yet also acknowledge the stresses and emotional toll inherent in entrepreneurship (Monsen & Boss, 2009; Mitchell et al., 2008; Jenkins et al., 2014).

Scholars have delved into the psychological mechanisms linking entrepreneurship and well-being (Shir, 2015; Williams & Shepherd, 2016), emphasizing the critical role of mental health in entrepreneurial success (Wach et al., 2016; Shir, 2015; Stephan, 2018). Additionally, the entrepreneurial actions and decision-making processes that sustain economic and social gains are under scrutiny (Shepherd & Patzelt, 2015; Stephan, 2018). While much research focuses on the individual entrepreneur, understanding the well-being of those working with or for entrepreneurs is equally vital. Neglecting employee well-being can lead to dysfunctional organizational dynamics amid rapid business changes (Peterson & Wilson, 2002), underscoring the interconnectedness of entrepreneurial success and the collective well-being of the organizational team.

While the emphasis on the entrepreneur's psychological well-being is warranted, this focus often overlooks the organizational context and those working with or for entrepreneurs. Employees are not merely passive participants; they play a central role in the venture's operations, culture, and long-term viability. Their experiences may be shaped by conditions distinct from those affecting either the entrepreneur or employees in larger, more structured organizations, making them worthy of specific and dedicated study.

Well-Being in Small Entrepreneurial Firms

Unlike corporate environments, small firms often lack formalized HR policies, leading to highly personalized and variable employee experiences (Kotey & Folker, 2007). Employees frequently assume multiple roles, contributing to both job satisfaction and stress. The social environment in small firms, including relationships with colleagues, customers, and the entrepreneur, plays a central role in shaping well-being (Peterson & Wilson, 2002). While these firms foster strong relational ties, they also present challenges such as unclear expectations, job insecurity, and inconsistent managerial approaches (DeJoy et al., 2010; Farrell & Geist-Martin, 2005).

Recent studies highlight that job flexibility and close-knit teams enhance employee resilience in small firms (Atkinson & Hall, 2011), yet these same characteristics can also contribute to role ambiguity and increased stress (Raya & Panneerselvam, 2013). Unlike larger organizations, where job roles are more clearly defined, employees in small firms often find themselves managing multiple responsibilities without clear boundaries, contributing to both positive and negative well-being outcomes (Johnson et al., 2017). This highlights the paradox of flexibility: while autonomy fosters innovation and engagement, the absence of structured support mechanisms can result in burnout and job dissatisfaction.

Workplace well-being in small entrepreneurial firms emerges as a pivotal factor influencing not only employee satisfaction but also organizational innovation and business performance (Mitra, 2020). While small firms offer dynamic and engaging work environments, they also present challenges in terms of job security, workload management, and emotional labor. Employees frequently engage in diverse roles and responsibilities, sometimes collaborating closely with entrepreneurs in strategy formulation and opportunity identification (Chell et al., 1991). However, the reliance on a small team to fulfil multiple roles can create a stressful work environment characterized by high expectations, fast-paced workflows, and a lack of formalized career progression pathways (Sparks et al., 2001).

The impact of organizational culture on employee well-being in small firms is significant. While strong team cohesion and shared values can enhance job satisfaction (Schumpeter, 1934; Chell & Baines, 2000), dysfunctional small firms may cultivate a culture of stress and anxiety, ultimately undermining long-term sustainability and growth prospects (Johnson et al., 2018). Research suggests that successful small entrepreneurial firms strategically nurture creativity and resilience among their workforce to thrive in competitive environments (Chamberlain, 2017). Conversely, firms that neglect well-being may experience high turnover, reduced innovation, and lower overall productivity.

In summary, while small entrepreneurial firms provide employees with greater autonomy and creative freedom, they also pose unique challenges in terms of job security, work–life balance, and stress management. Unlike large organizations with formal HR policies, small firms rely on informal structures, making employee well-being highly dependent on workplace culture and leadership approaches.

This chapter builds on existing research by examining how these factors interact in a real-world entrepreneurial setting, shedding light on the dual nature of well-being in small firms.

Case Study: Well-Being in a Small Craft Brewery, The Green Tap[1]

Being entrepreneurial involves creating and growing both value and ventures. The Green Tap, a community-oriented pub business in Essex, UK, exemplifies this ethos by emphasizing the creation of social and cultural capital. Founded in 2015 by an entrepreneur passionate about brewing, the pub offers nearly 50 unique beers, carving out a niche in the market. The entrepreneur fosters a distinctive workplace culture where employees are encouraged to express their personal identities, including artistic and musical talents showcased during pub events. This approach supports both professional and personal growth, reflecting a commitment to employee well-being and development.

Operating with a flat organizational structure, The Green Tap allows direct communication between employees and the entrepreneur, promoting openness and idea sharing. While this flat structure enhances creativity and innovation, it also presents challenges with accountability, as noted by employees. The firm operates without strict policies, reflecting a commitment to freedom and creativity, despite occasional tensions with the owner's wife, who advocates for more structured procedures.

Recent expansion plans include converting a neighboring shop into a café, underscoring the entrepreneur's vision to enhance community engagement. However, concerns over health and safety, particularly for female employees facing harassment, highlight operational challenges that require attention. While well-being strategies are not explicitly outlined, the entrepreneur's focus on community and external impact contrasts with employees' holistic well-being concerns encompassing mental, physical, and spiritual health.

Data Collection and Methodology

To better understand the dynamics of well-being in this small entrepreneurial firm, an exploratory research approach was adopted. The methods used for data collection included in-depth interviews and participant observation, as they help examine behavior within specific social contexts, including how it is shaped and constrained by these settings and how individuals interpret their experiences (Wilson & Chaddha, 2009). All ten employees were interviewed, including the entrepreneur. This provided a comprehensive perspective on workplace well-being from multiple vantage points.

The employees interviewed had varying levels of tenure at The Green Tap. Some had been with the pub since its inception in 2015, while others had joined more recently, within the past few years. This mix of perspectives allowed for a nuanced understanding of how well-being has evolved over time within the firm. Additionally, observational research was conducted to assess workplace interactions, routines, and informal dynamics beyond the formal interview discussions.

Interpretation of Findings

The analysis was conducted using an inductive qualitative approach, allowing key themes to emerge organically from the data (Gioia et al., 2013). Instead of testing a predefined hypothesis, the study sought to explore how employees perceive and experience well-being within the unique context of a small entrepreneurial firm. Recurring themes were identified across interviews, which were then compared to observations to ensure consistency and reliability. This approach aligns with existing research methodologies in workplace well-being studies, where understanding subjective experiences is critical to contextualizing broader patterns and dynamics. To enhance credibility, interview themes were triangulated with observations, and patterns were iteratively reviewed to ensure that they reflected employee perspectives rather than researcher assumptions. This approach, common in inductive workplace studies, prioritizes depth, contextual sensitivity, and the emergence of meaning from lived experience.

In summary, The Green Tap blends a passion for craft brewing with community building, fostering a dynamic workplace culture despite operational challenges and differing perspectives on organizational policies. By analyzing employees' experiences through direct engagement and observation, this case study provides rich insights into the complex interplay between entrepreneurial leadership, organizational informality, and workplace well-being.

Findings: Navigating Well-Being in Small Firms

Relational Resources

Work-Based Relationships

Work relationships significantly impacted employee well-being in the small entrepreneurial firm. Employees often encountered minimal structured interaction, leading to misunderstandings, disengagement, and frustration. The lack of accountability and mutual respect in the workplace negatively affected team dynamics. Elena, for instance, expressed her dissatisfaction: "I hate it when they [another employee and his friends] leave takeaway . . . everyone's just so relaxed and nobody cares." This frustration stemmed from a lack of communication and relationship-building opportunities, resulting in dysfunction within the firm. Research highlights that strong interpersonal relationships at work enhance job satisfaction and engagement (Robertson et al., 2011), yet small firms often lack structured mechanisms to facilitate these interactions (Kotey & Slade, 2005).

Despite these challenges, some employees found fulfillment in collaborative opportunities and social connections. When given the chance to work closely with colleagues, employees reported a greater sense of purpose. Small entrepreneurial firms have the potential to foster close-knit, supportive relationships, but without structured approaches, these interactions may become inconsistent and even counterproductive. Previous research has found that informal workplace cultures in small firms can foster both positive and negative well-being effects, depending on the level of cohesion within the team (Schjoedt, 2009).

Knowledge Sharing and Recognition

Employees valued informal learning and the ability to share their expertise, yet the lack of formal acknowledgment led to frustration. Elena illustrated this issue:

"I am fairly experienced in hospitality and stuff... but when I do something, no one cares . . . I get really pissed when I do not get any credit for what I do here." The absence of recognition created a disconnect between employee contributions and workplace appreciation, ultimately reducing motivation. Research suggests that knowledge sharing without formalized reward mechanisms can create disengagement (Dyer & Singh, 1998), reinforcing the need for small firms to cultivate an environment where contributions are acknowledged and valued. In line with self-determination theory (Ryan & Deci, 2001), the lack of recognition may inhibit employees' intrinsic motivation, affecting both job satisfaction and professional development.

Customer Relationships and Community Engagement

Customer relationships and community engagement were central to employee well-being. Many employees derived motivation and a sense of belonging through interactions with customers and the broader community. Tate described this experience: "We have an amazing relationship with our customers . . . they are like a part of us." These relationships provided employees with fulfillment beyond their immediate work responsibilities. Prior studies suggest that customer interactions can enhance hedonic well-being by fostering positive affect and social connection (Diener, 1984; Fisher, 2010).

The entrepreneur further encouraged community ties through cultural and artistic events, strengthening both external and internal relationships. Danny, the entrepreneur, stated: "Being a proper part of the community . . . it gives me a high . . . like a drive, then I am extremely happy and motivated to do more and more." This suggests that well-being in small firms extends beyond internal relationships to include community integration, which can enhance employee engagement and job satisfaction. The concept of social embeddedness (McKeever et al., 2014) supports this finding, as networks and community ties contribute to employees' sense of identity and belonging in entrepreneurial firms.

Organizational Systems and Practices

Autonomy, Flexibility, and Role Ambiguity

The autonomy and flexibility that characterized the work environment had a dual impact on well-being. Employees not only reported that high levels of autonomy fostered creativity and job satisfaction but also led to confusion and stress. Randolph noted: "I would say everyone who works behind the bar brings a bit of personality. . . . Danny gives us that freedom." However, autonomy without guidance resulted in role ambiguity and inefficiencies. This aligns with research on job flexibility in small firms (Peters et al., 2009), which indicates that while autonomy fosters innovation, it can also create uncertainty and frustration when job roles are not clearly defined. Stephan et al. (2023) argue that too much autonomy without structure can lead to psychological strain, reducing the overall benefits of flexibility in small business environments.

Accountability and Lack of Structure

The absence of formalized policies and procedures presented challenges for employees. Many found that the lack of clear expectations led to inconsistencies in workplace responsibilities and performance evaluation. Elena highlighted these frustrations:

> It [flexibility] needs to be managed properly . . . nobody puts [beer] in the fridge . . . [and] I'm embarrassed if someone asks for a beer, if I have to say, I am sorry I have not got any that's cold.

This illustrates how flexibility without boundaries can lead to operational inefficiencies and stress. The balance between autonomy and structured accountability is essential for maintaining both employee satisfaction and business success. Research suggests that clear organizational structures can mitigate stress by providing employees with well-defined expectations (Peterson & Wilson, 2002).

Entrepreneurial Passion and Its Impact

The entrepreneur's passion for brewing and creativity not only inspired employees but also contributed to stress and instability. Employees respected Danny's dedication but struggled with his unstructured leadership style. Rachel observed: "Danny and his wife have some issues . . . that affects the employees . . . most of us feel they should do this outside of work." Entrepreneurial leadership, often driven by passion, can boost motivation and team engagement, yet may also generate uncertainty and tension in the absence of clear organizational structures (Florin et al., 2003; see also Schumpeter, 1934). To optimize well-being, entrepreneurs must ensure that their vision translates into clear expectations and fair workplace dynamics. Previous studies have shown that entrepreneurial passion can not only drive commitment but also lead to burnout if not managed appropriately (Cardon et al., 2012).

Positive and Negative Well-Being Outcomes

Findings from this study illustrate the dual impact of workplace factors on well-being in small entrepreneurial firms. Employees valued creativity, community engagement, and customer relationships, which contributed to their sense of fulfillment and motivation. Autonomy and flexible work arrangements fostered innovation and job satisfaction, while entrepreneurial passion inspired commitment. However, challenges such as role ambiguity and lack of communication led to stress and disengagement. The absence of formalized workplace structures contributed to accountability issues and operational inefficiencies, making it difficult for employees to maintain consistency in their work. The entrepreneur's passion not only created enthusiasm but also introduced instability, as employees found it difficult to predict workplace dynamics.

These factors directly influenced employee performance and business innovation. Strong community ties and customer relationships contributed to brand loyalty and business growth. However, the lack of formalized workplace structures created inefficiencies that limited the firm's ability to scale sustainably. While employees felt motivated by creative autonomy, they also required clearer guidance and support mechanisms to perform effectively. Recognizing both the benefits and risks of informal workplace structures allows small firms to develop well-being strategies that support employees while maintaining business agility.

This study highlights that well-being in small entrepreneurial firms is deeply interconnected with workplace relationships, autonomy, and organizational practices. Small firms not only offer unique advantages such as creative freedom and community-driven engagement but also pose challenges related to role ambiguity, accountability, and emotional labor. By implementing structured yet flexible workplace policies, entrepreneurs can optimize both employee well-being and business performance.

Discussion: Theoretical and Practical Contributions to Well-Being in Small Entrepreneurial Firms

This study highlights the complex and nuanced nature of well-being in small entrepreneurial firms. The findings suggest that employee well-being is shaped by a combination of relational resources, organizational structures, and entrepreneurial leadership. Employees in small firms value autonomy, creative expression, and strong workplace relationships, yet they also face challenges such as role ambiguity, lack of recognition, and inconsistent leadership. The dual nature of these experiences illustrates the intricate balance required to maintain positive workplace well-being while ensuring business sustainability.

Theoretical Contributions

This study contributes to the literature on workplace well-being by extending existing models of hedonic, eudaimonic, and negative well-being within the specific context of small entrepreneurial firms. While previous research has focused predominantly on entrepreneurs' mental health (Stephan et al., 2023; Wiklund et al., 2019), this study shifts the focus to employees, offering insights into how workplace structures and relationships influence well-being beyond the entrepreneur.

Hedonic Well-Being

Hedonic well-being was observed in employees who derived enjoyment from autonomy, customer interactions, and creative work environments. The strong relational ties with customers and community engagement provided a sense of fulfillment and happiness, reinforcing findings by Fisher (2010) that positive affect and job satisfaction are enhanced in social and supportive work settings. Employees who had the freedom to engage in self-expression through work, such as showcasing artistic and musical talents, also experienced higher levels of workplace happiness, aligning with the concept of job crafting (Wrzesniewski & Dutton, 2001). However, while flexibility contributed to job satisfaction, the lack of structure sometimes led to inefficiencies and frustration, which reduced hedonic well-being.

Eudaimonic Well-Being

Eudaimonic well-being was evident in employees who found fulfillment in knowledge sharing, community engagement, and creative autonomy. Employees who were encouraged to develop skills and take on meaningful roles within the firm reported an increased sense of purpose. This aligns with self-determination theory, which posits that fulfilling intrinsic psychological needs such as competence and relatedness fosters higher well-being (Ryan & Deci, 2001). The entrepreneurial environment, which allowed employees to innovate and take ownership of their work, further enhanced their professional development and engagement, as supported by Ryff and Keyes (1995).

Negative Well-Being

Despite the benefits of autonomy and creativity, negative well-being emerged in employees who struggled with role ambiguity, inconsistent leadership, and lack of recognition. Frustration and stress arose when employees felt their contributions were undervalued or when workplace expectations were unclear. Research suggests that inconsistencies in policy adherence and mismatches in person-organization fit contribute to job dissatisfaction and disengagement (Peterson & Wilson, 2002). The findings highlight that workplace structures play a critical role in moderating stress; clear communication and defined expectations can mitigate the negative well-being outcomes associated with entrepreneurial informality (Welter et al., 2017).

The role of entrepreneurial leadership also shaped negative well-being. While the entrepreneur's passion inspired commitment, the lack of structured management and clear delegation of tasks resulted in stress and uncertainty. This aligns with previous research on entrepreneurial passion, which suggests that while passion can drive commitment, it can also create instability and emotional exhaustion if not managed effectively (Cardon et al., 2012). Thus, entrepreneurs must strike a balance between fostering enthusiasm and providing structured guidance.

Practical Contributions for Entrepreneurs and Managers

Beyond theoretical insights, this study offers practical guidance for entrepreneurs and managers aiming to create supportive and sustainable small business environments. The findings offer valuable insights for small business owners and entrepreneurs seeking to enhance workplace well-being while maintaining business growth. One of the primary implications is the need for structured yet flexible policies that provide employees with clear expectations without stifling creativity and autonomy. While flexibility is an asset in small firms, its benefits are maximized when accompanied by defined roles, communication protocols, and recognition mechanisms.

One critical aspect that emerged from this study is the importance of interpersonal relationships in shaping workplace well-being. Employees who felt valued and engaged in their work communities exhibited higher levels of job satisfaction and motivation. Entrepreneurs should actively foster knowledge-sharing environments and encourage strong team cohesion to promote both individual and organizational well-being. Providing resources for employees to cope with well-being issues arising from work relationships is crucial, as teams are vital for positive entrepreneurial outcomes.

Another key takeaway is that customer and community engagement can be leveraged as a source of workplace well-being. Employees who interacted regularly with customers and engaged in community events expressed a deeper sense of belonging and purpose. In small firms, where team sizes are often limited, there may be fewer opportunities for high-quality internal relationships simply due to the small number of colleagues. As a result, interactions with customers and community stakeholders can serve as important supplemental sources of social connection, meaning, and emotional support. This finding is particularly relevant for scholars and practitioners interested in relational well-being, as it broadens the traditional focus on coworker relationships to include external networks that are often central to small business operations.

Finally, the findings suggest that entrepreneurs must balance passion with structured leadership. While a strong entrepreneurial vision can inspire employees, inconsistent leadership and lack of formalized management processes can introduce stress and uncertainty. Implementing clear but adaptable management frameworks can help reduce employee burnout and increase job satisfaction.

Policy and Organizational Implications

Beyond individual firm-level applications, these findings have broader policy implications for organizations supporting small business development. Given the challenges associated with workplace well-being in entrepreneurial environments, policymakers should consider incentivizing small firms to adopt structured well-being initiatives. Providing resources such as employee training programs, mental health support, and workplace development initiatives could contribute to more sustainable small business environments.

In addition, entrepreneurship education programs could emphasize the importance of balancing flexibility with structured management, equipping future entrepreneurs with the tools to create workplaces that support both business innovation and employee well-being.

Conclusion

This chapter highlights the multifaceted nature of employee well-being in small entrepreneurial firms, shaped by a combination of autonomy, informal structures, close interpersonal relationships, and leadership style. The case study reveals that while small firms can foster creativity, community connection, and personal fulfillment, they also carry risks linked to role ambiguity, emotional strain, and lack of recognition.

Importantly, the findings suggest that in firms with limited internal social networks, external relationships particularly with customers and local communities may serve as alternative sources of connection and meaning. This dynamic presents a valuable direction for future research, particularly for scholars interested in relational well-being and workplace design in smaller organizations.

Going forward, it is essential for researchers and policymakers to explore how well-being in entrepreneurial firms can be supported through context-sensitive practices and policies. Attention to the interplay between leadership, structure, and employee experience can help inform a new generation of well-being-centered entrepreneurial thinking one that sustains not only business growth but also the people who make it possible.

Note

1 Names of the organization and employees are pseudonymized.

References

Aspinwall, L. G., & Staudinger, U. M. (2003). *A psychology of human strengths: Fundamental questions and future directions for a positive psychology*. American Psychological Association.

Atkinson, C., & Hall, L. (2011). Flexible working and happiness in the NHS. *Employee Relations*, *33*(2), 88–105.

Baron, R. A. (2008). The role of affect in the entrepreneurial process. *Academy of Management Review*, *33*(2), 328–340. https://doi.org/10.5465/amr.2008.31193166.

Cameron, K. S., Dutton, J. E., & Quinn, R. E. (2003). Foundations of positive organizational scholarship. In K. S. Cameron, J. E. Dutton, & R. E. Quinn (Eds.), *Positive organizational scholarship: Foundations of a new discipline* (pp. 3–13). Berrett-Koehler Publishers.

Cardon, M. S., Foo, M. D., Shepherd, D., & Wiklund, J. (2012). Exploring the heart: Entrepreneurial emotion is a hot topic. *Entrepreneurship Theory and Practice*, *36*(1), 1–10.

Chamberlain, A. (2017). What matters more to your workforce than money. *Harvard Business Review*. https://hbr.org/2017/01/what-matters-more-to-your-workforce-than-money.

Chell, E., & Baines, S. (2000). Networking, entrepreneurship and microbusiness behaviour. *Entrepreneurship and Regional Development*, *12*(3), 195–215. https://doi.org/10.1080/089856200413464.

Chell, E., Haworth, J. M., & Brearley, S. (1991). *The entrepreneurial personality: Concepts, cases, and categories*. Cengage Learning (EMEA).

DeJoy, D. M., Wilson, M. G., Vandenberg, R. J., McGrath-Higgins, A. L., & Griffin-Blake, C. S. (2010). Assessing the impact of healthy work organization intervention. *Journal of Occupational and Organizational Psychology*, *83*, 139–165.

Dewe, P. J., O'Driscoll, M. P., & Cooper, C. L. (2012). *Theories of psychological stress at work. In Handbook of occupational health and wellness* (pp. 23–38). Springer.

Diener, E. (1984). Subjective well-being. *Psychological Bulletin*, *95*(3), 542–575. https://doi.org/10.1037/0033-2909.95.3.542.

Dyer, J. H., & Singh, H. (1998). The relational view: Cooperative strategy and sources of interorganizational competitive advantage. *Academy of Management Review*, *23*(4), 660–679.

Farrell, A., & Geist-Martin, P. (2005). Communicating social health: Perceptions of wellness at work. *Management Communication Quarterly*, *18*, 543–592.

Fisher, C. D. (2010). Happiness at work. *International Journal of Management Reviews*, *12*(4), 384–412. https://doi.org/10.1111/j.1468-2370.2009.00270.x.

Florin, J., Lubatkin, M., & Schulze, W. (2003). A social capital model of high-growth ventures. *Academy of Management Journal*, *46*(3), 374–384.

Foo, M. D. (2011). Emotions and entrepreneurial opportunity evaluation. *Entrepreneurship Theory and Practice*, *35*(2), 375–393.

Foo, M. D., Uy, M. A., & Baron, R. A. (2009). How do feelings influence effort? An empirical study of entrepreneurs' affect and venture effort. *Journal of Applied Psychology*, *94*(4), 1086–1094. https://doi.org/10.1037/a0015599.

Gioia, D. A., Corley, K. G., & Hamilton, A. L. (2013). Seeking qualitative rigor in inductive research: Notes on the Gioia methodology. *Organizational Research Methods*, *16*(1), 15–31.

Hahn, V. C., Frese, M., Binnewies, C., & Schmitt, A. (2012). Happy and proactive? The role of hedonic and eudaimonic well-being in business owners' personal initiative. *Entrepreneurship Theory and Practice*, *36*(1), 97–114. https://doi.org/10.1111/j.1540-6520.2011.00490.x.

Jenkins, A. S., Wiklund, J., & Brundin, E. (2014). Individual responses to firm failure: Appraisals, grief, and the influence of prior failure experience. *Journal of Business Venturing*, *29*(1), 17–33. https://doi.org/10.1016/j.jbusvent.2012.10.006.

Johnson, S., Robertson, I., & Cooper, C. L. (2017). *Well-being: Productivity and happiness at work*. Springer.

Johnson, S., Robertson, I., Cooper, C. L., Buxton-Cope, V., & Desbonne-Smith, B. (2018). On track for wellbeing: Everyone fit for the future. In S. Johnson, I. Robertson, & C. L. (Eds.), *Well-being: Productivity, and happiness at work* (2nd ed., pp. 173–177). Palgrave Macmillan.

Kotey, B., & Folker, C. (2007). Employee training in SMEs: Effect of size and firm type—Family and nonfamily. *Journal of Small Business Management*, *45*(2), 214–238.

Kotey, B., & Slade, P. (2005). Formal human resource management practices in small growing firms. *Journal of Small Business Management*, *43*(1), 16–40.

Lopez, S. J., Pedrotti, J. T., & Snyder, C. R. (2018). *Positive psychology: The scientific and practical explorations of human strengths* (4th ed.). Sage Publications.

McKeever, E., Anderson, A., & Jack, S. (2014). Social embeddedness in entrepreneurship research: The importance of context and community. In *Handbook of research on small business and entrepreneurship* (pp. 222–236). Edward Elgar Publishing.

Mitchell, R. K., Mitchell, J. R., & Smith, J. B. (2008). Inside opportunity formation: Enterprise failure, cognition, and the creation of opportunities. *Strategic Entrepreneurship Journal*, *2*(3), 225–242. https://doi.org/10.1002/sej.51.

Mitra, J. (2020). *Entrepreneurship, innovation and regional development: An introduction* (2nd ed.). Routledge.

Monsen, E., & Boss, R. W. (2009). The impact of strategic entrepreneurship inside the organization: Examining job stress and employee retention. *Entrepreneurship Theory and Practice*, *33*(1), 71–104.

Peters, P., Den Dulk, L., & Van Der Lippe, T. (2009). The effects of time-spatial flexibility and new working conditions on employees' work–life balance: The Dutch case. *Community, Work & Family*, *12*(3), 279–297.

Peterson, M., & Wilson, J. F. (2002). The culture-work-health model and work stress. *American Journal of Health Behavior*, *26*, 16–24.

Raya, R. P., & Panneerselvam, S. (2013). The healthy organization construct: A review and research agenda. *Indian Journal of Occupational and Environmental Medicine*, *17*, 89–93.

Robertson, I. T., Cooper, C. L., & Johnson, S. (2011). *Well-being: Productivity and happiness at work* (Vol. 3). Palgrave Macmillan.

Ryan, R. M., & Deci, E. L. (2001). On happiness and human potentials: A review of research on hedonic and eudaimonic well-being. *Annual Review of Psychology*, *52*(1), 141–166. https://doi.org/10.1146/annurev.psych.52.1.141.

Ryff, C. D., & Keyes, C. L. M. (1995). The structure of psychological wellbeing revisited. *Journal of Personality and Social Psychology*, *69*(4), 719–727.

Schjoedt, L. (2009). Entrepreneurial job characteristics: An examination of their effect on entrepreneurial satisfaction. *Entrepreneurship Theory and Practice*, *33*(3), 619–644.

Schumpeter, J. A. (1934). *Change and the entrepreneur. Essays of JA Schumpeter*. Harvard University Press.

Seligman, M. E. P., & Csíkszentmihályi, M. (2000). Positive psychology: An introduction. *American Psychologist*, *55*(1), 5–14. https://doi.org/10.1037/0003-066X.55.1.5.

Shepherd, D. A., & Patzelt, H. (2015). The "heart" of entrepreneurship: The impact of entrepreneurial action on health and health on entrepreneurial action. *Journal of Business Venturing Insights*, *4*, 22–29. https://doi.org/10.1016/j.jbvi.2015.08.001.

Shir, N. (2015). *Entrepreneurial wellbeing: The payoff structure of business creation*. Stockholm School of Economics.

Sparks, K., Faragher, B., & Cooper, C. L. (2001). Well-being and occupational health in the 21st century workplace. *Journal of Occupational and Organizational Psychology*, *74*, 489–509.

Stephan, U. (2018). Entrepreneurs' mental health and well-being: A review and research agenda. *Academy of Management Perspectives*, *32*(3), 290–322. https://doi.org/10.5465/amp.2017.0001.

Stephan, U., Rauch, A., & Hatak, I. (2023). Happy entrepreneurs? Everywhere? A meta-analysis of entrepreneurship and wellbeing. *Entrepreneurship Theory and Practice*, *47*(2), 553–593. https://doi.org/10.1177/10422587211072799.

Uy, M. A., Foo, M. D., & Song, Z. (2013). Joint effects of prior start-up experience and coping strategies on entrepreneurs' psychological well-being. *Journal of Business Venturing*, *28*(5), 583–597. https://doi.org/10.1016/j.jbusvent.2012.04.003.

Wach, D., Stephan, U., & Gorgievski, M. (2016). More than money: Developing an integrative multi-factorial measure of entrepreneurial success. *International Small Business Journal*, *34*(8), 1098–1121. https://doi.org/10.1177/0266242615608469.

Welter, F., Baker, T., Audretsch, D. B., & Gartner, W. B. (2017). Everyday entrepreneurship—a call for entrepreneurship research to embrace entrepreneurial diversity. *Entrepreneurship Theory and Practice*, *41*(3), 311–321.

Wiklund, J., Nikolaev, B., Shir, N., Foo, M. D., & Bradley, S. (2019). Entrepreneurship and well-being: Past, present, and future. *Journal of Business Venturing*, *34*(4), 579–588. https://doi.org/10.1016/j.jbusvent.2019.01.002.

Williams, T. A., & Shepherd, D. A. (2016). Victim entrepreneurs doing well by doing good: Venture creation and well-being in the aftermath of a resource shock. *Journal of Business Venturing*, *31*(4), 365–387. https://doi.org/10.1016/j.jbusvent.2016.04.002

Williamson, O. E. (2000). The new institutional economics: Taking stock, looking ahead. *Journal of Economic Literature*, *38*(3), 595–613.

Wilson, W. J., & Chaddha, A. (2009). The role of theory in ethnographic research. *Ethnography*, *10*(4), 549–564. https://doi.org/10.1177/1466138109347009.

Wrzesniewski, A., & Dutton, J. E. (2001). Crafting a job: Revisioning employees as active crafters of their work. *Academy of Management Review*, *26*(2), 179–201.

14 The Toll of Leadership

Mental Health Challenges of Leaders

Hooria Jazaieri

From business to sports, leaders exist in public and private corporations, and in for-impact nonprofit sectors. The term "leader" can be broadly construed as "one life [positively] influencing another" (Maxwell & Dornan, 1997), whereby the opportunity and responsibility of leadership do not fall on a few, but rather on many. However, for purposes of this chapter, I refer to "leader" as *positional leadership* wherein a person has an official title, is in a position of formal authority, and occupies the upper echelons of an organization's flowchart. From this vantage point, leaders are increasingly faced with unprecedented challenges and are expected to produce extraordinary results (e.g., growth, profit, rankings) for a broadening pool of stakeholders. Leaders are responsible for not only continuing to "be better" themselves but also encouraging, guiding, and inspiring others around them to "be better." After all, from John Quincy Adams to leadership scholars, it is an accepted truism that the best leaders create more great leaders. All the while, leaders are also called to treat their workforce like "family" and attend to the mental health and well-being of their employees (e.g., McKinsey, 2022). Simultaneously, leaders need to manage their own mental health. While there has long been a fascination with the private lives of leaders, relatively little attention has been paid to their mental health specifically (e.g., van Doorn et al., 2023). In part, this is due to the difficulty in obtaining such sensitive information from leaders about their psychological experiences, which has likely contributed to the lack of research in this area (e.g., Mannor et al., 2016).

This chapter first reviews the existing research highlighting the unique stressors and pressures that come with leadership, acknowledging the internal and external expectations and demands to consistently perform at a high level and how this manifests as psychological conditions. Importantly, most of the literature in this space neglects to consider the unique challenges for those who are not traditionally seen as "leaders," including women, persons of color, or those who identify with other marginalized identities. Next, the chapter considers the societal and organizational cultural factors that perpetuate silence and stigma around mental health for those leading organizations and the consequences of this. This silence and stigma of unaddressed leader mental health challenges

DOI: 10.4324/9781003491170-18

have a substantial organizational impact. The chapter concludes with an invitation to reimagine leader mental health, making specific suggestions for individuals, teams, organizations, and business education. I approach this topic both as a management professor who teaches classes on leadership to undergraduate business students and MBAs, as well as a licensed psychotherapist in California.

The Perils of Leadership

While leadership is often "romanticized" and painted in an "overly heroic" manner (e.g., Fulop et al., 2004; Meindl, 1995), there are unique stressors and pressures that come with leadership given the complex and ambiguous situations that leaders face. In an increasingly polarized society, including workplaces (e.g., Martin & Reeves, 2022; Minson & Gino, 2022), it is inevitable that some of a leader's decisions will alienate important stakeholders who are both internal and external to the organization. Given that society and organizations still tend to shift blame and responsibility in order to attribute fault, those in positional leadership are often the ones who are assigned blame and ascribed responsibility when failures, setbacks, and mistakes occur. Additionally, for positional leaders, when involuntary turnover occurs, there are generally a limited number of alternative work opportunities available to the leader, meaning that involuntary turnover is quite consequential and may result in not only an employment gap but also reputational harm. Thus, the stakes continue to rise for those in formal positions of leadership, exacerbating the pressure and mental health difficulties.

While it has always been the case that leaders faced extraordinarily high expectations and demands to perform at an exceptional level (e.g., Li et al., 2018), given the rise of social media, leaders face immediate, unrelenting, and often anonymous, public scrutiny for every decision (or indecision) made, which adds to the pressure to perform without errors. Thus, it is no surprise that leaders experience a plethora of mental health challenges. According to the Gallup 2024 State of the Global Workplace, compared to those who are not in formal positions of leadership, leaders are more likely to experience negative affective states such as stress, anger, sadness, and loneliness. As briefly described later, these mental health challenges are consequential not just for the leader but those they interact with at work as well as the larger organization.

While some degree of stress is adaptive for peak performance (e.g., McGonigal, 2016; Yerkes & Dodson, 1908), it is well documented that leaders experience higher levels of stress and burnout compared to the general population (Gallup, 2024). Thus, some suggest that leadership and stress are "inextricably linked" (Harms et al., 2017, p. 178). The stress that leaders experience not only influences their own behaviors but also influences their relationships with others (for a meta-analysis, see Harms et al., 2017). It is important to note that the source of the leaders' stress may be work related or nonwork related (and yet still spillover into the leaders' work–life). Related to stress is burnout. Burnout consists of three key components—overwhelming exhaustion, cynicism and detachment, and a sense of ineffectiveness (Maslach & Leither, 2016). Experts suggest that burnout "represents an erosion in values, dignity, spirit, and will—an erosion of the human soul" (Maslach & Leiter, 2000, p. 17). Perhaps unsurprisingly, there is an inverse relationship between CEO burnout and firm performance (Sirén et al., 2018). Thus, from a strictly financial standpoint, leader burnout is bad economics.

Beyond stress and burnout, many leaders also experience anxiety. The experience of anxiety may be more situational in nature—related to more transient or fluctuating factors that tend to be temporary in nature (e.g., an upcoming earnings call), or more dispositional, static, or constant experience of anxiety (e.g., Cheng & McCarthy, 2018). Similar to stress, while some degree of anxiety is adaptive, too much anxiety can interfere with productivity and performance (e.g., Cheng & McCarthy, 2018). The anxiety leaders' experience not only has profound implications for them as individuals but also impacts others in the organization. For example, leaders' anxiety influences decision-making such that these executives take fewer strategic risks (e.g., Mannor et al., 2016). Leaders' anxiety is also related to higher abusive supervision (e.g., Byrne et al., 2014; Xi et al., 2022). Given that leaders' mood and emotions can be transferred to others (see Barsade et al., 2018), new research shows that a leader's anxiety can be contaged to their followers even through electronic (rather than face-to-face) communication (Gruda et al., 2022). Again, similar to stress, the leaders' anxiety may be work related (e.g., about their own performance or that of the organization) or nonwork related (e.g., college preparation for their adolescent) that spills over into the leaders' work–life.

Leadership can also feel "lonely at the top." When considering the experience of loneliness, a misconception that persists is that loneliness occurs when a person is isolated and alone; however, it is possible to also experience loneliness with frequent interactions with others (e.g., Hadley & Wright, 2024; Ozcelik & Barsade, 2018). While employees at all levels experience loneliness (e.g., Ozcelik & Barsade, 2018), somewhat embedded into the position of leadership is the experience of loneliness. Leader loneliness is defined as "feelings of lacking companionship from one's followers at work" (Gabriel et al., 2021, p. 1517). Leaders, while interacting frequently with others, tend to have more formal and less familiar interactions with others in their organization, and are generally expected to be the ones providing support for others (as part of their role), rather than receiving support from others (e.g., Toegel et al., 2013). Providing support for others, and not receiving support oneself, understandably has consequences for the leader's emotions (e.g., Lanaj & Jennings, 2020). Loneliness can turn into more severe experiences such as depression. The negative consequences of leaders' depressive symptoms may only exist at the individual level but in many cases can also affect others; for example, leaders' depressive symptoms are related to higher abusive supervision (e.g., Byrne et al., 2014).

While mental health issues such as depression can create problems for the leader, often the response or attempt to experience symptom relief can exacerbate the existing issue and create new issues. For example, approximately 10–25% of adults report consuming alcohol to cope with negative affective states (Cooper et al., 1992). Thus, like many employees (e.g., Martin et al., 1992), leaders also engage in self-medication attempts to address their symptoms by using substances (e.g., alcohol, drugs), which can exacerbate existing mental health issues and lead to other complications. As described previously, leaders are particularly stressed in their roles, and stress is considered to be a major risk factor for substance abuse and addiction (e.g., Frone, 2008; Harris & Heft, 1992; Sinha, 2008). Leaders' responses to stress can have a negative influence beyond the focal leader. For example, leaders' alcohol consumption is related to higher abusive supervision (e.g., Byrne et al., 2014). While silence and stigma around alcohol and substance use among top executives still persists, there are an increasing number of treatment facilities and rehabilitation programs that specifically target business executives (e.g., Sahadi, 2018).

Finally, it is important to note that while the perils of leadership exist for nearly all leaders, certain identity factors—being a woman, a person of color, coming from other marginalized groups, and intersectionality—can exacerbate the typical mental health perils of leadership. The reality of the additional mental health challenges for leaders who identify as women, minorities, and other marginalized groups has been historically neglected in research and in practice. Some research has shown that minority leaders who experience the common experience of workplace microaggressions experience heightened self-blame, isolation, emotional suppression, and negative health implications, among other consequences (Holder et al., 2015). Thus, it is important for research and practice in this space to recognize that while the perils of leadership exist for all, it is magnified for leaders from marginalized groups. This is an important area for future research to continue to develop.

Silence and Stigma Around Struggles

For leaders, there is often a sense that they are always performing, on stage, putting on a façade, and thus, separate from others—"I learned how to check most of my current worries with my hat and coat as I entered the wine and cheese party" (Jackson, 1977, p. 431). A leader experiencing mental health challenges violates the prototypes and expectations that people have of what it means to be an organizational leader (e.g., Cloutier & Barling, 2023). Similar to what is found in the general populations (e.g., Sickel et al., 2014), but to an extreme (e.g., Coe et al., 2021), there is stigma and reluctance among leaders to discuss the mental health challenges that they are experiencing (e.g., Barling & Cloutier, 2017). This lack of disclosure also contributes to the lack of research within this domain. In general, leaders seek to maintain their status (e.g., DeRue & Ashford,

2010; Foulk et al., 2018) and are thus unlikely to share their own struggles due to the "status penalty" incurred when disclosing information that may be interpreted by others as a "weakness" (e.g., Gibson et al., 2018). Some leaders I have encountered in my work have expressed fear of their mental health challenges being "weaponized" and "used" against them. The root of these fears is generally grounded in one's own past experiences, or the experiences of other leaders who have shared their mental health challenges and have been penalized. For example, one executive shared that his disclosure of mental health challenges resulted in his board of directors losing confidence in his ability to fulfil the duties of his job and holding a vote of no confidence, which resulted in him being let go from his job. In other cases, leaders may disclose and retain their jobs but may become the target of workplace gossip and experience a loss of respect from those whom they are leading. Thus, organizational environments with low psychological safety are unlikely to encourage leaders to share their mental health difficulties.

While stigma may prevent some leaders from disclosing and receiving mental health assistance, other leaders choose to remain silent for other reasons. Many leaders feel privileged to have the personal and professional lives that they have, which afford them many luxuries that most do not experience. Thus, for these reasons, these leaders may feel strong negative emotions such as guilt and shame about their mental health struggles. These emotions can cause leaders to actively avoid disclosure and, in some cases, prevent them from reaching out for mental health assistance. Thus, while leader mental health is left unaddressed for various reasons, the consequences of this lack of disclosure can have profound implications for leadership effectiveness, decision-making, communication, and organizational culture.

Invitation to Reimagine Leader Mental Health

The average employee spends approximately a third of their lives at work, and for leaders, it is even more. Thus, organizations can seize the unique opportunity to be change-agents in enhancing leader mental health. To do so, organizations and their members must reimagine leader mental health, not just from a standpoint of responding following onset and disclosure but also proactively taking action to help prevent or mitigate mental health challenges. It is important to note that while many leaders may be genetically predisposed to certain forms of psychopathology (similar to the general population), they may not necessarily develop symptoms that interfere with their ability to function, or meet criteria for a clinical disorder. Nevertheless, given that change efforts instantiated from the top tend to be more effective (e.g., Schein, 2010), a natural starting point for considering promoting mental health is through creating organizational cultures that prioritize leader mental health and well-being. According to Schein's (2010) widely accepted framework, organizational culture can be defined as consisting of three interrelated components—underlying assumptions and beliefs that are both implicit and explicitly held, norms and values (both espoused and enacted) about what constitutes appropriate attitudes and behaviors, and artifacts (e.g., language, symbols) that reflect the assumptions, beliefs, norms, and values.

When considering organizational artifacts, norms and values, and underlying assumptions, there are many opportunities to intervene in order to shift organizations from being contexts that are *depleting* for leader mental health and well-being to contexts that *promote* mental health. For instance, organizational artifacts are any visible features of the organization's culture which includes its physical spaces. Due to scheduling constraints, many leaders who seek out psychological services opt for telehealth appointments to address their mental health issues. While access to "therapy anywhere" seems ideal for busy working professionals, the physical spaces in most organizations are not set up for leaders to take private, personal calls. In open office plans or in-office spaces that are highly visible with little privacy (e.g., transparent glass, thin walls), this can be challenging for those who wish to take telehealth appointments from the office. Organizations can consider having dedicated soundproof spaces where all employees, leaders or otherwise, can take private, personal calls.

When considering norms and values, certain norms (e.g., no days off, long days with little sleep) and values (e.g., productivity, high energy) may be counter to best practices to preserve mental health and well-being. Instead, organizations can reconsider the norms around frequent travel, scheduling back-to-back events with long hours (and often without healthy, nutritious food), and the prevalence of substances at work events. When considering organizational values, organizations can choose to prioritize flourishing of organizational members above everything else (e.g., Dutton et al., 2010). When truly valuing the flourishing of organizational members, businesses are committed to keeping the health and well-being of their people as the number one strategic objective of the organization.

Assumptions about the appropriateness of emotions also influences organizational culture. Recent literature on organizational culture has emphasized the emotional component of culture—emotional culture (Barsade & O'Neill, 2014). Emotional culture refers to "the behavioral norms and artifacts, as well as the underlying values and assumptions, that guide the expression (or suppression) of specific emotions and the appropriateness of displaying those emotions within a social unit" (O'Neill & Rothbard, 2017, p. 78). Many organizations' emotional culture implicitly or explicitly promotes a culture, whereby the experience and expression of positive emotion are emphasized—at the extreme of "toxic positivity" (i.e., "the excessive and ineffective overgeneralization of a happy, optimistic state across all situations") that "results in the denial, minimization, and invalidation of the authentic human emotional experience" (Quintero & Long, 2019, para. 4), and any mention of negative emotions is to be avoided and suppressed (e.g., Gross & Levenson, 1997). The mention of negative emotional experiences is seen as detracting from the "positive culture" or "positive vibes" that many strive to have in their organizations. While organizational members still inevitably experience negative emotions—about the work, about each other, and about world events—the expectation is that it is swept under the rug and not shared or addressed. Decades of research on emotional suppression illustrates why such practices are problematic (e.g., Gross & Levenson, 1997; John & Gross, 2004; Srivastava et al., 2009). Furthermore, such cultures where negative emotions are not permitted communicate to organizational members that the workplace is not a context where such emotions can be disclosed or dealt with. Given how much time is spent at work, this seems like a missed opportunity. In fact, sharing one's own mental health challenges with others can help not only the leader but also others in the organization (e.g., Greenwood, 2023).

Rather than suppressing negative emotions, making conversation and dialogue about difficult mental health challenges an ordinary part of organizational life will have benefits not only for leaders but also for all organizational members across the organization. Currently, many leaders do not feel comfortable having open conversations about their mental health challenges. In fact, in some of my research looking at executives with bipolar disorder, many leaders experience fear and actively worry about potential adverse consequences if their organization found out about their mental health challenges (Hadley et al., 2024). During my time in my clinical private practice, while I did not accept insurance directly and was an out-of-network provider, I gave all patients a "superbill" (a document that summarizes services rendered). Depending on one's insurance plan and coverage, superbills can be submitted by the patient to obtain partial reimbursement, or meet annual insurance deductibles. Routinely, top executives would decline superbills (which typically meant forgoing a hefty five-figure annual insurance reimbursement) as they worried about their organizations finding out that they were seeking mental health treatment (superbills also include a diagnostic and procedure codes which discloses the nature of the patients' diagnosis and treatment). Normalizing conversations around mental health in workplaces and society more generally, and advocating for organizational members to proactively seek out mental health treatment is an important step.

These days, most organizations have many tools and resources available for employees to seek out support ranging from meditation rooms to tele-mental health to in-office exercise classes and trainers to employee resource groups (ERGs). At the same time, organizations should also consider the unique needs of leaders as they are often not the target of these programs and their needs are neglected (e.g., Barling & Cloutier, 2017). For instance, the professional training required of a clinician equipped to specifically address the mental health needs of leaders (who are often dealing with complex comorbidities) may necessitate additional intensive training that many clinicians do not have. Or the typical in-office exercise classes and physical training programs (which have been shown to improve mental health; e.g., Morres et al., 2019) held at lunchtime may not accommodate leaders who are often in meetings during the lunch hour. Thus, while these in-office perks and benefits are technically available to all organizational members, organizations should track the utilization of those who are using these resources and where they fall in the organizational hierarchy. Leaders often express that these resources, while technically available, are not designed to meet their unique needs.

Finally, organizations are encouraged to explicitly hold leaders accountable for prioritizing their own health and well-being. For example, organizations can set minimum vacation or mental health day requirements for leaders every quarter. Given that what is rewarded is repeated and what is punished is avoided (Clear, 2018), organizations can consider how to provide positive reinforcements or negative consequences (monetary or non-monetary in nature) to incentivize leaders to take their minimum vacation or mental health days each quarter. In order to promote such efforts organization-wide, organizations can set up creative ways to celebrate leaders taking vacation or mental health days (e.g., a designated Slack channel or internal group where leaders can post a photo from their time away from the office).

While taking a multi-day vacation to the beach or mountains can be awe-inspiring, and quite rejuvenating for leaders, it is important to note that vacation days or mental health days do not require physically leaving one's local area. Days away from the office can also include staying local and taking what Dr. Marsha Linehan calls a "mini-vacation" (Linehan, 1993; 2014). Mini-vacations can include engaging in any activity for a short period of time that helps an individual take a temporary break from daily stressors. Distress tolerance skills (i.e., skills that increase a person's capacity to experience and endure negative psychological states; Simons & Gaher, 2005), such as these mini-vacations, can help improve one's ability to regulate emotions and cope (e.g., Muhomba et al., 2017). Some examples of mini-vacations could include packing a picnic lunch and visiting a local park for a few hours, or engaging in a hobby that you do not normally make time for. Listening to beautiful, awe-inspiring music can also be beneficial (e.g., Monroy & Keltner, 2023). It is important that the mini-vacation truly feels like a vacation, even if brief. As Linehan describes (1993, 2014), this means being fully present and engaged in the mini-vacation (i.e., no checking work email at the picnic, ruminating about work problems while listening to Beethoven's Moonlight Sonata). Additionally, it is helpful to have an array of mini-vacation options available (e.g., with others or alone, non-weather-dependent activities, shorter or longer in duration). In sum, organizations have a distinct opportunity to envision, create, and encourage a work place where leader and employee mental health is the top business priority. Without prioritizing the people in the organization, it is difficult to meet the goals of other strategic objectives.

Conclusion

Just like all employees, leaders have a need to feel a sense of community and belonging in their organizations (e.g., Zumaeta, 2019). Business and society are at a crucial crossroads in addressing the mental health challenges facing leaders around the globe. If it chooses to do so, business can contribute to a valuable common good in society—not because of the products and technology it produces—but because of the way that business chooses to address the mental health and well-being of the leaders and employees within the organization. Demonstration of this commitment to the mental and emotional health and well-being of *all* employees, which includes those at the top of a business organizational chart, is the most profound act of courage and compassion.

References

Barling, J., & Cloutier, A. (2017). Leaders' mental health at work: Empirical, methodological, and policy directions. *Journal of Occupational Health Psychology, 22*, 394–406.

Barsade, S. G., Coutifaris, C. G., & Pillemer, J. (2018). Emotional contagion in organizational life. *Research in Organizational Behavior, 38*, 137–151.

Barsade, S.G., & O'Neill, O.A. (2014). What's love got to do with it? A longitudinal study of the culture of companionate love and employee and client outcomes in a long-term care setting. *Administrative Science Quarterly,* 59(4), 551–598.

Byrne, A., Dionisi, A. M., Barling, J., Akers, A., Robertson, J., Lys, R.,. . .& Dupré, K. (2014). The depleted leader: The influence of leaders' diminished psychological resources on leadership behaviors. *The Leadership Quarterly,* 25(2), 344–357.

Cheng, B. H., & McCarthy, J. M. (2018). Understanding the dark and bright sides of anxiety: A theory of workplace anxiety. *Journal of Applied Psychology, 103*, 537–560.

Clear, J. (2018). *Atomic habits: An easy & proven way to build good habits & break bad ones.* Penguin.

Cloutier, A. E., & Barling, J. (2023). Expectations of Leaders' Mental Health. *Journal of Leadership & Organizational Studies*, *30*(3), 276–296.

Coe, E., Cordina, J., Enomoto, K., & Seshan, N. (2021). Overcoming stigma: Three strategies toward better mental health in the workplace. *The McKinsey Quarterly*. July, 1–8. https://www.mckinsey.com/industries/healthcare/our-insights/overcoming-stigma-three-strategies-toward-better-mental-health-in-the-workplace#/

Cooper, M. L., Russell, M., Skinner, J. B., Frone, M. R., & Mudar, P. (1992). Stress and alcohol use: Moderating effects of gender, coping, and alcohol expectancies. *Journal of Abnormal Psychology, 101*, 139–152.

DeRue, D. S., & Ashford, S. J. (2010). Who will lead and who will follow? A social process of leadership identity construction in organizations. *Academy of Management Review, 35*(4), 627–647.

Dutton, J., Roberts, L,, & Bednar, J. (2010). Prosocial practices, positive identity, and flourishing at work. In S. Donaldson, M. Csikszentmihalyi, & J. Nakamura (Eds.), *Applied positive psychology: Improving everyday life, schools, work, health, and society* (pp. 427–431). Routledge.

Foulk, T. A., Lanaj, K., Tu, M. H., Erez, A., & Archambeau, L. (2018). Heavy is the head that wears the crown: An actor-centric approach to daily psychological power, abusive leader behavior, and perceived incivility. *Academy of Management Journal, 61*(2), 661–684.

Frone, M. R. (2008). Are work stressors related to employee substance use? The importance of temporal context assessments of alcohol and illicit drug use. *Journal of Applied Psychology, 93*,199–206.

Fulop, L., Linstead, S., & Dunford, R. (2004). Leading and managing. In S. Linstead, L. Fulop, & S. Lilley (Eds.), *Management and organization: A critical text* (pp. 324–363). Palgrave Macmillan.

Gabriel, A.S., Lanaj, K., & Jennings, R. E. (2021). Is one the loneliest number? A within-person examination of the adaptive and maladaptive consequences of leader loneliness at work. *Journal of Applied Psychology, 106*(10), 1517–1538.

Gallup. (2024). *State of the global workplace*. https://www.gallup.com/workplace/349484/state-of-the-global-workplace.aspx

Gibson, K. R., Harari, D., & Marr, J. C. (2018). When sharing hurts: How and why self-disclosing weakness undermines the task-oriented relationships of higher status disclosers. *Organizational Behavior and Human Decision Processes, 144*, 25–43.

Greenwood, K. (2023). Leaders, sharing your own mental health story can help you become a better ally. *Harvard Business Review*. https://hbr.org/2023/05/leaders-sharing-your-own-mental-health-story-can-help-you-become-a-better-ally

Gross, J. J., & Levenson, R.W. (1997). Hiding feelings: The acute effects of inhibiting negative and positive emotion. *Journal of Abnormal Psychology, 106*(1), 95–103.

Gruda, D., Ojo, A., & Psychogios, A. (2022). Don't you tweet me badly: Anxiety contagion between leaders and followers in computer-mediated communication during COVID–19. *PLoS One*, *17*(3), e0264444.

Hadley, C. N., Jazaieri, H., & Elfenbein, H. A. (2024). Lessons from leaders with bipolar disorder. *Harvard Business Review*. https://hbr.org/2024/06/3-ways-to-support-employees-with-bipolar-disorder

Hadley, C. N., & Wright, S. L. (2024). We're still lonely at work: It's time for organizations to take a new approach. *Harvard Business Review*, *102*(6), 68–77.

Harms, P. D., Credé, M., Tynan, M., Leon, M., & Jeung, W. (2017). Leadership and stress: A meta-analytic review. *The leadership Quarterly, 28*(1), 178–194.

Harris, M. M., & Heft, L. L. (1992). Alcohol and drug use in the workplace: Issues, controversies, and directions for future research. *Journal of Management, 18*, 239–266.

Holder, A., Jackson, M. A., & Ponterotto, J. G. (2015). Racial microaggression experiences and coping strategies of Black women in corporate leadership. *Qualitative Psychology, 2*(2), 164–180.

Jackson, P. W. (1977). Lonely at the top: Observations on the genesis of administrative isolation. *School Review*, *85*, 425–432.

John, O. P., & Gross, J. J. (2004). Healthy and unhealthy emotion regulation: Personality processes, individual differences, and life span development. *Journal of Personality, 72*(6), 1301–1334.

Lanaj, K., & Jennings, R. E. (2020). Putting leaders in a bad mood: The affective costs of helping followers with personal problems. *Journal of Applied Psychology*, *105*(4), 355–371.

Li, W. D., Schaubroeck, J. M., Xie, J. L., & Keller, A. C. (2018). Is being a leader a mixed blessing? A dual-pathway model linking leadership role occupancy to well-being. *Journal of Organizational Behavior, 39*, 971–989.

Linehan, M. M. (1993). *Skills training manual for treating borderline personality disorder*. Guilford Press.

Linehan, M. M. (2014). *DBT skills training manual* (2nd ed.). Guilford Press.

Mannor, M J., Wowak, A. J., Bartkus, V. O., & Gomez-Mejia, L. R. (2016). Heavy lies the crown? How job anxiety affects top executive decision making in gain and loss contexts. *Strategic Management Journal, 37*(9), 1968–1989.

Martin, J. K., Blum, T. C., & Roman, P. M. (1992). Drinking to cope and self-medication: Characteristics of jobs in relation to workers' drinking behavior. *Journal of Organizational Behavior, 13*(1), 55–71.

Martin, R. L., & Reeves, M. (2022, November/December). Strategy in a hyperpolitical world. *Harvard Business Review, 100*(6), 47–52.

Maslach, C., & Leiter, M. P. (2000). *The truth about burnout: How organizations cause personal stress and what to do about it*. John Wiley & Sons.

Maslach, C., & Leiter, M. P. (2016). Understanding the burnout experience: Recent research and its implications for psychiatry. *World Psychiatry, 15*(2), 103–111.

Maxwell, J. C., & Dornan, J. (1997). *Becoming a person of influence: How to positively impact the lives of others*. Thomas Nelson.

McGonigal, K. (2016). *The upside of stress: Why stress is good for you, and how to get good at it*. Penguin.

McKinsey. (2022). *Present company included: Prioritizing mental health and well-being for all*. https://www.mckinsey.com/mhi/our-insights/present-company-included-prioritizing-mental-health-and-well-being-for-all

Meindl, J. (1995). The romance of leadership as a follower-centric theory: A social constructionist approach. *Leadership Quarterly, 6*(3), 329–341.

Minson, J. A., & Gino, F. (2022, March/April). Managing a polarized workforce. *Harvard Business Review, 100*(2), 63–71.

Monroy, M., & Keltner, D. (2023). Awe as a pathway to mental and physical health. *Perspectives on Psychological Science, 18*(2), 309–320.

Morres, I. D., Hatzigeorgiadis, A., Stathi, A., Comoutos, N., Arpin-Cribbie, C., Krommidas, C., & Theodorakis, Y. (2019). Aerobic exercise for adult patients with major depressive disorder in mental health services: A systematic review and meta-analysis. *Depression and Anxiety, 36*(1), 39–53.

Muhomba, M., Chugani, C. D., Uliaszek, A. A., & Kannan, D. (2017). Distress tolerance skills for college students: A pilot investigation of a brief DBT group skills training program. *Journal of College Student Psychotherapy, 31*(3), 247–256.

O'Neill, O. A., & Rothbard, N. P. (2017). Is love all You need? The effects of emotional culture, suppression, and work–family conflict on firefighter Risk-taking and health. *Academy of Management Journal, 60*, 78–108.

Ozcelik, H., & Barsade, S. G. (2018). No employee an island: Workplace loneliness and job performance. *Academy of Management Journal, 61*(6), 2343–2366.

Quintero, S., & Long, J. (2019). *Toxic positivity: The dark side of positive vibes*. https://thepsychologygroup.com/toxic-positivity/

Sahadi, J. (2018). *Addiction in the C-suite*. https://www.cnn.com/2018/10/17/success/addiction-c-suite-executives/index.html

Schein, E. H. (2010). *Organizational culture and leadership* (4th ed.). John Wiley & Sons.

Sickel, A. E., Seacat, J. D., & Nabors, N. A. (2014). Mental health stigma update: A review of consequences. *Advances in Mental Health, 12*(3), 202–215.

Simons, J. S., & Gaher, R. M. (2005). The Distress Tolerance Scale: Development and validation of a self-report measure. *Motivation and Emotion, 29*(2), 83–102.

Sinha, R. (2008). Chronic stress, drug use, and vulnerability to addiction. *Annals of the New York Academy of Sciences, 1141*(1), 105–130.

Sirén, C., Patel, P. C., Örtqvist, D., & Wincent, J. (2018). CEO burnout, managerial discretion, and firm performance: The role of CEO locus of control, structural power, and organizational factors. *Long Range Planning, 51*(6), 953–971.

Srivastava, S., Tamir, M., McGonigal, K. M., John, O. P., & Gross, J. J. (2009). The social costs of emotional suppression: A prospective study of the transition to college. *Journal of Personality and Social Psychology, 96*(4), 883–897.

Toegel, G., Kilduff, M., & Anand, N. (2013). Emotion helping by managers: An emergent understanding of discrepant role expectations and outcomes. *Academy of Management Journal, 56*(2), 334–357.
Van Doorn, S., Heyden, M. L., & Reimer, M. (2023). The private life of CEOs; A strategic leadership perspective. *The Leadership Quarterly, 34*(1), 101679.
Xi, M., He, W., Fehr, R., & Zhao, S. (2022). Feeling anxious and abusing low performers: A multilevel model of high performance work systems and abusive supervision. *Journal of Organizational Behavior, 43*(1), 91–111.
Yerkes, R. M., & Dodson, J. D. (1908). The relation of strength of stimulus to rapidity of habit formation. *Journal of Comparative Neurology of Psychology, 18*(5), 459–482.
Zumaeta, J. (2019). Lonely at the top: How do senior leaders navigate the need to belong? *Journal of Leadership & Organizational Studies, 26*, 111–135.

Section V

Organizational Responses and Paths Forward

15 Well-Being as Workplace Culture

A Brief Examination of One Firm's Approach to Changing Its Landscape of Well-Being

Samantha G. Deane, Renée D. Edwards, Abigail Clemson, Lisa Schur, and Douglas L. Kruse

American workers are suffering. According to a report by the medical journal Lancet, rates of depression have risen by 28% because of the COVID-19 pandemic, and anxiety has increased by 26% over pre-pandemic levels (Institute for Health Metrics & Evaluations, 2021). Because 60% of the population is working, these issues manifest themselves in the workplace. According to a report by Mental Health America, 71% of employees in 2022 found it difficult to concentrate at work, compared with 65% in 2021 and 46% in 2018 (Mental Health America, 2022).

In line with this, worker demand for employers' attention to mental well-being is also escalating. Eighty-one percent of workers reported that they will be looking for workplaces that support mental health in the future (U.S. Surgeon General, n.d.). COVID-19 made it overtly clear that the workplace directly affects mental health, and a lack of effective structures and support at work can affect workers' ability to do their job well (Fabius & Phares, 2021; O'Brien et al., 2022). These shortfalls can undermine people's attendance at work, lead to higher levels of turnover, and even prevent people from getting a job in the first place (Redekopp & Huston, 2019).

Many companies are struggling to find the most appropriate responses. A 2022 survey of 50,000 employees by Mental Health America (Mental Health America, n.d.) found that employees reported only two in five managers encouraged them to take time off when under stress. Additionally, while 47% of workers know about their employer's mental health services, only 38% feel comfortable using them. Clearly the stigma of mental illness still weighs heavily on workers' willingness to disclose their difficulties and get help.

According to the National Organization on Disability (NOD) Employment Tracker™, a confidential benchmarking survey on workplace disability inclusion practices, 95% of employers now have senior leaders who promote mental health initiatives in some fashion, and 64% say that they have staff responsible for serving as a mental health ambassador. However, only 20% require managers to take part in an annual mental health awareness training.

DOI: 10.4324/9781003491170-20

This chapter considers efforts by one large professional services firm, Ernst & Young LLP (EY US),[1] to change the landscape of well-being within its workplace culture. Seven semi-structured interviews[2] were conducted with six firm representatives over the course of two weeks in March 2023. Using data from those interviews and quantitative, deidentified data provided by EY US, this case examines relevant academic research and frames the firm's efforts within research-identified best practices and challenges.

Mental Health and Well-Being in the Workplace

Research has indicated that mental illness, depression, and anxiety are prime causes of work absence, and that work-related factors can maintain or improve well-being and mental health (Redekopp & Huston, 2019). Studies also indicate organization-level benefits to maintaining a healthy workforce, including increased productivity and lower healthcare costs (Langlieb et al., 2021). Some research even points to cultures of health and well-being as indicators of marketplace performance (Fabius & Phares, 2021). This suggests that the development of a positive culture of health and well-being can have important benefits for employees, organizations, and their performance.

Universal Design

The concept of universal design is grounded in public space planning and is focused on accessibility (Story et al., 1998). For example, rather than adding elements to existing structures to increase accessibility for people with disabilities, a universal design accommodates all people from planning through execution (Preiser & Smith, 2011). This may include designing with ramps, cutaways, and accessible doorways—designs that make spaces usable by all—rather than steps, physical barriers, and doorknobs—elements that restrict use by certain populations and require modification for accessibility. A ramp is useful not only for people who use wheelchairs but also for people with strollers and those who have difficulty in climbing steps. This principle of accessibility, or designing with all people in mind, extends beyond physical design to the design of programs and services (Story et al., 1998). EY US's journey on its mental well-being evolved over the course of many years from a design meant to fix problematic employee situations to a more universal design approach, with prevention and up-stream utilization the goal.

The Evolution of Well-Being at EY US

Starting With an Employee Assistance Program

As early as the 1970s, the firm offered benefits that included mental health support through an internal and external Employee Assistance Program (EAP) that offered no-cost counseling sessions. However, the EY US EAP experienced low utilization due to societal stigma related to mental illness and substance misuse, and the reluctance to ask for help.

Approaching De-Stigmatization of Mental Health Issues Deliberately

In early 2016, the internal clinical team and disability employee resource group (ERG) developed a program to create awareness of the signs someone might be struggling with a mental health or substance issue. Designed as locally based events that combined storytelling, training, and tools/resources, these efforts focused on a "leaders first" model in which leaders shared personal stories of their own or family members' challenges, and began to de-stigmatize mental health issues, build trust, and normalize talking about mental health and addiction. Events of this type are generally unsuccessful without high levels of organizational trust (Dirks & Ferrin, 2001). While EY US did not report acute issues with trust firmwide, representatives indicated that levels of trust varied across teams of employees. Because leadership recognized the need for a strong foundation of trust, they included trust as an essential component to the well-being model. One firm representative said, "Without trust and a basic level of psychological safety, team members will never be able to speak up about wellbeing areas the team needs to address." The events served as one method of trust-building within the organization.

About the events, an EY US representative said,

> The internal [EAP] team conducted hundreds of presentations and interactive sessions addressing the stigma of mental health and the importance of prioritizing wellbeing . . . [and] connected with tens of thousands of EY [US] professionals during the past few years alone, and these efforts led to greater usage of our employee assistance counseling benefit.

During the period when the anti-stigma initiative was launched, the same representative noted: "Our program usage, which was flat in the low single digits for 30 years—similar to workplaces around the country—saw its first increase the very same month we began our anti-stigma initiative." This is a good example of universal design—leadership became aware that focusing on "fixes" to the existing structure was not a tenable way to transform culture.

Expanding the Scope of Well-Being

An e-learning curriculum was developed in 2016 that focused on normalizing conversations around mental health. In 2018, the content for the courses was expanded to include life events, caregiver struggles, parental transitions, financial challenges, loneliness, relationships, and other topics, with healthy sleep habits added in 2019.

Connecting Internally to Enable Relevance

The firm's internal group of EAP clinicians engaged with departments and groups across EY US, allowing them to provide well-being support tailored to specific communities and needs within the firm. Literature discusses multiple benefits of engaging with social networks within an organization to create change (Oreg, 2006). Social network theory argues that "individuals are embedded within social systems that function as reference points for the formation of attitudes" (Brown & Quarter, 1994; Burkhardt, 1994; Erickson, 1988; and Gibbons, 2004, as cited in Oreg, 2006). In other words, the social systems within which an employee works have a substantial role in determining the employee's attitudes (Burkhardt, 1994; Gibbons, 2004, as cited in Oreg, 2006). If an employee's social environment (such as colleagues, supervisors, and subordinates) tends to resist a change, the employee is more likely to resist as well (Brown & Quarter, 1994, as cited in Oreg, 2006). But if an employee's social environment reacts positively toward the change, or feels instrumental in creating it, the opposite can occur.

Responding to New Challenges and Opportunities From the Pandemic

While the COVID-19 pandemic added anxiety and mental health challenges for employees, it also helped normalize talking about well-being and mental health. Additionally, working from home created an atmosphere of authenticity that made work feel more personal. One participant said:

> You were coming into people's homes on [video conference calls], you were hearing dogs barking, you were hearing children, you were hearing roommates or spouses . . . we saw people's lives in a way we hadn't before, which led to a degree of openness and sharing and authenticity; the walls were down. And that made it easier for people to be more real, including for people to share their fears and their concerns, and some of the challenges they were having.

The firm continued to hold well-being events and storytelling throughout the pandemic, shifting to a virtual format that had the unexpected benefit of increasing capacity. One participant said, "we've had webcasts where thousands of people are on, and someone is telling a personal story around the mental health initiative."

Increasing Adoption With Leadership Buy-In

In 2021, EY US created a Chief Wellbeing Officer position to indicate the permanence of its well-being focus, making it, as one participant said, "a business imperative." Research highlights leadership vision and adoption as important to successful organizational change (Oreg & Berson, 2019). The installation of a Chief Wellbeing Officer reinforced commitment to well-being at the firm level and, matched with the firm's "leaders first" approach, helped combine top-down and bottom-up implementation to encourage safe spaces and build trust. A participant noted how instrumental the move was: "Bringing in this role was signaling long-term commitment to wellbeing as an important part of our business strategy."

Another representative said, "our Chief Wellbeing Officer helped expedite buy-in from our leaders to all of our wellbeing efforts." The Chief Wellbeing Officer said, "Creation of the Chief Wellbeing Officer role was really a focus on 'how are we going to transform our culture and our organization with [wellbeing] at the center of it?'" Research finds that in complex situations—such as organizational culture change—visible involvement and commitment by leadership can help by "providing structure that is more absent in purely bottom-up approaches" (Burgemeister et al., 2023).

Normalizing Well-Being at the Team Level

In 2022, EY US created and launched the Team Wellbeing Toolkit—a compilation of resources, programs, and guidelines that teams of employees could choose to implement. By allowing teams to choose ways to implement well-being in their respective teams, the firm created buy-in from teams and their leaders. Team members were involved in rolling out whatever form of well-being actions felt most useful to their individual team, choosing from a set of proposed "norms" (e.g., keeping Fridays free from meetings or not sending emails after 6:00 pm to allow teams to wrap up the workday without interruption). Research highlights this as an effective practice; one study found "engaging and involving others in the process of change is more likely to lead to successful implementation of the change" (Oreg & Berson, 2019, p. 284). Other literature states "situational interactions on an issue from the bottom-up result in increased emotional energy, understanding of the topic, and intention to allocate time and effort to the issue" (Soderstrom & Weber, 2020, p. 255).

Elevating Well-Being in the Business Model Using Well-Being-Focused Performance Goals

EY US adopted the well-being initiative as part of its business model, collecting well-being metrics in a "Vitality Index" and creating specific well-being-focused performance goals for partners and other leaders. Leaders have a formal goal on which their performance is evaluated, related to (1) how they are modeling well-being in their own lives and (2) how they are supporting well-being for their teams.

Solidifying Well-Being at the Team Level by Leveraging the Wellbeing Champions Network

In July 2022, EY US invited employees to become part of a volunteer network of Wellbeing Champions. Wellbeing Champions attend monthly meetings and receive further training on the Team Wellbeing Toolkit, specific firm well-being and mental health benefits, resources, and initiatives which they are able to bring back to their teams. They are then able to better lead their teams in well-being discussions, strategies, and best practices. Wellbeing Champions are recognized by peers and leaders as knowledgeable and approachable well-being advocates who can guide team members to benefits, programs, and resources.

Literature identifies that new initiatives face challenges when they are focused just on individuals and not at the team or organizational level (O'Brien et al., 2022, p. 7). The Wellbeing Champions Network, however, carried out the firm's well-being practices at the team level. One Wellbeing Champion said, "Many people think that team norms and dynamics and how a team works must come from the top down. I think we've been proving that is not the case, [because] we're able to really empower people of all ranks." In considering elements of universal design, deployment at the team rather than individual level takes more perspectives into account and thereby helps create a universal but tailored approach to well-being.

Literature discusses organizational change in teams, stressing that "the team level is where strategic goals are translated into an implementation plan," as mid-level managers must "agree to 'buy-in' or fully accept the change vision themselves and then be able to inspire others. This requires accurately determining the change impact to their team and diagnosing team weakness and strengths" (Heckelman, 2017, p. 17).

Framing Well-Being Within the Team to Create Buy-In and Accountability

The firm's well-being team developed a framework with four "pillars of healthy work" to shape workplace culture and support well-being at the team level. The four pillars are (1) focus, or a culture of well-being, so team members can focus on their work as well as maintain overall wellness; (2) connections, or building healthy relationships with team members to increase inclusion and belonging; (3) predictable flexibility, or having intentional flexibility within the team relative to workload; and (4) efficient impact, or effectively collaborating and focusing on the things with the most impact.

The firm's current goal is to imbed well-being in how teams work together and redefine team norms. Representatives of EY US stress that well-being is a permanent part of how employees relate and interact and that the creation of norms and behaviors that generate well-being for all team members has been framed as a team responsibility. As seen in Figure 15.1, this has been encompassed in the firm's well-being mantra: "wellbeing is a team sport."

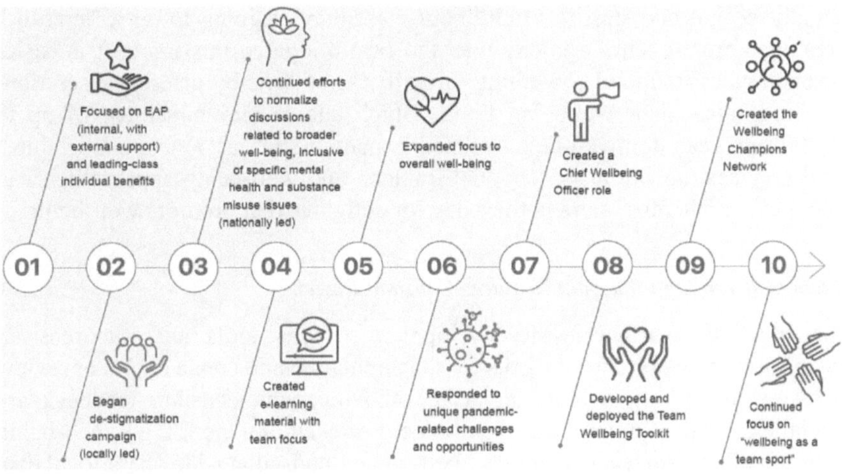

Figure 15.1 Progression of Key Activities in the Evolution of the EY US Well-Being Model.

Challenges

Organizational Culture Change Is Difficult

It involves layers of engagement, buy-in, trust, time, resources, and myriad other elements. Organizations must consider risk, resource investment, and other factors when considering tackling a culture shift (Oreg, 2006; Oreg & Berson, 2019). An interview participant discussed how the firm's teams of experts initially approached the idea of encouraging proactive conversations about mental health with caution. One consideration was the role of the organization in employees' mental health and substance misuse: how involved should an employer be in these issues? Is disclosure of sensitive issues something the firm should be promoting? Few organizational precedents were available.

The firm was also a successful organization with a well-established organizational culture, which presented potential difficulties for teams attempting to implement norms that would change the way work gets done. One participant described the process of change at the firm level, saying "we've got a group of people who've been highly successful operating one way. And we're asking them to reflect on how they've operated and start operating differently, which is just always really hard to change."

Making Time for Well-Being Can Be Difficult

"People are really busy," one representative said, noting that it is therefore difficult "to get to them in forums where they're tuned in and listening and can actually hear it and start to think about what they're going to do differently." Creating virtual events was one way the firm mitigated this issue; it is easier for employees to attend something virtually. Another is by offering discretionary funds through a Wellbeing Fund, which allows reimbursement of up to $1,000 per year, for well-being-related expenses such as gym memberships, meal services, nutritionists, personal trainers, and well-being apps, which can help them create more time in their day for activities that promote well-being.

Staying Current and Relevant Requires Constant Review

Challenges also surface in the development of apps, tools, and resources: an organization must find what works for the population and create cycles of review to assess usefulness. Monitoring usage and receiving constant feedback are crucial elements of maintaining relevance. For example, the EY US well-being team and other firm leaders monitor well-being trends alongside operational data through their Vitality Index dashboard. This dashboard provides insights into the state of vitality, or well-being, across various portions of their operations and across EY US overall. Additionally, the well-being team focuses on data-driven indicators of success in new programs to monitor their effects on employees' well-being scores.

Impact

Success/Impact Metrics

Academic research studying the effects of organizational change highlights several ways to measure impact. These include monitoring employees' awareness and interest in programs/initiatives, normalization of the issue of focus—in this case, mental health and well-being—and attendance or usage of the program or initiative.

Awareness/Interest

Interview participants discussed the high level of awareness of the well-being initiative and resources. One participant said: "I think people love the benefits. They use them. There's so much awareness. People know that we are serious about this." One participant commented:

> I think we've done a lot with awareness around what is mental health, what is wellbeing, what is psychological safety, why it's important to not just wait—have an open-door policy and just expect people to come in and talk about mental problems, you have to go out there because a lot of people don't show signs until it's too late.

This aligns with the principles of universal design, as the well-being initiatives and resources are accessible for everyone and the awareness and language keeps all employees in mind, not just those with diagnosed disabilities (Story et al., 1998). By promoting mental health and well-being for everyone, EY ensures that those with disabilities have the resources they need, while also providing those resources to other employees who could benefit from a focus on their mental health, creating a psychologically safe and inclusive environment for employees to utilize those resources.

Normalization

There seems to be an increased acceptance of well-being as a priority at EY US. One participant said, "we began to see a real shift when we launched our anti-stigma efforts. Over time, there was less discomfort approaching these issues." Another said:

> In the past, people didn't necessarily feel like they might have had the permission to say, "we should do this." They felt like that would have been inappropriate to go to the partner and say, "should we be talking about our team norms and talking about wellbeing?" And now we're creating an environment where everybody feels like, "it's actually OK for me to go and have that conversation."

This illustrates the universal design principles of equitable use—allowing everyone to use the practices—and flexibility in use—accommodating a wide range of preferences and abilities.

Attendance/Usage

A challenge many firms meet when attempting culture change is maintaining initiative relevance and keeping employees engaged. In 2022, EY US created a webcast series to address current issues that may increase anxiety/stress for employees, covering different topics throughout the series. One participant commented: "We've had over 28,000[3] views of these webcasts. And it's continuing, it's growing."

The internal EAP team continues that momentum, increasing the number of benefits overviews, professional network meetings, group support, and other presentations each year, growing the number of sessions by 180% between 2019 and 2022. Across that four-year span, sessions have drawn over 80,000 attendees. The EAP team leads these presentations at the request of ERGs, business units, teams, local offices, and other natural communities within the firm, illustrating the benefits of a combined grassroots and human resources department (central) approach in broadening reach and adoption of content. The Wellbeing

Champions Network has also continued to grow, with current membership of approximately 1,000 employees.

Informing Action

Collecting impact measures has limited benefits unless the organization is willing to act. An interview participant discussed an example of how the Vitality Index has been used to inform action:

> One of our teams had some low wellbeing scores. People didn't feel like they had the time to balance personal and professional demands, and people didn't feel like they had the time to take care of themselves from a health and wellbeing perspective. We were assuming that this team [was] working extensively more hours than anybody else. But when we got into the data, they weren't working any more hours. They also were taking time off at the same rate or more than other teams. They were feeling a disconnect between their level of effort and the level of impact. We're trying to enroll a lot more of that team into the Pathway to Purpose program, and we also have a team purpose program to help teams define their purpose together as a team, and we're pushing [the members of that team] to do that team purpose exercise.

Literature indicates that employees perceive the meaningfulness of their work relative to three dimensions: (1) perceived significance of work, (2) self-realization, and (3) broader purpose (Martela & Pessi, 2018). These three elements combine to help employees find a purpose in their work and a desire to continue working. How employees perceive purpose in their work can directly affect their well-being as well as their attitudes toward their work in general (Hill et al., 2018).

Well-Being Metrics

The EY US well-being team and firm leadership rely on data collected via various surveys to assess the effectiveness of their well-being programs and initiatives and to monitor the overall levels of employee-reported well-being.

Overall Well-Being Sentiment

With nearly a 50% response rate (49% in 2021 and 46% in 2022), the firm's People Pulse survey serves as a reliable check-in for many employee opinions. The percentage of EY US employees who indicated that they agreed or strongly agreed with the prompt "I am comfortable with the personal and professional demands for my time" increased by a highly significant eight percentage points between 2021 and 2022.[4]

In the year between the two surveys, EY US streamlined its survey, combining two well-being questions, as they had historically similar favorability response rates. The questions asked about employees' abilities to dedicate time to their "mental and emotional health needs" and "to practice health habits." The combined question asked about their ability to dedicate time to their "health and wellbeing needs." Looking at both questions in 2021 and the combined question in 2022, the percentage of EY US employees who responded positively (i.e., strongly agree or agree) increased by over ten points.[5]

Program-Level Efficacy

The firm also monitors metrics at the program level. These metrics are used to gauge programs' effects on employees' overall sense of well-being and to monitor program usage. For the EY Fit to Perform well-being program, the proportion of program participants who responded positively that "I can experience a level of wellbeing that is right for me" increased by an average of seven percentage points after program completion across the 2022 and 2023 cohorts.[6]

The Mindful Leadership program also saw improvements in measures of mindfulness, well-being, and empathy when comparing program participant responses from before and after the program. The surveys included 6 questions related to mindfulness, 13 questions related to well-being, and 1 question related to empathy. Looking at overall scores for the three measures, as a percent of maximum possible scores, Figure 15.2 shows the average scores improved by four percentage points for mindfulness, and nine percentage points

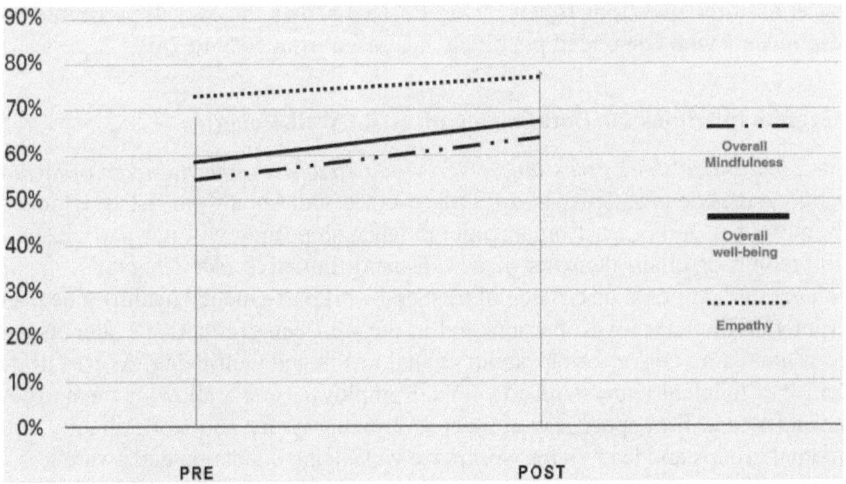

Figure 15.2 Employee Scores Before and After Participation in Mindful Leadership at EY Program.

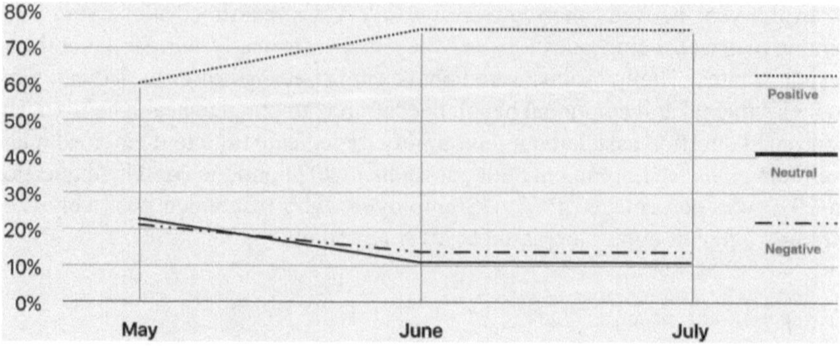

Figure 15.3 Aggregate Trend in Responses of Team Wellbeing Toolkit Pilot Participants to Wellbeing Questions.

for well-being and empathy, representing improvements of 6% in mindfulness and 16% in well-being and empathy.[7] The greatest improvement was seen in the well-being prompt "I've been feeling I'm not thinking clearly," which saw an average improvement of 20%.

When EY US introduced the Team Wellbeing Toolkit, they conducted a pilot and used the People Pulse Survey questions (the 2021 version) to track changes in the pilot teams over the course of three months (May through July 2022). Trends were similar across the three questions, with the percent of respondents who answered positively increasing by 25% for comfort with demands on their time, 27% for ability to dedicate time to support mental and emotional health, and 38% for ability to dedicate time to practice healthy physical habits. Looking at all three questions together, Figure 15.3 shows the overall percentage of respondents who responded positively increased from 59% to 76%.[8]

Recommendations for Building a Culture of Well-Being

First, *build a culture of trust and employ and enable an internal team of mental health professionals*. Trust is difficult to create but should not be overlooked. If employees do not trust organizational leadership, they will not participate in storytelling or other elements of a well-being initiative (see Chapter 8 in this volume for additional discussion of trust and workplace mental health). The team of internal clinicians was instrumental in the well-being initiative's success and de-stigmatizing conversations about mental health and well-being. As part of the firm, the clinicians understand how EY US employees work, allowing them to better understand firm-specific workplace well-being issues and work directly with internal groups and leaders for workplace well-being education and awareness.

Consider well-being for all rather than concentrating on individual "fixes," while promoting well-being in a combined bottom-up and top-down manner. A key element of universal design is to roll out plans focused on everyone in addition to changing existing elements to meet the needs of an individual, such as establishing "wellbeing for all." Asking employees what well-being means to them and engaging individuals and teams are principal elements of well-being culture change. Well-being is not something that can be driven only by the human resources department or firm leadership.

Finally, *invest in a well-being officer or similar executive leadership role focused on well-being and create and monitor measures of success.* Leadership must be involved and engaged for well-being to become institutionalized. Intentional and permanent well-being officers signal that an organization is dedicated to well-being. Organizations should establish research-based well-being metrics that will allow for constant measurement of programs and initiatives. These should include not only numeric measures but also ways to hear qualitative—contextual—evidence of success or failure through avenues of feedback such as focus groups or anonymous written reviews.

Conclusion

The application of a universal design approach helped EY US deploy a well-being model that continues to evolve and improve. Three key elements to the well-being model implementation were as follows: (1) teaming natural firm communities with internal mental health clinicians to create a norm of openness and authenticity in discussing mental health and well-being concerns; (2) ongoing leadership engagement as well-being role models, storytellers, and initiators of well-being dialogue and investment in an executive well-being role; and (3) empowerment of individuals and teams to influence well-being norms and behaviors to fit their specific needs.

EY US continues to refine its well-being initiatives, increasing focus on team well-being to promote boundaries between work and personal time and increasing "bandwidth" for individuals and teams to employ norms and tools. They continue to promote, refine, and assess available well-being tools and programs.

NIDILRR Disclaimer

This chapter was developed under a grant from the National Institute on Disability, Independent Living, and Rehabilitation Research (NIDILRR grant numbers 90DP0086 and 90DPAD0004). NIDILRR is a Center within the Administration for Community Living (ACL), Department of Health and Human Services (HHS). The contents of this brief do not necessarily represent the policy of NIDILRR, ACL, HHS, and you should not assume endorsement by the Federal Government.

Acknowledgments

This publication is supported by the Administration for Community Living (ACL), U.S. Department of Health and Human Services (HHS) as part of a financial assistance award totaling $4,375,000 with 100% funding by ACL/HHS. The contents are those of the author(s) and do not necessarily represent the official views of, nor an endorsement by, ACL/HHS, or the US Government.

The authors would like to thank many people who contributed to this chapter. We appreciate the ongoing partnership with the National Organization on Disability, whose staff assisted with coordination efforts and support. We also appreciate the cooperation and collaboration of Ernst & Young LLP (EY US) throughout planning and data collection efforts. The authors are solely responsible for any errors.

Notes

1 EY is a global organization of member firms, each of which is a separate legal entity. This study applies to the US member firm, Ernst & Young LLP.
2 Interviews were conducted via video conferencing technology and recorded. Transcripts were cleaned using speech-to-text transcription software and coded for themes and categories.
3 In the time between conducting the interviews and the writing of this chapter, views have reached over 31,000.
4 The percentage agreeing or strongly agreeing with this statement increased from 54.0% in 2021 to 61.9% in 2022. The sample sizes were 24,231 in 2021 and 26,119 in 2022. The *T*-statistic for the difference in proportion of favorable responses is 18.0, with a p-value $< .0001$.
5 The average percentage agreeing across the two 2021 statements was 52.8%, and the percentage agreeing with the 2022 statement was 63.3%. The sample sizes were 24,231 in 2021 and 26,119 in 2022. The *T*-statistic for the difference in proportion of favorable responses is 24.1, with a p-value $< .0001$.
6 The average percentage responding positively to this statement was 72.6% before participation and 79.3% after participation. The sample sizes were 1,236 for the pre-participation surveys and 663 for the post-participation surveys. The *T*-statistic for the difference in proportion of favorable responses is 3.34, with a p-value $< .001$.
7 Responses to Mindfulness and Wellbeing questions were on a 6-point scale, and Empathy was on a 5-point scale. The average percentage of the maximum score rose from 54.7% to 63.3% for Mindfulness, 59.3% to 66.9% for Wellbeing, and 73.0% to 77.2% for Empathy. The sample size was 648 for both pre- and post-workshop surveys. The *T*-statistics are 12.04, 10.10, and 3.86, respectively. These increases are statistically significant at the $p < .001$ level.
8 The sample sizes were 218 in May and 140 in June. The increase in proportion who responded positively is statistically significant at the $p < .001$ level.

References

Burgemeister, F. C., Crawford, S. B., Hackworth, N. J., Hokke, S., & Nicholson, J. M. (2023). Implementation of evidence-based programs within an Australian place-based initiative for children: A qualitative study. *Journal of Child & Family Studies, 32*(2), 357–372.

Dirks, K. T., & Ferrin, D. L. (2001, July–August). The role of trust in organizational settings. *Organization Science, 12*(4), 450–467.

Fabius, R., & Phares, S. (2021). Companies that promote a culture of health, safety, and wellbeing outperform in the marketplace. *Journal of Occupational & Environmental Medicine*, *63*(6), 456–461.

Heckelman, W. (2017). Five critical principles to guide organizational change. *OD Practitioner*, *49*(4), 13–21.

Hill, P. L., Almeida, D. M., Sin, N. L., Turiano, N. A., & Burrow, A. L. (2018, February). Sense of purpose moderates the associations between daily stressors and daily well-being. *Society of Behavioral Medicine*, *52*.

Institute for Health Metrics & Evaluation. (2021, October 8). *The Lancet: COVID-19 pandemic led to Stark rise in depressive and anxiety disorders globally in 2020, with women and younger people most affected*. http://www.healthdata.org/news-release/lancet-covid-19-pandemic-led-stark-rise-depressive-and-anxiety-disorders-globally-2020

Langlieb, A. M., Langlieb, M. E., & Xiong, W. (2021). EAP 2.0: Reimagining the role of the employee assistance program in the new workplace. *International Review of Psychiatry*, *33*(8), 699–710.

Martela, F., & Pessi, A. B. (2018, March). Significant work is about self-realization and broader purpose: Defining the key dimensions of meaningful work. *Frontiers in Psychology*, *9*.

Mental Health America. (2022, April 12). *MHA releases 2022 mind the workplace report, finds increasing number of employees have difficulty concentrating at work*. https://mhanational.org/mha-releases-2022-mind-workplace-report-finds-increasing-number-employees-have-difficulty

Mental Health America. (n.d.). *2022 Mind the workplace: Employer responsibility to employee mental health*. http://www.mhanational.org/mind-workplace

O'Brien, N., Flott, K., Bray, O., Shaw, A., & Durkin, M. (2022, February). Implementation of initiatives designed to improve healthcare worker health and wellbeing during the COVID-19 pandemic: Comparative case studies from 13 healthcare provider organisations globally. *Global Health*, *18*(1), 24.

Oreg, S. (2006). Personality, context, and resistance to organizational change. *European Journal of Work and Organizational Psychology*, *15*(1), 73–101. https://doi.org/10.1080/13594320500451247

Oreg, S., & Berson, Y. (2019). Leaders' impact on organizational change: Bridging theoretical and methodological chasms. *Academy of Management Annals*, *13*(1), 272–307.

Preiser, W. F. E., & Smith, K. (Eds.). (2011). *Universal design handbook* (2nd ed.). McGraw-Hill.

Redekopp, D. E., & Huston, M. (2019). The broader aims of career development: Mental health, wellbeing and work. *British Journal of Guidance & Counselling*, *47*(2), 246–257.

Soderstrom, S. B., & Weber, K. (2020). Organizational structure from interaction: Evidence from corporate sustainability efforts. *Administrative Science Quarterly*, *65*(1), 226–271.

Story, M. F., Mueller, J. L., & Mace, R. L. (1998). *The universal design file: Designing for people of all ages and abilities*. Center for Universal Design.

Workplace well-being. (n.d.). Office of the U.S. Surgeon General website. http://www.hhs.gov/surgeongeneral/priorities/workplace-well-being/index.html

16 Employee Perceptions of HRM and Burnout

Steven Kilroy, Janine Bosak, Patrick Groulx, and Patrick C. Flood

Introduction

Burnout, a work-related state of exhaustion, depersonalization, and reduced professional efficacy (Bakker et al., 2023), poses a critical concern for organizations. About 10% of workers in European countries and 17% in non-European countries experience burnout as per data from the 2015 European Working Conditions Survey (Schaufeli, 2018). Recent events such as the COVID-19 pandemic have worsened the situation, leading to a sharp rise in the number of workers experiencing symptoms of burnout (Gabriel & Aguinis, 2022). The consequences of burnout are substantial with detrimental outcomes at the individual level (e.g., mental health issues; Salvagioni et al., 2017) and organizational level (e.g., lower employee morale and financial costs; Salvagioni et al., 2017; Swider & Zimmerman, 2010).

To effectively reduce burnout and its associated costs, organizations are actively exploring different Human Resource Management (HRM) strategies (high-performance, high-involvement, or high-commitment work systems) as potential factors to mitigate it (Kilroy et al., 2017). These strategies, while often having a different focus,[1] largely involve the adoption of progressive people management practices in the realm of involvement/empowerment, recruitment and selection, training and development, and rewards and performance management, which aim to foster improved attitudes and behaviors as well as performance among employees. Evidence suggests that such progressive HR strategies can lead to beneficial organizational outcomes such as improved retention, heightened productivity, and enhanced financial performance (Wright & Ulrich, 2017), whereas the impact of such practices on employees' health-related outcomes including burnout is less clear. On the one hand, an "optimistic" perspective has emerged which stipulates that HRM strategies improve employee well-being, including decreasing burnout (Kilroy et al., 2016). On the other hand, a "pessimistic" perspective exists suggesting potential adverse effects of HRM strategies on employees (e.g., Van De Voorde et al., 2012). Specifically, research findings indicate that HRM strategies might increase workload (Wang et al., 2021) and

DOI: 10.4324/9781003491170-21

burnout (Kroon et al., 2009). The question of whether, and if so how, HRM reduces employee burnout is therefore a topic that it not fully clear and knowledge on this issue is important to illuminate whether practitioners should invest in such practices seeking to curb ill-being.

In light of these challenges, this chapter examines the link between HRM strategies and employee burnout. The first section briefly defines burnout and discusses its antecedents and detrimental consequences. Then, we define HRM and critically review the existing literature pertaining to the impact of HRM strategies on burnout, focusing especially on the mixed findings and possible explanations. Future research directions are then outlined to provide a way forward to better understand the relationship more fully. Finally, we conclude by highlighting a number of practical implications that stem from our overview.

Burnout: Antecedents and Consequences

Employee burnout is a well-established topic in the academic literature (Schaufeli et al., 2009). The most common approach to conceptualizing and measuring burnout has been advanced by Schaufeli and colleagues (1996) whereby burnout is believed to consist of three dimensions: exhaustion (the depletion of one's mental resources at work), cynicism (a distant attitude toward the job), and reduced professional efficacy (a lack of achievement and productivity at work). The Maslach Burnout Inventory General Survey (MBI-GS) was developed to measure these dimensions. Although still the most common approach to conceptualizing and measuring burnout, later years have also seen the emergence of approaches to defining burnout which also consider cognitive weariness and physical fatigue (Shirom & Melamed, 2006) or cognitive impairment (Schaufeli et al., 2020) as core burnout symptoms. Although burnout has been researched extensively for many years, the World Health Organization (WHO) only recently recognized burnout as an occupational phenomenon (and not a medical condition) in the 11th edition of the International Classification of Diseases (ICD-11) (WHO, 2019). The WHO definition views burnout in accordance with the three-dimensional conceptualization of Schaufeli et al. (1996). This formal recognition of burnout as an occupational phenomenon is critical to strengthen prevention measures in workplaces and avoid the adverse effects of burnout.

Research has shown that burnout can yield negative consequences for both the individual and the organization in which the individual is employed. Regarding individual consequences, burnout has been found to negatively affect employees' physical and mental health. For example, a systematic review of 61 prospective studies by Salvagioni and colleagues (2017) showed that burnout led to various physical consequences including cardiovascular diseases (i.e., coronary heart disease, hospitalization due to cardiovascular disorder), hypercholesterolemia, type 2 diabetes, musculoskeletal pain, changes in pain experiences, prolonged fatigue, headaches, gastrointestinal issues, respiratory problems, severe injuries, and mortality below the age of 45 years. In addition, the review also found psychological effects including insomnia, depressive symptoms, use of psychotropic and antidepressant medications, hospitalization for mental disorders, and psychological ill-health symptoms.

Regarding consequences for organizations, burnout is associated with employee withdrawal and poorer job performance. For example, meta-analytical findings from Swider and Zimmerman (2010) showed that the most proximal predictors of absenteeism, turnover, and job performance were emotional exhaustion, depersonalization, and personal accomplishment, respectively. Moreover, with regard to occupational outcomes, the review of 61 prospective studies by Salvagioni and colleagues (2017) showed that burnout increases sickness absence days and sickness absence spells while also demonstrating that it causes employee presenteeism too (attending work while ill).

Given these detrimental effects of burnout, it is critical to understand what factors contribute to and prevent burnout. While these factors can be differentiated into individual factors and contextual factors (see Bakker et al., 2023), we focus on the latter for the purpose of this chapter. However, examples of important individual factors evident from meta-analyses include personality traits (e.g., neuroticism), self-esteem, self-efficacy, locus of control, and coping style (Alarcon et al., 2009; Swider & Zimmerman, 2010). Regarding contextual factors, different systematic reviews (e.g., Schaufeli & Taris, 2014) as well as meta-analyses (e.g., Alarcon, 2011; Aronsson et al., 2017) have provided insights into critical contextual predictors of employee burnout. Findings across these different reviews and meta-analyses show that major job demands including role conflict, role ambiguity, role stress, workload, work pressure, work–family conflict, and emotionally intense situations are positively associated with burnout (e.g., Maslach et al., 2001). In addition, burnout is associated with a lack of job resources. For example, in their systematic review on the relationship between work environment factors and burnout symptoms, Aronsson et al. (2017) found moderately strong evidence that both workplace support and job control were negatively related to emotional exhaustion. They also reported limited evidence in support of an association of workplace justice, low reward, low supervisor support, and low coworker support with changes in emotional exhaustion and cynicism. The burnout dimension of reduced personal accomplishment was only associated with low reward. Finally, leadership is a critical resource in the work environment as leaders play a crucial role in job design and the provision of resources (Bakker & Demerouti, 2018), with transformational leadership—one of the most extensively studied leadership styles—being negatively associated with burnout (e.g., Bosak et al., 2021).

In recent years, the focus on burnout research has widened from the individual context to the broader organizational context including organization management, organizational climate, and HR practices (Bakker et al., 2023; Kilroy et al., 2022). Indeed, while an overwhelming number of studies have sought to investigate the role of individual interventions in reducing burnout (e.g., stress management programs; mindfulness practice; resilience training), recent evidence suggests that the impact of such individual interventions tends to exert very moderate to low effects (Fleming, 2024). Moreover, addressing burnout requires a fundamental change in organizational-level structures to address the underlying causes of burnout rather than treating its symptoms (Awa et al., 2010). One solution believed to be at the center of organizational attempts to reduce and prevent burnout is the adoption of progressive or strategic HRM strategies.

HRM Strategies and Burnout

HRM strategies focus on attracting, motivating, and retaining employees through various practices including selective recruitment and selection, training, rewards and performance management, and empowerment/involvement, and are designed to boost employee efficiency and organizational competitiveness (e.g., Guest, 2011). Terms like high-performance, high-involvement, and high-commitment work practices are used interchangeably to refer to these strategies, despite slight nuances in their focus and how they might enhance performance (Boxall & Macky, 2009). These strategies are, nevertheless, seen as progressive people management practices that boost organizational performance and employee well-being. We will use the term HRM throughout to refer to these strategies, although later we revisit the importance of distinguishing between different HRM approaches.

The link between HRM and burnout is a pressing topic in the HRM field for a number of reasons. Given the increasing prevalence and challenges associated with burnout, organizational strategies like HRM that aim to restructure the work environment can have significant impacts. These approaches are considered to be primary prevention measures, tackling the root causes of burnout rather than merely addressing its symptoms through individual interventions after the fact, when it's often too late or more difficult to manage (Fleming, 2024). Moreover, there is an ongoing and intense debate about the role of HRM and employee well-being more generally (Peccei & Van De Voorde, 2019). The mainstream or "optimistic perspective" of HRM considers HRM strategies to benefit both employee well-being and organizational performance (Van De Voorde et al., 2012). Conversely, the "pessimistic perspective" considers HRM strategies to be exploitative in nature since they can intensify work for employees and thereby harm their well-being (e.g., Ramsay et al., 2000). To unravel the role of employee well-being in the relationship between HRM strategies and organizational performance (i.e., the nature of the mediation effects), Van De Voorde and colleagues (2012) carried out a meta-analytic review. In doing so, employee well-being was categorized into happiness (e.g., job satisfaction, engagement), relationship (e.g., coworker and manager support, trust), and health (e.g., stress, burnout) well-being dimensions. Interestingly, their review indicated that the impact of HRM on employee well-being depended on the type of well-being studied, that is, for the happiness and relationship well-being outcomes, they found more support for a "mutual gains perspective" (i.e., both workers and organizations benefit) whereas for health-related well-being outcomes, they found more support for the "conflicting outcomes perspective" (i.e., organizations benefit but employees' health is harmed). A subsequent review by Peccei and Van De Voorde (2019), which included more recent studies, supported these earlier findings. However, both reviews acknowledged that the number of studies which investigated health-related well-being outcomes was limited. Given the dearth of studies focusing on health-related well-being outcomes (i.e., burnout), and given the importance of addressing the rising prevalence and issues surrounding burnout due to current and pan-global crises to come (Gabriel & Aguinis, 2022), this chapter focuses on the relationship between HRM and the outcome of burnout in its own right. In this regard, we will now present studies that have addressed this topic and critically review them to more fully understand this complex relationship.

Consistent with the "optimistic" perspective of HRM, studies have supported the notion that HRM yields significant benefits in terms of ameliorating employee burnout. Kilroy et al. (2016) found that HRM was directly and indirectly associated with lower levels of burnout via reduced role overload and role conflict among healthcare employees. Follow-up studies, also in healthcare, have revealed that HRM is associated with lower burnout via increasing employees' person-organization fit (Kilroy et al., 2017) and psychological empowerment (Kilroy et al., 2022). In the call center context, Castanheira and Chambel (2010) found that HRM was associated with lower levels of burnout through its role in reducing emotional dissonance and quantitative demands. Sun and Pan (2008) further found that HRM was associated with reduced emotional exhaustion, a core dimension of burnout, in the construction sector. More recently, Bartram et al. (2023) studied a set of well-being-oriented HRM practices (e.g., employment security, training and development/learning, job quality, involvement, information-sharing, use of teams, and relationship with the immediate manager) that were positively associated with employee thriving and negatively associated with burnout. The effectiveness of HRM practices in reducing employee burnout is supported by several theories. Conservation of Resources (COR) theory (Hobfoll, 1989) and Job Demands–Resources (JD-R) theory (Demerouti et al., 2001), for example, view HRM as essential resources that help employees manage job demands and conserve energy, thereby reducing burnout (Kilroy et al., 2016). Social exchange theory (Blau, 1964) also suggests that HRM can be perceived by employees as a form of organizational support, prompting them to reciprocate with improved well-being and positive workplace behaviors.

Departing from these positive results, some studies have also revealed that HRM can lead to higher levels of burnout, which is consistent with the "pessimistic perspective" of HRM. Kroon and colleagues (2009) found that HRM (as rated by managers) was associated with increased job demands (quantitative demands), thereby leading to higher levels of emotional exhaustion. Other studies have also revealed that some HRM practices (e.g., those targeting ability and motivation) are associated with heightened burnout (emotional exhaustion) by increasing workload and job responsibility (Oppenauer & Van De Voorde, 2018). Among call center employees, Teo et al. (2021) found no direct relationship between a set of high-commitment HRM practices and burnout, but rather an increase in job demands, which in turn, lead to burnout.

These findings can also be interpreted through the lens of the aforementioned theories: COR, JD-R, and social exchange theory. According to COR and JD-R theories, HRM practices, rather than solely being resources, can also function as job demands that drain employees' energetic resources, triggering a "loss spiral" that may lead to burnout (Hauff et al., 2022). For instance, the pursuit of goals established through rigorous performance management, coupled with the increased responsibilities arising from involvement and empowerment initiatives, can intensify employees' workloads (Ramsay et al., 2000). From a social exchange theory perspective, where HRM is perceived negatively rather than positively, employees can experience negative well-being and thereby elicit negative reactions toward the organization. Broadly speaking, this critical perspective of HRM is underpinned by labor process theory. According to this view, managerial practices including HRM practices are regarded as part of a broader managerial agenda to control workers and extract maximum value from them. This elevates work pressure often accompanied by a reduction in autonomy and a deskilling of work (Ramsay et al., 2000). The next section delves into the presented research earlier and other prevailing insights with the aim to reconcile the conflicting findings regarding the HRM–burnout relationship.

Reconciling Conflicting Findings

The flavor of the aforementioned studies paints a slightly murky picture of the relationship between HRM and employee burnout. Indeed, some studies reveal that HRM reduces burnout while others indicate that HRM increases burnout. These inconsistencies raise important questions about the factors influencing these varied outcomes, and we now explore key dimensions that help to clarify this complexity: (1) the importance of contextual factors as well as the accompanying theoretical perspectives to explain the impact of HRM in positive and negative terms (and how it is influenced by contextual factors) and (2) the conceptualization of HRM from a measurement and analysis perspective.

Studying contextual factors to decipher the conditions under which HRM leads to improved or impaired well-being is one way in which researchers have attempted to reconcile conflicting findings in the HRM field more generally (Peccei et al., 2013) and is therefore especially relevant for the HRM–burnout relationship. For example, Kilroy et al. (2020) investigated the moderating effect of psychological detachment and showed that the beneficial impact of HRM is enhanced when psychological detachment is high and weakened when psychological detachment is low. Jyoti and Rani (2019) found that HRM reduces burnout especially when mentoring is also in place. A recent study by Kilroy et al. (2023) also found that HRM resulted in lower levels of daily emotional exhaustion through its role in increasing daily bonding social capital and reducing daily work pressure. However, these effects were completely undermined when engaging leadership (inspiring, connecting, strengthening, and empowering behaviors) was low.

In addition, in an attempt to unearth the contradictory findings with respect to the impact of HRM on employee well-being (burnout), Shantz et al. (2016) introduced the concept of HRM attributions. The authors proposed that the impact of HRM on employee emotional exhaustion would be dependent on the specific attributions employees make regarding the organizations' intention in implementing them. Their findings supported their overall propositions that when employees perceived that their organizations' HRM practices are intended to improve their performance, they experience higher levels of job involvement, thereby leading to lower levels of emotional exhaustion. Conversely, when employees believe that the organizations' HRM practices are intended to reduce organizational costs, they experience work overload, which translates into higher levels of burnout (emotional exhaustion).

Theoretically speaking and as previously noted, JD-R theory and COR theory are informative in enabling us to comprehend why HRM could have this differential effect on employee burnout in the first instance, and why this might be dependent on contextual factors too. From a more "optimistic perspective," the JD-R model (Demerouti et al., 2001) postulates that job resources (of which HRM practices can be considered) can lead to improved well-being (i.e., lower burnout) and also buffer the impact of job demands on burnout (buffer hypothesis) (Bartram et al., 2012). In the same vein, the model also suggests that job demands can strengthen the impact of job resources, such as HRM, on employee well-being (burnout) (resource salience hypothesis) (De Reuver et al., 2019). From a more "pessimistic perspective", the JD-R model also recognizes that job demands, which HRM has been considered in previous research (e.g., Wang et al., 2021), can cause a health impairment process whereby employees' energetic resources are depleted resulting in burnout. In other words, certain aspects of HRM can create additional job demands for workers and thus foster heightened levels of burnout (Kroon et al., 2009). However, there is the potential that other job resources (e.g., social support or positive leadership styles) can buffer the deleterious impact of HRM on burnout, that is, "the buffer hypothesis" (Wang et al., 2021). Likewise, other job demands that employees encounter in their work can ensure that the health impairment effect of HRM on burnout is even further pronounced. COR theory (Hobfoll, 1989) is often used to further theoretically explain the links in the JD-R model (Schaufeli & Taris, 2014). COR theory posits that individuals are motivated to obtain, retain, and protect resources and that stress occurs when their resources are threatened with loss (and lost) or when they fail to gain resources after substantive resource investment (Hobfoll, 2002). Using the same line of argumentation earlier, HRM has the potential to activate a "resource gain" or "resource loss" spiral among employees, thereby increasing or ameliorating burnout, depending on whether it is perceived as a resource or demand (Hauff et al., 2022). Practically, these theories provide insights on why HRM can improve or impair employee burnout, and what can be done to enhance their positive effects and minimize their negative effects, on workers.

While contextual factors and these various theoretical approaches further elucidate the HRM–employee burnout relationship, additional features of the studies reviewed earlier can also be disentangled to provide additional insights (and to better discern why and when HRM might be conceived of as either resources or demands). The first issue concerns the measurement and analysis of HRM. Indeed, it is noteworthy that many different types of HRM have been used in prior studies such as high-performance (e.g., Kroon et al., 2009), high-involvement (e.g., Kilroy et al., 2016), and high-commitment (e.g., Sun & Pan, 2008) HRM practices. While all constituting a progressive approach to people management, the nature of the approach (and practices within them) may account, to some degree, for their inconsistent effects on employee burnout. It is particularly noteworthy that when high-involvement or well-being-oriented HRM practices are adopted, they tend to be more beneficial for employee burnout, while when high-performance work systems are used, the findings tend to be more negative. Perhaps this is not surprising since a broader approach encompassing high-performance work systems often incorporates an additional array of practices (not always included in the high-involvement or high-commitment approach) which are more demanding on employees (e.g., more rigorous performance management and extensive teamwork). As such, the lack of consistency in the particular HRM approach and subsequent measurement, may account for some of the differential effects. The absence of some HRM practices in various bundles of HRM, for example, when testing their influence on burnout, can lead to the so-called construct underrepresentation issue whereby the instruments used to measure HRM are too narrow and fail to include all the key components (Etchegaray et al., 2011). This can potentially lead to HRM having either exaggerated positive or negative effects.

HRM practices are typically grouped together and tested as "best practices" that are expected to consistently enhance various employee and organizational outcomes (Ogbonnaya & Ayree, 2021). However, these practices can act as both resources that benefit employees and demands that challenge them, resulting in varied effects on employee well-being (Boxall & Macky, 2009). To differentiate the effects of HRM practices, Li et al. (2024) integrated the job demands–resources (JD-R) model with the challenge-hindrance demand framework. They highlight that some HR practices serve as hindrance demands that impair well-being (i.e., happiness, health, and relationship quality), while others present challenging demands that may boost happiness and relationship quality but could also negatively impact health-related well-being outcomes, such as burnout. This differentiation of HRM and well-being indicates potential trade-offs; some HRM practices may improve certain aspects of employee well-being while damaging others (e.g., Hauff et al., 2022). Overall, the inconsistent measurement and analysis of HRM make it difficult to build a reliable evidence base for practitioners, complicating decisions about effective HRM strategies to mitigate burnout. This may suggest a need for HR professionals to adopt an isolationist (practice-based) approach too (Ogbonnaya & Ayree, 2021), recognizing that each practice can have independent and differential effects on outcomes.

The conflicting evidence concerning the relationship between HRM practices and employee burnout can also be affected by the perspective from which HRM practices are measured. Specifically, the source of employees versus managers and how HRM is implemented by line managers is key. It appears that when HRM is assessed from the employee's perspective, they typically show a positive impact by their effect on reducing emotional exhaustion (e.g., Castanheira & Chambel, 2010). Conversely, when HRM assessments are based on managers' perceptions, the impact on burnout is often non-significant (Vanhala & Tuomi, 2006) or even negative, that is, increasing burnout (Kroon et al., 2009). HRM scholars claim that understanding HRM's effect requires capturing the employee's experience, as they are the direct recipients of HRM practices (Guest, 2011). Solely relying on managers' reports of HRM may not accurately reflect the actual implementation of HRM and in particular how it is perceived by employees, thereby leading to biased results (Ogbonnaya & Ayree, 2021). The overall implementation of HRM is indeed crucial, and while the practices may or may not be beneficial in reducing burnout, their ultimate impact will depend on whether line managers are capable of effectively bringing them to life (Purcell & Hutchinson, 2007). Recent studies highlight that the effects of HRM on burnout depend significantly on how HRM intentions are communicated, and the leadership behaviors enacted (Shantz et al., 2016; Wang et al., 2021). Taken together, the areas highlighted earlier point to several areas for further research to better understand the role of HRM in influencing burnout.

Future Research Directions

Using our earlier review of research, we derive the following observations which then specifically point to possible areas for future research.

First, the majority of studies exploring the HRM–burnout relationship have focused on a limited number of burnout dimensions (the majority of studies focusing solely on emotional exhaustion). Exploring how HRM leads to all three components of burnout and in particular how burnout unfolds as a process over time (i.e., emotional exhaustion could lead to depersonalization, and in turn, reduced professional efficacy) would reveal additional insights about how workers cope with burnout and the specific loss or gain spiral that is activated (Williams et al., 2020).

Second, the impact of HRM on burnout is not always universal but instead is subject to numerous contextual influences. However, researchers have only scratched the surface regarding the potential contextual influences that might enhance or undermine (or determine the direction) of the relationship between HRM and burnout. Especially worthy of investigation going forward is the role of personal resources and leadership. Numerous personal resources including specific personality traits (e.g., the Big Five personality factors) and other psychological variables (e.g., self-efficacy, self-esteem, locus of control) might shape employees' reactions to HRM and determine their ultimate (positive or negative) impact on burnout (Kilroy et al., 2020). Another contextual factor of significant interest concerns the role of leadership styles (behaviors) in the HRM–burnout relationship. It is abundantly clear that line managers play a key role in implementing HRM practices in organizations (Purcell & Hutchinson, 2007). One study demonstrated that servant leadership can reduce the detrimental effect of HRM on health-related well-being outcomes (Wang et al., 2021), while another study revealed that the beneficial impact of HRM in ameliorating burnout can dissipate when engaging leadership is low (Kilroy et al., 2023). As such, uncovering which specific leadership styles universally help harness the benefits of and reduce the stressful components of HRM would greatly contribute to theory and practice and address a broader call in the HRM literature to explore the complementarities and potential substitutes involving HRM and leadership (Kilroy et al., 2023).

Third, most studies to date have explored the relationship between HRM and burnout or the relationship between HRM and performance, separately. However, studying the impact of HRM on burnout and performance outcomes in the same model would enable more nuanced insights. Indeed, existing research in this area of strategic HRM suggests that the impact of HRM on happiness and relationship well-being is largely positive and consistent with a "mutual gains" perspective (i.e., benefits organizations and employees) while for health-related well-being, the impact tends to be negative for employees although beneficial for organizations, consistent with a "conflicting outcomes" perspective (Peccei & Van De Voorde, 2019). However, these findings are considered tentative since the number of studies that incorporate health-related well-being outcomes, such as burnout, is limited. Addressing this issue (including burnout as a mediator between HRM and performance) will answer questions about potential trade-offs that might emerge between well-being and performance arising from HRM.

Fourth, it is clear that the HRM–burnout relationship has predominantly been tested in a linear fashion, whereby it is expected that increased investments in HRM should lead to either higher or lower levels of burnout. This ignores the possibility of curvilinear relations (Ho & Kuvaas, 2020). In other words, the extent to which HRM might lead to either higher or lower levels of burnout might depend on the amount or intensity of the practices deployed. This line of argumentation is consistent with the vitamin model of Warr (1987) which purports that certain job resources might initially lead to improved well-being but when they reach a certain point, that is, too much investment (saturation point), they either have no additional benefits or might even have a damaging effect on employees' well-being. This reality has also been recognized by Pierce and Aguinis (2013), who coined the term "too-much-of-a-good-thing effect" (TMGT) and proffers that testing curvilinear relations has significant potential to explain contradictory findings that pervade much of the management literature. Ho and Kuvaas (2020) investigated and found support for a curvilinear relationship between HRM and job satisfaction (happiness-related well-being). However, focusing on health-related well-being such as burnout represents a promising avenue for future research.

Finally, it is clear that the majority of research studies are predominantly cross-sectional in nature, and there is a notable absence of both structured workplace interventions and field experiments, diary studies that capture within-person fluctuations as well as qualitative research. This undermines our capacity to confidently conclude what impact HRM has on burnout. The lack of longitudinal studies (including diary studies) and intervention studies make it impossible to determine causality as well as ruling out alternative explanations for possible cause–effect connections. Non-randomized quasi-experiments would constitute a realistic and robust way of further building the evidence base. Moreover, more qualitative studies would provide more depth and unravel additional nuances with respect to how employees experience HRM and their effects.

Practical Implications

This chapter presents a number of implications for practice. It is clear that burnout is on the rise and its costs are substantial, ensuring that combating this workplace phenomenon should be a central priority for organizations. HR professionals and line managers need to be equipped to tackle the problem head on and in particular to avoid creating conditions conducive to burnout. Based on the review of studies, a number of specific practical recommendations are highlighted in Table 16.1.

Conclusion

In this chapter, the potential important role of HRM strategies to prevent and ameliorate burnout was highlighted, on the basis that adopting individual interventions to reduce burnout is unlikely to be sufficient on their own. However, it is apparent that evidence on the impact of HRM strategies on burnout is mixed, and we attempted to reconcile these conflicting findings by critically analyzing and deriving insights from the plethora of studies carried out to date as well as from a number of theoretical approaches developed in the occupational health

Table 16.1 Recommendations for Future Research on Burnout and HRM

• Utilization of the Maslach Burnout Inventory (MBI) and the Burnout Assessment Tool (BAT) are recommended to assess burnout among staff, the latter recognizing that cognitive impairment is also central to the burnout construct.
• It is critical for managers to assess burnout (and the influencing role of HRM) using such validated instruments, and they should do so for overall (long-term) levels and short-term fluctuations (given that burnout can also vary from week to week and even day to day).
• Addressing the problem of burnout comprehensively requires going beyond individual interventions and taking action to restructure the work environment.
• HRM strategies (especially high-involvement HRM) can play a key role in burnout reduction. However, HRM strategies might need to be accompanied with the appropriate environmental (support) conditions to be effective.
• It is possible that individual HR practices as part of an HRM system can have diverse effects on employee burnout, making it important for managers to understand this and provide additional resources and training to employees to cope with the demanding nature of these practices.
• Effective implementation by line managers can fundamentally determine whether HRM strategies will work as intended to ameliorate burnout. Preliminary research suggests that servant leadership and engaging leadership are particularly potent leadership styles that assist HRM strategies in improving burnout or reducing its stressful components. These styles should therefore be targeted in leadership development efforts.
• Given the stigma associated with burnout, organizations should have structures in place so that employees can openly report it and provide the appropriate occupational health services. Education and training efforts can also be targeted more specifically in the realm of effective recovery from work.

psychology field. To further build the evidence base, we outlined a number of future research directions and concluded with a number of practical recommendations for managers.

Note

1 While these terms are used interchangeably in the literature, each approach to HRM is purported to have a slightly different focus. For example, high-involvement work practices seek to foster enhanced participation and involvement from employees and to decentralize decision-making processes. High-commitment HRM seeks to foster greater commitment from employees by offering job security as well as internal promotions and incentives. High-performance work practices are focused on selective hiring, extensive training/development as well as group and individual incentives, in order to maximize employee performance.

References

Alarcon, G. M. (2011). A meta-analysis of burnout with job demands, resources, and attitudes. *Journal of Vocational Behavior*, *79*(2), 549–562. https://doi.org/10.1016/j.jvb.2011.03.007

Alarcon, G. M., Eschleman, K. J., & Bowling, N. (2009). Relationships between personality variables and burnout: A meta-analysis. *Work & Stress*, *23*(3), 244–263. https://doi.org/10.1080/02678370903282600

Aronsson, G., Theorell, T., Grape, T., Hammarström, A., Hogstedt, C., Marteinsdottir, I., Skoog, I., Träskman-Bendz, I., & Hall, C. (2017). A systematic review including meta-analysis of work environment and burnout symptoms. *BMC Public Health*, *17*(1), 264. https://doi.org/10.1186/s12889-017-4153-7

Awa, W. L., Plaumann, M., & Walter, U. (2010). Burnout prevention: A review of intervention programs. *Patient Education and Counselling*, *78*(2), 184–190. https://doi.org/10.1016/j.pec.2009.04.008.

Bakker, A. B., & Demerouti, E. (2018). Multiple levels in job demands-resources theory: Implications for employee well-being and performance. In E. Diener, S. Oishi, & L. Tay (Eds.), *Handbook of wellbeing*. DEF Publishers.

Bakker, A. B., Demerouti, E., & Sanz-Vergel, A. (2023). Job demands–resources theory: Ten years later. *Annual Review of Organizational Psychology and Organizational Behavior, 10,* 25–53. https://doi.org/10.1146/annurev-orgpsych-120920-053933.

Bartram, T., Casimir, G., Djurkovic, N., Leggat, S., & Stanton, P. (2012). Do High Performance Work Systems influence the relationship between emotional labour, burnout and intention to leave? A study of Australian Nurses. *Journal of Advanced Nursing*, *681*, 1567–1578. https://doi.org/10.1111/j.1365-2648.2012.05968.x

Bartram, T., Cooper, B., Cooke, F.L., & Wang, J. (2023). Thriving in the face of burnout? The effects of wellbeing-oriented HRM on the relationship between workload, burnout, thriving and performance, *Employee Relations*, *45*(5), 1234–1253. https://doi.org/10.1108/ER-06-2022-0273

Blau, P. M. (1964). *Exchange and power in social life*. John Wiley and Sons.

Bosak, J., Kilroy, S., Chênevert, D., & Flood, P. C. (2021). Examining the role of transformational leadership and mission valence on burnout among hospital staff. *Journal of Organizational Effectiveness: People and Performance*, *8*(2), 208–227. https://doi.org/10.1108/JOEPP-08-2020-0151

Boxall, P., & Macky, K. (2009). Research and theory on high-performance work systems: Progressing the high-involvement stream. *Human Resource Management Journal*, *19*(1), 3–23. https://doi.org/10.1111/j.1748-8583.2008.00082.x

Castanheira, F., & Chambel, M. (2010). Reducing burnout in call centers through HR practices. *Human Resource Management*, *49*(6), 1047–1065. https://doi.org/10.1002/hrm.20393

Demerouti, E., Bakker, A. B., Nachreiner, F., & Schaufeli, W. B. (2001). The Job Demands-Resources model of burnout. *Journal of Applied Psychology*, *86*(3), 499–512. https://doi.org/10.1037/0021-9010.86.3.499

De Reuver, R., Van De Voorde, K., & Kilroy, S. (2021). When do bundles of high-performance work systems reduce employee absenteeism? The moderating role of workload. *International Journal of Human Resource Management*, *32*(13), 2889–2909. https://doi.org/10.1080/09585192.2019.1616594

Etchegaray, J. M., Cynthia, T., & Eric, J. (2011). Measures and measurement of high-performance work systems in health care settings: Propositions for improvement. *Health Care Management Review*, *36*(1), 38–46. https://doi.org/10.1097/HMR.0b013e3181f685a4

Fleming, W. J. (2024). Employee well-being outcomes from individual-level mental health interventions: Cross-sectional evidence from the UK. *Industrial Relations Journal*, *55*, 162–182. https://doi.org/10.1111/irj.12418

Gabriel, K. P., & Aguinis, H. (2022). How to prevent and combat employee burnout and create healthier workplaces during crises and beyond, *Business Horizons*, *65*(2), 183–192. https://doi.org/10.1016/j.bushor.2021.02.037

Guest, D. E. (2011). Human resource management and performance: Still searching for some answers. *Human Resource Management Journal, 21*, 3–13. https://doi.org/10.1111/j.1748-8583.2010.00164.x

Hauff, S., Felfe, J., & Klug, K. (2022). High-performance work practices, well-being, and supportive leadership: Spillover mechanisms and boundary conditions between HRM and leadership behavior. *International Journal of Human Resource Management, 33*(10), 2109–2137. https://doi.org/10.1080/09585192.2020.1841819

Ho, H., & Kuvaas, B. (2020). Human resource management systems, employee wellbeing, and firm performance from the mutual gains and critical perspectives: The wellbeing paradox. *Human Resource Management, 59*(3), 235–253. http://doi.org/10.1002/hrm.21990

Hobfoll, S. E. (1989). Conservation of resources: A new attempt at conceptualizing stress. *American Psychologist, 44*(3), 513–524. https://doi.org/10.1037//0003-066x.44.3.513. PMID: 2648906

Hobfoll, S. E. (2002). Social and psychological resources and adaptation. *Review of General Psychology, 6*(4), 307–324. https://doi.org/10.1037/1089-2680.6.4.307

Jyoti, J., & Rani, A. (2019). Role of burnout and mentoring between high performance work system and intention to leave: Moderated mediation model. *Journal of Business Research, 98*, 166–176. https://doi.org/10.1016/j.jbusres.2018.12.068

Kilroy, S., Bosak, J., Chênevert, D., Flood, P. C., & Hill, K. (2022). Reducing burnout among nurses: The role of high-involvement work practices and colleague support. *Health Care Management Review, 47*(2), 1150–1124. https://doi.org/10.1097/HMR.0000000000000304.

Kilroy, S., Bosak, J., Flood, P. C., & Peccei, R. (2020). Time to Recover: The moderating role of psychological detachment in the link between high-involvement work practices and burnout. *Journal of Business Research, 108*, 52–61. https://doi.org/10.1016/j.jbusres.2019.10.012

Kilroy, S., Flood, P. C., Bosak, J., & Chênevert, D. (2016). Perceptions of high-involvement work practices and burnout: The mediating role of job demands. *Human Resource Management Journal, 26*(4), 408–424. https://doi.org/10.1111/1748-8583.12112

Kilroy, S., Flood, P. C., Bosak, J., & Chênevert, D. (2017). Perceptions of high-involvement work practices, person-organization fit, and burnout: A time-lagged study of health care employees. Human Resource Management, *56*(5), 821–835. https://doi.org/10.1002/hrm.21803

Kilroy, S., Fu, N., Bosak, J., Hayes, R., & Schaufeli, W. B. (2023). Reducing day-level emotional exhaustion: The complementary role of high involvement work systems and engaging leadership. *Human Resource Management Journal, 33*(4), 846–867. http://doi.org/10.1111/1748-8583.12482

Kroon, B., Van De Voorde, K., & van Veldhoven, M. (2009). Cross-level effects of high-performance work practices on burnout: Two counteracting mediating mechanisms compared. *Personnel Review, 38*(5), 509–525. https://doi.org/10.1108/00483480910978027

Li, M., Fu, N., Chadwick, C., & Harney, B. (2024). Untangling human resource management and employee wellbeing relationships: Differentiating job resource HR practices from challenge demand HR practices. *Human Resource Management Journal, 34*(1), 214–235. https://doi.org/10.1111/1748-8583.12527

Maslach, C., Schaufeli, W. B., & Leiter, M. P. (2001). Job burnout. *Annual Review of Psychology, 52,* 397–422. https://doi.org/10.1146/annurev.psych.52.1.397

Ogbonnaya, C., & Aryee, S. (2021). HRM practices, employee well-being, and organizational performance. In P. Brough, E. Gardiner, & K. Daniels (Eds.), *Handbook on management and employment practices*. Handbook Series in Occupational Health Sciences. Springer.

Oppenauer, V., & Van De Voorde, K. (2018). Exploring the relationships between high involvement work system practices, work demands and emotional exhaustion: A multi-level study. The International Journal of Human Resource Management, *29*(2), 311–337. https://doi.org/10.1080/09585192.2016.1146321

Peccei, R., & Van De Voorde, K. (2019). HRM–well-being–performance research revisited: Past, present, and future. *Human Resource Management Journal*, *29*(4), 539–563. https://doi.org/10.1111/1748-8583.12254

Peccei, R., Voorde, K. V. D., & Veldhoven, M. V. (2013). HRM, well-being and performance: A theoretical and empirical review. In J. Paauwe, D, Guest, & P. Wright (Eds.), *HRM and performance: Achievements and challenges*. Wiley.

Pierce, J. R., & Aguinis, H. (2013). The too-much-of-a-good-thing effect in management. *Journal of Management*, *39*(2), 313–338. https://doi.org/10.1177/0149206311410060

Purcell, J., & Hutchinson, S. (2007). Front-line managers as agents in the HRM-performance causal chain: Theory, analysis and evidence. *Human Resource Management Journal*, *17*(1), 3–20. https://doi.org/10.1111/j.1748-8583.2007.00022.x

Ramsay, H., Scholarios, D., & Harley, B. (2000). Employees and high-performance work systems: Testing inside the black box. *British Journal of Industrial Relations*, *38*(4), 501–531. https://doi.org/10.1111/1467-8543.00178

Salvagioni, D. A. J., Melanda, F. N., Mesas, A. E., González, A. D., Gabani, F. L., & Andrade, S. M. (2017). Physical, psychological and occupational consequences of job burnout: A systematic review of prospective studies. *PLoS One*, *12*(10), e0185781. https://doi.org/10.1371/journal.pone.0185781

Schaufeli, W. B. (2018). *Burnout in Europe: Relations with national economy, governance, and culture. Research Unit Occupational & Organizational Psychology and Professional Learning (internal report)*. KU Leuven.

Schaufeli, W. B., Leiter, M. P., & Maslach, C. (2009). Burnout: 35 years of research and practice. *The Career Development International*, *14*(3), 204–220. https://doi.org/10.1108/13620430910966406

Schaufeli, W. B., Desart, S., & De Witte, H. (2020). Burnout assessment tool (BAT)—Development, validity, and reliability. *International Journal of Environmental Research and Public Health*, *17*(24), 9495. https://doi.org/10.3390/ijerph17249495

Schaufeli, W. B., Leiter, M. P., Maslach, C., & Jackson, S. E. (1996). The Maslach burnout inventory—General survey. In C. Maslach, S. E. Jackson, & M. P. Leiter (Eds.), *MBI manual* (3rd ed., pp. 19–26). Consulting Psychologists Press.

Schaufeli, W. B., & Taris, T. W. (2014). A critical review of the job demands-resources model: Implications for improving work and health. In G. F. Bauer & O. Hämmig (Eds.), *Bridging occupational, organizational and public health: A transdisciplinary approach* (pp. 43–68). Springer Science + Business Media. https://doi.org/10.1007/978-94-007-5640-3_4

Shantz, A., Alfes, K., & Whiley, L. (2016). HRM in healthcare: The role of work engagement. *Personnel Review*, *45*(2), 274–295. https://doi.org/10.1108/PR-09-2014-0203

Shirom, A., & Melamed, S. (2006). A comparison of the construct validity of two burnout measures in two groups of professionals. *International Journal of Stress Management*, *13*(2), 176–200. https://doi.org/10.1037/1072-5245.13.2.176

Sun, L.-Y., & Pan, W. (2008). HR practices perceptions, emotional exhaustion, and work outcomes: A conservation-of-resources theory in the Chinese context. *Human Resource Development Quarterly*, *19*, 55–74. https://doi.org/10.1002/hrdq.1225

Swider, B. W., & Zimmerman, R. D. (2010). Born to burnout: A meta-analytic path model of personality, job burnout, and work outcomes. *Journal of Vocational Behavior*, *76*(3), 487–506. https://doi.org/10.1016/j.jvb.2010.01.003

Teo, S., Nguyen, D., Shafaei, A., & Bentley, T. (2021). High commitment HRM and burnout of frontline food service employees: A moderated mediation model. *Employee Relations: The International Journal*. https://doi.org/10.1108/ER-06-2020-0300.

Van De Voorde, K., Paauwe, J., & Van Veldhoven, M. (2012). Employee well-being and the HRM–organizational performance relationship: A review of quantitative studies. *International Journal of Management Reviews*, *14*(4), 391–407. https://doi.org/10.1111/j.1468-2370.2011.00322.x

Vanhala, S., & Tuomi, K. (2006). HRM, company performance and employee well-being. *Management Revue*, *17*(3), 241–255.

Wang, Z., Xing, L., & Zhang, Y. (2021). Do high-performance work systems harm employees' health? An investigation of service-oriented HPWS in the Chinese healthcare sector. *International Journal of Human Resource Management*, *32*(10), 2264–2297. https://doi.org/10.1080/09585192.2019.1579254

Warr, P. (1987). *Work, unemployment, and mental health*. Oxford University Press.

WHO (World Health Organization). (2019). *International classification of diseases (ICD-11)*. WHO.

Williams, E. S., Rathert, C., & Buttigieg, S. C. (2020). The personal and professional consequences of physician burnout: A systematic review of the literature. *Medical Care Research and Review: MCRR*, *77*(5), 371–386. https://doi.org/10.1177/1077558719856787

Wright, P. M., & Ulrich, M. D. (2017). A road well traveled: The past, present, and future journey of strategic human resource management. *Annual Review of Organizational Psychology and Organizational Behavior*, *4*, 45–65. https://doi.org/10.1146/annurev-orgpsych-032516-113052

17 Respect and Mental Health

A Case Study and Multilevel Model

Emily H. Rosado-Solomon and Jordon Babcock

Introduction

An important, yet often overlooked, component of understanding mental health and work is the extent to which respect is present in an organization. This is a curious omission, as research on work has emphasized the importance of respect for meaningful outcomes, including positive organizational identity development (Rogers & Ashforth, 2017; Rogers et al., 2017), engagement, and job satisfaction (LaGree et al., 2023; van Quaquebeke & Eckloff, 2010). At the same time, clinical psychologists have recognized the critical importance of respect for promoting well-being, which is particularly evident in the recovery process for those with mental illness and other mental health challenges (Dixon et al., 2016).[1] This is notable because of the highly stigmatized nature of mental illness compared to other medical conditions (Corrigan et al., 2007), which often results in treatment that has less respect for patients' dignity (Ross & Goldner, 2009).

Despite the established importance of respect across both organizational and psychological research, the issue of respect has yet to be emphasized in literature concerning mental health challenges in organizations. This omission is notable because organizations are complex systems where phenomena spread and transform, and therefore dynamics in these contexts require explicit examination (Klein & Kozlowski, 2000). In other words, while much is known about the positive role that respect plays in interactions for those with mental health challenges (Watson et al., 2008), it is not possible to take this knowledge and assume that it functions exactly the same in a complex organizational system (Klein & Kozlowski, 2000). Given the complexity of organizations, alongside the importance of respect in organizations and for dealing with mental health conditions, this chapter illuminates how respect functions in various ways within an organization to improve mental health challenges for multiple stakeholders.

To facilitate this illumination, we review extant literature and then introduce a case study that describes prioritizing respect in a behavioral health facility. We have chosen this context because mental health challenges in behavioral health facilities are simultaneously pervasive and important to address. For employees,

DOI: 10.4324/9781003491170-22

mental health challenges are pervasive as work in a behavioral health facility involves unique challenges, such as the requirements for deep emotional labor from nurses, doctors, and social workers (Edward et al., 2017; Yanay & Shahar, 1998) in order to support patients' recovery. While one might assume that organizations that professionally specialize in the treatment of mental health challenges would have an easier time promoting the mental health of their own employees, extant research suggests that this is not the case. In fact, professions like social work and nursing, which are prominent in behavioral health facilities, have notoriously difficult problems with mental health challenges such as burnout (Brotheridge & Grandey, 2002). Despite their professional knowledge about mental health, challenges persist due to the uniquely difficult nature of working in this context (Gwain et al., 2022).

This chapter proceeds by briefly reviewing the literature on respect as it relates to both organizational settings and mental illness recovery, which is a context in which the impact of respect on mental health is particularly prominent. Following this review, we examine a case of respect in a psychiatric care facility, which is context where mental health challenges are salient for multiple stakeholders, such as patients who experience acute mental illness and staff members who often experience burnout and other mental health challenges. Following this examination, based on extant literature and the case study themes, we propose a multilevel model of respect and mental health in organizations, noting how respect that stems from leadership and human resource practices can spread and transform throughout the organization to improve the mental health of multiple stakeholders. Taken together, this chapter provides an important perspective on the role of respect in promoting mental health in organizations.

Literature Review

Respect in Organizations

In the organizational literature, scholars have noted that there are myriad considerations in determining what respect is and how it applies to organizational stakeholders. In this chapter, we adopt the general definition of Spears and colleagues (2006), who suggest that respect is the "perceived worth accorded to one person by one or more others" (p. 179, see also Rogers & Ashforth, 2017). This is distinct from, yet related to, constructs such as trust, justice, status, and civility, which refer to related sentiments in organizations and often co-occur with respect in generally positive organizational climates (Martinson et al., 2025; Rogers & Ashforth, 2017). Readers interested in an extended distinction between respect and related constructs should consult extant reviews (e.g., Rogers & Ashforth, 2017) for more detail.

Beyond the general definition of respect, organizational scholars have recognized that there are multiple forms of respect in organizations. In particular,

Rogers et al. (2017) differentiated between generalized respect, which refers to a broad sense of respect for all individuals, and particularized respect, which refers to the respect accorded to one person as a unique individual. Decker and Van Quaquebeke (2015) similarly noted differences between horizontal respect, "a personal attitude of treating others as equals or, at least, extending them equal dignity," and they clarify that this "is (or should be) unconditionally guaranteed to every human being" (p. 544) and vertical respect, which they define as "paid to people for reasons such as their expertise, excellence, or status; it is conditional in the sense of being based on differences between people" (p. 544). While distinct in their manifestation, both types of respect are important in organizational contexts.

A key concern in organizational studies on respect has been the extent to which leaders demonstrate respect for their subordinates. In their landmark study on leaders' respect, Van Quaquebeke and Eckloff (2010) identified 19 specific categories of ways that subordinates perceived their leaders as demonstrating respectful behavior. Of particular relevance to the present chapter, these manifestations included categories such as trusting behavior, supportive behavior, and appreciating employees' work, in addition to more tactical behaviors such as granting autonomy and conferring responsibility to employees while being and understanding in the event that they make an occasional mistake.

Mental Health and Respect

The role of respect in promoting mental well-being cannot be overstated. It is particularly evident in the context of mental illness recovery, where the promotion of respect can greatly enhance people's ability to navigate mental health challenges, while the absence of respect can undermine therapeutic treatment. In the case of recovering from mental illness, the goal is often not to eradicate the mental illness completely, as such an outcome may be unattainable, particularly for those with severe mental illness (Davidson & Roe, 2007). Instead, recovery often involves a goal to live a meaningful life in which the individual can function without major impairment and find fulfillment. Stated differently, meaningful recovery in mental illness is often described as "recovery *in* mental illness" as opposed to "recovery *from* mental illness" (Davidson & Roe, 2007). Such a state of recovery has been characterized as promoting an increased sense of agency and involving participation in meaningful aspects of life, such as employment and education (Drake & Whitley, 2014).

There is significant research to support the fact that being treated with respect is related to a variety of mental health outcomes (for a review, see Allan & Davidson, 2013). Correspondingly, treating patients with respect has been noted as a prominent obligation of medical professionals across all subspecialties, with many professional organizations explicitly including respect as a component of professionalism (Beach et al., 2007). Despite this wide acknowledgment, there is a recognized pattern of people not being shown appropriate respect while undergoing mental health treatment. For example, while people with mental health challenges often have unique barriers that conflict with theoretical "best practices" for treatment (e.g., inconsistency in communication and medicine adherence; Dixon et al., 2016), practitioners do not always demonstrate the flexibility in treatment approach that would be necessary to respect patients' autonomy, instead pressuring them or failing to acknowledge their holistic needs and preferences (Dixon et al., 2016). This issue of lacking respect for those experiencing mental illness is further compounded by the pervasive stigma against people with mental illness, which can be held by practitioners despite their medical training (Ross & Goldner, 2009). Given the importance of respect for those experiencing mental illness (Allan & Davidson, 2013) and the lack of universal respect for people with mental illness and other related mental health challenges (Dixon et al., 2016), it is particularly necessary to examine the role of respect in organizations serving those with mental health challenges.

Case Study: Behavioral Health Facility

To illuminate the importance of respect in the context of organizations and mental health, we consider the case of respect in a behavioral health facility. The data for this case study are semi-autoethnographic, in that it emerged in a series of reflective, critical discussions between the first and second authors over the course of approximately one year, and represent the second author's lived experience as the CEO of the behavioral health facility. Data from these discussions were supplemented with archival data, such as publications and social media posts about the facility. The reflection and subsequent critical discussions focused on leadership during the COVID-19 pandemic, when mental health challenges were especially prevalent across society (Mind Share Partners, 2023). During this period, healthcare workers in particular faced unique challenges because they worked in close proximity with others, thereby increasing their risk of infection and exposure to vicarious trauma (Shreffler et al., 2020). Given the combination of type of organization and unique period, the dynamics around organizational factors that influence mental health were particularly salient, thereby clearly illuminating the relevant phenomena to this inquiry.

Although the data were autoethnographic, reflections centered on how leadership behaviors influenced multiple stakeholders, with a focus on both employees and patients. In focusing on the intended effects of multiple stakeholders, we set the stage for producing a multilevel model that suggests how respect can spread and transform throughout the organization to positively impact the mental health of multiple stakeholders. Prior to that exploration, we briefly describe the context of the behavioral health facility.

Context

Behavioral health facilities are a type of medical facility that treats people with psychological health concerns. In many ways, it is similar to other types of medical facilities, and the behavioral health facility we reviewed shares a number of logistical features with conventional hospitals. There is an emergency room that provides emergency assessment and treatment for individuals with acute psychological distress. This parallels services offered in a hospital's emergency room, with the distinguishing factor being that behavioral health facility focuses exclusively on psychiatric emergencies. Similar to general emergency rooms, patients with acute health problems are assessed to determine the appropriate level of care. Patients requiring intensive, immediate care (e.g., those who pose a risk to themselves or others) may be admitted to an inpatient section of the hospital, whereas people who present less acute symptoms may be given recommendations for outpatient follow-up care.

Beyond the emergency room, there are a variety of services such as therapy (both individual and group), medication management, family support services, and more. In order for these services to operate, there are a number of job roles that make up the workforce of the behavioral health facility. There are those who work directly with patients, including a clinical staff that is composed of doctors with mental health specialties (e.g., psychologists and psychiatrists), as well as various forms of therapists, social workers, and nurses. There are also medical professionals separate from the clinical staff who provide support for the general health concerns of the inpatient population, such as treating colds, physical injuries, and other maladies. Finally, there is a group of employees who do not provide direct services but are nevertheless vital within the organization. These include staff who perform business and administrative functions, such as those in charge of billing insurance, enacting human resource practices (e.g., hiring, training, and reviewing performance of the facility's employees), ensuring compliance with state and federal regulations, and those in various leadership and administrative positions.

There are several ways in which mental health challenges are salient in this context. Most obviously, the facility's primary purpose is to serve patients impacted by mental health challenges including mental illness, psychiatric distress, and related conditions. Beyond this, many of the jobs in the facility are jobs that include inherent and unavoidable risks to employees' mental health, including the requirement to display certain emotions, close contact with patients' suffering, and challenging work schedules. Taken together, this context is ideal for examining how mental health challenges might be impacted for various stakeholders in an organization.

Activities

In this facility, the promotion of respect, and its connection to mental health, begins during employees' onboarding process. During the focal period, the CEO of the organization took part in the first few stages of employees' orientation and training, and was vocal during that process about the values of the organization.

In particular, he was vocal about the importance of a respectful organizational climate, which involved employees supporting both their patients and one another. The CEO's discourse about a respectful climate was framed in terms of relationships, emphasizing that cultivating positive relationships with colleagues was an important value of the organization, and that new employees were expected to treat their colleagues with respect and compassion. While it was equally important for employees to be respectful to patients, leadership found it easier to assess employees' ability to deal with patients in the hiring phase, where such interactions are often considered a job-related competency. However, the CEO found it harder to assess potential employees' contribution to respectful culture during the hiring and performance evaluation processes, which was why it was emphasized at the beginning of employees' tenure with the behavioral health facility.

The CEO was aware that HR and other professional trainers could tell new employees about the importance of respect, as many organizations use HR to enact behaviors intended to promote a climate of respect (Koys, 1988). However, he felt that respect-oriented messaging given by the CEO was uniquely impactful because it sent a signal to employees about the priority of establishing a respectful climate. The fact that the CEO spent so much time in the onboarding process was meant to convey to employees that the organization truly prioritized maintaining a respectful culture. Through his physical presence, he hoped that employees would understand that establishing a respectful culture was the most important part of his job, and that they would similarly prioritize behaviors that contributed to the desired respectful climate.

Alongside emphasizing the importance of respect and relationships in orientation, the CEO also conveyed that employees' well-being is a primary concern of the company. The CEO's philosophy in this role was that "it's more important if employees are okay than that they get the job done today," noting that where there were tensions between short-term performance and well-being, he prioritized well-being. This is not driven purely by altruism, although he believes in a moral imperative to care for employees' well-being. He also noted that it would ultimately result in improved long-term performance as employees feel respected and suffer from fewer work-induced mental health challenges (e.g., burnout).

Beyond the CEO's participation in the initial employee onboarding, he aimed to foster a climate of respect through his ongoing interaction with employees. This was related to his efforts in onboarding, as he prioritized consistency between the experience that employees are promised vis-à-vis working in a climate of respect, and the actual reality of their day-to-day experiences. In order to continue direct modeling of respect through interpersonal interactions, he broadly participated in meetings to ensure that he maintained a face-to-face relationship and went beyond this to make himself visible in the facility outside of formal meetings. In so doing, he aimed to demonstrate his concern for employees' well-being through regular interaction and modeling of respect in interpersonal communications. This opportunity for regular interactions also meant that he was able to discuss neutral or positive subjects with employees, instead of predominantly focusing on contentious or negative issues that may disproportionately dominate town hall discussions and other formal meetings.

The CEO was also able to get a sense of the ongoing norms of the facility's respectful culture, which enabled him to be sensitive to changes that may occur over time. This was particularly beneficial during the COVID-19 pandemic, which disproportionately affected healthcare workers such as those at the facility (Prasad et al., 2021). Because of the emphasis on respect and well-being, alongside the frequent leader visibility in employees' day-to-day work, the facility was able to withstand the unprecedented challenges that were brought by the pandemic.

At the same time, the CEO notes that a balanced approach was required to maintain respect in the context of interpersonal communication. Importantly, he felt that maintaining a culture of respect required him to set boundaries so he did not develop personal relationships that might compromise his ability to lead the organization. This is consistent with extant research on workplace friendships (Methot et al., 2016; Pillemer & Rothbard, 2018), which finds that people who are both friends and coworkers are more likely to have situations in which their personal and professional roles conflict. This is especially salient in the context of leaders and subordinates, as leaders must maintain impartiality and the ability to convey unpleasant decisions when they are in the best interest of the organization (Kark, 2011). To that end, the CEO's participation in respectful culture creation and maintenance exemplified a balance of frequent, personal communication with a strong awareness of avoiding communication and relationships that he characterized as "too personal."

Finally, the CEO of the behavioral health facility observed that the culture of respect created in the institution influenced the way that patients received care during their treatment. Because employees were treated with respect by their superiors and peers, they achieved two potential benefits that could improve their care of patients. One benefit was that they were less likely to experience burnout or have other mental health challenges that result from organizational mistreatment, such as the problems that result from abusive supervision or incivility (see Rosado-Solomon et al., 2023, for a review of these challenges). Additionally, the climate of respect in which they work reinforced the norm of respectful communication, and the employees in this climate were more likely to use that communicative norm when dealing with colleagues and patients alike. By communicating with patients more respectfully, the CEO believes that employees were likely to provide more useful care than if they enacted the same therapeutic behaviors in a tone that was not respectful.

Multilevel Model of Respect and Mental Health

Jointly considering extant research on respect, mental health, and organizations alongside the case study of the behavioral health facility, we now turn to articulate

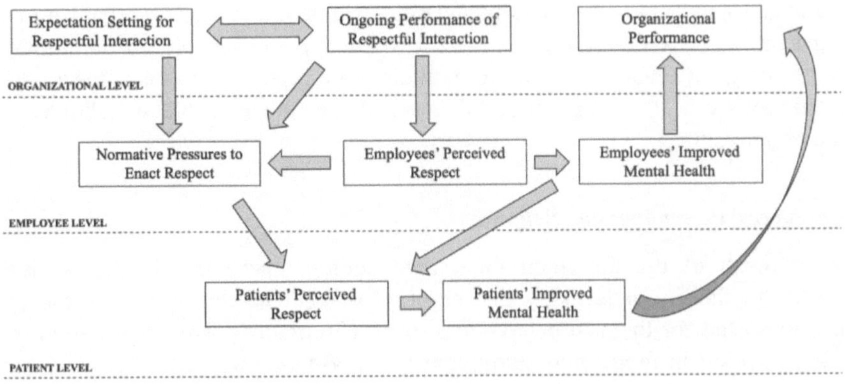

Figure 17.1 Multilevel Theoretical Model of Respect in Organizations.

a multilevel theoretical model of respect and mental health in organizations. By multilevel model, we mean that we examine respect and mental health at various levels of the organization and articulate how they spread and transform between levels (see Klein & Kozlowski, 2000, for a more detailed description of multilevel modeling). A multilevel perspective in this case is critical because respect and well-being do not manifest in the same way across levels; for instance, the CEO enacts a different set of behaviors to establish a culture of respect with new employees than nurses would use to establish a relationship of respect with a patient. We demonstrate our model graphically in Figure 17.1 and then explain it in the sections that follow.

Organizational-Level Influences on Respectful Interaction

As demonstrated in the aforementioned case study, the behavioral health facility we examined utilized both HR functions—especially onboarding—and the personal participation and actions of the CEO to set expectations for, and demonstrate, the importance of a respectful climate. Importantly, these are mutually reinforcing activities. Whereas it may be effective for short-term respect if HR and leadership set an initial expectation during the onboarding procedure, such an expectation is not sufficient to direct employees' behavior throughout their tenure with the organization. Indeed, if employees believe that they are joining a respectful organization and then come to find out that the day-to-day culture does not truly embody respect, then leadership and HR may be perceived as disingenuous, and employees may be less motivated to enact respectful behaviors than they would be if leadership had not said anything at all (Rosado-Solomon et al., 2025). Correspondingly, if leadership were to enact respectful behavior but did not explicitly set initial expectations for the importance of such behavior, then employees may misinterpret respectful interactions as simply indicative of the leader's individual personality and not attribute it to a broader organizational expectation. Given these possibilities, it is uniquely consequential and mutually reinforcing for leaders and HR to explicitly set expectations for respect while continuously performing respectful interactions with multiple stakeholders in the organization.

Employees' Perceptions and Behaviors

As a result of the aforementioned organizational activities in the behavioral health facility, it is likely that employees received the clear message that it is expected for them to behave in a respectful manner. This expectation was made explicit in their onboarding, and its importance was underscored by the participation and presence of the CEO. The ongoing performance of respectful interaction from leadership and HR personnel highlights that this is not merely corporate jargon but rather an integral part of the organization's values. Given that employees generally act in accordance with the normative expectations of their workplace (Schneider, 1987), it is likely that employees in an environment such as the behavioral health facility would also enact behaviors that manifest respect.

Moreover, respect afforded to employees by senior management and other employees is likely to promote feelings of felt respect on behalf of the employees themselves. This is instrumental in our model for two reasons. First, employees who feel that they have positive interpersonal relationships, such as those found in respectful interaction, generally have fewer challenges with mental health at work (see Rosado-Solomon et al., 2023, for a review of this association). Conversely, employees who experience various manifestations of disrespect at work, such as abusive supervision, bullying, and harassment, have poorer mental health than those who do not have such aversive experiences. The other reason that felt respect is important in this model is that employees who feel respected are more likely to enact respectful behavior themselves as pervasive generalized respect is appreciated and normalized.

Impact on Patients

In the context of the behavioral health setting we examined, an important consideration was the overall quality of treatment that is provided to patients, which was a determinant of patients' improved mental health resulting from treatment. As illustrated in our graphical model, employees' performance of respectful behavior, both through generalized respect for all patients and particularized respect within the context of specific interpersonal interactions, is likely to promote a feeling in patients that they are respected. This may be a uniquely salient concern in the behavioral health setting, as those with severe mental illness often face stigmatization and discrimination related to their condition that systematically undermines their feelings of being respected in other contexts. Indeed, there is even evidence of stigma against those with mental illness in other medical settings and among behavioral health professionals in other organizations. To that end, the respect displayed at the behavioral health facility we studied is notable given pervasive stigma in the mental health industry.

Of note, these dynamics apply to contexts that are quite different from the behavioral health facility that is the focus of this chapter. While mental health outcomes are uniquely salient in a behavioral health setting, many other customer-facing organizations are similarly concerned with the well-being and satisfaction of those they serve. This is clearly true for other types of medical organizations, such as hospitals, clinics, and other medical practices, as well as for social service organizations that are explicitly formed to improve people's mental health. Yet even beyond these organizations, other customer-facing organizations want their employees to behave in ways that are in the best interest of the customer, patient, or client they are serving. From this broader vantage point, the behavioral health facility's priorities represent a common organizational imperative.

Impact on Organizational Performance

As demonstrated in Figure 17.1, there are two elements of our multilevel model that are uniquely impactful for driving organizational performance. The first is improved employee mental health that comes from operating in a climate of respect. When employees are in a place of good mental health, they are more able to leverage their knowledge, skills, and abilities to support the organization's functioning. Of note, this refers to employees with lower levels of subclinical mental health concerns; it is well established that employees who have high levels of burnout and strain (the aversive psychological condition resulting from too much stress; Lazarus & Folkman, 1984) have systematically lower performance compared to employees who do not have these concerns. To clarify, this does not mean that employees with chronic mental illness (e.g., bipolar disorder) have systematically lower performance; there is no evidence for a systematic link between chronic mental illness and performance (Rosado-Solomon et al., 2023).

Conclusion

Consistent with increasing calls for organizations to proactively take steps that are likely to promote well-being and mental health (Gabriel et al., 2022; Rosado-Solomon et al., 2023), the current chapter underlines the importance of creating respect in both organizational norms and discrete interpersonal interactions. By using themes from the case of a behavioral health facility to consider how respect operates and influences outcomes across multiple levels of an organization, the present chapter sheds insight on the importance of promoting respect for mental health among a variety of stakeholders in organizational settings.

Note

1 The term "mental health challenges" is used throughout the chapter to refer to a range of people who have notably suboptimal mental well-being, including people who have diagnosed mental illness and those with other forms of poor mental health such as burnout, strain, and subclinical symptoms of depression and anxiety.

References

Allan, A., & Davidson, G. R. (2013). Respect for the dignity of people: What does this principle mean in practice? *Australian Psychologist*, *48*(5), 345–352,

Beach, M. C., Duggan, P. S., Cassel, C. K., & Geller, G. (2007). What does 'respect' mean? Exploring the moral obligation of health professionals to respect patients. *Journal of General Internal Medicine*, *22*, 692–695.

Brotheridge, C. M., & Grandey, A. A. (2002). Emotional labor and burnout: Comparing two perspectives of "people work". *Journal of Vocational Behavior*, *60*(1), 17–39.

Corrigan, P. W., Larson, J. E., & Kuwabara, S. A. (2007). Mental illness stigma and the fundamental components of supported employment. *Rehabilitation Psychology*, *52*(4), 451–457.

Davidson, L., & Roe, D. (2007). Recovery from versus recovery in serious mental illness: One strategy for lessening confusion plaguing recovery. *Journal of Mental Health*, *16*(4), 459–470.

Decker, C., & Van Quaquebeke, N. (2015). Getting respect from a boss you respect: How different types of respect interact to explain subordinates' job satisfaction as mediated by self-determination. *Journal of Business Ethics*, *131*(3), 543–556.

Dixon, L. B., Holoshitz, Y., & Nossel, I. (2016). Treatment engagement of individuals experiencing mental illness: Review and update. *World Psychiatry*, *15*(1), 13–20.

Drake, R. E., & Whitley, R. (2014). Recovery and severe mental illness: Description and analysis. *The Canadian Journal of Psychiatry*, *59*(5), 236–242.

Edward, K. L., Hercelinskyj, G., & Giandinoto, J. A. (2017). Emotional labour in mental health nursing: An integrative systematic review. *International Journal of Mental Health Nursing*, *26*(3), 215–225.

Gabriel, A. S., Arena, D. F., Calderwood, C., Campbell, J. T., Chawla, N., Corwin, E. S., Ezerins, M. E., Jones, K. P., Klotz, A. C., Larson, J. D., Leigh, A., MacGowan, R. L., Moran, C. M., Nag, D., Rogers, K. M., Rosen, C. C., Sawyer, K. B., Shockley, K. M., Simon, L. S., & Zipay, K. P. (2022). Building thriving workforces from the top down: A call and research agenda for organizations to proactively support employee well-being. *Research in Personnel and Human Resources Management*, *40*, 205–272.

Gwain, G. C., Amu, H., & Bain, L. E. (2022). Improving employee mental health: A health facility-based study in the United States. *Frontiers in Public Health*, *10*, 895048.

Kark, R. (2011). Workplace intimacy in leader–follower relationships. In K. Cameron & G. Spreitzer (Eds.), *Oxford handbook of positive organizational scholarship* (pp. 423–438). Oxford University Press.

Klein, K. J., & Kozlowski, S. W. (2000). A multilevel approach to theory and research in organizations: Contextual, temporal, and emergent processes. In *Multilevel theory, research, and methods in organizations: Foundations, extensions, and new directions* (pp. 3–90). Jossey-Bass

Koys, D. J. (1988). Human resource management and a culture of respect: Effects on employees' organizational commitment. *Employee Responsibilities and Rights Journal, 1*, 57–68.

LaGree, D., Houston, B., Duffy, M., & Shin, H. (2023). The effect of respect: Respectful communication at work drives resiliency, engagement, and job satisfaction among early career employees. *International Journal of Business Communication, 60*(3), 844–864.

Lazarus, R. S., & Folkman, S. (1984). *Stress, appraisal, and coping.* Springer Publishing Company.

Martinson, B. C., Smallfield, J., Magley, V. J., Thrush, C. R., & Gunsalus, C. K. (2025). Climate of Accountability, Respect, and Ethics Survey (CARES): Development and validation of an organizational climate survey. *Frontiers in Research Metrics and Analytics, 10*, 1516726.

Methot, J. R., Lepine, J. A., Podsakoff, N. P., & Christian, J. S. (2016). Are workplace friendships a mixed blessing? Exploring tradeoffs of multiplex relationships and their associations with job performance. *Personnel Psychology, 69*(2), 311–355.

Mind Share Partners. (2023). *Mental health at work report.* www.mindsharepartners.org.

Pillemer, J., & Rothbard, N. P. (2018). Friends without benefits: Understanding the dark sides of workplace friendship. *Academy of Management Review, 43*(4), 635–660.

Prasad, K., McLoughlin, C., Stillman, M., Poplau, S., Goelz, E., Taylor, S., Nankivil, N., Brown, R., Linzer, M., Cappelucci, K., Barbouche, M., & Sinsky, C. A. (2021). Prevalence and correlates of stress and burnout among US healthcare workers during the COVID-19 pandemic: A national cross-sectional survey study. *EClinicalMedicine, 35*.

Rogers, K. M., & Ashforth, B. E. (2017). Respect in organizations: Feeling valued as "we" and "me". *Journal of Management, 43*(5), 1578–1608.

Rogers, K. M., Corley, K. G., & Ashforth, B. E. (2017). Seeing more than orange: Organizational respect and positive identity transformation in a prison context. *Administrative Science Quarterly, 62*(2), 219–269.

Rosado-Solomon, E. H., Koopmann, J., Lee, W., & Cronin, M. A. (2023). Mental health and mental illness in organizations: A review, comparison, and extension. *Academy of Management Annals, 17*(2), 751–797.

Rosado-Solomon, E. H., Thatcher, S. M., & Strizver, S. D. (2025). Navigating mental illness at work using disengagement and engagement pathways. *Academy of Management Journal*. https://doi.org/10.5465/amj.2023.0430

Ross, C. A., & Goldner, E. M. (2009). Stigma, negative attitudes and discrimination towards mental illness within the nursing profession: A review of the literature. *Journal of Psychiatric and Mental Health Nursing, 16*(6), 558–567.

Schneider, B. (1987). The people make the place. *Personnel Psychology, 40*(3), 437–453.

Shreffler, J., Petrey, J., & Huecker, M. (2020). The impact of COVID-19 on healthcare worker wellness: A scoping review. *Western Journal of Emergency Medicine, 21*(5), 1059–1066.

Spears, R., Ellemers, N., Doosje, B., & Branscombe, N. R. 2006. The individual within the group: Respect! In T. Postmes & J. Jetten (Eds.), *Individuality and the group: Advances in social identity* (pp. 175–195). Sage Publications.

Van Quaquebeke, N., & Eckloff, T. (2010). Defining respectful leadership: What it is, how it can be measured, and another glimpse at what it is related to. *Journal of Business Ethics, 91*, 343–358.

Watson, A. C., Angell, B., Morabito, M. S., & Robinson, N. (2008). Defying negative expectations: Dimensions of fair and respectful treatment by police officers as perceived by people with mental illness. *Administration and Policy in Mental Health and Mental Health Services Research, 35*, 449–457.

Yanay, N., & Shahar, G. (1998). Professional feelings as emotional labor. *Journal of Contemporary Ethnography, 27*(3), 346–373.

18 Conclusion

Charting a Course for Future Research on Mental Health Challenges and Work

Emily H. Rosado-Solomon

If this book serves its purpose, you should come away with at least as many questions as answers. Research has long recognized that poorly designed work—as well as other aversive experiences during the workday—can cause or exacerbate mental health challenges (Kelloway et al., 2023; Rosado-Solomon et al., 2023). Increasingly, scholars also recognize that good work can have benefits for people with mental health challenges (Modini et al., 2016). But the closer we look, the more complicated those relationships become. Table 18.1 contains illustrative examples of research questions that one might ask after reading each section of this book, which represent only a small fraction of the important questions that should be addressed in future research.

Section 1 of the book began with the most fundamental question: what *are* mental health challenges, anyway? How do we measure them in a way that is rigorous? What measurement and conceptual insights can management scholars borrow from psychology to improve the scope of research on established bodies of research, such as issues surrounding narcissism and work? Future research might leverage these insights by making more informed considerations about the assessment tools that are used in management research, or by using established measurements that are not normative in the management literature. Research might also draw on the information in Section 1 to ask questions about topics in the other sections of this volume, such as investigating whether certain measures are more or less valid in different occupational contexts or for employees with varied attributes. There is reason to think that questions on the latter subject are particularly important. For example, previous research has found that people who identify as Asian American have systematic differences in their symptoms of depression compared to those from European backgrounds, such that they are less likely to report certain affective symptoms (e.g., crying often, feeling depressed; Kalibatseva et al., 2014). Given this, research on workplace mental health challenges in specific populations might find that certain validated tools are more or less sensitive depending on the proportion of affective symptoms they measure.

DOI: 10.4324/9781003491170-23

Table 18.1 Future Research Questions Derived From This Volume

Book Section	*Exemplar Future Research Questions*
I: Issues of Measurement and Construct Clarity	- Directly comparing established assessment tools, which common measures are most valid in different employment contexts? - How does incorporating a broader view of the lifespan into management research inform novel management research? For instance, are there trauma-based treatments that might reform managers who are highly narcissistic or those who display related maladaptive behaviors such as abusive supervision or bullying? - What opportunities exist for deepened interdisciplinary collaboration in research on workplace mental health challenges, particularly between researchers from psychology and management disciplines? How might collaborating with scholars from domains such as public health, social work, and psychiatry further strengthen management research on mental health challenges?
II: Intersectionality	- What are the unique issues surrounding mental health challenges and work for different racial and ethnic groups? - How does cultural background change the way that mental health challenges manifest? In what ways does culture impact the types of supports that people find effective in addressing these challenges? - How does systematic marginalization of certain groups—such as employees who are neurodivergent, those with disabilities, and those with varied immigration statuses—uniquely influence workplace mental health challenges? - What are distinct issues surrounding mental health for other generations, including older employees who are about to retire, or Millennial employees who are juggling the demands of caring for children and older parents alongside their work responsibilities?
III: Navigating Mental Health Challenges in the New World of Work	- What is the role of AI in promoting, exacerbating, or mitigating mental health challenges at work? - How does precarious work, such as gig work, impact the mental health challenges that employees face at work? Does this impact the type of challenges directly, or does it alter the coping tools available to deal with known challenges? - How does virtual communication with colleagues from different cultural backgrounds promote or hinder the ways employees manage their mental health challenges?

(*Continued*)

Table 18.1 (Continued)

Book Section	*Exemplar Future Research Questions*
IV: Psychological Hazards in Unique Contexts	- What additional work contexts contain unique psychological hazards? What is the nature of these hazards, and how are they similar and different to known workplace hazards? - Given the equivocal findings in extant research on resilience training, how can employees be prepared to deal with psychological hazards that are inevitable in certain occupations, such as the close contact with trauma inherent in high-risk occupations? - How might leaders be better prepared to manage their employees' mental health challenges while balancing their own well-being? How might this preparation differ for leaders in different types of organizations or industry contexts? - How might unique psychological hazards in seemingly "safe" occupations, such as academia, be made more visible to practitioners and researchers in a way that promotes enhanced attention to addressing these challenges?
V: Organizational Responses and Paths Forward	- How might interpersonal efforts to support employees' mental health, such as managerial or coworker support, interact with organizations' systematic and procedural supports for employees' mental health? Are the benefits of one type of support contingent on other types of support, or can strong interpersonal support supplement lower procedural supports (or vice versa)? - What barriers exist to leaders and organizations enacting evidence-based responses to address employees' mental health challenges? How can these barriers be overcome? - What is the impact of organizational responses to employees' mental health challenges over time? Which organizational actions create a permanent benefit, and which offer temporary relief from mental health challenges? - How do organizational responses differentially impact employees with various mental health challenges, including distinct components of burnout, chronic mental illness, and symptoms of depression or anxiety?

Section 2 complicates the topic of mental health challenges and work further by illuminating the fact that mental health challenges manifest differently for people with different characteristics. In some cases, the differences manifest because the nature of mental health challenges themselves are distinct, such as the issues surrounding maternal mental health that Heskiau and colleagues describe in their chapter. In other cases, the challenges might be similar to other groups, but they may be caused by unique factors such as systematic racism (Rorie, this volume; Ryu et al., 2024), or they may manifest differently in the workplace, as with the disproportionate comfort that early-career employees of Gen Z have talking about their mental health (Turner et al., this volume). While chapters in this section do an excellent job highlighting the importance of an intersectional approach that simultaneously considers people's mental health challenges alongside their other attributes and identities, curious readers might also start to see how this is just the tip of the iceberg. There are unique dynamics around workplace mental health challenges that apply to multiple racial and cultural backgrounds, as well as those from different generational backgrounds, performance achievement groups, and family statuses.

There are several interesting questions that might jointly relate to both Sections 2 and 4, potentially considering whether there are unique mental health challenges that impact employees with certain attributes differently in different contexts. For example, simultaneously considering both Heskiau and colleagues' research and Jazaieri's research on leadership and mental health, one might wonder whether mothers in managerial positions face unique workplace challenges. It is foreseeable that other groups of employees, such as the high performers that Fezzey and colleagues discuss in their chapter, might have unique challenges and successes in non-traditional contexts such as the small entrepreneurial firms that Gopinath highlights in her chapter. In this example, it would be foreseeable that the dynamics of mental health challenges would shift as there is not only less clarity about what success looks like but also fewer institutional constraints to achieving success.

In Section 3, the overarching themes of mental health challenges are made more complex by acknowledging that the nature of work is changing, and these changes create unique barriers and opportunities for addressing workplace mental health challenges. As work is increasingly geographically distributed yet interdependent (Malhotra, 2021), there are new questions to ask about whether workplace relationships are fundamentally different than they were a generation ago. Given the emerging body of research about computer-mediated work relationships (e.g., Schinoff et al., 2020), virtual coworker relationships might promote or hinder employees' ability to manage mental health challenges compared to employees who primarily work in person. Elraz's chapter begins to explore some of these themes, and it is imperative that future research continues investigating this topic. Sawyer and Gabriel's chapter on the role of trauma in the career lifecycle also acknowledges that awareness about trauma, which is becoming more broadly acknowledged as a public health concern that promotes mental health challenges (Magruder et al., 2017), has implications for how employees' mental health challenges might influence their work throughout a career. As both work and society jointly evolve, research on mental health challenges must evolve, too.

As with the themes in other sections, there is ample opportunity for future research at the intersection of Section 3's themes and themes in other sections of the volume. For instance, jointly considering the fact that trust is uniquely formed—and crucial—in high-risk situations, future research might investigate the dynamics of relational influences, such as those discussed in the chapter by Kavanagh and colleagues, on managing mental health challenges in high-risk contexts, building on the themes that Britt and colleagues discuss in their chapter. Additionally, the acknowledgment of trauma that Sawyer and Gabriel discuss clearly relates to the themes that Dobrow and colleagues discuss in their chapter on narcissism in Section 1. By considering broader causes for undesirable workplace behaviors, such as the impact of trauma on promoting high levels of narcissism, future research might develop a more holistic understanding of the complex factors that contribute to mental health challenges at work.

In Section 4, a selection of four chapters demonstrates that mental health challenges often manifest in unique ways, and for unique reasons, in various occupational contexts. Some risks are obvious, such as those in the high-risk contexts that Britt and colleagues review in their chapter. As other chapters demonstrate, some of these occupational contexts may initially seem safe but nevertheless hold unique risks to employees' mental health that may cause or exacerbate challenges. For instance, the stereotype of professors sitting at desks and teaching classes may not initially spark worries about well-being, but as Martin and colleagues explain in their chapter, there are unique hazards that must be acknowledged and addressed in academia to protect employees' mental health. Similarly, while people might initially think of leaders as having positions of relative power and privilege in an organization, Jazaieri's chapter highlights unique risks to leaders' mental health that do not parallel hazards in non-managerial roles.

While connections between themes in Section 4 and themes in the previous sections have already been discussed, it is notable that there is also opportunity to conduct important future research by integrating themes from Section 4 with Section 5, which focuses on the organization's role in addressing mental health challenges. For instance, employees in certain industries (e.g., construction, police) may hesitate to participate in mental health training programs if there is an occupational stigma against discussing emotions or challenges, and small firms such as the one investigated by Gopinath might not have the resources to offer formal mental health support. Leaders may also hesitate to bring their own mental health challenges into the workplace if they think that it will damage others' perceptions of their legitimacy (Rosado-Solomon et al., 2025). As these examples demonstrate, future research is clearly needed to identify what constraints to organizational responses might exist in unique employment contexts and, crucially, what effective alternatives might be available in these situations.

Section 5 highlights the unique role that organizations can play in influencing employees' mental health challenges, for better or worse. As Deane and colleagues illustrate in their chapter, successful efforts to support employees' mental health should be integrated as part of a holistic, multi-pronged approach to supporting employees' overall wellness, recognizing that the type of work, relationships with colleagues, and other stressors (physical challenges, financial stressors, etc.) have complex relationships with employees' mental health (Granger & Turner, 2025; Mind Share Partners, 2023). The other two chapters in Section 5 also highlight the critical role that human resource functions can play in employees' mental health challenges at work. Future research would do well to draw from these insights and conduct empirical testing of organizational interventions, especially those that focus on modifying HR functions such as onboarding and performance evaluation practices, so that organizations have the information they need to make informed cost-benefit decisions about how to leverage resources to promote desired results.

While the focus of Section 5 on organization's role in mental health challenges can clearly be integrated with all other themes in this volume, there are some areas of integration that might yield particularly important future research. For instance, jointly considering Rosado-Solomon and Babcock's chapter on the behavioral health facility that highlights the role of the executive in promoting a culture of respect, and Jazaieri's chapter in Section 4 on leaders' mental health, future research should investigate how managers can balance their opportunity to support employees while not becoming over-extended themselves. Similarly, Kilroy and colleagues' chapter on the dual perspectives of HR and burnout might be integrated with themes from Section 2, propelling research on how employees might experience mental health outcomes differently in response to the same HR practices, where such differences are based on their demographic, cultural, or other systematic differences in attributes.

As an editor compiling the research of chapter authors in this book, I gained an increased appreciation and understanding for facets of mental health challenges and work that I had not previously considered. I hope this book has similarly expanded the perspective of readers and sparked a desire to conduct meaningful research on addressing mental health challenges at work. Beyond that, for readers who are also members of organizations—employees, faculty, or graduate students—I hope the insights contained in the book's chapters provide ideas about steps you might individually take to make your context better for the mental health of those in your own organization. While continued research in this field is sorely needed, so is individual action by informed, compassionate individuals.

References

Granger, S., & Turner, N. (2025). Work injuries and mental health challenges: A meta-analysis of the bidirectional relationship. *Personnel Psychology*, *78*(1), 11–57. https://doi.org/10.1111/peps.12649

Kalibatseva, Z., Leong, F. T. L., & Ham, E. H. (2014). A symptom profile of depression among Asian Americans: Is there evidence for differential item functioning of depressive symptoms? *Psychological Medicine*, *44*(12), 2567–2578. https://doi.org/10.1017/S0033291714000130

Kelloway, E. K., Dimoff, J. K., & Gilbert, S. (2023). Mental health in the workplace. *Annual Review of Organizational Psychology and Organizational Behavior*, *10*(1), 363–387. https://doi.org/10.1146/annurev-orgpsych-120920-050527

Magruder, K. M., McLaughlin, K. A., & Elmore Borbon, D. L. (2017). Trauma is a public health issue. *European Journal of Psychotraumatology*, *8*(1), 1375338. https://doi.org/10.1080/20008198.2017.1375338

Malhotra, A. (2021). The postpandemic future of work. *Journal of Management*, *47*(5), 1091–1102. https://doi.org/10.1177/0149206321100043

Mind Share Partners. (2023). *Mental health at work report.* https://www.mindsharepartners.org/.

Modini, M., Joyce, S., Mykletun, A., Christensen, H., Bryant, R. A., Mitchell, P. B., & Harvey, S. B. (2016). The mental health benefits of employment: Results of a systematic meta-review. *Australasian Psychiatry*, *24*(4), 331–336. https://doi.org/10.1177/1039856215618523

Rosado-Solomon, E. H., Koopmann, J., Lee, W., & Cronin, M. A. (2023). Mental health and mental illness in organizations: A review, comparison, and extension. *Academy of Management Annals*, *17*(2), 751–797. https://doi.org/10.5465/annals.2021.0211

Rosado-Solomon, E. H., Thatcher, S. M., & Strizver, S. D. (2025). Navigating mental illness at work using disengagement and engagement pathways. *Academy of Management Journal*. https://doi.org/10.5465/amj.2023.0430

Ryu, J. W., Gonzalez-Mulé, E., & O'Boyle, E. H. (2024). Taking a heavier toll? Racial differences in the effects of workplace mistreatment on depression. *Journal of Applied Psychology*, *109*(5), 611–621. https://doi.org/10.1037/apl0001170

Schinoff, B. S., Ashforth, B. E., & Corley, K. G. (2020). Virtually (in) separable: The centrality of relational cadence in the formation of virtual multiplex relationships. *Academy of Management Journal*, *63*(5), 1395–1424. https://doi.org/10.5465/amj.2018.0466

Index

Page numbers in *italic* indicate a figure and page numbers in **bold** indicate a table on the corresponding page. Page numbers followed by n refer to notes.